THE REAL
VALKYRIE

ALSO BY NANCY MARIE BROWN

Ivory Vikings

Song of the Vikings

The Far Traveler

THE REAL
VALKYRIE

THE HIDDEN
HISTORY *of*
VIKING WARRIOR
WOMEN

NANCY MARIE BROWN

St. Martin's Press
New York

First published in the United States by St. Martin's Press, an imprint of
St. Martin's Publishing Group

THE REAL VALKYRIE. Copyright © 2021 by Nancy Marie Brown. All rights
reserved. Printed in the United States of America. For information, address
St. Martin's Publishing Group, 120 Broadway, New York, NY 10271.

www.stmartins.com

Design by Meryl Sussman Levavi

Library of Congress Cataloging-in-Publication Data

Names: Brown, Nancy Marie, author.
Title: The real Valkyrie : the hidden history of Viking warrior women /
    Nancy Marie Brown.
Description: First edition. | New York : St. Martin's Press, 2021. | Includes
    bibliographical references and index.
Identifiers: LCCN 2021006973 | ISBN 9781250200846 (hardcover) |
    ISBN 9781250200839 (ebook)
Subjects: LCSH: Women, Viking—History. | Women—Scandinavia—
    History—To 1500. | Vikings—History. | Civilization, Viking.
Classification: LCC DL65 .B775 2021 | DDC 948.7/3—dc23
LC record available at https://lccn.loc.gov/2021006973

Our books may be purchased in bulk for promotional, educational, or
business use. Please contact your local bookseller or the Macmillan
Corporate and Premium Sales Department at 1-800-221-7945, extension
5442, or by email at MacmillanSpecialMarkets@macmillan.com.

First Edition: 2021

1 3 5 7 9 10 8 6 4 2

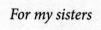

For my sisters

CONTENTS

A NOTE ON LANGUAGE

I have standardized and Anglicized the spelling of foreign words and names (even within quotations) throughout this book, dropping all accents and diacritical marks. To make my speculations about the tenth century clear, I use quotation marks only for direct references to a text, medieval or modern; these are cited in the endnotes.

The holes in the record present one hazard, what we have constructed around them another.

—Stacy Schiff, *Cleopatra*

Objectivity is not a possibility. Our definition of the past is part of the way we define ourselves.

—Anthony Faulkes, "The Viking Mind, or In Pursuit of the Viking,"
Saga Book XXXI

THE REAL
VALKYRIE

INTRODUCTION

THE VALKYRIE'S GRAVE

All I have are her bones. I don't know her name, or precisely where or when she was born. I don't know how she died, though bones often do betray such secrets. All I have are her bones, now boxed and stored in a museum in Sweden, bones gathered by an archaeologist in 1878 from a grave beside a hillfort overlooking the Viking town of Birka, where she was buried in the mid-tenth century in a spacious, wood-lined pit.

To tell her story, all I have are her bones—and what was unearthed with her: an axe blade, two spearheads, a two-edged sword, a clutch of arrows, their shafts embellished with silver thread, a long sax-knife in a bronze-ringed sheath, iron bosses for two round shields, a short-bladed knife, a whetstone, a set of game pieces (bundled in her lap), a large bronze bowl (much repaired), a comb, a snip of a silver coin, three traders' weights, two stirrups, two bridles' bits, and spikes to ride a horse on the ice, along with the bones of two horses, a stallion and a mare. Of her clothing all that remains are an iron cloak pin, a filigreed silver cone, four baubles or buttons of coiled silver wire, strips of silk embroidered with silver, and a scattering of mirrored sequins.

Until 2017, when DNA tests proved the bones were female, this grave, numbered Bj581, was held up as the classic Viking warrior's grave. "The position of the skeleton," wrote a Swedish archaeologist in 1966, "gave the impression that he had been sitting in the grave, rather than laid out. . . . The equipment indicates that this is a warrior's grave rather than that of a merchant. . . . The date of a silver coin, found underneath the skeleton of the dead man, provides a fairly good idea of the date of the grave: 913–980 A.D."

The implications of the "dead man" turning into a dead woman dazzle me. They ignite my imagination. A burial with weapons and horses, an archaeologist claimed as late as 2008, used "a widely recognised symbolic language of lordship, one that was unquestionably masculine." To assume all such "weapons graves" are male now seems to me to be a mistake—one that has skewed our image of the Viking Age. How does history change if we turn that assumption on its head?

There are other ways to interpret the grave, other ways to explain a female body buried with weapons. But the simplest seems to me the most likely. Defending their findings in 2019, the team that tested her DNA said Bj581 "suggests to us that at least one Viking Age woman adopted a professional warrior lifestyle." They added, "We would be very surprised if she was alone in the Viking world."

A Viking is a raider from the sea. During the Viking Age, roughly 750 to 1050, Europe was plagued by such pirates in their swift dragonships. The Vikings were traders and explorers, too. They were farmers, poets, engineers, artists—but their place in history was carved by their swords. "From the fury of the Northmen, O Lord, deliver us!" wrote a French monk around the year 900. They "ransacked and despoiled, massacred, and burned and ravaged," wrote another, who witnessed the Viking attack on Paris in 885. In Ireland in the mid-800s, a monk praised the safety of a storm:

Bitter is the wind tonight,
White the tresses of the sea;
I have no fear the Viking hordes
Will sail the seas on such a night.

Archaeology backs up the Vikings' violent image: Across Northern Europe, from Russia in the east to Iceland in the west, Vikings are found buried with swords. Three thousand Viking swords are known from Norway alone. Assuming all sword-bearers are male, writers limn the Viking Age as hypermasculine: a time when "shiploads of these huge and brawny men would suddenly appear out of the sea mists. They would pillage at will, mercilessly cutting down all opposition."

Let's set aside, for a moment, the idea that mercilessness is a masculine trait. How does an archaeologist know a buried Viking is male? The bones found beside the buried swords, if any, are degraded. Sexing them by their robustness or by the shape of the skull or pelvis is often not possible—and is always open to interpretation. There's no internationally agreed-upon definition of "robust"; there's no absolute scientific scale for pelvic structure. DNA sexing is difficult and expensive and, so, rarely done. Instead, "sexing by metal" has been standard procedure since 1837, before archaeology as a science even existed. Graves with weapons—even cremation graves in which the bones have been crushed after burning—are catalogued as male; those with jewelry are female. The thirty-some Viking graves in which slender, female-looking bones were unearthed beside weapons are ignored as "noise in the data."

The result? Historians and novelists write confidently of ships carrying only "huge and brawny *men*." Museum designers and filmmakers and Viking reenactors re-create in exquisite detail a male-dominated Viking world. When we hear the word "Viking," we imagine a well-armed man.

Yet most people who died in the Viking Age were buried with nothing that will sex them. Even the elite, the people whose graves announce their high status, often hide their sexual identity, as if their gender mattered not at all. Half of the elite burials in some Viking graveyards contain neither weapons nor jewelry. Their grave goods, though rich, are horses and boats and knives and tools: things that cannot be gendered.

And now, in Birka grave Bj581, we have a woman buried as a Viking warrior. What does her grave tell us? That we don't know the Vikings as well as we thought.

In December 2012, a man using a metal detector near the village of Harby in Denmark found a small face peering up at him from a lump of frozen dirt. His find, cleaned up, was an intricately detailed figurine of gilded silver, about an inch tall, in the shape of a woman with long hair twisted into a ponytail. She carries a sword and shield.

I know of seven flat metal images of a woman with weapons, and seventeen showing a shield-carrier facing a horse rider armed with sword

A three-dimensional Viking warrior, just over an inch tall, from Harby, Denmark.

and spear, both perhaps female. These images were found in Denmark, England, Germany, and Poland. Similar images of women with weapons, fashioned from thread or carved in stone, come from Norway, Sweden, and Russia.

The figurine from Harby is the first three-dimensional portrayal to appear. Like the others, she is dismissed as a "valkyrie." By that the experts mean *she is not real.*

The Old Norse word *valkyrja* combines *valr,* "corpse," and *kjósa,* "to choose." The standard definition comes from Snorri Sturluson. Writing in Iceland between 1220 and 1241, this Christian-educated lawyer, politician, and poet described valkyries as pagan battle-goddesses with shield and sword (or spear) who ferried dead heroes to Valhalla, the otherworldly feast hall of the god Odin, and there served them celebratory cups of mead. Trusting Snorri (who was well known, in his lifetime, for being untrustworthy), modern scholars classify valkyries as "mythological." They are "firmly supernatural" or, at most, "semi-human."

Why, when we see the Harby figurine, do we not assume, instead, that it depicts an actual woman—that carrying a sword and shield was "a perfectly ordinary aspect of a woman's life" in the Viking Age? A 2013 museum exhibition in Copenhagen did suggest that—and sparked a storm of rebuttal. The argument devolved to one point: Said a specialist on women of the Viking Age, "We know that warriors were men."

How do we know that?

Norse culture in the Viking Age, I was taught, was divided along strict gender lines. I described it that way myself in my previous books. The woman ruled *innan stokks*, "inside the threshold," where she held considerable power, for she was in charge of clothing and food. In lands where winter lasts ten months and the growing season two, the housewife decided who froze and who starved. The larger the household, the more complex her job. Keeping house for a chieftain with eighty retainers, as well as family and servants, she was the CEO of a small business.

But for all that, the man held the "dominant role in all walks of life," I was taught. His duties began at the threshold of the house and expanded outward. His was the world of public affairs, of "decisions affecting the community at large." He was the trader, the traveler, the warrior. His symbol was the sword.

The woman's role, in turn, was symbolized by the keys she carried at her belt.

Except she didn't.

Our picture of everyday life in the Viking Age is largely drawn from later written sources, from laws, poems, and the long prose Icelandic sagas, all of which survive only in manuscripts from the 1200s or later—more than two hundred years after the people of the North converted to Christianity and their culture radically changed. There are more than 140 Icelandic sagas; only one, recounting a feud from 1242, refers to a housewife's keys. A Danish marriage law from 1241 says that a bride is given to her husband "for honor and as wife, sharing his bed, for lock and keys, and for right of inheritance of a third of the property." A bawdy poem, in an Icelandic manuscript dated after 1270, describes the hypermasculine thunder god, Thor, disguised as a bride with a ring of keys at his belt.

These three are the only mentions of housewives with keys I can come up with: two women and a man in drag. They might reflect a pagan truth from before the year 1000. They might equally reflect the values of the medieval Christian world in which they were written. No one can say for sure.

Women with weapons appear in these same texts much more

frequently than women with keys: I can name twenty warrior women from sagas and histories, another fifty-three in poems and myths. The earliest Icelandic lawbook (dated 1260 to 1280) considers women with weapons a threat to society—which implies they existed. You don't write laws to control myths.

Why then did keys become the symbol of Viking womanhood? Because our image of the Viking world took shape in the nineteenth century. Keys reflect the values of Victorian society, when upper-class women were confined to the home and told to concern themselves only with children, church, and kitchen. The iconic Viking housewife with her keys first appeared in a Swedish history book in the 1860s, replacing an earlier historical portrait of Viking women who were strikingly equal to Viking men. The Victorian version of Viking history has been presented ever since as truth—but it is only one interpretation.

Surely archaeology backs up the image of the Viking housewife with her keys, doesn't it?

It does not.

Keys have been found in some Viking women's graves. But they are not common, nowhere near as common as the symbol chosen for Viking men, the sword. Against the three thousand swords from Viking Age Norway, a Norwegian archaeologist in 2015 sets only 143 keys, half of which were found in men's graves. An archaeologist in Denmark in 2011 found that only nine out of 102 female graves she studied contained keys. Calling keys the symbol of a Viking woman's status, these researchers say, is "an archaeological misinterpretation," "a mistake," "a myth"—and a dangerous one.

By accepting the Victorian stereotype of men with swords and women with keys, we legitimize the idea that women should stay at home.

We reduce the role models for every modern girl who visits a museum or reads a history book.

We make it hard to even imagine a Viking warrior woman like the one buried in Birka grave Bj581.

Viking society was not like Victorian society. It was not like our own. It was a martial society, in which vengeance was praised and war was glorified. An insult to one's honor—as slight as a nasty poem, as serious as the killing of kinsfolk—was repaid with violence or, at least, by the threat of violence until blood money was paid. Of heroes it's said they "fled not," but fought as long as they could hold a weapon. Fearlessness was the highest virtue. Death was met with laughter. The winner in any conflict was the one who wouldn't give up.

No one is immune to violence in such a society. No one is a noncombatant, no one is safe, inside the threshold or out.

In medieval texts depicting this martial Viking society, women "do battle in the forefront of the most valiant warriors." "Like a son," they avenge the killing of their kinsmen. They kill berserks, break shields, kill one king and help another. They say, "As heroes we were widely known— with keen spears we cut blood from bone. Our blades were red."

These women are called trolls or giants, valkyries, or shield-maids— but not shield-*maidens*, as in many modern translations. The Old Norse word *skjaldmær* joins "shield" to "girl," "daughter," or "virgin." Another term for a warrior woman, *skjaldkona*, "shield-woman," makes it clear that sexual experience has nothing to do with warrior status. The comparable word for male warriors is *drengr*, literally "boy" or "lad" (which originally meant one who is "led by a leader"). *Drengr* is occasionally applied to women, too. The issue is not sex, but status. These warriors are not householders. They have no economic responsibilities. They have no obligations except to their war leader. They are professional fighters.

The warrior women in these texts are portrayed as human, semi-human, or supernatural. But so are their male counterparts: the berserks (or "bear-shirts"), whom iron cannot bite, the half trolls and dragon-slayers, the shape-shifters who turn into wolves. Male or female, many warriors in Icelandic sagas and Old Norse poetry talk to gods (or birds), use magic, have inordinate luck or strength that increases after sunset, are matchless athletes, outlive a normal life span, and serve mead to heroes in Valhalla. Only the females are explained away by modern scholars as fantasy or wish fulfillment. Only the females are considered as fabulous as dragons.

The Victorian stereotype blinds us.

We need to clear our eyes. The sources depicting Viking women with weapons—the Christian-era texts, the images, the ambiguous burials, and stray archaeological finds—are the same sources depicting Viking *men*. To write about the Viking Age at all means to connect the dots. To make educated guesses. To interpret and to speculate.

Reading itself is a form of interpretation. Words like *menn* in Old Norse, *manna* in Old English, and *homines* in Latin have been casually translated for hundreds of years as "men"—but they also mean "people," no genders implied. When these *menn* are warriors, translators have assumed they were all masculine. Yet Old Norse can be gender-specific when it matters. When a warrior using the masculine name Hervard killed a man in a king's hall, in one saga, the king's warriors egged one another on to go after him. Then the king spoke up, calling out information they'd apparently missed: "I think he is a *kvennmann*," the king said. "I think, moreover, that with the weapon she has, each of you would find it dearly bought to take her life." As the king's shift in pronouns reveals, *kvennmann* means "female person"; *kvenn* is our word "queen." Its opposite, *karlmann*, "male person," is also used in the sagas—when gender matters.

"Was femaleness any more decisive," mused one saga scholar as long ago as 1993, "in setting parameters on individual behavior than were wealth, prestige, marital status, or just plain personality and ambition?"

I think it was not.

Mercilessness is not a masculine trait.

What would the Viking world look like if we revised our assumptions? What would it look like if roles were assigned, not according to Victorian concepts of male versus female, but based on ambition, ability, family ties, and wealth?

In this book, inspired by a warrior woman's bones, I reread the texts and reexamine the archaeological finds with that question in mind. I use what my research uncovers to re-create the world of one warrior woman in the Viking Age.

I don't know her name, so I've given her one: I call her Hervor. Other famous skeletons have names. There's Lucy the Australopithecus, named for a Beatles song, and Otzi the Iceman, named for the valley he was found in.

I could have named her Lagertha, after the shield-maid who Saxo Grammaticus, writing his *Gesta Danorum* (or *History of the Danes*) in Latin around the year 1200, said "would do battle in the forefront of the most valiant warriors." But Lagertha has already been brought to life by the actress and martial artist Katheryn Winnick in the History Channel television series *Vikings*. I could call her Brynhild, Geirvifa, Svava, Mist, Thogn, or Sigrun, the names of valkyries in sagas and poems, names that mean Bright Battle, Spear Wife, Sleep Maker, Fog of War, Silence of Death, or Victory Sign. But I call her Hervor, after the warrior woman in the classic Old Norse poem *Hervor's Song. Her* means "battle." *Vör* means "aware." Hervor, then, means Aware of Battle, Warrior Woman.

Who was this Hervor, buried in grave Bj581 outside the Swedish town of Birka sometime between 913 and 980? What might her life have been like? To tell her story, all I have are her bones, but bones can be eloquent. If complete, a skeleton speaks not only of its sex; it whispers of its life and death. Diseases—if they don't kill quickly—can mark bones, as can repeated motions like rowing or riding or stringing a bow. Injuries and accidents are recorded in bones.

Yet to read cut marks as killing blows—the edges of the wound "sharp and splintery," not the smooth, rounded traces of earlier, healed injuries—the surface of the bones must be pristine. Bones buried for a thousand-plus years are rarely pristine. Like wood, cloth, leather, food, and other biodegradable objects placed in Viking Age graves, bodies rot—that's the point of burial, after all, to return to earth. It takes less than twenty-five years (sometimes much less) for a buried body to be reduced to bones. How long those bones last depends on the chemistry of the soil they're set in.

Hervor's bones, the bones in grave Bj581, are too degraded for any signs of action, illness, or battle trauma to be seen. Bone preservation at Birka is generally poor. The soil is too acidic. The mineral constituent of the bones simply breaks down into calcium and phosphorus salts that leach away. Microbes and fungi carve fissures and tunnels. The bones break into bits and dissolve into dust.

In many of Birka's eleven hundred excavated graves, all that remained by the time they were opened in the late 1800s were loose teeth. In Bj581, by contrast, were bones from all parts of Hervor's body. Compared to her neighbors, she is remarkably well preserved. She is one of the few Birka skeletons to have a complete backbone. She has two ribs, bones from each arm and each leg, part of her pelvis, and her lower jaw. Her bones are characteristically female—as osteologists pointed out at least twice (and were ignored) before the DNA test confirmed her sex.

When she was dug up in 1878, her skull was also recovered; it has since gone missing. Anatomical collections were in fashion in the late 1800s, and archaeologists often lent or traded bones with their friends. Skulls were particularly popular: Their shape was thought to reflect race, intelligence, and even criminal tendencies. Archaeologists still use the shape of the skull to sex a skeleton. Women's skulls are thought to be smoother and more rounded, while men's have a more prominent brow ridge and a more muscular jaw, though hormone fluxes can cause older women's skulls to resemble men's.

DNA sexing leaves less room for doubt. If DNA can be extracted at all, it can usually be sexed. In Hervor's case, university researchers from Stockholm and Uppsala extracted DNA from one tooth and one arm bone recovered from grave Bj581. They sequenced the DNA and searched for Y chromosomes, the genetic signal of maleness. Their results fell far to the female end of the spectrum.

The mature appearance of certain bones and the level of wear on her molars say Hervor was at least thirty when she died—she could have been as old as forty. Her bones tell us, too, that Hervor ate well all her life, which means she came from a rich family, if not a royal one. At over five foot seven, she was taller than most people around her: Five foot five was the average man's height in tenth-century Scandinavia; King Gorm the Old, who ruled Denmark during Hervor's lifetime, was considered tall at five foot eight.

The chemistry of her teeth tells us Hervor was not a native of Birka, where she was buried, on an island in Lake Malaren a short boat ride from present-day Stockholm. She came from away. As teeth develop, they pick up isotopes of strontium (which mimics calcium) from the local water. The strontium signature of a tooth will thus match that of the bedrock where the child lived when the tooth's enamel formed. Hervor's first molars (mineralized before she was three) reveal that she was born somewhere in the western part of the Viking world, in what is now southern Sweden or Norway. Her second molars say she sailed from there, before she was eight, to somewhere else in the west. She did not arrive in Birka until she was over sixteen.

Where did she travel between her birthplace and her tomb? If all I had were her bones, I could only wonder. But I can also study what was buried with her. She was seated in her grave surrounded by weapons. None of them are overly fancy. None are simply for show. They are sturdy weapons, crafted for killing.

The two-edged sword beside her left hip is an uncommon type, rare in Norway and Sweden, but more often found along the Vikings' East Way, the trade route through what is now Russia and Ukraine to Byzantium, Baghdad, and beyond.

Birka grave Bj581, as imagined by artist Þórhallur Þráinsson based on archaeologists' interpretations.

Her long, thin-bladed sax-knife, or scramasax, in its elaborate bronze-and-silver ornamented sheath, is also Eastern, a rare and prestigious weapon—some say a status symbol—inspired by the equipment of the Magyar horse archers who haunted the steppes and harassed the Viking traders along the East Way.

Hervor was an archer, too, and may have shot from horseback. Hers is one of only eighteen graves at Birka—out of the eleven hundred excavated—to contain a horse, and hers are clearly riding horses. One of them was bridled with an iron bit; a second bit was found nearby. A pair of iron stirrups are all that remain of her wood-and-leather saddle. By her side were twenty-five spike-headed, armor-piercing arrows with elegant silver accents. Between the arrows and her scramasax was a bare spot, a gap, the right shape for a bow, which had disintegrated.

It may have been a Magyar bow. Though not preserved in her own grave, the distinctive metal rings and fittings of Magyar bow cases and quivers were recovered from other Birka graves of Hervor's generation, as well as from the remains of the town's fortress, which burned down a few years after she was buried and wasn't rebuilt. Magyar bows, sometimes called horn bows, were composites of wood, sinew, and horn, bent into a reflex shape. Small and handy on horseback, they were equally suited to fighting on shipboard or defending a hillfort like the one that guarded Birka: They shot twice as far as an ordinary wooden bow. At close range they offered the skilled archer greater accuracy, speed, and penetration.

But Hervor was not solely a mounted archer. An archer's weapon kit consisted of bow, arrows, spear, and shield. Hervor was buried with almost every Viking weapon known: sword, scramasax, arrows and bow, axe, two spears, and two shields. She was buried with more weapons than any other warrior in Birka; more than almost every Viking in the world. Of those Vikings found buried with any weapons at all, 61 percent have one weapon; only 15 percent have three or more.

Hervor's grave is remarkable not only for its complete weapon set and sacrificed horses. Its location is equally impressive. From the main gate of the hillfort that crowned the island, an avenue led north or south. North, it passed between two groups of elite graves. South, it went to the Warriors' Hall, where Birka's garrison lived. Hervor's grave lay west of the road, beside the hall. It was hard to miss: It was the only grave marked with a tall standing stone. It was also the grave set farthest west, perched to look down over the harbor and town, and out across the waters of Lake Malaren to the royal manor on the neighboring island of Adelso. From Hervor's grave you could see everyone who came or went, to or from the busy town of Birka. Whoever Hervor was, the warriors of Birka honored her memory. They wanted her near to keep watch.

The prominent location of her grave, her panoply of weapons, the double sacrifice of valuable horses—these mark Hervor as a warrior of high status. A final touch elevates her rank to war leader: the full set of pieces for the board game *hnefatafl*, or Viking chess, that was placed in her lap. From the Roman Iron Age through the high medieval era, from Iceland to Africa to Japan, the combination of game pieces, weapons, and horses in a grave has indicated a war leader. Game pieces symbolize authority and a "flair for strategic thinking." They express "the idea that success in warfare is not dependent on physical strength and dexterity alone but also on intelligence and the ability to foresee the actions of one's opponents," scholars say. In Viking terms, particularly, they attest to the warrior's good luck.

Until the bones in Bj581 were determined to be female, no one doubted the warrior in the grave was a war leader. She was buried as a war leader—her gender seems not to have been worth mentioning. Individuality was not highly prized in the Viking Age. What mattered was not your unique and special self but your role in life. If you had the required qualities, physical and mental, you could fill any role; you became that role.

One role Hervor may not have filled is mother. Viking women are often found buried with two large oval or box-shaped metal brooches by their collarbones. These brooches, experts think, clasped the shoulder straps of a wool dress, cut like an apron or pinafore, worn over a low-necked linen shift. It was a practical design that made breastfeeding easy. Hervor did not wear an apron-dress; there are no brooches in her grave.

Based on what little does remain of her clothing, she dressed like the other Birka warriors. They affected an urban style, distinctive to the fortress towns along the East Way; it was a mixture of Viking, Slavic, steppe-nomadic, and Byzantine fashions. Under a classic Viking cloak, clasped with a ring-shaped iron pin at one shoulder, Hervor wore a nomad's kaftan, a riding coat that wrapped in the front and was closed by a belt or buttons. It might have been made of Byzantine silk; in her grave was a scrap of fabric woven from silk and silver threads. It might have been decorated with mirrored sequins, a scattering of which were also found in her grave.

On her head she wore a close-fitting silk cap with earflaps that could be fastened up with silver buttons. It was topped by a filigreed silver cone that might have stuck up straight like a spike or flopped over like a tassel, depending on the cut of the cap. Only the buttons and cone and a scrap of silk remain of Hervor's cap, but a silk cap perhaps like it was found in a fabric-rich grave in the Caucasus. An exact match for her cap's filigreed silver cone was buried with another Birka warrior. A third matching cone was buried with a warrior near Kyiv.

Who was this valkyrie buried in grave Bj581? What might her life have been like? To tell Hervor's story, I have to use my imagination. I have to make assumptions. I have to connect the dots.

Her bones say she lived to be thirty or forty. Archaeologists can rarely date their finds within a span of thirty years. Historians have a similar difficulty. The medieval sources are chronologically confused. Most were written down well after the events they record, and the accounts in different texts simply do not sync. Like anyone else studying the Viking Age, I'll have to approximate. In Hervor's case, the items in her grave suggest she died around the middle of the tenth century, when Birka was at its height and its connections to the East Way were strongest. The location of her grave implies she was buried after the Warriors' Hall was built, around 930 or 950, but well before it burned down, between 965 and 985. To tell the best story, I'll guess she was buried a little after 960 and born around 930.

Where exactly was she born? Science tells me only that she came from southern Sweden or Norway. Looking at the Viking world from a warrior woman's point of view, I've opted for the kingdom of Vestfold, on the west side of the Oslo Fjord. Here, a hundred years before Hervor's birth, two powerful women were buried in the most lavish Viking grave ever uncovered, the Oseberg ship mound. Here, when Hervor was a child, the great hall guarding the cosmopolitan trading port of Kaupang was destroyed—perhaps by Eirik Bloodaxe and Gunnhild Mother-of-Kings, who conquered Vestfold around that time.

Where would a small girl, born in the town of Kaupang to a rich family, if not royal, end up? Science suggests she went west, possibly to the British Isles—as did Eirik and Gunnhild sometime between 935 and 946, having lost Norway's throne. From their base in the Orkney Islands, the royal pair meddled in the politics of the main Viking towns in the west, Dublin and York. Ruthless, ambitious, and fiercely intelligent, Gunnhild Mother-of-Kings makes a fine role model for a young valkyrie. Another role model is the Viking chieftain known as the Red Girl, active in the Irish Sea at that time.

When Eirik Bloodaxe was killed in England in 954, Gunnhild sought allies in Denmark. When the Danish king Harald Bluetooth helped put her sons on Norway's throne in 961, Gunnhild ruled beside them for fourteen years: One medieval historian called it the "Age of Gunnhild." Long before then, however, Hervor had quit Gunnhild's court and become a Viking. She was already in Birka, defending the town, if she died there as war leader before the Warriors' Hall burned down.

Yet, before her death, Hervor traveled on the East Way to Kyiv and back, if Kyiv is where she got the silver cone for her silk cap. If so, she met Queen Olga, who ruled the Vikings, or Rus, in Kyiv from about 945 until 957, when her son, Sviatoslav, came of age. In 971 Sviatoslav took the Rus south to challenge Byzantium, a raid that ended in disaster on a Bulgarian battlefield, where the Byzantine victors found warrior women among the Viking dead. Hervor was not among them; she had already been buried in Birka.

Besides this conjectural outline of Hervor's life, what links Dublin and York to Kaupang, Birka, and Kyiv? The Viking slave trade, through which young men and women were exchanged for Byzantine silk and Arab silver. The Viking slave route passed the Danish island of Samsey, where perhaps Hervor stopped to plunder her father's grave and retrieve his sword, as did her namesake in the poem *Hervor's Song*. Let's begin by imagining her there.

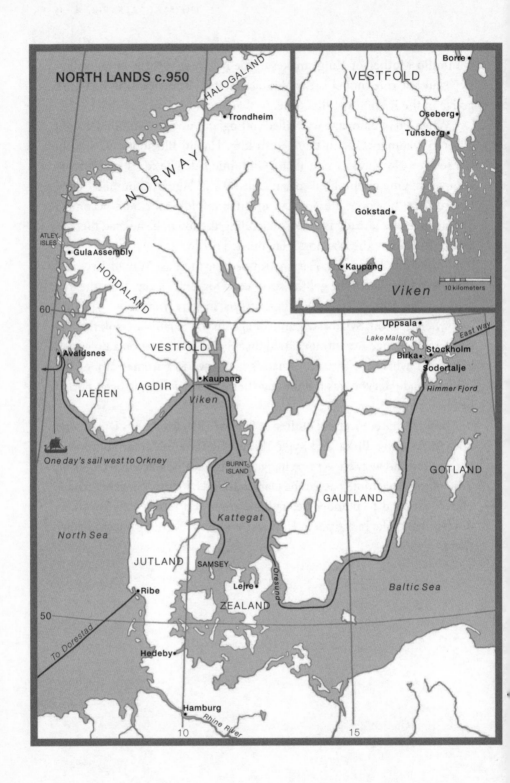

NORTH LANDS c.950

VESTFOLD

Borre

Oseberg

Tunsberg

Gokstad

Kaupang

Viken

10 kilometers

HALOGALAND

Trondheim

N O R W A Y

ATLEY ISLES

Gula Assembly

HORDALAND

60

VESTFOLD

Uppsala

Lake Malaren

East Way

Avaldsnes

Birka

Stockholm

Sodertalje

Himmer Fjord

AGDIR

Kaupang

JAEREN

Viken

One day's sail west to Orkney

BURNT ISLAND

GOTLAND

Kattegat

GAUTLAND

North Sea

JUTLAND

SAMSEY

Lejre

Oresund

Baltic Sea

Ribe

50

ZEALAND

To Dorestad

Hedeby

Hamburg

Rhine River

10

15

HERVOR'S SONG

Sunset on the isle of Samsey. A cold mist rolls in off the Kattegat. A shepherd gathering his flock for the night pauses on the dunes, alert, always alert on this small island famed as a meeting place of Vikings. And indeed, those sounds he hears, that rhythmic splashing, that groan and creak of oars, mean a ship is nearing—one or more. He throws himself flat in the long grass and listens.

He hears his sheep bleating as they trot homeward down the forest path, the bellwether leading. He wishes he were with them. He isn't sure which is worse to meet here after dark: the Vikings in the approaching ships, or those buried under the mounds. Twenty years ago, two rival bands met here and fought: Angantyr and his eleven brothers against Arrow-Odd and his companions. All died except Arrow-Odd—people say he used magic. The dead haunt the shoreline still.

Beneath the raucous chatter of gulls, he listens to the breeze worrying the grass. An owl hoots, and the forest birds fall silent. The sun sinks lower; the mist thickens.

Now he hears voices, raised, and the rattle of weapons. A knocking of ships' hulls, one bright and empty, the other weighty and dark. More oar splash. He is ready to run.

But what comes out of the mist is only a small boat rowed by a single warrior. The boat grounds and the warrior leaps out, drawing the vessel higher on the stony shingle. In spite of himself, the shepherd is curious. He lifts his head.

Immediately, the warrior spots him. You! she calls. Come down.

He rises to his feet, brushes off his bare knees, and slides down the dune to the beach. You're crazy, coming here alone at nightfall, he says. Get to shelter before it's too late.

The warrior gathers her gear from her boat. There's no shelter for me here, she replies. I know no one living on this island.

When she turns toward him, he instinctively steps back. She is taller than he is, and much more muscular. Much wealthier, too. She wears a ringmail byrnie—he knows how heavy those are—but moves as if it were weightless. Beneath it she wears a good wool tunic, padded and embroidered, over wide wool pants, cross-gaitered below the knee. Silver glints at her throat. Her long hair is knotted at her nape.

Get back to your ship, he says. You can't stay on the beach, not at night. It's not safe to be alone here.

She claps a battered helm on her head, slips a hand axe into her belt. She picks up her shield and spear. You're here with me, she says. Carry those. She points the spear tip at the rest of the pile: a broad axe, a shovel, a coil of rope.

The shepherd laughs. Only fools walk by the barrows at night. He gestures west, where the land is rippled by rows and clusters of grave mounds, some marked with tall upright stones, others shadowed by brush and trees. Two mounds stand higher than the rest, one by the shore, the other a little inland, on the edge of the salt marsh. Already he sees fires flickering in the mist as the sunset paints the sky red.

They're scared too, she says, glancing over her shoulder at the invisible Viking ship. She turns back toward the mounds. Which is Angantyr's?

We shouldn't be standing here talking, he says. We should be heading home as fast as we can.

She unlinks a silver arm-ring and dangles it from a finger. I'll give you this if you tell me where to dig.

The shepherd snatches it. He points to the nearer of the big mounds. Arrow-Odd buried his friends there in their boat, he says, and over there he buried his enemies, Angantyr and his brothers, in a wood-walled chamber. He claimed he did it alone, but of course we islanders helped him. We covered both graves with wood and turf and heaped sand over them. We left the dead with all their weapons, I swear it. But still they walk. At night, their graves open. This whole point of land bursts into flames.

It's her turn to laugh, a scoffing laugh. I don't faint at the crackling of a fire, she says.

Tossing her shield on the sand, she picks up the shovel and sets off for the barrow. She doesn't look back, doesn't see the shepherd disappear down the forest path.

Framed by the sunset, the barrow *is* on fire. Mist swirls around its base like smoke. She wades through it, unafraid. Circling the mound, she prods it with her spear. The turf and sand are not deep—you can't expect much of a monument when your enemies bury you. Her spear tip touches wood and in one place pokes into it; the timbers are rotten. She won't need the rope. She strips off her gear and starts digging at ground level. She takes her hand axe to the wood. Soon she breaks through.

When the tunnel is wide enough, she arms herself again and slips into the barrow—and only then realizes what she's forgotten: light.

The grave is darker than night. She waits for her eyes to adjust, but not a glimmer from the sunset sky seeps in. Death surrounds her.

I will not tremble before you, Father, she says. Speak to me.

She closes her eyes but hears only silence and the wind in the world outside. One hand on the damp wooden wall of the tomb, she shifts forward until she can stand.

Awake, Angantyr! Angantyr, awake! she calls out. I am Hervor, Svava's daughter, your only child. Give me your sword, the great sword Tyrfing, the Flaming Sword the dwarfs forged in their halls of stone.

Again, no answer. She takes another step forward and stumbles to one knee. She steadies her balance with her spear shaft, but one hand still comes down upon bones. She jerks her hand away.

May you writhe within your ribs, she curses. May your barrow be an anthill in which you rot. May you never feast with Odin in Valhalla, unless you let me wield that sword. Why should dead hands hold such a weapon?

And this time she thinks she hears an answer. *You do wrong to call down evils upon me. No dead hands hold that sword. My enemies built this barrow. They took Tyrfing.*

It could be true, though the shepherd swore not. She calls out again into the darkness: Would you cheat your only child? Tell the truth! Let Odin accept you only if the Flaming Sword is not here, in the tomb.

Silence. She opens her eyes and now flames do flash and flicker about her. She reaches for them, but they dance away.

Not for all your fires will I fear you, Father. It takes more than a dead man to frighten me.

You must be mad. Go back to your ships! No woman in the world would wield that cursed sword.

She knows of the curse: Once drawn, the sword must kill before it can be sheathed again. If not, it will doom her sons, destroy her family line— but what does she care about that? She has no sons, and no intention of marrying. She is a shield-maid. A warrior woman. A valkyrie.

People thought me man enough, she quips, before I came here.

Twelve bodies were buried in this barrow, her father and his eleven brothers. Angantyr, she reasons, was laid on top. Using her spear as a probe, she finds the edges of the pile, then its highest point. She pokes and prods until something falls to the floor that is not bone.

She shimmies out through the tunnel, her treasure tight in her fist: It *is* her father's sword, gold-hilted Tyrfing, the Flaming Sword.

The mist has disappeared. The starlight seems so bright.

You've done well, Father, to give me your sword, Hervor says. I'd rather have it than rule all Norway.

Hervor's Song was the first Old Norse poem to be translated into English, in 1703. As such, it crafted the image we hold today of the fearless Viking warrior who laughs in the face of danger—and that warrior is a woman.

My dramatization isn't exact: The original includes no shovel. Instead, I've described what might have happened if *Hervor's Song* reflected a real event—if, let's say, this Hervor was the real warrior woman buried in grave Bj581 beside the Swedish town of Birka.

In the poem, the flames are real. The grave magically opens; the dead rise like smoke. Hervor conjures up her ghostly father and demands he hand over the family heirloom, the famous Flaming Sword. When he refuses, fearing the sword's curse will destroy his family line, she scoffs and finally bends him to her will. "Now," she brags, brandishing the sword, "I have walked between worlds." The poem is eerie and otherworldly and has been popular, in English, for hundreds of years. Some say this poem inspired the first Gothic novel.

But the prose *Saga of Hervor*, which quotes the poem—and so preserved it for us to read—confounds modern readers. We like our genres clear-cut. Is it history? Is it fantasy? Is it *true*?

Medieval Iceland's writers made no such distinctions. Those few sagas that do not mention dragons or ghosts, witches or werewolves, prophetic dreams or dire omens, dwell instead on the miracles of saints. The name "saga" implies neither fiction nor fact; it derives from the Old Norse verb *segja*, "to say." A good saga seamlessly integrates the two. Some saga authors were witnesses to the events they relate; others retell stories from hundreds of years in their past. Some list their sources: folktales, poems, genealogies, or interviews with wise grandmothers. Others don't. Some mimic foreign tales of chivalry; others focus on Icelandic farmers and their petty feuds.

All I can say for certain about the sagas is that they were first written down, in prose, after Christian missionaries created an Old Norse alphabet soon after the year 1000—no sagas are written in the ancient Norse runes—and that the copies we have were created in Iceland in the 1200s, 1300s, or even later.

A manuscript can be dated by what it's written on (skin or paper), by the chemistry of its ink, by the shape of its letters and the abbreviations used, and by its vocabulary (though an ancient word hoard can be faked). Dating the stories and poems a manuscript contains is trickier. They are older than the parchment or ink, for sure. But how much older? For *Hervor's Song*, I have a few clues.

The oldest copy of the *Saga of Hervor* was penned by an Icelandic lawyer named Haukur Erlendsson, as he tells us in letters from 1302 and 1310, though he only copied down the bits he liked. A longer (but much later) manuscript suggests the *Saga of Hervor* was first composed around 1120 for Queen Ingigerd of Sweden, whose mother was a princess from Kyiv. This version ends with a long list of kings descended (in spite of the sword's curse) from Hervor, and the last on the list is Ingigerd's husband.

The saga itself is set in a mythic Viking past that is impossible to date. Its story ranges from Norway east through Russia to the Black Sea and, as sagas go, it is not particularly well written. It could use "a ruthless rewriting" to smooth out its "many inconsistencies" and tie up its "loose ends," according to its modern translator, and I have to agree. But it was apparently quite popular in the Middle Ages: Many manuscripts include a copy.

During the general "sorting frenzy" of the Victorian Age, the *Saga of Hervor* was classified as a Saga of Ancient Times, a genre created to dismiss a group of "mythical" or "romantic" tales "that have little or no historical authenticity," as the translator put it. Yet, perversely, he prized the *Saga of Hervor* for its historical elements, which "come down from a very remote antiquity." Those elements include *Hervor's Song* and three other poems quoted in the text.

Saga scholars since the Middle Ages have deemed poems more authentic than prose. It was common for Viking kings and queens to retain court poets to record their deeds. "People still know their poems," wrote the Icelandic author Snorri Sturluson in the 1200s. Like sonnets or haiku, Viking Age poetry had elaborate rules for rhyme, rhythm, and alliteration. These rules made poems harder to tinker with—and easier to memorize—than prose. "If a verse is composed correctly," Snorri asserted, "the words in it will remain the same, even as they are passed down from person to person" for hundreds of years.

Modern readers tend to agree with him: Most of what we think we know about the Viking mind comes from Viking poetry. Much of Viking history derives from poetry as well. For his *Heimskringla* (or *Orb of the World*), a collection of sixteen sagas about Norway's kings, Snorri expanded upon "what is said in the poems recited before the rulers themselves or their sons." Of course, he admitted, poets exaggerate: "It is the way of poets to praise most those to whom they are speaking," he said (and Snorri was himself a poet). But no one would dare to recite a poem praising the rulers for things that they—and everyone listening—knew were false. "That would be mockery, not praise." For that reason, Snorri took to be true "all that can be found in those poems about their travels or their wars."

If I apply Snorri's rule to the *Saga of Hervor*, it's hard not to conclude that some Viking women were warriors.

The first poem in the saga tells how the Viking warrior Angantyr came to be buried on the Danish isle of Samsey before his only child was born. Hervor, says the prose between the poems, grew up with her grandfather, a chieftain, thinking she was the swineherd's bastard. A difficult child, she preferred archery and swordplay to sewing and embroidery. As a teen she ran off and lived wild in the woods, robbing and killing passersby before being hauled back to court, where she annoyed everyone with her rudeness. When she finally learned her father was a famous Viking warrior, not a swineherd, she resolved to be like him. She ordered a new shirt and cloak, demanding her mother give her "everything you would give to a son." She renamed herself Hervard, the masculine form of her name—and the saga author follows suit, referring to her as "he," not "she."

Hervard joined a Viking band and quickly rose to lead it. Raiding in the Kattegat, among the Danish islands, he led his band to Samsey and proposed they break into the grave mounds to reclaim his family treasure. His crew feared waking the dead, so he rowed to the island alone. Here the saga writer inserted *Hervor's Song*, in which Hervard reveals himself to be Angantyr's daughter and declares she would rather have her father's sword "than rule all Norway."

In the saga, this Hervard-Hervor eventually gives up the Viking life, marries, and has two sons. The third poem quoted in the saga is a set of riddles associated with one of them, King Heidrek the Wise. One riddle, aptly, refers to warrior women:

> *Around a weaponless*
> *king, what women*
> *are fighting?*
> *The fair attack him,*
> *the red defend him,*
> *day after day.*

The answer to the riddle is the board game *hnefatafl*, or Viking chess. Hervor, the saga says, was an expert player, better than the king under whose banner she fought.

Her skill explains how she could become a Viking leader: Not only had she trained with weapons since childhood, she displayed that flair for strategic thinking so prized in the Viking Age. Success depended on surprise—a Viking band was often outnumbered. But surprise depended on skill. A good leader took care of logistics: Her band was well fed and rested, and their ship and equipment in good shape before a raid. She could read the weather and water; she didn't get lost. Her contacts (and spies) kept her well informed of which kings were at war (and so looking elsewhere). She knew her enemies' tactics, and how to trick them. She knew when fairs were held and harvests brought in, the routes of the tax collectors and traders. She could rouse her fighters to battle frenzy, make them laugh at defeat, and engineer their escape. She had good luck—in a pinch, she could be counted on to make the right choice—and she never gave up. She dressed as a man for practical reasons, not to fool anyone—there's no privacy on a Viking ship, not even a deck to go below. She announced her sex the first time she pissed. She took a man's name to announce her role: She was a warrior.

The final poem in the *Saga of Hervor* features a second shield-maid named Hervor. In the saga she is the first Hervor's granddaughter, but scholars think the chronology's mixed up. This poem, they believe, tells of an ancient war some four hundred years before the Viking Age began. If so, *The Battle of the Goths and the Huns* may be "the oldest of all the heroic lays preserved in the North."

The poem is set beside the forest of Mirkwood, on the border between the Goths, who were ruled by one of this Hervor's two brothers, and the Huns, from whom her second brother had raised an army to challenge his sibling's rule. Hervor commanded the border fortress. One morning, from the tower above her fortress gate, she watched as a great cloud of dust rolled out from the shadows under the trees. It glittered as it moved. She called her trumpeter. "Summon the host," she said, and when her warriors gathered: "Take up your weapons and prepare for battle." By the time the Huns arrived on their fast horses, glittering in ringmail and helmets and wielding their deadly horn bows, Hervor was ready. She rode out at the head of her army, and the battle began. But she was badly outnumbered. She and her captains were killed, all but one; he rode night and day to bring the news to the king of the Goths. The king took no time to mourn his sister—she had been happier in battle than other women were when chatting with their suitors, the poem says—but set forth at once to avenge her. He met the Huns on the plains of the Danube. The battle raged for days, until the Goths, their ranks constantly reinforced as the news spread, repelled the Hun invaders, leaving so many dead that the rivers were dammed with corpses and overflowed their banks.

If *The Battle of the Goths and the Huns* is truly the oldest epic song of the north, then the idea of the warrior woman was embedded in Viking culture from its very start.

A Viking rider and a standing warrior, less than an inch tall, from Tisso, Denmark. Near-identical amulets have been found in England and Poland.

The Christian writer of the *Saga of Hervor*, stitching four ancient poems into a tale in twelfth-century Sweden, struggled with that idea and ultimately rejected it. Though the Gothic Hervor who guards the border remains a hero (if a failed one), her grave-robbing namesake in *Hervor's Song* is thoroughly undermined. She is cruel, willful, self-centered, greedy, light-minded, and not, in the end, a good leader. Her role in the saga, it seems, is to warn against letting your daughters run wild.

In the poem, the shepherd on Samsey is not surprised to see a warrior woman, only to see anyone foolhardy enough to face the ghost-fires. Neither is Hervor's ghostly father, Angantyr, surprised to see her in armor or commanding a fleet of Viking ships. He finds her "not like other people" (another translation is "hardly human") not because she wants to wield a sword, but because she wants *this* sword: the cursed sword that will destroy all their kin. Even the saga writer, introducing the poem, matter-of-factly identifies Hervor as the leader of a Viking band. Yet after winning her father's sword, the saga says, Hervor returned to the shore to find her companions had deserted her.

It's unlikely. A Viking band was a team, its success dependent on cooperation and trust. Its members were closer than kin.

Though fighters from the same families often joined the same bands, Viking bands were notable for their diversity. Bands included men and women, young and old, rich and poor, warriors from the same region and those from far off, even those who spoke different languages and worshipped different gods, all brought together by a leader's reputation for good luck.

Viking bands were notable, too, for their loyalty: They swore a binding oath. Elaborate rites and symbols also bound them: They painted their ships or shields with certain colors or patterns, affected a certain style of dress, followed a single banner. They wore or carried amulets or badges fashioned as miniature ships, spearheads, hammers, swords, falcons, dragons, wolves, and people, both men and women, tearing out their hair or bearing weapons, standing or riding or both. These may have been lucky charms or religious totems, or they may have functioned like the challenge coins modern soldiers must produce on demand to prove they belong to a certain unit.

Most of all, the members of a Viking band were bound by common experiences: the spiritual release of rituals, the trauma of the battlefield, the dangers of sea travel, and the overindulgence that defined a good feast, where boasting and storytelling both created and expressed their shared identity, and oaths were sealed with a drink.

If the Christian author of the *Saga of Hervor* had believed in the reality of Viking warrior women, if that writer had known what it meant to be a Viking leader—or had understood Hervor's meaning when she quipped she was thought "man enough"—her story might have continued like this:

When Hervor returned from the grave mounds, she found her ship moored in a creek on the lee side of the cape. Her crew had butchered a stolen sheep and were stewing bits of it in an iron pot over their campfire— all but the warriors left guarding the ship. Hervor joined their circle and set to cleaning Tyrfing, the Flaming Sword, scraping away the moldering remains of the wood-and-leather sheath, oiling away the rust and tarnish, and honing the edge with her whetstone. Finished, she raised a horn of beer and recounted—in verse—how she had taken the sword from her ghostly father.

The sword buried with the warrior woman in Birka grave Bj581, the Hervor of this book, was not the gold-hilted Tyrfing. It was a simple, sturdy weapon, of a style most often found in Sweden, Russia, and Ukraine.

I can only guess how she earned it.

Perhaps, like her poetic namesake, she took it from a grave. The Persian historian Miskawayh, who chronicled a Viking raid on a town in Azerbaijan in 943, noted that the slain Vikings were buried with their swords. But these swords were in high demand "for their sharpness and excellence," so as soon as the rest of the Vikings left town, their enemies reopened the graves, picked out the swords, and sold them.

In the Icelandic sagas, grave robbing is not so simple—or safe. Some attempts involve terrifying confrontations with reanimated corpses, zombies who can only be overcome if their heads are cut off and set between their buttocks. The poetic Hervor's argument with her ghostly father is tame by comparison. Yet archaeologists have found breaking into Viking barrows to be common—nearly every large grave mound from the Viking Age shows signs of intruders. It may have been the usual practice to retrieve heirlooms like swords.

Not all Viking swords were buried, even temporarily. Many were passed down from generation to generation. Such was the case with Tyrfing before Hervor's father, Angantyr, took it to the grave. According to the *Saga of Hervor*, Tyrfing was made by two dwarfs (under duress) for a Viking chieftain in Russia. He gave it to the Swedish Viking who married his daughter. They took Tyrfing to Sweden, and some twenty years later the Viking gave it to his eldest son, Angantyr, before he and his brothers set off to challenge their enemies on the Danish isle of Samsey. "I think you will have need of good weapons," their father said. The poetic Hervor was the fourth generation to wield the Flaming Sword; her last act in the saga is to give it to her son.

The hero of *Grettir's Saga* had a sword with a similar lineage. He received Jokul's Gift from his mother, secretly, because his father did not think he deserved a weapon. As Grettir set out from home, his mother "took a sword out from under her cloak; it was her most valuable possession. She said, 'My grandfather Jokul owned this sword, and other Vatnsdalers before him, and it brought them victory.'" She added, "I think you will have need of it."

Swords were won in battles and duels; they were also traded among friends. In *Egil's Saga*, Egil gave his friend Arinbjorn two gold arm-rings. In return, Arinbjorn gave Egil a sword named Slicer. Arinbjorn had received Slicer from Egil's brother, who in turn had received it from Egil's father; he had it from his brother, who got it from a friend, who got it from his own father—altogether, Slicer had seven owners over three generations.

The sword's biography added to its value: It tied its owners together in a web of friendship. "Long friendships follow frequent gifts," says the Viking creed, *Havamal*, or *The Words of the High One*. "If you have a friend you fully trust and want good to come of your friendship, share your thoughts, exchange gifts, and go to visit often."

A gift was an invitation—and an obligation. "To your friend, be a friend, matching gift for gift," the Viking creed continues. The rule concerned not only cloaks and swords, but intangible gifts as well: match laughter with laughter, but lies with lies.

Most of all, the Vikings' gift rule concerned whom you fought for or against. Says a poem written for Harald Fairhair, king of Norway when Hervor was born:

> By their gear,
> their gold rings,
> you can see
> they're the king's friends.
> They have red cloaks
> and colored shields,
> silver-clad swords
> and ring-woven shirts
> gilded sword belts,
> engraved helmets,
> rings ready to hand,
> that Harald gave them.

"The king's friends," here, means his army. But Harald Fairhair, who died around 932, was one of the last kings to hold power this way, by giving his friends gifts.

By the time Hervor earned her sword in the mid-900s, *The Words of the High One*, along with other tenets of paganism, were fading in the face of new ideas of kingship coming north from Christian Europe. A Christian king like Harald Bluetooth, who came to power in Denmark in about 958, ruled by divine right. Bluetooth didn't need to persuade warriors to support him through gifts and acts of friendship—he commanded them. To disobey a Christian king was to disobey God and be damned. And, as the earthly representative of God the Father Almighty, the Christian king was, by definition, a man.

It wasn't always so in the Viking world.

The Viking Age was an age of endings. It was indeed Ragnarok, the Twilight of the Gods, when the ancient pantheon of deities and spirits was exchanged for the Christian one-in-three. It did not come at once, this Change of Ways, as the sagas call it, but in waves. The sun did not darken, nor the earth sink; the sky was not scorched by fire, nor the stars blotted out, as the wisewoman predicts in the poem *Song of the Seer*, written in Iceland around the year 1000, when converting their subjects to Christianity was the policy of Viking kings. But when the Viking Age began, in the eighth century, the people of the North were pagan. When it ended, three hundred years later, they had abandoned Freyja and Freyr, Odin and Thor, and put their faith in Christ.

What changed? Their entire way of looking at the world. The roles of women and men were radically altered. What had once been ordinary became taboo. Hervor, our valkyrie, our shield-maid, the skeleton buried in Birka grave Bj581, was a relic by the time she died. By the time the *Saga of Hervor* was written, religion was a monopoly and patriarchy ruled. A warrior woman was as odd as a dragon.

But when Hervor was born, around 930, a woman's opportunities were far wider. "You've done well, Father, to give me your sword," says the warrior woman in *Hervor's Song*. "I'd rather have it than rule all Norway"—which implies that for her, as for the Viking Age poet, a woman *could* rule.

And, indeed, if Hervor was born around 930 in Vestfold in southern Norway, as I speculate, she would have known a woman who *did* rule all Norway: Gunnhild Mother-of-Kings.

2

GUNNHILD
MOTHER-OF-KINGS

Her earliest memory is of fire. The whoosh and crackle of it overhead, the embers drifting down like brilliant snow to be stamped or swatted out with cloth soaked in whey or stale urine or even beer, the water barrel being already bone dry. The smoke smarting in her eyes and seizing her breath.

Stand still! barks her mother as she layers clothing onto her. Most are not even Hervor's clothes but belong to King Bjorn's daughter, who is already so overdressed she can hardly waddle.

Quit wriggling! Her mother loops a long string of beads three times around Hervor's neck and tries to clasp her cloak with an enormous brooch that must be the queen's.

There, in the chest, is a knife in a jeweled sheath. Hervor grabs it—and her mother slaps her, her own mother, whom Hervor will never see again after this night. Hervor spins away. Cloak and brooch drop to the floor as she darts for the door, brandishing the knife. *Hervor!* she hears her mother shriek as she slips between the legs of the warriors guarding the exit and runs into the tumult of the night.

Smoke and flames all around, horses screaming and cattle bawling as folk herd them away. People filling carts and wagons with plunder from the storehouses: barrels and sacks and chests and tubs, a bloody heap of dead geese.

A rhythmic chanting and banging mingles with the roar of the fires:

Bjorn's warriors, pinned inside the burning feast hall, have torn down a beam and are ramming a cornerpost, seeking a way out before the roof caves in.

A trumpet blares. At its sound, a small woman in a glittering robe strides to the center of the courtyard. She signals with one upraised hand, and four warriors race off in four different directions. The line of carts and wagons advances down the hill toward the town, following the herds. Fires flare up behind them as the storehouses are set alight.

The small woman turns to speak with her companion—a taller woman in a simple shift, her long hair loose, her feet bare. She looks like a slave, Hervor thinks, then startles: It's the Queen of the Shining Hall herself. She rushed from her bed at the first moment of the attack, to sue for peace for all those whose honor does not require them to fight. Has she been taken captive?

Hervor runs toward her, clutching her knife in one hand, the sheath in the other. She has nearly reached the two women when a strong arm circles her waist and she is lifted off the ground. She jabs down with her knife—

The kitten has teeth! the warrior says, laughing. She twists the knife out of Hervor's grasp and flips her sideways, pinning her securely against one hip, in spite of her efforts to escape. Is this wildcat yours? she asks the Queen of the Shining Hall.

No, says the queen. Hervor is our guest.

Then she will become my guest, says a third voice, soft and soothing, yet somehow it takes all the fight out of Hervor. She goes limp—startling the warrior enough that Hervor slips out of her grasp. She falls to the ground and sits there, looking up in awe at the small woman with the voice of power. The woman glances down and meets Hervor's gaze.

Give her back her knife, the woman orders. I admire a girl with guts. But tie her up so she can't use it again. Then bring out the rest of Bjorn's people so I can choose which others I'll claim. They've had time enough to fetch their things—and that roof is about to fall in.

She flicks her eyes to the queen. You go in too, she says. You need to dress.

The small woman returns her gaze to Hervor and drops her voice to a whisper. She won't fetch much of a bride-price, will she, if she looks like a slave.

The wedding is held at dawn. The Shining Hall lies in ruins, its roof collapsed, only two walls standing. Scraps of burned tapestries flutter above a smoking pile of broken beams and blackened bodies. The stench is horrible.

Huddled with the other children the small woman claimed, Hervor watches as the Queen of the Shining Hall is given as wife to one of her attackers.

A good match, says the small woman with the powerful voice.

The queen stands tall as a tree beside her, glittering herself, now, with beads and jewels, and swathed in a rich blue cloak. She looks down on the small woman and coldly says, King Bjorn will not come back from Valhalla. As things stand, Gunnhild, what choice do I have but to let you and Eirik have your way?

A good match, the small woman with the powerful voice repeats. And perhaps your daughter will marry one of my sons.

She glances at the group of captive children and catches Hervor's eye. Too bad that wildcat isn't yours, she adds. She shows promise.

Did it happen like that? Is that how Hervor came to the notice of Gunnhild Mother-of-Kings?

Perhaps.

Like Snorri Sturluson writing of Norway's kings hundreds of years after the events he describes, I'm weaving together poems and sagas and things experts tell me to imagine Hervor's early days. It's the only way. The events that shaped the warrior woman buried in Birka grave Bj581 will always be hidden in shadow, a thousand years on. She left no letters, no pictures. No descendants retold her tale. All I have are her bones.

These tell me she was well fed all her life, so grew up in a rich or royal household. She came from the western side of the Viking world—the kingdom of Vestfold in southern Norway fits the facts—and moved as a child, west again. She died, aged thirty to forty, before 970, and so was a child in the 930s when, archaeologists say, the Shining Hall in Vestfold burned to the ground. It was not rebuilt. By 950, both the hall on the hill and the market town beneath it were abandoned. What happened? Eirik Bloodaxe and Gunnhild Mother-of-Kings arrived in Vestfold, the sagas say, and fought to control it for five—or fifteen—years.

The story of Gunnhild Mother-of-Kings is told by Snorri Sturluson in the *Saga of Harald Fairhair*, the third of sixteen sagas about kings in the collection *Heimskringla* (or *Orb of the World*). An eloquent and unscrupulous lawyer, Snorri was the wealthiest and most powerful chieftain in thirteenth-century Iceland. He wanted to be Iceland's king—or at least its earl, under the rule of Norway—and wrote *Heimskringla*, after two years of travel and research, to gain influence at the Norwegian court. He is a captivating storyteller, and his books are treasures, among the finest literature of the Middle Ages. He is not a historian by modern standards, but he spoke with learned men and women, studied genealogies, and collected stories and poems.

He had a prodigious memory. In *Heimskringla* and in his *Edda*, a handbook on poetry and myths, Snorri quotes apt lines from nearly a thousand poems, most of which had never been written down before. Because he wrote for an audience of one—the young king of Norway, brought to the throne at age fourteen—his tales in these two books skew toward the interests of a boy. Because that boy was brought up by Christian bishops and remained largely under their control, Snorri gilds his Viking lore with Christian values.

As his books and his biography show, Snorri was also a misogynist. Gunnhild is one of the few women whose stories he tells in *Heimskringla*. She was too powerful to leave out: In other histories of Norway, the years 961 to 975, when she ruled Norway alongside her sons, are known as the "Age of Gunnhild."

But Snorri's account is not flattering. Gunnhild, he writes, was "intelligent and well-educated, charming, but very deceitful, and the grimmest person," by which he seems to mean uncompromising or fierce. He does not consider these to be good traits in a queen. She appears, as well, in *Egil's Saga*, which Snorri wrote for an Icelandic audience. There, as the villain, Gunnhild attempts to kill the Icelandic hero of the saga, Egil the Poet, several times. She is so malevolent, conniving, and cruel that modern scholars charge Snorri with conducting a "smear campaign."

An earlier history of Norway identifies Gunnhild as a princess, a daughter of the powerful Danish king Gorm the Old. Snorri explains Gunnhild's power differently. According to the wild tale he tells, Eirik Bloodaxe and his Viking band had raided east in the Baltic Sea and west among the British Isles, even all the way north along the North Way into the Barents Sea and the northernmost shores of Russia, where breeding walruses crowded the beaches and could be butchered for their valuable ivory tusks and thick skins, the best leather for making ships' rigging. On his way back south along Norway's coast, Eirik met the formidable woman who would become his wife—and provide the skills he lacked.

Gunnhild was so beautiful, the men who found her "had never seen the like of her." She was also small and delicate, and so had learned to protect herself with her wits. Eirik's men had found her alone in a Sami hut. They dared not capture her, she warned, speaking sweetly to them, for she was the ward of two sorcerers, who were then out hunting. Like other Sami, these two could follow a track like a dog, even over ice. They skied so fast and were such good shots that nothing escaped them. Nor did they need arrows to kill: With an angry look they could turn the land upside down. Any living thing they glared at fell dead. No, Eirik's men could not capture her—but they could *rescue* her, suggested the sweet young girl. Both sorcerers wanted to marry Gunnhild, and she did not plan to waste her life in the snowy woods, far from the halls of power.

She hid Eirik's men under some blankets and sprinkled ashes all about, making them invisible. When the Sami sorcerers came home from the hunt, tired and weary, she invited them to lie beside her, one on each side. She put her arms lovingly around their necks and sang them a magical lullaby. They slept so soundly they didn't even wake when she slipped two sealskin bags over their heads and tied them tight. Then she motioned to Eirik's men, who rushed out of their hiding place and stabbed the sorcerers to death.

In the morning, they escorted Gunnhild to Eirik. He took one look at the pretty girl and declared he would marry her. She said he must first ask her father's permission, so they sailed south to Halogaland, where the chieftain Ozur Toti gave his blessing.

How did Gunnhild arrive in the far north of Norway? Was Ozur Toti her real father, or her foster father, or the Viking who had captured her previously? Had she gone to the Sami on her own initiative, or was it common to send chieftains' daughters north to learn magic? Or was she, in fact, Sami herself? Snorri's tale leaves these questions unanswered.

Gunnhild Mother-of-Kings appears in many other stories, playing a part in eleven Icelandic sagas and several histories. She is always powerful, and always portrayed as the villain. All the writers were Christian, writing in the twelfth century or later. They picture Queen Gunnhild as proud and ambitious, lecherous and moody, ruthless, calculating, and cold. They also attest to her beauty and small size, her resilience, her ability to manipulate people with her voice, her organizational skill, her generosity, her humor, her knowledge of potions, rituals, poems, and stories, and her belief that the best way to neutralize her enemies was to adopt their children. She was good at raising children. Her own eight sons, unlike Eirik and his brothers, never turned on one another but shared the rule of Norway, when it finally came to them, with one another—and with her. As Snorri himself reports, from 961 to 975 Gunnhild and her sons "often met to talk things over together and to decide how to rule."

With her husband, Eirik Bloodaxe, Gunnhild was less successful. Eirik was a handsome man, strong and bold, a great warrior "blessed with victory," Snorri writes. But he was not like his father, King Harald Fairhair. He did not have his father's easy way around people. He was no charmer, but short of speech, and often sat silent in the feast hall, watching, a frown creasing his broad brow; his eyes in the moonlight "gleamed, dragon-like, terrible to look at," as Egil the Poet would later say. He had a quick temper.

He was also rather stupid. Faced with a difficult decision, time and again Eirik threw up his hands and refused to pass judgment, despite Gunnhild's best efforts to give him good advice. If Bloodaxe could not solve a problem with force, it didn't get solved.

And the problem Eirik was trying to solve when Hervor came into his orbit—how to become the sole king of Norway—was not succumbing to brute force.

Eirik's father was the first king of all Norway. In the late 800s, he united Norway's hundreds of chieftains and petty kings under his own rule. It was Harald Fairhair whose "friends" you could recognize, according to the contemporary poet Thorbjorn Horn-Cleaver, by their red cloaks, their "silver-clad swords . . . rings ready to hand, that Harald gave them." It was Harald Fairhair who amassed armies through gifts and friendship—and who was one of the last Viking kings to do so.

But it was tricky to be Harald's friend—he burned down the feast halls of friends he found too ambitious. When he conquered a district, Snorri writes, Harald gave the landowners and rich farmers "and anyone else who might cause trouble" three choices: They could become his friends, swearing to support him, or they could leave the country. "Otherwise, they could expect the harshest terms, even death." It was during Harald's reign, several sagas agree, that Iceland was settled and many Norwegian warriors and their families decamped to the British Isles.

Besides gifts, another way Harald Fairhair turned his enemies into friends was to marry their daughters. When he contracted to marry Eirik Bloodaxe's mother, Ragnhild the Powerful, Harald divorced nine of his wives, Snorri says: Ragnhild was the granddaughter of the king of Denmark, a most useful ally. By then the danger of his earlier strategy must have become clear. Through his many marriages, Harald had indeed united Norway under his own rule. But when his sons grew up—twenty of them, with seven different mothers—he was forced to divvy it up again.

By Norwegian law, any king's son could be elected king, with the consent of the chieftains and the landed farmers. That only an eldest son could inherit, and that only one marriage at a time was legitimate, were Christian ideas; they did not apply. In 930, when Hervor was born, there were nine Norwegian kingdoms—not twenty only because some of Eirik's brothers were dead, some had agreed to share the title of king, and Harald's youngest son was being raised in England. Each of Norway's nine kingdoms had to pass on half its taxes and tolls to Harald Fairhair, the high king.

Eirik Bloodaxe was Harald's favorite son, meant to be high king after his father's death. But the old man seemed in no hurry to die. Meanwhile, Eirik's brothers were entrenching themselves in their kingdoms. Eirik and Gunnhild decided to take matters into their own hands and kill off as many of Eirik's brothers as they could. Gunnhild arranged for one to be poisoned. Eirik burned two in their halls.

Brother Bjorn, king of Vestfold, might have avoided that fate if he'd been more hospitable. One autumn, Snorri says, Eirik swept into Vestfold with a fleet of dragonships and confronted his brother, demanding Bjorn give him the revenues owed to King Harald. He demanded Bjorn feed him and his warriors and, above all, get them something to drink.

Snorri, writing in the 1200s, says this confrontation happened outside Tunsberg, twenty miles north of the Shining Hall. But archaeologists say Tunsberg was not a center of power until late in the tenth century, nor are there signs that a feast hall was burned there in the 930s. Eirik's likely target was the Shining Hall and the rich market town, or *kaupang*, at its feet, for Bjorn was known by the nickname "the Merchant King."

Bjorn was no fighter. He was intelligent, calm, and "expected to make a good ruler," Snorri says. He owned a fleet of merchant ships "and so acquired for himself the various treasures and other things he thought he needed." Bjorn did not let Eirik upset him. He had always delivered the Vestfold revenues to their father himself, and he intended to continue doing so. Nor was he prepared to play host to Eirik's rowdy Viking band. The brothers quarreled. Eirik did not get his way and left in a rage.

Late that night, in the episode I've dramatized, Eirik surrounded the hall where Bjorn was staying and set fire to the roof. Bjorn and his warriors were still up drinking, the saga says. They armed themselves and burst out of the building.

In *Heimskringla* Snorri does not describe the fight, but a similar scene appears in *Egil's Saga*, when Eirik's father killed his ambitious friend Thorolf.

The king, like Eirik, came late at night, when everyone had been drinking for some time. He surrounded Thorolf's feast hall, unfurled his standard, blew his trumpets, and shouted his battle cries. Thorolf and his friends ran for their weapons and armor. Thorolf's wife, Sigrid, left the hall and petitioned the king. He agreed to let the children and old people, the slaves and servants, Sigrid and her women—everyone except Thorolf and his warriors—leave the building.

"Is there no chance of reaching a settlement between you and Thorolf, my lord?"

"If Thorolf gives himself up and asks me for mercy, I'll spare his life. But his warband must be punished."

Sigrid conveyed the king's terms to her husband. He refused them.

"Set fire to the hall," said the king.

The trapped warriors broke down the partition separating the main room of the hall, with its high ceiling, from the entryway. "They took one of the beams, as many as could grab hold of it, and rammed one end of it at a corner post so hard that the joints gave way and the walls burst apart," Snorri writes.

Thorolf's warriors rushed out, but the king's troops held them pinned against the burning building. For a while, they used it to shield their backs. But as the fire blazed hotter they pressed forward, and soon many had been killed. Thorolf himself charged at the king's banner, striking out to left and right. He reached the shield-wall—the braced shields of the warriors who surrounded the king—and killed the standard-bearer by the king's side. "He was wounded by both swords and spears, but the king himself dealt him his death-wound, and Thorolf fell dead at the king's feet." His last words, in suitable Viking fashion, were, "I'm just three feet short."

At once, the king stopped the killing—as Eirik Bloodaxe did when his brother, Bjorn the Merchant, was dead. As the hall burned to the ground, the king gave quarter to the warriors who survived, provided they swear fealty to him and join his warband. He had the dead buried, the wounded treated, and the queen of the hall quickly remarried—it is Sigrid in *Egil's Saga* who "realized that as things stood she had no choice and must let the king have his way."

Eirik's attack on his brother's hall was not a Viking raid (though he certainly plundered the storehouses). Eirik intended to rule the people of Vestfold as king of Norway. Setting fire to Bjorn's feast hall was symbolic.

Feast halls throughout the Viking world were much alike. Though some had roofs of thatch and others of bark or shingles, though some had thick outer walls of well-insulating sod and others thin wooden walls of tarred or whitewashed planks or the basketweave of twigs plastered with mud known as wattle and daub, their basic layout changed little for hundreds of years. They were oblong—roughly boat-shaped—and divided into three parts (not counting the occasionally attached stables): the kitchen and storeroom, the ruler's private quarters, and the open public space where lordship was symbolically enacted.

Within the hall were held the rituals through which the bonds between rulers and people were renewed. Some rituals were religious, held to propitiate the deities or speak with ancestors, to foretell the future, decide a course of action, pray for good luck or a good harvest, or give thanks for a victory. Others were political: The order in which people were seated or given something to eat and drink. What they ate or drank and how much. The storytelling, poetry, music, boasting, and oath taking that accompanied the meal. The gifts received on arrival or departure, such as clothing and jewelry, chests of silver coins, ships and horses, weapons and armor, control of estates and harbors, opportunities for plunder and monopolies on trade, offers of marriage alliances, or prospects for revenge. All these were ways in which individuals were melded into a people, and all took place, at least in part, inside the feast hall.

Feasting itself was a gift—being invited to accompany your ruler to a feast was a mark of high status. For a hall was not a palace. A Viking ruler had no fixed abode, but circulated among several halls, each on an estate managed by a chieftain who counted him- or herself among the ruler's friends. It was these friends who provided the meat and drink for the feast. Friendship had little to do with affection and much to do with politics.

A chieftain's hall was costly to build. Like a grave mound, it announced the chieftain's command of labor and wealth. It was a statement of power. Its exceptionally high roof, like those of later cathedrals, made the inside space feel larger than expected and, consequently, made those who entered feel small. Its position in the landscape added to this effect: A chieftain's hall was set on a hill, to see and be seen. Exposed to wind and storm, it was placed not to be comfortable, but to be commanding. It metaphorically oversaw the realm, controlling trade routes and access to resources like iron ore, fertile fields, and timber.

And so its destruction by fire was equally commanding. When the Shining Hall was destroyed, the merchants and artisans living in the town below watched it flare and flame like a fiery dragon. But they did not fear it. Like Bjorn's queen they had understood that, "as things stood," they would have to change their allegiance. Even before the fires were lit, they had, in essence, done just that: Gunnhild's ships rocked at the town's wharves, waiting for plunder; Eirik's warriors patrolled the town's lanes. The townsfolk did not foresee that this change of rulers (unlike the last one) would mean the end of the town they called Kaupang. They could not know that this time the Shining Hall would not be rebuilt.

3

THE TOWN BENEATH
THE SHINING HALL

Hervor tries to wriggle around so she can see forward, but the wagon is too tightly packed with boxes and barrels and bags. And with other children. All the children she is used to playing with. Even some of the older ones. They look like strangers to her: dirty, exhausted, resigned, frightened. Some of them, like King Bjorn's overdressed little daughter, scream and struggle as the wagon draws away from the Shining Hall, away from the people clustered around Bjorn's queen, a queen no more. Hervor looks away.

They drive south through the graveyard, where King Bjorn's barrow will soon rise, and enter the town. Squeezed here between the wattle fences surrounding each house plot, the lane is deeply rutted, the mud churned up, so many carts and herds have passed through ahead of them. Their going becomes painfully slow. She could run to the sea nine times in the time the wagon will take.

But from her slow-moving perch, nothing escapes her. She sees pigs running loose, rooting through rotting garbage. Geese and goats being herded out to pasture by shouting children and barking dogs. Every house has a tall loom standing near the door, to catch the best light, and a pair of weavers hard at work. As the wagon crawls toward the harbor, she watches jewelers drawing beads from glowing rods of glass, carving them from amber, and setting nuggets of red stone into nests of gold. A combmaker cuts delicate teeth from reindeer antler. A ropemaker plaits hempen cord.

A silversmith melts coins to mold a silver ingot. Above the whine of the wind and the seagulls' chatter, Hervor hears blacksmiths' hammers and shipwrights' axes, the rumble of querns and the shriek of whetstones. The crowded boardwalks are filled with people haggling in all different languages—and ignoring the wagonload of captives passing by. You'd never think the town had just been conquered. The only change Hervor can see is in the warriors patrolling the beach: They bear different symbols on their shields and sheath ends.

At the tide line, Hervor and the other children are ordered out onto the sand. She struggles to hop down, with her hands tied and her legs tangled in layers of extra clothing. With a casual wave, Gunnhild orders a warrior to assist her. She does—and, grinning, drops Hervor unceremoniously into a foul-smelling pit of human feces. Hervor shouts with rage until she recognizes her: It is the warrior she stabbed. Then Hervor grins back. The warrior grabs her tied hands and hoists her to her feet. While their wagon continues on into the water, clattering over the cobbled landing stage to a ship whose workers wait to load the plunder, Hervor lets herself be led along a wooden jetty to another ship.

When Gunnhild's party is all aboard, the rowers run out their oars, and the ship, guided by a pilot from the town, makes its winding way past the rows of sharpened stakes, and the rocks and shoals and silted-up channels that guard the marketplace. They raise the sail and head out to sea. The last Hervor sees of the place of her birth are the rows of rounded grave mounds at the harbor's mouth and the dark pillar of smoke still rising from the ashes of the Shining Hall.

The Shining Hall, or Skiringssal, is mentioned in an Anglo-Saxon account: Ottar, a Norse merchant who presented King Alfred of England with a gift of walrus ivory in the year 890, frequented a market, or *kaupang*, there. It was a month's sail south from his home in Halogaland—the northern district Gunnhild Mother-of-Kings also came from—and five days, with a fair wind and few stops, from there to the Danish town of Hedeby, he told the English.

The truth of Ottar's tale was unknown until archaeologists investigated a coastal farm named Kaupang in Vestfold. Beginning in the 1950s, they unearthed thousands of artifacts from across the Viking world. They found, too, a curved grid of house plots, each about twenty by thirty feet and stacked two deep, paralleling the tide line. On each plot had been built a house of wattle and daub. Combining living space with a workshop, it had an earthen floor, a fire pit, and a door in the gable end that looked toward the sea. Outside there was room for a kitchen garden, a pig pen, and a garbage pile.

The houses were small, smoky, cold, and damp, but the town itself showed proof of careful planning: The plots were fenced and ditched. Lanes and boardwalks led up to a timber-cased well at the foot of a hill and down to wooden wharves that fingered into the sea. Where the shore was soft, cobblestones were laid in a great fan, fifty feet into the water, to make a stone paving onto which carts could be rolled. Pits had been dug along the tide line: They still smelled of feces a thousand years later. "People were evidently not particularly concerned about matters of modesty," the archaeologists note.

In 1999, the ruins of the Shining Hall itself were uncovered. Rising from a flattened platform on the crest of a ridge a half mile from the harbor, the structure was 120 feet long and roughly boat-shaped, thirty-eight feet wide in the center, tapering to twenty-six feet at each end. Lines of sturdy posts set on stones held up its roof and defined its walls, which, like those in the town's much smaller houses, were fashioned of wattle and daub—though the hall's were likely lime-washed to shine bright white. The wings of the building housed living space and a textile workshop. The central space was a vast, high-ceilinged hall where the chieftain's warriors feasted and drank: In the floor litter were found bits of glass beakers and fine pottery jugs, armor-piercing arrows, and a fragment of a silver amulet portraying a valkyrie.

Burned bits of daub testify to the hall's fiery end sometime after 925, though the town below shows no signs of having been plundered or burned. Yet between 930 and 950, the settlement entirely disappeared. All that was left were its graves.

Like Birka in Sweden, where Hervor was buried, the Viking town of Kaupang was surrounded by graveyards. Rows of grave mounds guarded the harbor's mouth; more barrows bordered the road to the hall. Travelers approaching the market were meant to be cowed by this display of power. The message was clear: Kaupang had wealth to burn (or bury). Kaupang's graves also displayed its notable equality. Many of the richest ones gave no hint of gender—then or now. But some clearly did: Some rich women were buried in long oval barrows, some rich men in barrows that were round. The women's barrows match the men's in splendor, location, and size, and nearly in number. Kaupang's women were buried as powerful landowners and as members of the chieftain's retinue, some with weapons. Kaupang's men were buried with cooking equipment and keys as often as its women were; tools, horses, and equestrian gear were also not gender-linked. And while Kaupang's women were more often buried with weaving tools—and seem to have controlled a vast textile industry—these tools were found in men's graves too. "The Kaupang burials speak very clearly of a society where gender was unlikely to have been a determining factor in choice of occupation," writes one archaeologist. Nor did it determine one's status.

Hervor would not have noticed Kaupang's gender equality. The modern idea that a woman could not be a landowner, warrior, artisan, trader, or political leader would never have occurred to her—for the women she grew up around performed all these roles. As was true throughout Scandinavia in the Viking Age, the town's girls and women were as healthy and well fed as the boys and men. Testing teeth from more than a hundred sites in Europe spanning two thousand years, researchers found Viking women to be unusually "strong, healthy, and tall" compared to women elsewhere. Said one scientist, "Such women in the Nordic countries may have led to popular myths about the valkyries." Or to more than "myths."

When Hervor was born, before the burning of the Shining Hall, Kaupang was at its peak of population. Up to a thousand people lived and worked in the town. Six to eight hundred fertile Vestfold farms provided them with beef, mutton, and pork, which they preferred to eat stewed, not roasted; milk, drunk as buttermilk or sour whey or eaten as butter, yogurt-like skyr, and several varieties of fresh and dried cheese; cabbages and other vegetables, often pickled; dried peas and beans; turnips, which also could be dried; herbs and flavorings like angelica, caraway, coriander, dill, garlic, leeks, mustard, thyme, juniper berries, and spruce buds; and grains such as flaxseed, wheat, rye, oats, and, most of all, barley, which they ate as porridge or bread and brewed into beer.

They drank lots of beer. They also imported wine from vineyards along the Rhine River; the number of broken wine jugs found in the town proves not all of it was drunk in the Shining Hall by the chieftain's noble guests. Mead, considered the best liquor, was harder to get. The Norwegians did not keep bees, so making mead depended on finding a wild swarm in the woods or trading for honey with England or other lands where beekeeping was practiced. Thanks to its town of traders, the Shining Hall likely did serve mead on occasion—a Viking feast hall is often referred to as a mead hall, after all.

Vestfold, the kingdom surrounding the Shining Hall, was the warmest, most fertile part of Norway. Its population throughout the Viking Age was dense, its chieftains rich: From the 600s on, more than 147 rulers in this one kingdom alone were buried under great barrows more than sixty-five feet across, each grave mound, like an Egyptian pharaoh's pyramid, representing a spectacular outlay of labor and wealth.

But Vestfold could afford it: Its grain fields were wider, its harvests more reliable; its pastures supported greater and more diverse flocks and herds than most other parts of Norway. Vestfold had thick forests of shipbuilding timber and ample supplies of iron, too, while its island-studded coast offered rich fishing grounds and innumerable safe harbors for cargo ships.

Vestfold was one of several kingdoms in Viken, from which the word Viking—meaning "people of Viken"—was once thought to have come. Viken means "the bay"; it described what we call the Oslo Fjord, its coastal lands now split between Norway and Sweden.

In the Viking Age, Denmark claimed Viken. Around the year 800, the Danish king Godfrid established a town in Vestfold to anchor what he considered his northern border. He did the same in the south. Among his many skirmishes with the emperor Charlemagne was Godfrid's descent on the Frankish town of Reric, a major port on the Baltic Sea. Given the choice of death or a change of venue, Reric's merchants and artisans moved to the newfound Danish town of Hedeby, at the mouth of the river Schlei; the site is now in Germany.

Guarded by a hillfort and encircled by a rampart, Hedeby had wood-paved streets and more than twenty jetties. You could buy a flute or game pieces made in the town out of Norwegian elk antler or walrus ivory. Or you could buy a leather belt with metal strap ends made in England. You could pay for your purchase with hacksilver: bits of rings or chains or ingots weighed on a scale. You could pay with a silver coin struck in the town itself. Or you could pay with a silver Arab dirham.

In Vestfold, the site Godfrid chose was Skiringssal. Here, on that rocky hillock above a harbor, some generations before, a chieftain had erected the first Shining Hall, flattening a grave mound—the barrow of a powerful woman, though he may not have known that—and bringing in tons of soil to create a large platform. The wooden hall he built could be seen far out to sea, its whitewashed walls and yellow pine-shingled roof shining in the sun. This chieftain was one of the Ynglings, said to descend from the fertility god Freyr. Calling himself Yngvi, Freyr had established a dynasty at Uppsala in Sweden in ancient times. From there the Ynglings, or "people of Yngvi," had moved west, bringing with them the fashion for building feast halls on platforms.

By the time King Godfrid claimed Vestfold and established Kaupang at Skiringssal, the Ynglings had moved their royal seat north to Borre, where the Oslo Fjord narrows—or Godfrid may have pushed them there. The Danish king held a new concept of lordship, a Christian concept he learned from Charlemagne: A king did not lead warriors; he controlled land and ruled over everyone who lived there. A kingdom was a fixed territory. It had borders, and these needed to be watched.

Kaupang became Godfrid's port of entry, a place to tax ships plying the ancient North Way: the thousand-mile trade route that gave Norway its name. Sheltered by barrier islands from Viken nearly all the way up the west coast of Scandinavia to the arctic, the North Way was a thoroughfare bringing goods and people south to Denmark and, from there, along the East Way, to Byzantium and beyond.

Godfrid was even more keen, though, to skim off profits from the new route west, linking the North Way to the isles of Britain.

In 793, says the *Anglo-Saxon Chronicle*, Vikings arrived like a "bolt from the blue" at an English abbey seventy miles south of Scotland:

> In this year dire forewarnings came over the land of the Northumbrians, and miserably terrified the people: There were excessive whirlwinds and lightnings, and fiery dragons were seen flying in the air. A great famine soon followed these tokens; and a little after that, in the same year, on the sixth of the Ides of January, the havoc of heathen men miserably destroyed God's church on Lindisfarne, through rapine and slaughter.

English histories often begin the Viking Age on this date—despite the dragons, the *Anglo-Saxon Chronicle* generally counts as a historical

An inch-wide pendant in the Borre style of Viking art, named for Borre in Vestfold, where the first examples were found. This pendant from Birka, Sweden, matches one found in Norfolk, England.

source. Yet archaeologists noting changes in the imported goods buried in Viking graves, the style of their houses, and the fashions in Scandinavian art suspect Vikings were engaging in trade throughout the British Isles for a half century before that.

This new trade route into the west began at Avaldsnes, a royal estate on an island near modern Bergen. Avaldsnes had long been a node on the North Way. There, where the shipping lanes narrowed, a row of burial mounds up to sixteen feet high announced the island's ancient authority—an authority put into practice by halting every ship that passed. In return for a fee, the rulers of Avaldsnes offered a safe port. At the trading post by the chieftain's hall, sailors found a place to bunk, a horn of beer (the island warehoused barley and malt), and an opportunity to discuss the weather, for the next day's sail, no matter your destination, was the most dangerous. To the north was Stad, the windiest promontory in Norway. To the south was the high surf off Jaeren, where low-lying fields and white-sand beaches met storms head-on. To the west was the "vicious tumble of short waves for which the North Sea is famous"—but to the west lay also the lucrative new Viking markets of Dublin in Ireland and York in England.

Godfrid's neighbors in Vestfold, the Ynglings and their allies, were not pleased to have him muscle in on this new West Way. Before Kaupang was established, merchant ships had always sailed to the royal estate at Borre, situated beside another bottleneck marked by a high-roofed feast hall and rows of ancient grave mounds.

It was worth going to war over. In 813, Godfrid's sons skipped a meeting with Charlemagne's emissaries; instead, the Danes "set out for Vestfold with an army," the *Frankish Annals* report. "That region is at the edge of their kingdom, located between the north and west, and, facing into the North Wind, looks toward the top of Britain. The leaders and people of that region were refusing to be their subjects." The geography lesson is clear: To the Danes, Vestfold was key to controlling trade on this new route between the Franks and the British. And the Danes, that time, must have won: for Kaupang was not destroyed.

Kaupang at Skiringssal was the first true town in what is now Norway. Earlier markets were held on any handy beach, or timed to coincide with rituals and assemblies. Traders were based on family farms, traveling in the slack time between sowing and harvest. Artisans worked on chieftains' estates, where their silver, steel, ivory, and other valuable supplies were safe.

Protection did not presume total control. Artisans prized their independence, as the story of Volund shows. An elf, Volund was "the finest craftsman of anyone in the ancient sagas," explains the poem *Volund's Song*. He was married to a valkyrie named Hervor the Wise (not Angantyr's daughter), who could transform herself into a swan. After nine years of marriage, this Hervor flew away to take part in a battle, leaving Volund at home to work gold and jewels into rings to please her when she returned home. But when an evil king learned the artisan was no longer protected by his valkyrie wife, he captured him. He slit Volund's hamstrings so he could not leave, but was forced to stay and craft treasures for the king. Volund's vengeance was awful: He killed the king's sons, turning their skulls into silver-footed drinking cups, then flew away on mechanical wings he had made.

At Kaupang, King Godfrid did not force artisans to stay in his towns. Instead, he offered them more independence than they had previously enjoyed. Traders, likewise, were freed of the necessity to farm. The king, or his representative in the Shining Hall, saw that the town was supplied with food from the countryside and protected from attack (for a price). Their connection was to the advantage of each—though not to the Yngling chieftains, who saw their ability to reward their "friends" with well-crafted and exotic gifts impaired.

A town not only concentrated population; it focused power—which is why King Godfrid was so thorough. To lay out his towns, he engaged professional planners. Kaupang and Hedeby look very much like Ribe, an earlier Danish town, or Birka in Sweden, with which the Danes had strong trade connections. The sloping meadow below the Shining Hall was leveled—dips filled in with sand and clay, banks shored up with walls—before the house plots were laid out.

Along with town planners, Godfrid may also have recruited merchants and artisans—or, as at Hedeby, captured them. By the artifacts found inside it, archaeologists can tell that one large house by Kaupang's harbor belonged to a family of Frisians. They may have come from Dorestad, a large market town on the Rhine River, near modern-day Utrecht in Holland. Controlled by the Franks, Dorestad was at its peak around the year 800, commanding trade routes west to York in England and east through the Baltic Sea to Birka. One of its specialties was wine; another was cloth, especially fine diamond twill, a luxury wool fabric with a metallic sheen. Both came to Kaupang in quantity, as did Frankish swords, Irish horse harnesses, Baltic amber, jet from York, lead from mines in southern England, glass goblets from the Rhineland, copper ingots from the Middle East, and beads of carnelian and amethyst from the Orient. Blacksmiths and glass-bead makers worked at Kaupang, as did shipwrights and metal casters, who mass-produced cheap brooches of brass. Iron ingots, soapstone pots, and whetstones of light or dark schist (the light for grinding, the dark for polishing) were produced nearby, while from the Norwegian arctic along the North Way came furs, hides, feathers and down, falcons, dried fish, walrus ivory, reindeer antlers, and ships' rigging of sealskin or walrus hide.

Kaupang's heaviest traffic, however, was in humans—as was true for most Viking towns. Slavery was a main driver of the Viking economy. Along with looting and pillaging, one purpose of a Viking raid was to capture people to sell into slavery. Anyone, if their luck failed, could become a slave. Rich or poor, male or female—but usually young and healthy—anyone could suddenly lose their freedom and find their status reduced to the lowest rank in society. The reverse was also true in the Viking world: Kings' sons and daughters became slaves, but slaves also became kings or queens. Slaves were mistreated and looked down upon, but they were not considered subhuman. "Slave" was a role a person could fall into and, with luck, climb out of.

Trade—especially in this kind of slaving culture—requires trust. To acquire exotic goods means dealing with strangers, whose ideas of right or wrong might not be yours. Trade is essentially risky: Each side hopes to profit at the other's expense; each side hopes not to be cheated. While a generous gift radiates goodwill, an easy sale invites suspicion: *Buyer beware.* Are the goods flawed? The coins counterfeit? (In Kaupang, as well as in Birka and Hedeby, archaeologists have found fake Arab dirhams, the silver tainted with baser metals.)

It was to reduce the risk of trade that Kaupang looked to the Shining Hall.

First, the merchants' physical safety must be assured. In Vestfold's clan-based society, strangers had few rights or protections except while in Kaupang, where the chieftain's well-armed warriors policed the marketplace. Graves containing weapons (both men's and women's graves) are more common at Kaupang than anywhere else in Norway. Though no hillfort or ramparts protected the town, as at Birka and Hedeby, the harbor was barricaded with underwater shoals and stakes. The area was protected by the townspeople's ancestors and deities as well. On the far side of the Shining Hall sat the assembly grounds, beside a sacred lake, watched over by the Holy Mountain. Weapons were taboo there and in the graveyards that ringed the town, guarding every entrance. In such places of peace, robbers or murderers would be cursed or outlawed.

Second, the rules of trade must be made plain. In some Viking markets, the chieftain fixed commodity prices. In others, witnesses were required for all sales. Elsewhere deals were sealed with a handshake or a drink. No one knows Kaupang's rules. But buyer and seller needed to be sure the same ones applied to both stranger and kin; to both Christians from Dorestad and pagans from the arctic north; to those who bartered goods for goods, those who paid with silver arm-rings, and those who paid with silver coins; and to those who weighed that silver with the old-style rounded weights, based ultimately on the weight of a barley grain, as well as to those who used the new-style eight-sided cubes, based on the standard weight of an Arab silver dirham.

Finally, those coins and weights and measures must be periodically checked for accuracy, and cheating punished.

But after Eirik Bloodaxe killed his brother Bjorn, he did not—as expected—perform Bjorn's duties. Neither he nor Gunnhild stepped into the Merchant King's shoes. They did not have the chance.

For Bjorn the Merchant was not the last of Eirik's brothers to challenge him and Gunnhild for the kingship of Norway. Harald Fairhair's youngest son, Hakon the Good, was still safely out of the way in England, where he was the foster son of King Athelstan. But Bjorn's full brother, Olaf Haraldsson, remained at large in Vestfold, and Sigrod Haraldsson, who ruled the region around Trondheim, was on his way south to aid him, according to the reports of Gunnhild's spies.

Eirik and Gunnhild sailed off to confront them, and Hervor, perhaps, went too.

4

LITTLE "HEL-SKINS"

A s soon as they are well underway, the warrior unties the cord binding Hervor's hands and lets her use it as a knife belt. She peels off Hervor's extra clothes, rinses the soiled dress in seawater, and bundles everything up with her own gear. She takes the long string of beads that burdened Hervor's neck and stuffs it into her own belt pouch.

Then she lets Hervor loose.

Hervor runs from one end of the great ship to the other, back and forth, from the high, coiled dragon's head at the prow to the high, coiled serpent's tail at the stern.

She climbs onto the steering deck—but the captain orders her off.

She climbs over the bales and bundles and barrels of cargo in the ship's broad waist, leaps from rowing bench to rowing bench, dips a drink of water from the butt at the mast, shinnies up a little way to look at everything from that angle, and pauses for a moment to listen to the story with which Queen Gunnhild, in the shade of the upturned rowboat, is holding the other captive children transfixed:

With his new friend Hildir, Arrow-Odd continued his journey. Hildir was a mountain troll. He offered to row, and no one rows better or faster than a troll. But Odd had weather-luck and the wind was fair, so he raised the sail. The mountains raced past so fast it made Hildir dizzy. His courage snapped. He leaped for Odd and wrestled him to the deck.

I'll kill you if you don't stop this magic! he said. You'll sink us!

Calm down, Odd replied. You're just not used to sailing. Let me up, and I'll show you.

He lowered the sail, and the mountains stood still.

Hervor laughs. She's never sailed before either, but she isn't a coward like the troll.

She climbs a little higher, staring back the way they've come and ahead to where they're going, and now, from this height, she notices the fleet has split.

She slides down the mast, turns around—and there is the warrior who captured her, leaning on the gunwale, watching. Hervor realizes the warrior has not let her out of her sight since they left Kaupang harbor. She wonders if she is this warrior's booty now—her slave—or just her responsibility. She glances down at her knife, now strapped to her hip. Slaves aren't given back their knives. Especially not knives with jeweled sheaths, are they? She pushes the question out of her mind and turns to a more pressing one:

Where's everyone going?

Just as she reaches the boat's side, a great gout of spray drenches them both—and both of them laugh. The warrior lifts Hervor up so she can hang on the gunwale from her armpits, toes kicking the strakes, and side by side they watch as the first of the great striped sails disappears behind the islands.

They'll go up the fjord to Tunsberg, the warrior says, while we loop out and around and pinch off the Thread.

What thread? Hervor asks.

The Thread. The waterway that connects Tunsberg to Viken farther north. If the brothers flee by ship, they'll go that way.

The brothers are Olaf and Sigrod, two more of Harald Fairhair's sons who stand between Gunnhild Mother-of-Kings and the throne of Norway. Hervor has learned that already, listening to the rowers chat as they lounged between the benches, playing dice while the sails did their work.

Now, hanging over the gunwale, tired and wet and happy, watching the other sails shrink in the distance, Hervor remembers another question she wanted to ask: Can you sink a ship by sailing too fast?

If you sail the keel loose you can, the warrior replies. I've seen it happen. The ship was racing along and suddenly it lifted its prow out of the water like a horse rearing. The keel lost its grip. The ship spun sideways, plunged into the trough of the wave, and filled with water. The sailors were caught in the net of Ran, Queen of the Sea, and sank to her watery feast hall, where the lamps are lit by gold, not fire, and the beer serves itself. Not a bad death, really.

Were they our friends?

Our friends? The warrior smiles. No, they were not.

Their ship plunges into a trough and the bright spray drenches them again. *The bow chisels the smooth sea into spraystorm*, the warrior chants, her voice lifted into the rhythm of poetry. *The sea thuds on each side. Froth piles in heaps, the sea swells with gold, the waves wash the frightening dragon's head. The mane of the serpent glitters.*

Hervor repeats the lines until she's memorized them, the poetry sweet on her tongue.

They pass Sand Isle and Birch Isle, Goose Isle and Whale Isle, the great Island of Nut Trees, and enter the Thread. But then their ship and two others leave the fleet and turn up Slag-Bank River, skirting Tunsberg, the Fortress Rock, where Eirik Bloodaxe hopes to bring his brothers to battle. Queen Gunnhild's ship rows up the narrow river as far as it can go and docks beside a great burial mound circled with oaks.

When Snorri Sturluson wrote his sagas of the kings of Norway, *Heimskringla*, he saw no problem in making up dialogue for people long dead. Does that make his history unhistorical? It depends on how his readers understood it. Did they read Snorri's dialogue as direct quotes? As the gist of what was said so long ago? As obvious fakery—or artistry? No one knows. Quotation marks—the tools we use today to denote direct speech—weren't invented until the 1500s. The sagas had no such punctuation (though modern editors and translators add it). There was no way for a saga author like Snorri, writing in the thirteenth century, to indicate what he intended or how words of dialogue should be understood.

As Snorri did, I'm compiling a history from snatches of poetry and scraps of tales told and retold for centuries. I use quotation marks or italics if I'm citing an existing text, medieval or modern, and reference my source in the endnotes. Otherwise, you can assume I'm making the dialogue up—based, like Snorri's work, on the best sources I can find. From these I can guess what it felt like to sail on a Viking ship for the very first time, thanks to the *Saga of Arrow-Odd*. I can hear the Vikings' love of their ships in the lines of poetry Snorri and his peers collected. Plus, I have an advantage Snorri didn't: I can sail on a reconstructed Viking ship (and have done so). Until one was unearthed in 1880 from a Vestfold burial mound, no one knew what a Viking ship looked like.

But no poems or histories or archaeological finds tell me that Hervor, the warrior woman buried in Birka grave Bj581, as a young girl sailed north with Gunnhild Mother-of-Kings past Tunsberg, where Eirik Bloodaxe fought the battle that made him (briefly) Norway's king. The texts say nothing about Gunnhild's whereabouts during the fighting. The fates of the captives from Kaupang and the Shining Hall (assuming Hervor was one of them) went completely unrecorded. Was Hervor put into the care of Gunnhild's bodyguard—and did that guard include warrior women? I can only conjecture.

Did she embrace her new life so readily, leaving Kaupang and her mother behind so blithely? If she had the bold and aggressive character I imagine, it's likely she did. Though sources on childhood in the Viking Age are few, both texts and archaeology do give me some clues.

It seems the mother-child bond was not particularly strong. For example, in the *Saga of Hervor*, young Hervor leaves the company of her mother, who tried to teach her sewing and embroidery, "as soon as she was able" and went off to learn to fight "with a bow and a sword and shield." She doesn't approach her mother after that except to demand her inheritance.

Young children of every class, it seems, were raised communally. In one tale, Princess Ljufvina of Permia, in northern Russia, was captured by a Viking and forced to marry him. Her twin infant sons were raised with a slave's son of the same age, and not until they were three years old did the Viking ask which boy was his own. Ljufvina pointed to the slave boy. The father was disappointed. The handsome, fair-skinned boy was "a puny-looking thing," in his opinion, while the two swarthy twins looked strong and sturdy. He called them "Hel-skins." Maybe he meant they resembled the powerful queen of the underworld, Hel, who had an ugly face, half-dark, half-pale. But maybe the word meant "hell-raisers" or "hellions," a description that fits the boys' behavior. When Ljufvina admitted her deception, their father was delighted to acknowledge the little Hel-skins as his own.

Though the sagas do depict loving mothers, Viking children often seem to form closer attachments to the nurses and guardians and tutors they called their foster mothers or foster fathers. Two who grew up in their parents' homes, Egil and Hallgerd, were raised by slaves or servants of whom they became particularly fond. Egil's foster mother taught him songs and magic and how to write runes, and saved his life once during a ball game that turned deadly; when she was killed, he avenged her murder as if she were kin. Hallgerd's foster father petted and spoiled her and killed anyone who slapped her. She loved him in return, shielding him from retribution until he killed a man she was fond of; then ruthless Hallgerd sent him to his death.

Often Viking children were not raised in their parents' households. Sending a child away to be fostered was a way to cement relationships among families. It was also considered good for the child. One-year-old Halldor, who had several older brothers, was sent away to be raised by his father's elderly kinsman. Bersi had no children to inherit his farm, so the infant would become his heir. Because Bersi was a poet, a vignette of the infant's life was preserved: "That summer Bersi took sick, and he lay in bed a long time," the saga says. One day, while everyone else was out hay making, Bersi and the baby were left alone in the house. Halldor lay in a cradle, but he was apparently learning to stand and hauled himself up. "The boy tipped the cradle over and he fell"—screaming—"onto the floor, but Bersi wasn't able to do anything about it." As Viking heroes often do when they get into tight spots, Bersi made up a poem about it:

> We both
> lie abed,
> Halldor and I:
> We're no heroes.
> I'm too old,
> you're too young.
> You'll get over it.
> I won't.

Later, the saga says, someone came in and picked Halldor up off the floor, no harm done.

Both men and women were responsible for childcare. Several fathers or foster fathers, like Bersi, end up babysitting in the sagas. One took his infant son along when he went fishing. He dressed the boy in a sealskin bag that covered him, neck to toes, to keep him dry, and laid him in the prow of the boat. Luckily, little Seal-Thorir stayed at home in his mother's care on the next fishing trip, when his father drowned.

Sometimes mother and father were both irresponsible: The marriage between an Icelandic chieftain's daughter, Thurid, and a Norwegian merchant, Geirmund, was not a happy one. Geirmund was a dapper warrior: He wore a red tunic, a gray sea cloak, and a bearskin cap, and always carried the sword Leg-Biter, with its walrus-ivory hilt. He decided to leave Iceland and go back to Norway, but he not only refused to take Thurid and their one-year-old daughter with him, he refused to leave money behind to pay for their keep.

Thurid was outraged. Geirmund's ship was loaded and waiting for a fair wind when she snuck aboard late one night, carrying their daughter. She slipped the little girl into the skin sleeping bag in which Geirmund lay, grabbed Leg-Biter, and returned to her boat. Geirmund did not wake until the baby began to cry. He tried to go after Thurid, but she had drilled a hole in his ship's rowboat. As she and her crew rowed away, he called out, "Take the girl with you and whatever else you want from the cargo. I'd rather lose my fortune than my sword."

"Then you'll never get it back," said Thurid. She never saw Geirmund—or her daughter—again, as their ship sank off the Norwegian coast.

Whether raised by their kin or fostered out, Viking children were given a great deal of freedom. Boldness and initiative were rewarded. Risk taking was encouraged. Being a troublesome "Hel-skin" was not a bad thing— even when mischief devolved into violence.

When the heroine of the *Saga of Hervor* was a teenager, she ran away to the woods to escape her embroidery lessons. Briefly, she lived as an outlaw, attacking travelers and even killing them for their money. Her grandfather forced her to come home—but didn't otherwise punish her. As the description of another young saga heroine shows, such boldness and courage were valued in girls. Said to be the finest marriage prospect around, Hildigunn was not only handsome and a talented artist, "she was the fiercest of women and the most strong-willed"; she was both a *skörungr* and a *drengr*, the saga says—both a leader and a warrior.

A rare saga portrait of a much younger child gives us Egil's exploits as a boy of three (though he is said to be as big as a six-year-old). When forbidden to accompany his parents to a feast, he caught a horse and, though he had trouble managing the beast and almost got lost in a bog, rode nearly ten miles to the party. Greeted warmly by his grandfather, little Egil composed a poem about his adventure, for which he was rewarded with the gift of a seashell and three duck eggs.

When Egil, age seven, was bullied by bigger boys, Egil's mother praised him for fighting back. The scene was a ball game. Egil whacked his opponent with the bat. The boy threw Egil roughly to the ground, and the other boys jeered. Egil got an axe and, when his opponent was running with the ball, darted onto the field and struck him on the head. The boy died. Egil's mother said her son would make a fine Viking when he grew up. Egil was so proud he composed a poem:

> My mother said
> to buy me a ship,
> a fast one, with fine oars;
> to set off with Vikings:
> to stand in the stern,
> to steer the vessel,
> straight in to harbor,
> and kill a man or two.

Outright rebellion was tolerated as well. Olaf (who grew up to be Saint Olaf, king of Norway) was asked to saddle his stepfather's horse. When he saddled, instead, a billy goat, he was not punished. Grettir (who grew up to be an outlaw) was asked to take care of his family's flock of fifty geese. "It wasn't long before he learned how hard it was to get them all going in the right direction, with the slow-moving goslings and all. He got very annoyed at this." When passersby reported seeing geese with their wings broken and a pile of dead goslings, his father stoically announced, "We'll find another job for you."

According to an Irish legal text from the Viking Age, children were taught skills appropriate to their status. Sons of farmers (and most Vikings were farmers) were taught to dry malt and to cut wood. Their sisters learned to grind grain, to sieve the flour, and to knead the bread. Both were taught to take care of animals. Noble boys, by contrast, learned to play board games and to handle weapons, while their sisters learned to cut out and sew clothing and to weave decorative tapestries. Their status also determined what they ate: children of farmers flavored their porridge with buttermilk and salted butter, noble children got fresh milk and sweet butter, while royal children got milk and honey. Likewise, status determined the color of their clothing: farm children wore yellow, black, or undyed cloth; noble children wore red, green, or brown; royalty wore blue and purple. Babies of any class wore dark colors (to hide the stains).

Though these Irish laws come from a Christian culture, not a pagan one, people from Norway had been in Ireland since the late 700s, raiding and trading and marrying into Irish families. In the early 800s, they founded the city of Dublin. By the time Hervor was born, the Irish and the Norse had been influencing each other's cultures, as their artwork shows, for more than a hundred years. Some of these Irish rules might have applied to her.

But the strict division of tasks by gender—boys dry the malt, girls grind the flour, boys cut wood, girls sew—seems to me to be very impractical. Nor do the sagas support the idea. In one of the few descriptions of making bread, boys are charged with the task. When his sister's ten-year-old son wished to join him in his outlaw lair, the hero Sigmund tested the boy's mettle by handing him a sack of flour. "You make the bread, and I will go fetch firewood," he says. When he returns, the boy has done nothing. He didn't dare touch the flour because something was squirming in the sack. He was sent home. When his brother Sinfjotli reached ten, he too was tested. This time, when Sigmund returned with his load of wood, he found fresh-baked bread awaiting him. "Did you find anything odd about the flour?" he asked. "There was something alive in it when I began kneading," young Sinfjotli replied, "but whatever it was, I kneaded it in." Sigmund laughed. "It was the most poisonous of snakes," he said, and suggested the boy eat something other than poisoned bread for supper.

Vikings were travelers, and any traveler, male or female, needs to know how to split wood to make a fire and how to sew well enough to repair ripped clothing or patch a sail—which may mean first spinning the thread and carving a bone needle. Other things Hervor needed to know were how to sharpen a knife (and sharpening a sword is not so different); how to raise, capture, kill, butcher, and cook an animal; what plants can be eaten, which are poisonous, and which have medicinal uses; how to train and ride a horse; how to cut and dry hay or find other fodder for one's animals; how to row and sail and keep a boat seaworthy; and how to build a house—or at least fix a leaking roof.

Simply by being around when an extra hand was needed, Hervor could have learned a craft, such as making combs, pots, rope, or shoes, weaving, metalworking, wood carving (at least enough to repair a ship or reshaft a scythe), and blacksmithing (at least enough to shoe a horse). While some crafts required greater strength or dexterity than others, none were restricted to males or females. In some sagas, women are praised for their skill in carving scenes on wooden doors or fashioning art objects out of walrus ivory. Archaeologists have found tools for metalworking in several female graves, while textile-working tools are sometimes found buried with men. Tools, in general, are among those artifacts that can't be reliably sexed.

All these crafts were practiced in and around a chieftain's hall. Hervor, living near the town of Kaupang, may also have learned from a young age the basics of trade: how to value an item; how to weigh hacksilver with a handheld set of scales and convert it to a number of coins; how to dicker; and how to tell an honest trader from a thief.

Finally, Hervor was taught to memorize poems and stories and genealogies and laws—for the human mind was the repository of culture in the Viking Age. Only well after Christianity came to the North was the memory replaced by the book, and learning became something done seated, indoors, with quill in hand.

In many ways, Viking children seem to have raised themselves. Older children taught the younger ones to play those rough games with a bat and a ball in grassy meadows or on ice-covered lakes. They wrestled and learned to swim. They ran footraces and had jumping contests, raced on ice skates (made of a cow's shin bones), on wooden skis, and on horseback. They flew kites and had snowball fights. They competed in picking up heavy rocks and pitching stones. They learned to juggle (preferably with knives).

They challenged their balance: One day, they might be dared to walk on the moving oars of a longship.

They played as warriors, too. Archaeologists have found small swords and axes, spearheads, arrows, bows, and knives at Viking sites. Play weapons were made of stone and clay, sized for a child's hand. Practice weapons were made of wood, carved to look like real weapons currently in fashion. Fully functional children's weapons, of iron and steel, have also been found.

In the stories, Viking children proudly carry such weapons. Young Hervor in the *Saga of Hervor*, as we've seen, "practised more with a bow and a sword and shield" than at her embroidery. Kjartan was fascinated by the pool of blood spreading from the wounds of a dead man who had been dragged into the bushes. He "had a little axe in his hand. He ran up to the bushes and dipped the axe in the blood." Sviatoslav learned to cast a spear from horseback; the first time, it struck his leg and "barely cleared the horse's ears." Herjolf, a few years older, put his spear to good use: At eight, he killed a bear that attacked his favorite goat. Arrow-Odd "would never play games like other children"; instead he was obsessed with archery. He "asked everyone who was good at it to make arrows for him, but he was careless with them afterward, and left them lying around on the benches where people sat. Many people were hurt by them when they came into the dark room to sit down."

Viking children had toy ships, carved out of wood, and toy horses, of wood or bronze, that they took into imaginary battles. They laid out miniature farms on grassy hillsides and inhabited them with bones: Certain bones represented sheep, others cows or horses. They molded clay, making miniature pots. They played board games that taught them to think strategically: Some games required only two handfuls of pebbles and a gameboard scratched in the sand.

Sometimes, like modern children, they played "make-believe." On a rainy day, says one saga, two boys and a girl were playing on the floor beside the fire while their parents entertained some guests. The children were acting out a lawsuit heard by the judges at a recent assembly. The girl played Unn, who was suing her husband, Hrut, for divorce. Their marriage had been cursed by Gunnhild the Witch, Queen of Norway. "He cannot have sex with me because he was once her lover."

One of the boys played Unn's lawyer: "You must return her dowry, you gelding."

The other boy, playing Hrut, replied, "Not unless you can beat me in single combat!"

The people sitting around the fire laughed, tentatively at first, so the children repeated their play. Their silliness increased and the laughter grew raucous, until one of the onlookers picked up a stick and struck the "lawyer" in the face. "Get outside and stop ridiculing us," he shouted.

He was the real Hrut's brother, and Hrut was sitting beside him. Hrut took a ring from his finger. "Come here," he said, and gave it to the chastened boy. "Go away now, and never make fun of anyone again." The boy thanked him and ran out into the rain, his playmates hard on his heels.

Queen Gunnhild's love for Hrut—and the curse she laid on him when he lied to her, according to *Njal's Saga*—came well after Eirik Bloodaxe's death. Now, in our story, Gunnhild is a young woman pushing her husband Eirik to become sole king of Norway. As Snorri Sturluson writes in *Heimskringla*, Eirik's brothers Sigrod and Olaf were still mustering their forces when Eirik's fleet arrived: He "got such good winds he could sail day and night, and no news of his coming outran him."

He attacked his brothers just south of the great burial mound at Oseberg, beside the steep craggy hill where, much later, the fortress of Tunsberg was built. "Eirik had a much bigger army and won the victory," Snorri writes. "Both Olaf and Sigrod fell there, and each is buried in a mound on the slope of the hill, where they died." Eirik Bloodaxe could finally call himself king of Norway.

Snorri, again, says nothing of Gunnhild's whereabouts during the fight at Tunsberg. But twenty-some years later, when her sons won the kingdom, he places her on the battlefield itself. There, her errand runner is credited with killing the rival king somewhat magically—or perhaps the archer was Gunnhild herself. At a crucial moment, says Snorri, an arrow of an unusual kind "hit King Hakon in the arm, just below the shoulder. And it is said by many that Gunnhild's servant, the one named Kisping, ran through the crowd shouting: 'Make way for the king-slayer'—and shot the arrow at King Hakon, but others say no one knows who shot it." The arrow hit an artery and King Hakon the Good bled to death.

Now, in the 930s, Gunnhild likely did not attend the fighting. Her household was then encumbered by many children, both her own—she was pregnant with her seventh—and those she had taken in to foster, like Hervor. The Oseberg grave mound, a mile from the Tunsberg battlefield, seems a likely spot for her to establish her camp. A mere hundred years before, two powerful queens had been buried there in the most lavish Viking funeral known.

QUEEN ASA'S REVENGE

I t is the largest barrow Hervor has ever seen. Smooth and rounded on every
side, it springs from the shallow valley floor like a mountain—like the
Holy Mountain behind the Shining Hall, where the rituals were held on
the Winter Nights. She slips from the warrior's side and darts down the
ship's gangplank.

Ignoring the shouts behind her, dodging the well-dressed dignitaries
who, come to greet Queen Gunnhild, try to snag her, she runs to the top
of the grave mound and gazes around in awe. The whole world seems
to be looking at her: the ship and its bustling crew, the welcoming party
with their colorful cloaks and flags flapping in the wind, the farmhouses
ranked on the hills all around, even the whispering oaks, the bright streak
of the river, and the far-off sparkle of the fjord.

Who lives here? Hervor asks the warrior when she rushes up after her.

Treat her with some dignity, or you'll meet her sooner than you'd like.

Hervor blinks. There is no laughter in the warrior's voice this time. She
looks—could it be?—afraid. Hervor meekly follows her down the mound,
the unanswered question simmering inside her.

It comes to a boil at the banquet that night. Leaving the other children
playing on the floor, Hervor sneaks up behind the seat of honor where
Queen Gunnhild sits. She waits for a break in the conversation and,
when it comes, taps the queen's arm. Who lives there, in the mound?
she asks.

The queen turns and stares at the hand that touched her until Hervor self-consciously tucks it behind her back. The queen's eyes then shift to Hervor's own, boring into her head as if searching for secrets. Hervor stares back, unblinking.

Queen Gunnhild smiles. This, she says to the feast hall at large, is the boldest child for her size I've ever seen.

By then the warrior, Hervor's guardian, has reached them. She takes Hervor's hand and brusquely tugs her back to her own seat on the warriors' benches.

As bold as the queen in the mound, Gunnhild continues. She lifts her horn of beer: I drink to Asa, queen of Agdir, mother of Halfdan, father of Harald, father of Eirik, our king!

She takes a long draft of drink, then splashes the remainder on the fire.

But I curse the name, she mutters, her voice turning dark and harsh—though still filling the hall with its power—of the Hunting King, Gudrod the Generous, who killed her kinsmen and took Asa to wife without her consent.

And then she tells the tale.

Before books, there were stories. In them was distilled the knowledge each generation wished to pass on to the next. Storytelling was (and is) a form of power. It was time binding: It linked *then* to *now*. Told eloquently, at the right time to the right listeners, a story shaped the future. Told often enough, in as many ways as possible, a story became indelible. Such a story is the one Gunnhild told of Eirik Bloodaxe's great-grandmother, Queen Asa.

The story was still being told when Snorri Sturluson visited Vestfold nearly three hundred years later. As he relays it in *Heimskringla*, Asa was the only daughter of King Harald Redbeard, who ruled Agdir, Norway's southernmost kingdom. Gudrod, king of Vestfold and two other kingdoms at the head of Viken, sent messengers to Agdir asking for Asa's hand. Asa might have preferred to marry Gudrod's grown son, who was exceedingly handsome and tall, for the Hunting King had already seen one wife to the grave. Or Asa may have been a shield-maid who wished not to marry at all. Whatever the reason, her father refused Gudrod's suit.

The Hunting King swept down from the north with many ships. He took Agdir by surprise, surrounded the king's estate, fired the thatched roofs, and turned his Vikings loose to plunder. Fighting against heavy odds, Asa's father and brother were killed. Asa herself was captured and raped by her father's murderer. She kept her dignity and contained her rage. When she became pregnant, he made her his queen. When their son, Halfdan the Black, was a year old, she took her revenge.

The Hunting King and his queen were on their autumn progress, sailing from one chieftain's estate to another, enjoying a harvest feast at each one, dispensing justice, attending rituals, witnessing oaths and boasts, and generally reminding their subjects who was in charge. At Stiflu Sound (a place still unidentified by modern historians), Queen Asa saw her chance. At the end of the quay where they'd moored the royal ship she'd noticed a thicket of trees. That night there'd be no moon.

She posted her errand runner in the thicket. She ran her thumb up the edge of the spear she'd given him and was pleased to see beads of blood well up. He'd whetted it as sharp as her need for vengeance.

If he survived she'd make him rich. He wouldn't survive. She couldn't help that. The king's bodyguard were berserks—his best fighters. She refilled the king's mead cup and reentered the tent on the ship, where he slept.

Late at night the king went on land, looking for a woman, as she knew he would. He was very drunk—she'd seen to that. It was very dark. When he reached the thicket, the boy leaped out and ran him through. The Hunting King fell into the water, dead.

So far, the story of Queen Asa is what you'd expect of a Viking queen. She is tough, decisive, unbowed—but still helpless. She has, as sociologists say, no *agency*. She can plot revenge but not execute it. She can provide the spear but not make the thrust. She is reduced to getting her way through "deep-wrought wiles," in the words of the ninth-century Norwegian poet Thjodolf of Hvin, who preserved Asa's story for posterity. He called her wicked and the murder foul play.

Snorri Sturluson didn't say much more when he expanded on Thjodolf's poem in *Heimskringla*. Yet, for me, the few lines he added change everything.

The next morning the king's killer, hacked down at the quayside, was seen to be the queen's errand runner. King Gudrod's warriors confronted her. Queen Asa, said Snorri, "did not deny it was her plan." You'd expect her to be executed; instead, Snorri wrote, Asa "at once" took her infant son Halfdan and went south to Agdir. There, she "reigned over the kingdom

*Battle scene carved on the side of the wooden wagon buried
with the Oseberg queens in Vestfold, Norway.*

that her father, Harald Redbeard, had ruled" until Halfdan the Black grew
up. "He was eighteen years old when he took over the kingdom."

Given the length of Snorri's book, it's easy to overlook what Queen Asa's
revenge reports about women and power in the Viking Age. *At once* she
proceeded south. She established herself in Agdir as the ruling queen.
What does that say about her agency, her ability to act independently?

It says she needed no help from any man. Her father and brother and
most of their warriors were dead—or still south in Agdir if they had escaped the Hunting King's attack. She alone had been captured and kept
captive, though queen in name. Her son was an infant. Alone she faced
down her dead husband's warband. Alone she faced down her son's tall,
handsome half brother. She faced down the chieftain at whose quay they
were moored. She not only escaped punishment, she left *at once*. Regally.
Like a warrior queen no one dared cross. She must have taken the royal
ship. She must have taken all the ship contained, including its crew, whose
sworn oaths she exacted. She returned to the kingdom of her birth and
established herself there, ruling Agdir for seventeen years.

Perhaps her own mother was still alive and ruled alongside her. Perhaps the two queens traveled north with eighteen-year-old Halfdan, when he added Vestfold to his kingdom, as Snorri tells us, reconquering the territories his older half brother had let slip from his grasp. Perhaps Queen Asa fought beside her son. Perhaps she died in battle in Vestfold and was buried there in the most lavish Viking burial known, that of the Oseberg ship mound, up the Slag-Bank River near Tunsberg. Perhaps her mother died at about the same time and was buried in the same barrow—for two women were buried in the Oseberg ship.

There are many theories about who these two women were. A queen and her slave? A sorceress and her assistant? A king's mother and her companion? A queen and her mother, herself a queen? No one knows. One woman was between twenty-five and fifty-five, the other fifty to eighty, depending on how their ages are assessed; the higher the age at death, the less reliable are the estimates. One or both of the Oseberg women may have fought in battle: The younger woman had a broken collarbone that had begun to heal, as well as a fractured skull. The older woman badly injured her knee in her youth and had massive arm muscles; she died of cancer. Which one was Queen Asa? Probably neither. Though Asa has been linked to Oseberg since the ship burial was discovered in 1904 (one translation of "Oseberg" is "Asa's Mound"), the scientific dating of the burial to 834 does not sync with the dates historians have deduced from Snorri's sagas. DNA tests, likewise, kill the mother-daughter theory: The younger woman seems to have come from Persia.

Still, like the story of Queen Asa's revenge, the Oseberg burial underscores for me the power women held in ninth-century Vestfold: They ruled. When the warrior woman in *Hervor's Song* says of her father's sword, "I'd rather have it than rule all Norway," she was speaking of real options.

The Oseberg grave mound was built to impress. It called for coordinated teams of laborers and the destruction of enormous wealth. The process took months. A deep pit 144 feet long was dug into the heavy blue clay, its bottom below the water table. A dragonship was floated up the narrow river, then portaged over a roadway of logs into the pit—by then a muddy pool—and turned so its high spiral stem faced the fjord, before being moored to a large stone.

The ship alone was a symbol of wealth and power. It was built in the west of Norway, its keel and strakes shaped of oak from Hordaland, its accents of beech from the forest of Vollom, a beech woods so small and so far north of the species' natural range that it must have been planted. Hidden in Hordaland's maze of fjords, in a sheltered bay near the beech woods and with easy access to oak and pine, lay a revolutionary shipyard. Its shipwrights were artists, successfully marrying the north's swift, sleek rowing boats with the ponderous sailing ships then plying the English Channel. Using two-handed axes with thin, narrow blades to fell the trees, and bearded axes (so called because their long cutting edge made the blade look, side on, like a bearded chin) to shape the boards into ship strakes, they made the famous vessel now known as the Oseberg ship. I think of it as the first Viking ship, but it's merely the earliest one that's been recovered in excellent condition. It was long thought unseaworthy—a queen's pleasure barge, suitable for lakes—after a 1987 reconstruction sank in twenty seconds. But in 2006 an expert boatbuilder saw the pieces from the grave had been put together wrong. She oversaw the building of a new reconstruction, *Saga Oseberg*; a true warship, it easily sailed from Tunsberg, where it was built, to the Viking Ship Museum in Roskilde, Denmark, in 2015.

The original Oseberg ship took a master shipwright and ten smiths, working twelve-hour days, seven months to a year to create. Seventy feet long, it required twelve large oak trees: one giant trunk at least fifty feet long for the keel, and eleven logs, each three feet in diameter by sixteen feet long, to provide the twelve long, horizontal strakes that, laid up from keel to gunwales, created the ship's curving lines. The inch-thick strakes overlapped, giving the technique its name—lapstrake—and were clinched together with thousands of iron rivets. The ribs that stiffened the lapstrake skin against the pressure of the waves were carved from boughs with a natural bend and tied on with baleen from the jaws of whales. The stem and stern were part oak, part beech. The flooring of the deck was pine, as were the thirty oars and the tall mast. The square sail was woven from wool: It took the fleece of 150 sheep, handspun into more than 120 *miles* of thread, and handwoven into a thousand square feet of cloth. There was rigging to make too, ropes to plait of horsehair or walrus hide or hemp. And before the ship was coated with black pine tar, Oseberg's stem and stern down to the keel were carved with beasts and people laced into long scrolls, fantastic, ecstatic, dancing, fighting, and grimacing to warn Ran's daughters, the waves, away, like the "wave runes" the valkyrie Brynhild knew to carve, according to *Volsunga Saga*, so "no towering breakers, no waves of blue will fall, but you'll be safe from the sea."

After the beautiful Oseberg ship was moored in the valley floor, beside the narrow Slag-Bank River, a burial chamber of sturdy logs was erected on the ship's deck behind the mast. Aft of this chamber a complete kitchen was assembled, with iron pots, a frying pan, a dough trough, a quernstone, cups and platters, knives and spoons, and at least one black glass goblet. An ox was butchered and other foods were gathered: Archaeologists have found traces of rye flour, blueberries, apples, plums, and spices, including cumin, horseradish, and mustard.

The chamber itself was furnished as a royal bedroom. Long, narrow tapestries lined the walls, one showing a battle scene, the other a ritual procession. Carved wooden beds with feather pillows and blankets woven of red and white wool filled most of the floor space. There were iron lamps on long poles, a chair, a stool, and a bast-fiber floor mat. A line of chests along the far wall had once held clothing (scraps of wool and silk showed their fine quality). There were shoes and combs, but no jewelry except for seven glass beads.

The archaeologists who opened the grave in 1904 were also surprised to find no weapons, except for two hand axes. Instead there was a plethora of textile tools—looms, spindles, scissors, yarn—and other objects that seem to have had ritual use: a leather pouch of cannabis seeds for invoking a shamanistic trance; musical instruments, including a long wooden horn called a lur, whistles and a small bell, and five sets of rattles made of large, linked iron loops. One rattle was attached with rope to a splendidly carved wooden post topped with a snarling animal head. Four similar animal-head posts were found outside the bedroom.

Once the kitchen and bedroom were prepared, the aft end of the ship was sealed under a mound of turf blocks, laid up in rows like bricks to a height of twenty feet, leaving a sheer wall behind the mast and an A-framed opening into the now-buried bedroom. The prow of the ship remained clear, creating a stage on which the rituals of the burial ceremony were performed. These may not have taken place for months—even years: A king in Snorri's *Heimskringla* spends three summers overseeing the building of his own burial mound. Or one or both of the Oseberg queens may have died before the mound was begun and been laid to rest temporarily somewhere else, as was true for the funeral the Arab traveler Ibn Fadlan witnessed a hundred years later along the Vikings' East Way. But at some point, the bodies of the two Oseberg queens were sealed in the bedroom, hurriedly, haphazardly, by workers drunk on burial ale, it seems, for the carpentry shows none of the skill or care put into the chamber itself or its furniture. The doorway was closed with wood scraps in odd sizes, with bent and broken nails.

And then the gory spectacle began.

Equipment for a long journey was tossed on board—some of it literally thrown: barrels and buckets, tents and collapsible beds, a beechwood saddle and harness fittings, dog collars and chains. A gorgeous wagon—a close match to the processional wagon depicted on one of the tapestries in the burial chamber—was drawn on board, along with three similar sleighs, all exuberantly carved with interlaced lines and faces and the goddess Freyja's totem cats. The wagon and the sleighs were dragged through the traveling goods, smashing things indiscriminately.

And then the animals were sacrificed. Fifteen horses were beheaded, their heads carried into the middle of the ship, their bodies scattered. Five dogs were killed, one, at least, also beheaded—its head was attached to a horsehead with a long chain. The screams of the animals, the stench of guts and dung, must have been overwhelming. Everything was bathed in blood.

Finally, the beautiful ship and its contents were stoned—an enormous heap of stones was thrown onto the deck, crushing everything to splinters—before more blocks of turf were laid up some days or months later to complete the mound, leaving only the tip of the ship's mast visible.

The event would have been unforgettable. But it was not a unique occurrence. An almost identical burial took place at Gokstad, a mile from the Shining Hall, thirty years before Hervor was born. She would have known all about it.

The first people in the North burned their dead, Snorri writes in *Heimskringla*. They burned their possessions, too, for the god Odin had declared the dead could bring to Valhalla, the "Hall of the Slain," whatever was with them on their funeral pyres.

Two poems about the famous valkyrie Brynhild, who was betrayed by Sigurd the Dragon-Slayer and had him killed, describe the ritual in more detail. These poems, in the collection known as the *Poetic Edda*, may date from the Viking Age or might be later imitations. They were written down in Iceland by someone in Snorri's circle, perhaps one of his nephews; the earliest manuscript of the *Poetic Edda* can be dated to about 1270. "Build me a pyre on the plain," Brynhild says in one of these poems, ordering her own funeral before killing herself, "so broad that all who follow Sigurd to Hel find room beneath it. Cover it over with tents and shields and tapestries and many corpses"—five slave girls and eight slave boys were to be killed, plus her own (free) servant women, "adorned with jewelry," and two hawks. Sigurd was to burn at her side, a sword placed between them.

The second poem reveals that her people did not follow her orders. "After Brynhild's death," says the introduction to the poem, "two pyres were built; the one for Sigurd burned first. Then Brynhild was burned on the other pyre, and she was in a wagon covered with beautiful cloth. So it is said that Brynhild drove her wagon along the Hel-Road," Hel being both a place of the dead, like Valhalla, and the name of its queen. Stern and fierce and easily recognized, since one side of her face was light and the other dark, Hel had power over all the Nine Worlds of Norse mythology. Unlike in Greek myths, for example, the Norse underworld was not "a place in which women are silenced or pay brutal prices for the mistakes of men." No, the Norse underland was a place of brutal women: All who died of sickness or old age resided in Hel's cold, damp hall, eating off plates called "Hunger" and sleeping on cots called "Sickbed." Her realm was guarded by a high wall and a river, whose only bridge was guarded by a warrior woman, a giantess named Modgud, or "Battle Weary." When Brynhild took the road to Hel, Modgud barred her way: "You shall not pass by my rocky fortress," she insisted. "You have washed your hands in human blood." Brynhild answered, "Blame me not, lady of the rock, though I went on Viking raids." She had come to find the Dragon-Slayer and take him to Valhalla to join Odin's band of otherworldly warriors, for "we shall never be parted, Sigurd and I."

Once a funeral pyre burned out, Snorri continues in *Heimskringla*, the ashes were scattered at sea or covered with earth. Sometimes a memorial stone was erected. But after Yngvi-Freyr, the divine ancestor of the Yngling kings, "was laid in a mound at Uppsala, many chieftains chose to raise burial mounds as often as standing stones in remembrance of their kin."

Several rulers, according to Snorri, were buried at Borre in Vestfold, about six miles north of Oseberg. When he visited in 1217, there were nine large mounds up to 148 feet in diameter and twenty feet high; eight still exist, unexcavated. Most, like Oseberg, show signs that someone reopened the mound after the funeral, but how much later no one knows. Nor can anyone be sure of the grave robbers' motives. Were they recovering heirlooms, like the warrior woman in *Hervor's Song*? Were they collecting burned bones, or "bone coal," used as a source of carbon in making steel, to burn an ancestor's spirit into a sword? Were they testing their courage against zombies, as the sagas recount? The skeletons in the Oseberg mound (or what was left of them) were not found lying peacefully on their featherbeds when antiquarians opened the mound in 1904.

If the robbers were Christians, were they retrieving their ancestors' bones to rebury them in a Christian cemetery? Or were they destroying the graves' sacred power? Grave mounds were the focal point for many pagan practices: Rulers were crowned on grave mounds, assemblies met there to make laws and settle disputes, and individuals often sat on the mounds seeking inspiration or advice from their ancestors. In another poem, for example, a couple could not decide on a name for their son. One day the nameless boy was sitting on a grave mound when nine women rode by; the most magnificent of them stopped to talk with him. "She was a valkyrie and rode on the wind and the sea," says the poet. This line has usually been interpreted to mean she was a goddess—but it could just as well be a poetic description of a sailor. The poem continues, "She gave Helgi his name and shielded him often afterward in battle."

Or did the desecrators of Viking burial mounds have political, not religious, motives for opening the graves and ritually killing the dead? Some scholars think the Danish king Harald Bluetooth, who ruled during Hervor's lifetime, desecrated the Oseberg grave as part of his campaign to bring Christian ideas of kingship to the North. And it is true that, after Bluetooth became king in 958, no more large burial mounds were built in Vestfold.

No one knows how many Viking grave mounds honor queens, as only a few of the mounds have been excavated and their skeletons sexed. The most famous mound after Oseberg is at Gokstad, where, just outside Kaupang about thirty years before Hervor was born, a man was buried with the same ceremony as the Oseberg queens.

The size and construction of the Oseberg and Gokstad mounds are nearly identical. Both are positioned in the center of flat valleys facing the Oslo Fjord, interrupting a landscape of farms and fenced fields, sheep meadows, and well-traveled roads. In each case, the dead rulers were laid in a sumptuous burial chamber, with a kitchen and traveling gear, on a large, seagoing sailing ship. Instead of weaving tools and musical instruments, the Gokstad burial contained sixty-four iron-bossed shields, painted yellow and black, a gameboard and game pieces, and, in addition to twelve slaughtered horses—remarkably—two peacocks, announcing the chieftain's trade links to the East.

When the Gokstad mound was broken open in 1880, eight human bones were recovered. From those clues, an anatomist reconstructed a fifty- to seventy-year-old man of great height—over six foot two—who suffered from severe arthritis and might not have been able to walk or even to chew his food. In 1929 the bones were reburied, to be dug up again in 2007. A new analysis found the chieftain was not so old or so tall: only forty to fifty years old and five foot eleven. He was judged to be male, due to the bones' "extremely thick and powerful appearance with large muscle attachments, even if no 'sex specific' parts—like, for example, the pelvic bones—were preserved," the osteologist wrote. Calling this gender assignment into question, however, the same scientist read a deformity of the skull as sign of a growth hormone disease that would have given the chieftain "coarse features"—a big nose, protruding ears, fleshy lips, and huge hands and feet—as well as headaches, blurry vision, and "frequent muscular weakness." The chieftain did not suffer from arthritis, according to this reanalysis, though he may have walked with a limp and needed a crutch. Instead, several years before his death he injured his left knee "by jumping or falling from a great height." Nor was he bedridden and spoon-fed like a baby. He died, like a Viking, violently. "At least two persons with different weapons attacked the man and killed him," says the 2009 report. A sword cut to the shin of his bad left leg—when he was on horseback or lying helpless on the ground—made it impossible for him to stand. His right thigh was stabbed by an arrow or a knife and his right foot cut off. None of these battle wounds were noticed in the 1880s or when the bones were reexamined in 1907 or 1928.

Like Oseberg, the Gokstad mound contained no weapons (except the shields) and no jewelry when it was opened by archaeologists. The boggy, acidic blue clay into which the ships were sunk and the nearly airtight seal of the turf blocks used to build both mounds, however, preserved items of wood and, in the case of Oseberg, cloth. These materials usually rot faster than bone; they are rarely recovered from Viking graves. Yet items of wood or cloth can be more revealing than long-lasting metal jewelry or weapons. Such items let us look beyond stereotypes of gender to discover what roles the ruler filled in Viking society and how he or she exerted power. With such excellent preservation of cloth and wood, archaeologists can see that the space inside the Oseberg and Gokstad mounds was laid out like a chieftain's feast hall.

The arrival of the Oseberg queens, in their splendidly carved ship, to a chieftain's hall was always accompanied by the threat of violence. Power, for a Viking ruler, was a balance of give and take—and what was given to one person was often taken from another. The queens' itinerary was an exercise in authority. A chieftain who proved unfriendly—who failed to provide an appropriate feast when the ruler came to visit—could find himself evicted, or worse, as happened to the saga-hero Thorolf in *Egil's Saga*. His mistake was inviting five hundred of his neighbors to his feast for Harald Fairhair, when the king had only three hundred in his train. The king's rage at this insult smoldered (and was stoked by slander) until one spring, as we have seen, he arrived at Thorolf's hall unannounced, ringed it with warriors, and set it on fire. The hall was destroyed and Thorolf killed, though most of his people were spared, and the estate was given to another warrior who swore to be King Harald's friend.

Setting the Gokstad and Oseberg burials into this context of give and take, of promise and threat, explains to me why they are so alike and yet so different. Each represents one face of the Viking ruler. In Gokstad, I see the threat: the war leader, with his horses and game pieces, the shields standing in for his army. In Oseberg, I see the promise: the ritual leader, with her musical instruments and magical rattles, wagons and sleighs. Both are buried in magnificent ships, surrounded by extravagant wealth and everything needed for a feast.

Though Gokstad is the burial of a man and Oseberg of two women, I think it's a mistake to divide these two functions of a Viking leader along gender lines. In Norse mythology, Odin, the one-eyed god of war and poetry, leads ritual sacrifices, raises the dead, reads the runes to learn the future, and can leave his body in a shamanistic trance. Freyja, the goddess of love—and the one who taught Odin this ritual magic—rides to war in a chariot pulled by lions, claims half the dead, and oversees an endless battle in which the wounded are healed overnight to resume their fight at dawn. The tapestries found in the Oseberg mound illustrate both aspects of leadership, the ritual procession and the battle scene, suggesting to me that both roles were required, regardless of the sex of the rulers.

If so, when Hervor was growing up in southern Norway in the mid-tenth century, the twin roles of the Viking ruler were filled by Eirik Bloodaxe and Gunnhild Mother-of-Kings. Eirik was the war leader; he made the threats. Gunnhild was the ritual leader; she saw the future.

6

THE WINTER NIGHTS
FEAST

The way between worlds opens at the Winter Nights. The harvest is in, the beer is brewed, the farmers have assessed their hay stores and decided how many of their stock to keep over the winter. Each has offered a sacrifice: A horse of a special color. A boar to honor the goddess Freyja and her twin brother, Freyr. A bull, the bigger and straighter its horns, the better.

In the old days, Hervor knows, the sacrifice chosen was sometimes human. Queen Gunnhild taught her the lines from the poem of the Yngling kings:

> Long ago
> they reddened the land,
> the sword-bearers
> bloodied their swords
> with kings' blood,
> killing in hope
> of future harvests.

When Domaldi was king at Uppsala, Hervor learned, famine struck year after year, until at one Winter Nights feast it was his royal blood that reddened the altars, a gift to the goddesses, lifting the curse.

Generations later, the goddesses took King Adils, too, the poem said.

As he rode around the ritual hall, his horse stumbled and he was thrown. He hit his head on a rock and died, his blood mixing into the earth: A fruitful summer followed that winter.

Here on Atley Isle, the sacrifice is a magnificent bull. Hervor marches in the procession behind the great beast, her role a major one this year: She carries the blood bowl, while beside her young Ragnhild, Gunnhild's daughter, bears the bundle of twigs used to sprinkle the holy blood. They stand tall, stepping slowly in their long, trailing robes, as they were taught. Behind them come ranks of women and men walking or riding horses, carrying torches and oil lamps on long poles, wearing masks and headdresses, brandishing weapons and staffs, blowing long horns, and shaking large metal rattles lashed to elaborately carved poles, their ends carved as cats' heads in Freyja's honor. Queen Gunnhild herself comes last, driving the elaborately carved horse cart on which the goddesses themselves—in wooden form— are carried to the holy place.

Drugged and placid, the bull circles the barley fields, then is led back to the temple beside the feast hall. There, the idols are reverently unloaded and installed on their pedestals. With fire and sweet smoke, music and elaborate gestures, through the carving of runes and reciting of incantations, Gunnhild invites the goddesses to inspirit their wooden forms and receive the sacrifice.

The final act, as Hervor knows from years past, is thrillingly bloody and dramatic. The bull is led to the temple door. The best two warriors, chosen through fierce competition, stand on either side. The one with the hammer swings a heavy blow between the beast's eyes, stunning it or perhaps killing it outright—Hervor cannot tell which, for at the very same moment the second warrior swings a broad-bladed axe and cuts off the beast's head. Its blood gouts out in a fountain as the beast falls, pumped by the still-beating heart. Holding the bowl Hervor handed her, Gunnhild's arms are drenched with the sacred blood, her face and beautiful garments splashed.

When the bowl is full, Gunnhild passes it back to Hervor—*Don't you dare spill it*, the queen's narrowed eyes warn—and they circle through the celebrants. The queen dips the bunch of twigs Ragnhild hands her into the blood and flings the sacred droplets over the crowd, the idols, the temple walls. Other people, meanwhile, collect the rest of the bull's blood and paint the idols' pedestals; others butcher the bull and set its meat to boiling in many cauldrons; still others bring around beakers and buckets of ale to toast the deities, the rulers, and the ancestors in hopes of prosperity and peace.

Finally the time comes when Hervor can take off her long, blood-splattered robe and compete in the archery match—for the best parts of the Winter Nights for her, each year, are the contests and entertainments. The festivalgoers race horses and wrestle, bet on tests of strength like tug-of-war and weight lifting, and compete in several kinds of ball games, all of which are punctuated by heavy drinking and occasional injuries and deaths.

As the day darkens and the games move inside, people pose riddles and cap verses, creating impromptu ditties to a specified rhyme scheme and rhythm. Masked and wearing costumes, they act out poems about deities and ancient heroes. A *skáld* recites long ballads, accompanied by a lyre. Musicians sing, some chanting deep in their throats. Others play fiddles strung with horsehair, bone or wooden flutes, recorders and trumpets made from goat or cow horns or birchbark or bronze, and various drums, their tunes and tempos rousing the feasters to an ecstatic, drunken dance.

As the night wears on, the smoke from the fires and oil lamps collects, swirling like spirits in the high ceiling of the hall. The darkness deepens and becomes more beautiful, Hervor thinks—and also more terrifying. The guests press closer as Gunnhild again takes her place at the center of the ritual, on a platform surrounded by a chorus of singers. Her dress stiff with gleaming gold and silver embroidery and accented with glittering jewels and furs and feathers, bones and other fetishes, her staff of power in her hand, fortified by alcohol, cannabis, and other herbs she lets no one see her prepare, she sings the songs that unlock the doors to the spirit worlds.

For Gunnhild is a witch. Her song is a whirlwind, spinning part of herself out into the room until she snares everyone's attention and—this is what both thrills and terrifies Hervor—flings it out into the dark unknown. Over the drone of the long, trumpetlike lur, the dark knock of the drums, and the wild dance of the tongue horn, Gunnhild whispers, she keens, she chants, until Hervor rocks and sways to her rhythm; she breathes to it; her heart beats to Gunnhild's time. She is fascinated—and afraid, as all Gunnhild's listeners are, that the witch's staff will suddenly single her out in the crowd, the witch eye will fix on her alone, and she will reveal Hervor's fate.

But the staff passes by, touching a boy instead: *You won't wrestle with old age: A horse's skull will be your bane.* It touches a young widow: *From you will come a worthy family, for shining over your children I see bright rays of light.*

Singing is magic. To hold a room in thrall, a singer outmatches her audience. She grows bigger than the crowd. She pulls the song from her enormous heart and aims it at each of their little hearts. She inhales all the air in the room and sings it out, altered. She plays with that air, breathing out fear, boredom, courage, lust. She sings so loudly the air in her throat turns turbulent: a living whirlwind. She sings herself, and her listeners, to the point of pain, to exhaustion, and, finally, into ecstasy. Modern singers know this. If you sing something—if you say something—it becomes real. "That's the power of poetry," says one. "Your words are your will." Witchcraft, *seiðr* in Old Norse, is a synonym for song.

The mark of a witch, the sagas say, is her staff of power. It might be a twig or a reed or a sturdy stick, crooked or straight. It might be topped by a brass-bound knob studded with jewels or covered with cloth, feathers, and seeds. It might be carved with runes. It might be made of iron, like the rods archaeologists have found in Viking Age graves: Too fancy to be roasting spits, these rods were harder to make, and more valuable, than a sword. It might function as a metaphorical distaff, which held a spinner's raw fibers: In this case, the threads spun are the invisible threads of spirits, "mind-threads." It might function, at other times, as an actual measuring stick: The metal rods archaeologists have found are the length of an ell, about half a yard, the standard length by which cloth was sold. In later ages, such measuring rods were affixed to the door of the parish church, giving them the authority of the new Christian religion, as they once had borne that of the old pagan rites. The witch's staff was like a king's scepter of later ages—a mark of royal might and power. In some stories, that power becomes literal, as the staff transforms into a killing spear.

Several women in the sagas and poems are called *völva*, or "staff bearer," but there is no one single word in Old Norse for "witch." What translators call "witchcraft" was a constellation of powers—powers Christian priests sought to appropriate or deny. Witches were wise. They preserved old lore and kept ancient ritual practices alive. They taught right from wrong, explaining humanity's place in the Nine Worlds of Norse cosmography. They used second sight to foretell the future or find hidden things. With their voice of power, they could wound or bind with words. They could change shape (their own or someone else's) and control the weather. They could turn the land topsy-turvy with a look.

They were not all women: In the sagas, an equal number of men are named witches. They are both rich and poor, despised and well thought of. In most cases, their witchcraft is seen as a useful skill, accorded no moral judgment at all. Egil the Poet, the hero of *Egil's Saga*, for example, was taught magic by his foster mother. When handed a poisoned drinking horn at a feast, Egil not only detected the danger, he knew what to do: He carved runes onto the horn and gave them power with his blood and his words. He magically shattered the cup, and the poison spilled harmlessly to the floor.

It was Queen Gunnhild who tried to poison Egil. In this saga she is the chief villain, and her witchcraft—but not Egil's—is condemned. To Snorri Sturluson, writing for a Christian audience in the mid-1200s, it was beside the point that Egil had rudely disrupted an important ritual: a *dísablót* led by Gunnhild on Atley Isle during the Winter Nights in the late 930s. Snorri says little about the ritual in this saga, but he paints a fuller picture of the rites in *Heimskringla*. There he quotes the poem of the Yngling kings. There he describes the altars and the walls of the temple, both inside and out, as reddened with blood. Blood was borne around in a bowl and the people were splattered, too, using bundles of twigs "made like the sprinklers priests use for holy water." The meat of the sacrificed beasts was stewed in large cauldrons, and everyone was served beer with which to toast the deities. Other sagas describe the singing and soothsaying, the contests and sports that took place during the feasts held on the eve of winter, over three nights around the autumnal equinox. The bloody slaughter of the bull, in my dramatization, was reconstructed by archaeologists based on finds of cattle skulls beside a temple in Iceland, while the ritual procession is best depicted in one of the tapestries buried in the Oseberg ship.

Witch, seer, sorceress, shaman, wisewoman, woman of power, priestess—Gunnhild Mother-of-Kings is all of these, and none of them. I know of no English word that properly describes her role in the ritual. Nor, though

Reconstruction of the ritual procession shown in the Oseberg tapestry,
based on the work of artist Mary Storm.

I can describe some of what went on, thanks to Snorri, can I know what a *dísablót* signified in the mid-tenth century, when Hervor, the warrior woman buried in Birka grave Bj581, was growing up. Literally, the term means "a sacrifice," or *blót*, to or for the *dísir*—but no one today knows who the *dísir* were.

Freyja, the Norse goddess of love and good harvests, and Skadi, goddess of winter and the hunt, are both called *dís* (singular of *dísir*) by Viking Age poets. The word sometimes seems to be a generic term for "goddess."

The norns are *dísir*: These ancient female spirits rule the fates of both deities and humans; their judgment is law, final and unavoidable. Even the chief god, Odin, must abide by the word of these women.

Some valkyries are also called *dísir*—and at least one *dís* who is named a valkyrie is also called a norn. The valkyries in sagas and songs appear as armed and helmeted horsewomen (maybe mortal, maybe not), and as troll women pouring troughs of blood over a battlefield, and in the form of swans. The valkyries "choose the slain," as their name literally says, deciding who will die on the battlefield. Some stories say the god Odin tells them whom to choose and punishes them when they disobey; some say they report to Freyja, not Odin; and some stories say the choice of whom to kill is their own.

The *dísir* include nature spirits, living in rocks and hills, rivers and trees, or masquerading as humans; they are stewards of the earth's resources, safeguarding its fertile soils, its forests, its animal life, its salt and ores. Sometimes they are referred to as elves, sometimes as giantesses, and sometimes as fetches, a type of guardian spirit that can take the shape of an animal or a human.

The *dísir* have power over life and death, often guarding and guiding certain individuals or families—or even nations. Many place-names in Norway and Sweden refer to the *dísir*. These spirits, always female, are associated with rituals, assemblies, and marketplaces, but the picture I am left with is mostly a blur. It may be that the different names of the *dísir* describe not beings, natural or supernatural, but roles.

That I can discover so little about the *dísir* I chalk up to the biases of Snorri Sturluson. Author of our two best sources on Norse mythology, Snorri wasted few words on females, human or divine. They did not fit his audience or his purpose. He wrote his *Edda* in about 1220 for the sixteen-year-old Norwegian king to complete (or counteract) the boy's education by Christian bishops. Snorri's *Edda*—not to be confused with *The Poetic Edda*—was a handbook of myths and short quotations meant, ostensibly, to teach the young king to appreciate the court poetry of the ancient North, with its many allusions to mythology. Snorri's real goal was to gain an influential position as court poet himself and to become the king's counselor. Snorri wrote *Heimskringla*, his collection of sagas of the kings of Norway, during the same king's reign, again to impress the younger man. Women in both books are honored mothers or objects of lust, Mary or Eve, as they were in Snorri's own lifetime. It was the orthodox view of women in medieval Christian society, where even marriage and childbirth were considered matters for churchmen to control.

But Snorri gives us glimpses of the myths he left out, as do several poems he quotes. One of these is the Norse creation myth. In the beginning two driftwood logs, one elm and one ash, are found on the seashore by three wandering gods. These gods give the wood human shape and bring it to life with blood, breath, and curious minds. Unlike the Christian creation myth, where Eve is an afterthought, fashioned out of Adam's rib, in the Norse myth Embla (the female) and Ask (the male) are equal: They are made at the same time out of nearly the same stuff. As different as an ash tree and an elm, they make a good team.

Likewise when the Norse deities gather in council by the Well of Fate, each one sits on a chair or throne, a mark of authority. Portable chairs are scarce in Viking Age sources, but one was found in the Oseberg ship mound; its boxy, throne-like shape is uncannily like that of the tiny silver chair amulets found in some rich female graves in Birka and elsewhere. Sitting on their chairs in the council, the goddesses have an equal say in the issues under discussion. The goddesses are "no less holy" than the gods, Snorri concedes, "and no less powerful." In council, the gods and goddesses determined the calendar, planning when markets, festivals, and assemblies should be held. They determined the standards of weights and measures that transformed precious metals and lengths of cloth into currency. They determined how oaths should be sworn and when blood money should be paid for a crime.

Individually, the *dísir* have other powers. The norns (sometimes three, sometimes more) set down the laws and created the runic alphabet used for writing down ordinary speech—such as records of ownership—as well as for acts of magic and soothsaying. The goddess Eir is "an excellent physician," Snorri says—and tells us nothing else about her or her art. Likewise, the goddess Vor is so "wise and questioning" that "nothing can be hidden from her." The goddess Syn watches at the doors of the hall and locks out "those who should not enter"; she is also a lawyer, speaking for the defense "in court cases she wishes to prove untrue." Hlin guards people the goddess Frigg "wishes to protect from danger," and Gna rides a horse "over wind and sea" to attend to Frigg's business. What that business is remains unclear, but Frigg may sit beside her husband, Odin, on the high seat, a kind of watchtower from which they can see "over all the worlds," marking everyone's behavior and understanding everything they see. She—not Odin—also knows everyone's fate, though she chooses not to reveal it. Odin may be known for his wisdom, but his wife, having foresight, is wiser than he and gives better advice. The people of Hervor's day, in the tenth century, would have known stories of all these goddesses. The people of Snorri's day, in the thirteenth, knew some stories too—how else were their names remembered through two hundred years of Christian teaching? But Snorri chose not to record those stories. The mythology he bequeathed us is less than half the whole.

Snorri does tell an amusing tale about Skadi, the goddess of winter, of skiing, and of the hunt—its adolescent humor was certain to appeal to his adolescent male audience. He describes Skadi as a warrior woman, a shield-maid or valkyrie figure, and daughter of a giant. When her father was killed by the god Loki's tricks, Skadi "took up her helmet and ringmail byrnie and weapons of war" and set off to avenge him. To avoid a fight, Odin offered her compensation: In lieu of blood money, he would turn her father's eyes into two stars in the sky and Loki would make her laugh (unforgettably, by tying a rope around the beard of a goat and the other end around his own testicles). Finally, Skadi could choose a husband from among all the gods (by looking only at their feet). Skadi chose the sea god Njord, but their marriage did not work out. He hated the howling of wolves, she despised the cries of gulls, and they agreed to live apart; her realm was in the mountains, his down by the sea.

Skadi may be the winter face of the fertility goddess Freyja, who in Snorri's account is beautiful and sad, fond of love songs and gaudy jewelry, with a cat-drawn carriage and a wandering husband for whom she weeps tears of gold. In Snorri's tales, Freyja exists "primarily as an object of lust for male giants," notes one expert. It's easy to overlook Snorri's own comment, based on an older poem, that "wherever she rides in battle, she claims half of the dead, and half go to Odin," for Snorri tells us nothing more about Freyja as battle-goddess. Those enormous cats who draw her carriage? Picture them as mountain lions, not house cats.

The poem Snorri cites makes it clear that the spirits of all warriors slain in battle go first to Freyja: She decides which ones will stay in her roomy hall at Folkvang (Field of Warriors), and which ones she will send on to Odin's Valhalla (Hall of the Slain). From this it appears that the mythological valkyries must report to the goddess Freyja first—that she, not the god Odin, is the chief of these "choosers of the slain." These warrior women may originally have been Freyja's bodyguard or special forces, just as the berserks, those men who "threw off their ringmail and were mad as dogs or wolves, bit their shields and were strong as bears or bulls," as Snorri describes them, were the special troops of Odin. Men who are especially fierce and reckless fighters are called berserks in the sagas, without it meaning that they are truly superhuman. The same may be true of the warrior women called valkyries.

Odin's position as chief god of the Norse pantheon—the "All-Father," as Snorri names him—may, in fact, be a late development influenced by Christianity. Before the Viking Age, religion in the North was local. As many Scandinavian place-names reveal, the people in some places worshipped the fertility goddess Freyja and her twin brother, Freyr, while in other places they worshipped Thor the Thunderer or Njord, a god of the sea.

Odin, the latecomer, was worshipped mostly by chieftains and warrior kings with national ambitions: Fewer places are named after him. These aristocrats saw an advantage in having one high god—a god not linked to any specific place, one whose power lay not in blessing the land or in harnessing nature, but in the intangible rewards of the afterlife. Odin, like Christ, gave little to the living but much to the dead. Once the Norse accepted the notion of one high god, impersonal and remote, whose rewards were long delayed, might they not also accept the idea of a king who lived far away, one they rarely saw and got little good out of, who was chosen by or descended from that one high god and granted his power?

Though considered a warrior god, wisdom, not strength or courage, is Odin's chief attribute. He has many features of a shaman, the religious leader of the reindeer-herding Sami in the far north, with whom the Vikings traded for furs and walrus ivory. According to the myths, Odin gave up an eye for a sip from the well of wisdom. He stabbed himself with a spear and hung on a tree, without food, without drink, for nine nights—sacrificing himself to himself, the poet says—to gain access to the wisdom of the runes and other magic lore.

But Odin was not the first Norse deity to go through such an initiation rite. A goddess named Gullveig also sacrificed herself for knowledge, was stabbed and burned, but defied death and lived, becoming a seer and a practitioner of magic. Her name literally means Golden Drink or Golden Intoxication. She may be the original goddess of beer and of poetry and song, as Odin afterward came to be.

Gullveig, once initiated into these mysteries, taught them to other women, including the goddess Freyja, who then taught this witchcraft to Odin. A witch knew the battle magic that caused enemies to be blind or deaf or terrified and their swords to bite no better than sticks. She could shape-shift, like a shaman, into a bird or beast, fish or serpent, and travel to distant lands. She could disguise a person as a goat, a horse, a pig, a wooden chest, a distaff, or whatever she liked. She could make herself, or anyone else, invisible. She could carve and read runes, cast lots to tell the future, and interpret dreams. She knew charms to find buried treasure, to bring sickness, misfortune, or death. She brewed love potions and poisons, knew how to keep a woman from conceiving a child and how to ease a birth. She could heal wounds, set bones, and make someone proof against iron weapons. She could extinguish fires, calm the sea, and turn the winds with a word. She could conjure up darkness and mist, blizzards or earthquakes. She could fill the sea with fish.

As Odin's teacher, Freyja is the older and more powerful deity. Her name came to mean "lady," Snorri notes: not as in "wife of the lord" but as in "female ruler." "She became so famous," he writes, "that all noble women were called by her name, as they are now, also those women who control their own property or own a farm." *Frau* in German and *fru* in the modern Scandinavian languages are titles derived from Freyja's name.

As the original Norse fertility goddess, Freyja is an avatar of the Great Goddess, who is both Mother Earth and the goddess of the sun: In Norse mythology, unlike that of many other cultures, the all-powerful sun is female, while the changeable moon is male. Cult objects from before the Viking Age in Scandinavia prominently feature the sun. As the power of Odin rose, these sun symbols were replaced by images of warriors. Rites and sacrifices that used to be held outdoors, in wooded groves or hills or beside holy lakes, moved indoors, into a chieftain's hall or into a temple, or "god house," patterned on Christian basilicas. As the holy space moved from a natural, fixed site to an artificial, movable one, the focus of worship also changed, moving from the natural world to the human one—and from the many goddesses and gods of nature to a male, humanlike god. Power, not fertility, became the ultimate divine gift.

Hervor knew nothing of the waning of the power of Freyja and the presumption of Odin. If she did help Queen Gunnhild perform a *dísablót* as a girl, she would not have doubted that fertility *was* power, for Gunnhild herself embodied the goddess. In addition to giving Eirik advice, strengthening his ambition, organizing his traveling household, and taking matters into her own hands, when necessary, Gunnhild bore nine children—nine, that is, who lived past infancy. Five of them shared the title of king, earning her the name Gunnhild Mother-of-Kings.

What was Eirik's role as king? "Long ago," sang the poet, "the sword-bearers bloodied their swords with kings' blood . . . in hope of future harvests." When a king was killed, and his blood mixed into the earth, the famine would lift and a fruitful summer follow. In the oldest Norse texts, a king guaranteed his people's prosperity by shedding blood: sometimes his own. Prosperity was defined as a good harvest of grain, which in most of the Viking world meant barley. And barley meant beer.

THE VALKYRIES' TASK

G irl. Bring more beer.

Eirik Bloodaxe is black-haired and handsome, big, bold, and blessed with victory, the poets say, but Hervor finds him grim, glum, and cold. Quick to fly into a rage, he takes ages to reach any kind of a decision, sucking on it like a toothache. He could not be more unlike Queen Gunnhild, whose sharp mind snaps through the knottiest problems with the teeth of a wolf.

Still, Eirik Bloodaxe is king, so Hervor hustles to do his bidding.

It is the third night of the Winter Nights feast, and everyone is feeling the effects of too much drinking. Hervor's head pounds. Bard of Atley Isle, preparing to welcome his king and queen, brewed a huge vat of beer—not so huge as the legendary vat King Fjolnir drowned in, but large enough that everyone can drink a full hornful for each toast, instead of sharing one horn between two people, as usual. No one goes thirsty at Bard's feasts. No one goes clearheaded to bed. It's a matter of pride.

Still, by the third night, the beer vat is running low. Hervor has to lean down into it to fill a fresh bucketful. If she weren't so tall for her age, she'd need help. As it is, her tunic is wet where she bent over the vat's lip and her sleeve ends are dripping, her hands sticky, as she lugs the heavy bucket through the crowded hall, sidling between lolling bodies, climbing over limp limbs, taking special care not to spill it.

For the king, for the king, she hisses, when someone tries to stop her.

They pluck at her arms; they pat her back. She ignores them. All that exists is that tall, carved seat beside the longfire, where Eirik sits wrapped in his festival robes, brooding. All Hervor wants is to get there before Eirik's angry bellow makes the room ring with sudden silence. Queen Gunnhild is not at his side, and their host, Bard, keeps disappearing from the feast hall. Eirik's mood is as black as it gets.

Hervor knows that could be a problem. But she never expected it to be *her* problem. She is the queen's ward. Eirik doesn't even know who she is—except the girl bringing him beer. He glares at her as she reaches his side, as if to say, *What took you so long?* She smiles to appease him, though it has no effect, then concentrates on steadying the heavy bucket while he dips his silver-rimmed drinking horn, splashing beer over the side and dribbling it down her already sticky-slick hand.

Then King Eirik speaks. To her. He grabs her sleeve, sloshing more beer out of the bucket, and growls, Who does Bard have out in the barn? Who is he attending to, when he should be in here with me?

Hervor doesn't really know, but she realizes she'd better answer. Quick.

A boat came, she says. When it was raining. They were hungry and cold.

From somewhere in her pounding head a name pops out: Olvir?

Eirik nods. Olvir. His expression eases. Hervor begins to breathe again.

Tell him to join the feast, Eirik commands.

The old man, Olvir, comes in disheveled, as if he's just woken from sleep. His tunic is salt-stained and damp and definitely not festival garb. They landed on Atley Isle by accident, he says. The wind held them back, and by dark they'd rowed only this far. They had not intended to interrupt Eirik's Winter Nights Feast. They're headed elsewhere, to collect taxes owed Chieftain Thorir, Eirik's old foster father, who cared for him when he was three—

Eirik waves away Olvir's explanations. Sit and drink, he says.

The people on the benches across the longfire make room. Bard himself brings beakers of beer for Olvir and the big man who sits down next to him, a young fellow no one bothers to introduce.

That's a mistake, Hervor thinks. Though his beard is sparse, the boy is huge—even brawnier than King Eirik. He is uglier, too, with a frown even more menacing than the king's. He too is damp and disheveled, but while Olvir looks exhausted, this boy looks ready to erupt. He snatches the beer cup out of Bard's hand and drinks it down, toasting the king. On the next toast, he drinks both his own and Olvir's cups—the old man looks ready to pass out. Bard waves Hervor over, takes her beer bucket, and refills both cups.

You look thirsty, boy, Bard says. That won't do.

He pointedly hands one cup to Olvir.

Bard shouldn't have baited the boy, Hervor thinks. And, indeed, after draining his cup, the boy gets to his feet.

> *You told the trolls' foe*
> *you were flat out of ale—*
> *at a Winter Nights feast?*
> *You foul blasphemer.*
> *A cheap host it is*
> *who cheats a guest.*
> *Your lies, Bard, leave*
> *a bad taste in my mouth.*

Don't mock your betters, boy, Bard replies.

The boy takes Olvir's cup, drains it, and holds the two cups out again. I'm just thirsty, he says. But you, of course, are all out of beer, like you told us when we arrived—when you served us sour whey and said you wished you could offer us a better welcome.

When Hervor's beer bucket is empty, Bard pulls her aside. Go to the queen, he says. Tell her that ugly young man is mocking us, claiming to be thirsty no matter how much he drinks.

Queen Gunnhild is well aware of what is going on in the hall. She takes a vial of liquid from a pouch at her belt and pours a few drops into a horn of beer. She tells Hervor to take it to the boy.

Hervor walks straight and tall, her hands still, her face blank. Without the beer bucket, no one pays her any mind. It seems to take forever to squeeze her way through the crowd. When she reaches the boy, he is leaning over the drunken Olvir, trying to slap him awake. Hervor waits until he looks up.

She hands him the drinking horn. From the queen, she says.

The ugly boy glares at her, but she knows he will read nothing in her face.

Then he surprises her. He draws his eating knife and carves runes on the horn. He pricks his palm and reddens the runes with his own blood,

Vikings in long gowns, including a cup bearer, each less than an inch tall.

then whispers a verse. The horn splits apart, and the poisoned beer spills into the straw. He watches for Hervor to react, and when she doesn't, he hoists Olvir up and half drags, half carries the old man to the door.

Just as they reach it, Bard rushes up with a new beer horn. Olvir, he says, you must drink a parting toast to the king.

The boy grabs the horn and throws it on the floor, then draws his sword and thrusts it into Bard's belly. Bard and Olvir collapse at the same time, and by the time King Eirik has a light brought, he finds the one dead and the other passed out, the floor a pool of vomit and blood.

Find that boy and bring him to me! King Eirik says.

They search the island, seize all the boats, but Bard's killer has escaped.

The figure of a cup bearer appears on several Viking Age amulets and stone carvings. She is said to be a woman because of her long hair and long dress, yet many Viking kings and warriors, like Harald Fairhair, are famous for long hair, and several—including Egil the Poet—owned ceremonial silk gowns so long they dragged on the ground; Egil's was embroidered with gold and had gold buttons all down the front.

The cup bearer is often compared to the Lady with the Mead Cup, an archetype based on the character of Queen Wealhtheow in the Old English epic *Beowulf*. Scholars have written whole books on how Wealhtheow served the mead: Entering the hall with the intoxicating golden drink, she drew all eyes. By offering the cup first to the king, she enacted "an archaic ritual of lordship" that underscored his preeminence. As she brought the cup to the warriors, each in turn, she fixed their status, their rank in the king's band. By drinking, the warriors accepted that ranking and assented to the king's rule. "So did the queen act to help achieve cohesion and unity of purpose between lord and follower in the royal hall," says one scholar.

And so did Bard—not Queen Gunnhild—at the Winter Nights feast on Atley Isle, according to this scene I've retold from *Egil's Saga* (and in which I've substituted Hervor for the unnamed beer server). It was Bard who brought the ceremonial cup to the newcomers, Olvir and Egil, and Bard who insisted Olvir should not leave the hall without a final toast to King Eirik, assenting to the king's rule. A ritual of lordship the serving of alcohol may be; it was not necessarily a woman's task.

Amulets of a cup bearer are often found in women's graves. Despite this fact, the figure is commonly said to be a valkyrie welcoming a dead (male) warrior to Valhalla. Snorri Sturluson, once again, is the source of this misinterpretation. It was the valkyries' task to "serve in Valhalla, bringing drinks and taking care of the cups and beer casks," Snorri, writing in the thirteenth century, says.

Yet two tenth-century poems describe dead kings arriving at the doors of Valhalla, and neither one is greeted by a valkyrie with a cup. In one poem, the Christian King Hakon is met by a pair of pagan gods, who promise, "You will receive ale from the Aesir," a collective term for the male gods Odin, Thor, Tyr, and many others.

In the second poem, Odin is alarmed to learn that the great Eirik Bloodaxe himself has been killed in battle; the god cries out:

> *What did I dream?*
> *Just before daybreak*
> *I readied Valhalla,*
> *or so I imagined,*
> *for a host of the slain.*
> *I woke up the Einherjar:*
> *Get up! Scatter straw*
> *on all the bare benches,*
> *wash out the beer cups!*
> *Valkyries! Bring wine,*
> *for a war leader arrives!*

At the doors of Valhalla Eirik is met, not by valkyries carrying wine, but by the heroes Sigurd the Dragon-Slayer and his brother Sinfjotli.

Eirik Bloodaxe's death song is the earlier of the two poems. It may have sparked the tenth-century fashion for gone-to-Valhalla verses to commemorate Christian kings—for while ruling York in England, both Eirik and Gunnhild converted to the new faith. Eirik's eulogy, written after he died in England about 954, may have been composed by Queen Gunnhild, who is known to have been a poet. If so, her sense of humor has been sadly underappreciated. Here the great heroes and berserks of the Einherjar or "Lone-Fighters," the army of Odin, are "being forced out of bed early, like recalcitrant teenagers, to wash the beer mugs," as one scholar puts it, while the death-dealing valkyries masquerade as serving wenches. It's a spoof, a parody of pagan beliefs, not a portrayal by a true believer in Valhalla.

Analyzing those amulets and other images of a cup bearer, most scholars say the woman is offering the cup to someone unseen. It's not the only possible interpretation. "How close must a drinking horn be next to an (alleged) woman, before the idea comes to mind that she actually could have taken a sip herself?" asks a feminist critic. Couldn't she be raising her own cup to make a toast or take a vow? "Why is the thought of women drinking so utterly neglected?" The answer, again, is because our understanding of the Viking Age took shape during the Victorian Age, when well-bred ladies were excluded from rowdy drinking parties.

Yet even the misogynist Snorri gives a more balanced picture. It was the custom in some kings' halls, he writes in *Heimskringla*, "that in the evenings they should drink in pairs, two by two, one man and one woman, if possible, and those that were left over should drink all together." Toasts were drunk to the ancestors and to the gods, and boasts were made. At one feast, "King Ingjald stood up and lifted up a great drinking horn. He made this vow, that he would double the size of his realm in every direction, or else die. Then he drank the horn dry." At another feast, Hildigunn "took a silver cup, filled it, and took it over to King Hjorvard. 'All hail to the Ylflings, in memory of Hrolf Kraki,' she said. She drank off half the cup and handed it to the king."

Nor did the women shyly retire after a courteous sip. The widowed queen Sigrid the Strong-Minded invited a potential husband, a king, to a feast. "The king and the queen sat on the high-seat and drank together all evening. . . . And when the king had taken off his clothes and gone to his rest, the queen came in to him and filled his cup herself. She urged him to drink up—she was most agreeable. The king was completely drunk; both of them were."

Egil, whom Queen Gunnhild had failed to poison, attended a feast where people were to drink two by two, the pairs determined by lot. "The people threw their lots onto a square of cloth and the earl picked them out. The earl had a very handsome daughter who had just come of age. The way the lots fell, Egil was to sit beside the earl's daughter for the evening, but she wandered around the room, enjoying herself. Egil stood up and went to where she had been sitting all day. And when everyone took their seats, she returned to her old seat." Seeing Egil there, she challenged him in verse:

> Who said this seat was yours, boy?
> Seldom have you drawn sword.
> From you the wolf gets no flesh.
> My flesh likes sitting solo.
> You've never seen the crow caw
> on corpses slain at harvest;
> when shell-sharp swords came slashing
> you shied away, and stayed home.

Egil answered her with a boasting verse—*I've borne a bloodstained sword*—and "they drank together that evening and both had a fine time."

I imagine Hervor got drunk at feasts like other girls in tenth-century Norway. Nor was she stuck in the kitchen, as the Victorian model of the Viking Age led us to assume. Preparing a feast was a great deal of work, but it wasn't *women's work*. Pots and pans and festival food were found in both the Gokstad (male) and Oseberg (female) royal burials, while at Kaupang kitchen equipment appears in slightly more men's graves than women's.

Hervor would have been taught kitchen skills, of course. Boys and girls needed to know how to grind barley to make bread, for example, though they may not have been called upon to do it often. The tool used was a hand quern: two heavy discs of stone, each about a foot in diameter, the top one with a center hole and a side handle. While the top disc was rotated, seeds were fed into the center hole. The steadier the stream, the lower the friction; with less friction, the millstones lasted longer and the flour was less tainted with stone dust (which wore away the enamel on your teeth). About a pound of grain could be ground at a time. After two passes through the mill, one experimenter found, barleycorns were ground fine enough for porridge. To make bread flour called for another four or five passes, with the flour sieved each time and the coarser grains reground. "The time and effort needed," he writes, "suggests that one would produce only enough flour to cover the needs of the day." It was so strenuous that scientists blame habitual grinding when they find skeletons with tears in their shoulder joints.

It was the kind of work Vikings forced their captives to perform; two poems that mention querns point out that the grinders are enslaved. The warrior Helgi, cornered by his enemies, escaped capture by trading clothes with a slave girl and taking over her task. His enemy remarked, "That's no farm girl standing by the quern. The stones are cracking. The handle is flying around." That's not so surprising, Helgi's accomplice explained. His slave was a valkyrie: "She dared to fight as a Viking," before she was captured and put in chains.

In the second poem, King Frodi bought two strong women to grind his magic millstone, which produced not only flour, but "whatever the grinder wished it to." Frodi told them to grind out gold, first, and then peace and plenty. The women began their task cheerfully. They sang a working song, the poem says, and made the quernstone whirl around.

But the king gave them no rest. "Sleep no longer than it takes me to recite a poem!" he ordered.

The women got angry. "You were not very wise," they told Frodi, "when you bought your slaves. You chose us for strength and looks and asked nothing about our background." Before they were captured and enslaved, they had been warrior women: They killed berserks, broke shields, killed one king, and helped another. They said:

> *This went on*
> *for many years:*
> *As heroes we*
> *were widely known—*
> *with keen spears*

we cut
blood from bone.
Our blades were red.

They ordered the quernstone to grind out an army to overthrow Frodi. "Let's turn the mill-handle harder! We're not yet covered in corpse-blood."

This poem itself is a working song. I can imagine Hervor singing it as she ground the day's grain. It's a merciless song, a song to inspire a young warrior woman.

If she was taught to grind barley into bread flour, Hervor would also have learned to brew it into beer and ale. Bread was not essential for a Viking feast, but beer—or some other liquor—was, and most of the barley harvest in the North likely went for brewing. In some versions of the Icelandic law code, written down in the thirteenth century, brewing is a specifically female task. But other copies of the laws, as well as poems and sagas, show that men were just as likely to be brewers. In one poem, Thor the Thunderer ordered Aegir, a god of the sea, to provide a feast for all the deities.

Aegir disliked Thor's attitude. He sent Thor on a wild-goose chase: "Bring me a big enough cauldron," he said, "that I can brew beer for all of you." Unexpectedly, Thor succeeded, returning with a giant cauldron a mile deep. So Aegir set to work.

The process the sea-god followed, as Hervor would have learned it, began by turning barley into malt. The grain had already been harvested, then threshed and winnowed to separate the seed from the chaff. Handed a sack of barleycorns, Hervor set it in a stream to soak for several days. Then she spread the seeds in a single layer on the paved floor of a dark, breezy barn and allowed the grain to sprout. When rootlets appeared, she gathered the grain and dried it in an oven, then crushed it and warmed it with water in an iron cauldron, simmering over a fire, or in a wooden vat warmed by dropping in hot rocks heated in a fireplace.

Once the mash was sweet enough, Hervor strained it, collecting the malt liquid in a separate vessel. If the liquid was cloudy, she repeated this step—altogether a messy, sticky process—then boiled the sweet barley juice, or wort. After it cooled a bit, if she stirred it with the same stick used for the previous batch, the wort became infected with yeast—a good thing, allowing it, given three or four days in a warm, covered vat, to ferment into beer or ale (depending on the type of yeast).

But if she did not keep the vat and other tools clean, she introduced bacteria that ruined the batch, so constant fresh water was crucial. She might use ten times more water cleaning than went into her beer. The archaeological signs of a Viking Age brewhouse, like one found on Orkney, thus include a malting floor, a large fireplace, fire-cracked rocks, a drying oven, and a well-planned system of drains. The Orkney brewhouse, set next to the feast hall, was once identified, mistakenly, as a bathhouse.

At several points in the process, Hervor may have been taught to add herbs to the beer. Some herbs, like hops, which was known to the Vikings but was not widely available, acted as preservatives. Others gave the beer flavor, color, and other properties. Marsh rosemary turned it spicy and red; yarrow made it bitter and astringent. Bog myrtle gave beer a sour taste, balancing out the sweetness of the malt; it also enhanced the brew's alcoholic effect, acting as a sedative, even a narcotic: Some drinkers describe it as "stupefying." Overindulged, it produces a "whopping" headache. Psychotropic herbs added to beer might be what caused Viking warriors to go berserk.

Heavy drinking was standard at a Viking feast, yet drunkenness was frowned upon. When Sigurd the Dragon-Slayer asked the valkyrie Brynhild for advice, she taught him "beer runes" to carve on his drinking horn or on his fingernail or to tattoo onto the back of his hand. These would keep him from making drunken advances to a woman and protect him from beer "blended with poison." But the best way to stay safe at a feast, she warned, was to keep your wits about you and never fight while drunk. She said:

> Singing and drinking
> have brought sorrow to many:
> to some, death;
> to some, bad fortune.

The evils of drunkenness are repeated in the Viking creed, *The Words of the High One*:

It's not as good
as everyone says,
ale, for anyone.
The more you drink,
the less aware
you are of yourself . . .
Oblivion is the bird
hovering over the ale-hall:
It steals your good sense.

But if the sagas can be trusted, the Vikings, in general, ignored such advice. The value of a feast was measured by how much beer (or wine or mead) was poured, and the beer was judged by how drunk everyone got. To drink and drink but not grow drunk was itself an insult, implying your host had not served strong-enough beer. When Queen Gunnhild met Egil the Poet on Atley Isle, he insulted their host in that way. Gunnhild took it personally and sent a girl—perhaps Hervor—to hand him a horn of poisoned beer.

THE FEUD

Hervor is the fastest runner of all the children in Gunnhild's care. Taller than her age-mates among Gunnhild's sons, it is she who is chosen to run the queen's errands when they attend the Gula Assembly.

Make way! Make way for the queen's runner! she calls as she slips through the packed crowd, searching for this man or that woman summoned to see the queen. In a sweaty hand she clutches the queen's royal token.

Up to the edge of the dark woods she runs, where the craggy hillside looms over her. Down to the lip of the fjord, narrow here, a silver ribbon leading east toward blue ranks of mountains, the farthest and highest showing teeth of snow. She weaves among the market stalls that clutter the harbor, ignoring the pungent scents of simmering horsemeat and warming ale, ignoring the flash and dazzle of goods for sale. She circles the law court in the center of the great open field: The sacred space within which petitioners can safely stand is clearly defined by hazel poles and horsehair ropes.

There, at one end of the law court, Queen Gunnhild sits on her throne, King Eirik beside her, their warriors and counselors ranked behind them. Likewise, on the other three sides of the square sit the chieftains of Hordaland, Fjordane, and Sognefjord.

The Gula Assembly is the yearly meeting for the people of these three districts in western Norway. Eirik's father, Harald Fairhair, set it up so the farmers could meet him in a neutral spot and resolve any differences. Laws are debated here and fixed in memory. Lawsuits are settled. The chieftain of each district chooses twelve judges, to take oaths and rule on the legal issues of each case. Though the king has the final say, his decision is based on the numbers who swear oaths in support of each side—or who are willing to fight. Weapons are barred from the assembly grounds for good reason.

The assembly's location has been carefully chosen too, Hervor sees. The place itself reinforces the king's promise of peace. No one can feel trapped here: It is the best sort of meeting place and the worst battleground. The land at the mouth of the Sognefjord is cut up into countless points and islands, some linked by land bridges at low tide. Safe harbors are scattered behind every headland, and each seems to have its own escape route, around this island or that, out to the North Way. High, wooded hills hide entire inlets. Secret coves offer ample hiding places. Numbers—of ships, of warriors—do not equal victory, when it is so easy for small boats, skillfully sailed or rowed, to slip away.

Recognizing the big ugly man Queen Gunnhild tried to poison at the Winter Nights feast on Atley Isle, Hervor stops and stares when Egil the Poet steps over the holy ropes and enters the law court.

After he killed the queen's friend Bard, Egil was exiled from Norway. But here he is now, an outlaw, asking King Eirik to grant him half the wealth of a chieftain, recently deceased, whose granddaughter Egil has married.

And he is backed by Arinbjorn, the young chieftain of Sognefjord—Eirik Bloodaxe's foster brother and closest friend.

But Egil's opponent in this lawsuit is backed by Queen Gunnhild.

Returning to the queen's side to await her next errand, Hervor feels the tension in the air. The packed crowd that surrounds the law court is about to burst into action. It is wise, she thinks again, that they are all weaponless.

The argument turns on Egil's wife's legal status: Her mother eloped, marrying without the approval of her brother, Chieftain Thorir—Arinbjorn's father and King Eirik's foster father. Egil swears the marriage was, eventually, made valid. But his wife, the other side argues, was born before that. She is the child of an elopement, which gives her the low status of a slave. She cannot inherit. The judges bandy the matter back and forth.

Arinbjorn wants to call witnesses to swear the marriage was legalized, but King Eirik will not say yes or no. It is all too complicated for him. He is famous for brawn, not brains. He wants nothing more to do with the case.

Queen Gunnhild is disgusted. It amazes me, she says, how you let Egil, this big nobody, tie up your law court. Would you have anything to say, I wonder, if he decided to take the whole kingdom off your hands?

The queen sends Hervor to find her most loyal henchman. Tell him to break up the court, she whispers, and passes Hervor a token.

Hervor runs to where the man waits, beside a hazel pole. Seeing the token, he yanks the pole out of the ground, draws his knife, and cuts the holy rope. As Hervor watches, the court falls into chaos. The judges dart this way and that, as Egil, stranded in the middle, bellows with rage.

The feud between Gunnhild and Egil that began at the Winter Nights feast on Atley Isle lasted their entire lives. If Hervor was Gunnhild's foster child, it colored her life as well, teaching her not only the power of a queen, but also the limitations of the law. In one of his poems, Egil names his nemesis Gunnhild the Grim. To my mind, it was Egil who made her so, by murdering her ten-year-old son in cold blood, as we will see.

To Snorri Sturluson, the grim queen was a convenient villain. While in his *Edda* Snorri names a goddess who practiced law and controlled access to justice, he wrote *Egil's Saga* to glorify his ancestor and justify his own control, like Egil's, three hundred years earlier, of one-fourth of Iceland. He had no interest in Gunnhild as a person. Even so, his account of her feud with Egil reveals another side of this powerful Viking queen. She was not only a witch—a cult leader or shaman—and the mother of many children. She was also a politician, lawyer, counselor, and judge, with an excellent sense of strategy.

A good queen, say several sagas and songs, should offer her advice, on military as well as household matters. She should be wise and farseeing, bold and eloquent, persuasive in making her case, and have good political instincts, knowing when to negotiate and when to strike. She should be assertive and firm, taking matters into her own hands when necessary. She should know how to raise an army and how to defend—or take—a town.

The connection between women and wisdom is deeply embedded in Norse lore. The god Odin is taught witchcraft by the goddess Freyja and consults an anonymous wisewoman to learn the future. Sigurd the Dragon-Slayer asks the valkyrie Brynhild for news and advice.

A detailed picture of the wise Viking queen appears in the *Saga of Hrolf Gautreksson*. Like the *Saga of Hervor*, *Hrolf's Saga* is the story of a warrior woman; for this reason, among others, it has long been considered "unacceptable as history," though it might "contain historical elements." Taught to see the Viking world in terms of men's actions, scholars classify *Hrolf's Saga* as a Bridal-Quest Romance, reducing the saga's strong women to objects for the men to win. They tag it as "late," "popular," and—in case you didn't notice those words were insults—"entirely frivolous."

I fully agree that *Hrolf's Saga* is not a literary masterpiece like *Egil's Saga*, but it may have been written down no later than this exemplar of "realistic fiction in the classical saga tradition." *Egil's Saga* (with its magic spells, runic charms, curses, half trolls, berserks, and werewolves) is thought to have been written by Snorri Sturluson shortly before he died in 1241; the oldest manuscript, a fragment not in Snorri's handwriting, dates from about 1250. A bit of *Hrolf's Saga* appears on two scraps of parchment dated to around 1300. In another of the oldest saga manuscripts, dated 1300 to 1325, *Hrolf's Saga* and *Egil's Saga* appear together. The medieval scribe who collected and copied the stories clearly did not find the two sagas so very different in quality.

Just as clearly, readers' tastes have changed. *Hrolf's Saga* was extremely popular in the Middle Ages—it is still preserved in more than sixty manuscripts, while *Egil's Saga* is found in only thirteen.

When *Hrolf's Saga* was written, and for whom, is unknown. But one word choice hints that the author was a woman. The saga concludes, "People say this saga is true. Although it has never been *skrifaði í tabula*, wise people have kept it alive in their memories." Translators read *skrifaði í tabula* as "committed to parchment," but the word *tabula*—Latin, not Norse—is elsewhere used in the sagas to mean an embroidered altarpiece or other woven picture, while the verb *skrifa*, "to write," can also mean "to weave." Is the author saying this saga "has never been woven into a tapestry"? Weaving or embroidering a series of pictures, like the cartoons in the famous Bayeux Tapestry from eleventh-century England, was the best way of preserving a tale until writing became commonplace. In *Hrolf's Saga*, *Hervor's Saga*, and many other texts, such pictorial weaving was important cultural work assigned to women.

As for the tale's "frivolous" nature, the saga author addressed this point directly:

It may be so for this saga as for many another, that not everyone tells it the same way. But people are of many kinds, and some travel widely. One hears this and one hears that, and each may be true, though neither is quite the whole truth. . . . It seems to me best to not find fault with a story if you can't better it. Whether it's true or not, let those who enjoy it do so, while those who don't can look elsewhere for entertainment.

Stories told over and over and laboriously handwritten on parchment for generations are never "frivolous." They have meaning for someone.

Like all good stories, *Hrolf's Saga* both informs and entertains. Through five examples, the saga shows how a kingdom suffers without a wise queen—or when the king doesn't listen to the queen's advice— though, pointedly, the one kingdom ruled by a woman alone functions perfectly well until attacked by the bride-seeking hero. Overall, *Hrolf's Saga* is an extraordinarily feminist saga, affirming the ability of women to compete with men on all levels. More, it affirms the necessity for the sexes to share power. Though today it is known as the *Saga of Hrolf, Son of Gautrek*, it was likely known in Hervor's day by the name of its true hero, as the *Saga of Thornbjorg*.

The saga's theme is clear from the start: Once upon a time, King Gautrek had been a fine king, famous for his generosity; then his queen died. Now he spent his days sitting on her grave mound talking to her bones, and "his kingdom was like a ship with no one steering." His people convinced him he must remarry, so he asked for the hand of Ingibjorg of Norway. But negotiations were already underway for Ingibjorg to marry a young king from a neighboring land. Her father said, "I can avoid this hassle if I let her choose her own husband, as she's asked me before." Ingibjorg made her decision using reason and logic. She chose the well-tested older king, Gautrek, over the youthful but untried one, saying, "It's a bad idea to bet on hopes."

Later, both she and the anonymous queen of Denmark chastise their kings—and not gently, either—for being disloyal to a friend. Gautrek and Hring fell out when slanderers convinced each king the other was preparing to attack. "That's foolish talk," said Hring's queen. "You've long been the best of friends. Will you now listen to evil tongues and break up your friendship?" She suggested Hring sail to Gautrek's kingdom of Gautland (in what is now southern Sweden) in a single ship and patch up their friendship by offering to foster Gautrek's young son Hrolf. Hring followed her advice; but when his ship was spotted, Gautrek began spouting off about an attack. Queen Ingibjorg let him talk. "There's little wisdom in that diatribe," she said when he had finished. "Look at it this way, would King Hring come here with so few followers if he no longer trusted you?" They should welcome him with a feast, but keep a close eye on him to see if he seemed guilty of anything. Gautrek followed her advice, and the kings' friendship was saved.

Ingigerd, the third virtuous queen in the tale, not only demonstrates good logic and political skill; she could see the future in her dreams. When her husband, King Eirik of Uppsala, failed to listen, she predicted dire consequences—then told him how to repair the damage. "Well, that's turned out badly," said the queen, when she learned Eirik had insulted the saga's hero, Hrolf, then a young king seeking their daughter's hand in marriage. It would be "hard going to contend against him in any contest," she said of Hrolf, "since he has the backing of the Danish king, his foster father, King Hring, with whom he discusses everything." King Eirik had apparently not known of Hrolf's powerful connections. He answered, "It may be that I have made a mistake. What can I now say or do to placate him?" The queen said, "Here's my advice . . ."

Ingibjorg of Ireland, the final example, is perceptive enough to see through a spy's disguise. She shows compassion and kindness, rewards courage and honorable behavior, and is loyal to her father, despite his evil deeds, negotiating a peace that preserves his life.

The central queen of the saga, Thornbjorg of Sweden, shows all these good qualities (except for the prophetic dreaming), while adding to them skill in the martial arts. Says one character, "As far as her womanly accomplishments go, you could not find yourself a finer match anywhere in the North, while in some things, like jousting and fencing with shield and sword, she equals the hardiest knights. In that way she surpasses all other women I've heard of." The mention of knights, jousting, and fencing shows that *Hrolf's Saga* was written down after 1226, when French romances of chivalry became popular in the North; in those earlier versions preserved in the memories of learned people, Thornbjorg's skills in horseback riding and sword fighting were described in different terms.

A flavor of French romance (or Christian teaching) appears again, when her father finds her warrior training unwomanly and orders her to spend her days in the women's *skemma* like other kings' daughters. *Skemma* is one of those Old Norse words I can't adequately translate. A *skemma* was a small building, easily heated yet lavishly appointed, in which women gathered to work on fine weaving and embroidery; it may also have been used to store clothing and jewels. Some translators call it a "boudoir," but that word has unnecessary sexual overtones.

Thornbjorg did not scorn the work of the *skemma*; the saga says, "She was as accomplished at women's work as any girl anyone knew of." But she had also learned to handle weapons as well as any knight. She said to her father, "Given that you have no more than one lifetime to rule this kingdom and, as your only child, I will inherit everything after your death, it's likely I will have to protect the realm from other kings and their sons, once I have lost you."

Her father was so impressed with this argument that he gave Thornbjorg a third of Sweden to govern, letting her practice ruling while he was yet alive to advise her. He chose as her headquarters a fortified town near Uppsala—it could even be Birka—and provided her with "strong, hardy men who were willing to obey her and follow her orders." Not content with being appointed to rule, Thornbjorg held an assembly at which she presented her credentials and asked the local landowners to vote. After she was elected king (not queen), she assumed the masculine form of her name and insisted on the proper courtesy. At this point, as in the *Saga of Hervor*, the saga author begins referring to her as "he."

When a visitor to the town rudely pointed out the king was a woman and proposed marriage, Thornbjorg pretended not to understand. She said, "It seems to me that these 'delightful pleasures' that you crave from us are food and drink, and those we will deny to no needy person who asks them of us. You may direct your requests to the one who handles that task for us." When he persisted in addressing her, not her steward, she grabbed her weapons and chased him out of the hall.

Having learned that her impudent suitor was the famous Hrolf, king of Gautland, however, she prepared for his return. "Call for the smiths," she said, "and have them build walls around our whole town, with strong and sturdy defenses, and ready them with such devices that no one can break through, neither with fire nor iron." Afterward, the town was "so well protected that most people thought it unconquerable, so long as valiant warriors defended its walls."

After a hard-fought battle, however, Hrolf did manage to take the town and to capture Thornbjorg—though not in a fair fight. Hrolf's brother, Ketil, warned not to injure her, slapped Thornbjorg on the buttocks with the flat of his sword. She retaliated in the same fashion, turning her axe to hit him with the blunt end under his ear. Scholars often comment on the shameful sexual overtones of that slap on the ass but fail to react to the equally shameful way Thornbjorg treated Ketil: "He was flung head over heels. 'We beat our dogs like this when we're tired of their barking,' she said." Nor is it commonly noticed that, while Thornbjorg was proving herself an equal fighter to Ketil, matching her axe to his sword, Hrolf dishonorably snuck up behind her and wrestled her to the ground. To his credit, though (and her surprise), he did not press his advantage. If she agreed to a truce, he said, he would allow her father to decide if she must marry him.

Thornbjorg was impressed. "You must be a wise and patient man," she said. She accepted his offer and, her honor intact, rode to Uppsala, where she again symbolically changed sex. "He went before his father, King Eirik, lay his shield by his feet, took his helmet off his head, bowed to the king, and said: 'My dear father, I have been overcome by strong fighters and exiled from the kingdom that you gave into my hands, and for this reason I ask that you make those plans for my marriage that are most to your liking."

She married Hrolf, devoted herself to embroidery, had two sons, and—according to some scholars—her "submission to her husband is complete." But a parallel episode in the saga shows her "submission" to Hrolf to be no more conclusive or demeaning than that of a male warrior. While raiding in the British Isles, Hrolf attacked the fleet of a Scottish Viking named Asmund. The battle was going against Asmund's forces and he himself was badly wounded, but he continued to fight. Impressed by his bravery, Hrolf offered to call a truce if Asmund would swear friendship and become his blood brother. Asmund agreed, "if you lay no burden of shame on me or my followers." His honor safeguarded, Asmund sent most of his men home and, with one ship, joined Hrolf's fleet. Like Thornbjorg, he gave up his independence and accepted Hrolf's leadership, but the saga is clear that he was treated as an equal and that his friendship, like hers, was prized.

It was for Asmund's sake, in fact, that Hrolf returned to the British Isles, where he was defeated, captured, and imprisoned by an Irish king, the father of the woman Asmund wished to marry. When a year had passed with no news, Thornbjorg sent out a spy. Then she gathered an army of Swedes. She called upon Hrolf's brother, the king of Gautland, and another blood brother, the king of Denmark, and joined her forces to theirs, but "the queen had the rule and command" of their combined fleet of sixty ships.

When they reached the Irish kingdom and saw Hrolf's ships deserted by the shore, the army angrily rushed upon the town. Hrolf's brother, Ketil, said they should set fire to it. Thornbjorg argued—logically—that they might by accident burn down the house in which Hrolf was being held prisoner, but Ketil got his way, with near disastrous results. Hrolf was, in fact, hiding in the town, having been smuggled out of prison by the compassionate princess Ingibjorg. He and his men "took a log and rammed the door of the *skemma*, burst it in pieces, and rushed out. King Hrolf quickly recognized Gauts and Swedes among his attackers. Before him stood a most warlike man, fully armed. The man took off his helmet and stepped back—and King Hrolf realized it was Queen Thornbjorg." Together they put out the fires and captured the Irish king, accepting his daughter Ingibjorg and "much wealth in gold and silver and all kinds of treasure" as the price of his freedom.

And so the "bridal quests" end with another lesson on the importance of listening to the queen.

Hervor may have heard the saga of Thornbjorg told in Queen Gunnhild's *skemma*, where she—like the saga heroine—at a young age learned the arts of weaving and embroidery. This saga of wise queens had a moral Gunnhild liked. It is the kind of tale—entertaining and instructive—that she would have favored.

Eirik Bloodaxe, apparently, never learned the lesson. Again and again, in *Egil's Saga*, he ignores his queen's good advice, with the result that he loses the throne and is exiled from Norway.

Over her objections, he accepts blood money for the killing of their friend Bard.

Over her objections, he rescinds Egil's exile, allowing him to spend the winter in Norway with Arinbjorn. "It would be different, of course, if anyone else had taken Egil in," Eirik said.

Queen Gunnhild was not happy. "It seems to me, Eirik," she said, "that it's happening again just as before, and you're being taken in by fine talk. You're not thinking of what he's done."

The queen took matters into her own hands: She ordered two of her men to assassinate Egil. When they couldn't find him, they settled for one of his friends. The next summer Egil retaliated, and when he next landed in Norway, Arinbjorn counseled him not to stay: The queen "hates you bitterly," he said. Egil, suitably frightened, slipped off to Iceland with his Norwegian bride.

The court scene I've retold at the beginning of this chapter (adding a role for Hervor) takes place a few years later, after Egil's father-in-law died. When Egil and his wife returned to Norway to claim her inheritance, Arinbjorn deemed their case "pretty hopeless." Another relative, Berg-Onund, had claimed the land, and he had the queen on his side. "Gunnhild is your worst enemy, as you well know. She's certainly not going to order Berg-Onund to do right by you."

When that prediction came true, and Gunnhild's men broke up the court, Egil challenged Berg-Onund to a duel, calling him a coward. King Eirik, his blood up, said he'd fight Egil himself, but Egil—rational, for once—declined to face the king in combat. Instead, he cursed anyone, high or low, who took over the property at issue, calling down upon them the wrath of Odin.

Arinbjorn gave Egil a fast ship and told him to leave. King Eirik chased after him, but by switching ships several times—once rowing a dinghy over a sandbar—Egil eluded him.

Eirik could waste no more time hunting Egil, for his kingship was at stake: His youngest brother, Hakon the Good, had arrived from England. Eirik sailed south to face him, gathering an army along the way, and Arinbjorn chose to sail with him.

Meanwhile, Egil loaded his merchant ship and ostentatiously sailed out past the barrier islands. Then, hiding the ship in a snug harbor, he took a small skiff and snuck south as well.

Berg-Onund, for fear of Egil, did not sail with King Eirik. But, hearing his enemy had headed off toward Iceland, he relaxed his guard and invited some friends to a feast. Everyone was quite drunk when Egil arrived. He tricked Berg-Onund into stepping outside and killed him. He looted the farm and carried off everything he could. This time Egil did intend to sail to Iceland.

But coming down the fjord, he recognized a pretty little ship, gaily painted, with six oars on a side. It belonged to Eirik and Gunnhild's ten-year-old son, a "promising lad" who was being fostered in the area. Egil did not hesitate. He steered straight at it, ramming the prince's boat so hard it heeled over and filled up with water. Egil grabbed his spear. "Let no one escape alive," he cried. "Which was easy," the saga continues, "since no one put up a fight." In a pair of verses Egil boasted:

> Grim Gunnhild's to blame
> for my banishment—
> I was never slow
> to avenge a slight . . .
> my blade I smeared
> with her little boy's blood.

Then Egil went onto land and, to make his revenge complete, set up a magical curse-pole: He carried a hazel branch and led a horse up to a high cliff. He carved runes onto the wood, slaughtered the horse, cut off its head, and stuck the head on the pole. He jammed the pole into a cleft in the rocks and pointed the horse's nose toward the mainland. "I aim this curse at the land spirits who inhabit this country," he said, "so that they will all lose their way, coming or going, and find no rest until they have driven King Eirik and Queen Gunnhild away."

Who can say if Egil's curse worked, and turned the *dísir* against Gunnhild?

But when Hakon the Good arrived in Norway, people said he was the young Harald Fairhair come again, so different from the sulky and irresolute Eirik Bloodaxe. Strong, handsome, and eloquent, though only fifteen, Hakon the Good was also politically canny. He had been raised in England as the foster son of King Athelstan and knew how Christian bureaucrats ran a kingdom. He offered to revise Harald Fairhair's most hated law: that all ancestral estates belonged to the king, and that all farmers had to pay a land tax. Hakon "offered to give the farmers back the estates

King Harald had taken from them." At this, "a great roar swelled from the crowd and the farmers shouted and called for him to be their king." It was a marvelous political move. Hakon had said nothing about the taxes; he just returned the titles.

It was enough. The news "flew like fire through dry grass" and Eirik Bloodaxe found his support shrinking away. Around Viken, in Vestfold and the other kingdoms he had just conquered, his warriors stood ready to fight. But farther north, in the lands Eirik had long ruled under his father, the chieftains abandoned him. "When he saw no way of matching Hakon's forces," says *Heimskringla*, "he sailed west over the sea with whoever was willing to follow him."

Did Gunnhild cast lots to tell their future? Did she petition the *dísir* to learn what to do? No one knows. I can't even say when she and Eirik abandoned Norway, or where they went. Some sources place them in the Orkney islands north of Scotland, but for how long, even Snorri Sturluson doesn't say. Snorri "evidently had little interest in absolute chronology," write his translators. "It would be hard to fault him for inconsistency in his treatment of time within the framework of the narrative, but it has proved difficult to reconcile the timing of these narrative-events with historical dating."

An understatement. Based on *Egil's Saga*, Eirik is fighting to be king of Norway until 947. Based on *Heimskringla*, Eirik abandoned Norway around 935. Snorri wrote both texts in the mid-thirteenth century. He does not number the years in either one.

For their historical dates, scholars turn to the *Anglo-Saxon Chronicle*, written by Christian clerics who numbered years relative to the birth of Christ—as Anno Domini, or "the Year of Our Lord"; this dating system, still used today, came into fashion in Christian countries just before AD 800, replacing an older system that related dates to the creation of the world according to the Bible. Neither system, of course, made any sense in the pagan North. There, the passing of time was expressed through genealogies—lists of names, not numbers. In a manuscript of the *Anglo-Saxon Chronicle* copied in the mid-eleventh century, an Eirik (possibly not Bloodaxe) is acknowledged king of York, in northern England, from 946 to 948 and again from 952 to when he is killed, still a vigorous and dangerous man, in 954.

This chronological uncertainty means that, even if I assume Hervor became Queen Gunnhild's foster daughter, I can't say where she spent her formative years. Science doesn't help me either; the chemistry of the teeth recovered from grave Bj581 tells me only that she moved at least once as a child and arrived in Birka, Sweden, after she turned sixteen. To continue with her story, then, I will pick an arbitrary date—942—for twelve-year-old Hervor to arrive on Orkney, where she will mature from a bold child into a warrior woman, alongside Gunnhild's remaining seven sons and her only daughter, Ragnhild.

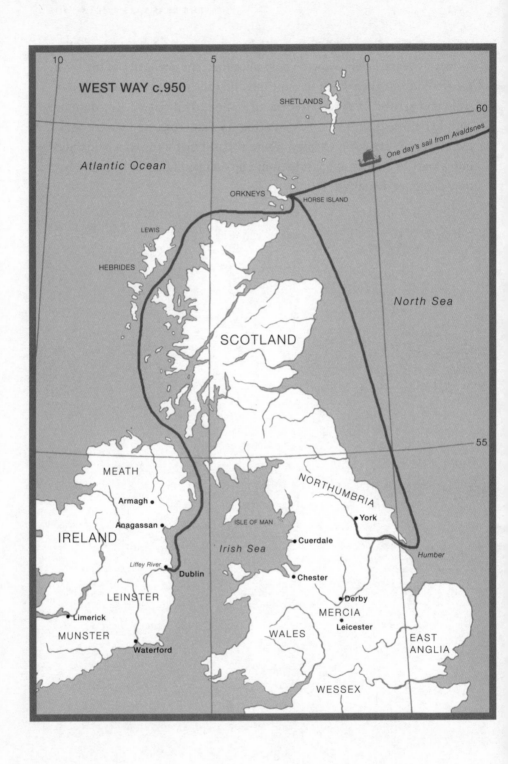

WEST WAY c.950

Atlantic Ocean

SHETLANDS

One day's sail from Avaldsnes

60

ORKNEYS

HORSE ISLAND

North Sea

LEWIS

HEBRIDES

SCOTLAND

55

MEATH

NORTHUMBRIA

Armagh

Anagassan

ISLE OF MAN

York

IRELAND

Liffey River

Dublin

Irish Sea

Cuerdale

Humber

LEINSTER

Chester

Limerick

MUNSTER

Waterford

WALES

Derby

MERCIA

Leicester

EAST
ANGLIA

WESSEX

9

THE QUEEN OF ORKNEY

They meet on Stone Ness, the headland named for its rings of stand-ing stones. The wind whips their garments and shreds their words so that, from where she stands, Hervor can hardly follow what is being said. Bored, she lets her eyes roam over the strangely stirring landscape.

There were standing stones in Vestfold, she remembers, but Vestfold is wooded. She recalls the day she discovered the stones, walking through the thick forest on a well-beaten path, stooping to pick the spindly fronds of club moss she was sent out to gather: The weavers used it when dyeing cloth to brighten the yellows and reds.

Above her, the intertwining twigs and leaves had woven a green screen against the sky. In the shadowy dimness, white-barked birches flashed. Pine boughs whispered, layering the air with their pungent scent. Acorns rattled underfoot. Birds sang, and unseen creatures rustled in the under-brush. She wandered over and down a hill. Suddenly she stepped into a sunny glade and stopped, awed by the aura of sacredness achieved by the rings of standing stones. They were ancient but seemed alive. To enter their sanctuary was to enter a mystery. She circled around them, parsing their patterns. Two stones were twice her height; they were stem and stern of the outline of a boat. Smaller stones were set in perfect circles. She was not afraid, only puzzled. What did they commemorate? What heroes were buried here? No one could tell her.

Orkney, where she is now to live, is not wooded. Orkney, named for its seals, lies bare to the vastness of the sky, a brave clutch of green islands laughing in the midst of the endless sea.

Clouds darken the rumpled bulk of the High Island, over there across the water, then suddenly dapple the acres of barley, oats, and flax here on Horse Island. The wind rushes through, setting the seed heads dancing. The wind booms in her ears, makes her eyes tear. It buffets the gulls, which battle it, diving and screeching. It whips up spray from the tops of the waves, salting the stone walls of the houses, salting her lips no matter how far she is from the shore. Sometimes, people say, the wind pulls the fish from the sea. The cows and sheep huddle against low walls. The dogs dig themselves hollows in the sand. The horses turn their tails to the wind.

Only the stones do not notice it, the two great rings of standing stones jutting from the purple heather, one on either side of the stream. Some tall stones are twice as tall as the tallest person she knows. Lichen-spotted slabs with sharp-angled tops, they are ancient and unknowable and sacred, still. One stone standing alone has a single eye—they call it Odin's Stone, though to Hervor the hole near its base looks more like a mouth than an eye, the mass of rock swelling above it like a blind skull. To clasp hands through the hole calls the god Odin as a witness to any bargain.

The Orkney islanders have no need of hazel rods or horsehair ropes to mark out their law courts, as in Norway. They hold their assemblies within these rings of stones, set so long ago between the sheltered sea cove and the freshwater loch. So it is here that her foster father, Eirik Bloodaxe, has chosen to address the people he has come to rule. He brought many ships and warriors from Norway, he tells the islanders—as if they cannot see that for themselves. But he also brought those warriors' families, as well as his own, he reminds them. He means not to rob these islands, but to enrich them. Allied with the warriors of Orkney and of all the islands in the Western Sea, down through the Hebrides to Man, Eirik means to be the greatest sea-king of the west. Not a speck of trade will travel from Dublin or York without his say-so—and without paying toll to Orkney.

So much Hervor understood before the wind picked up. Before her mind wandered.

Now Eirik Bloodaxe and the Orkney chieftain are clasping hands through Odin's Stone, and Hervor realizes she's missed something important. It's only when she sees the shocked look on her friend Ragnhild's face that she knows what bargain King Eirik has made.

Well before Eirik's father, Harald Fairhair, unified Norway in the late 800s and forced those chieftains who disagreed with his ambitions to emigrate, the islands off Scotland had known a strong Norse presence. A day's sail west from the Norwegian coast, and within easy striking distance of England and Ireland, Orkney, especially, was prized for its snug harbors and bountiful barley harvests (and thus plentiful beer).

The Vikings never conquered Orkney; they insinuated themselves into its society. In the 700s and early 800s, the islanders were Picts. Known since the Roman Empire as pirates, the Picts were famed for their seamanship and their tattoos—"Pict" means "painted." Remarkably, the Picts of the Viking Age were Roman Christians, following the hierarchical structure of the Holy Roman Empire rather than the looser, community-based Celtic Christian Church of the Scots and Irish to their south.

The ruler of Pictish Orkney was its bishop, supported by the Pictish king across the strait in northern Scotland. On each of Orkney's major islands, Christian chapels—not feast halls—crowned the mounds beside ruins of Stone Age round towers, or brochs. The church administered the king's law and collected the king's taxes. It owned a third of the islands' farmland, granting estates to war leaders in the king's name. By the mid-800s, most of those war leaders were Norse. Then, in 843, the Scots king conclusively defeated the mainland Picts. The Pictish church was "freed" from Rome, and Orkney's bishop was abandoned. The Norse stepped into the breach: Orkney became a Viking stronghold. When its sea-king threatened King Harald Fairhair, he invaded, the sagas say, and gave the islands to his friend Rognvald as a battle prize.

The first Norse earl of Orkney was Rognvald's brother, Sigurd the Powerful. He is remembered for his hapless death. Sigurd and his ally Thorstein the Red, whose father was the Viking king of Dublin, invaded northern Scotland and conquered it. Sigurd didn't celebrate for long. He had chopped off his enemy's head and hung it by his saddlebow as a trophy.

On the long ride north, the dead man's bucktooth scratched Sigurd's bare leg. The wound festered and finally killed him.

Thorstein the Red died soon after, ambushed by the Scots. He is remembered for his remarkable mother. As the Icelandic *Book of Settlements* says, Aud the Deep-Minded, long divorced from the Dublin king, was in Scotland when she learned of her only son's death. She had a ship built in the woods, secretly, and when all was ready she sailed to Orkney, where she married off one of her granddaughters. She married off another granddaughter in the Faroe Islands, then sailed to Iceland. There, she established herself as a chieftain, claiming an entire fjord and granting farms to twenty men who had followed her from Scotland.

Twenty or thirty years later, the gruesomely named Thorfinn Skull-Splitter met the equally gruesomely named Eirik Bloodaxe when he and his people descended on Orkney. I can imagine the two men instantly liked each other. They were a lot alike.

Thorfinn Skull-Splitter was a son of Turf-Einar, Rognvald's son, who took over Orkney after his uncle Sigurd's death by tooth. Thorfinn and his brothers were tall and ugly, like their father (who was also one-eyed), but as Orkney earls they were wealthy and well fed. Keen to make their names, they were eager to ally with Eirik Bloodaxe. Olaf Cuaran, the upstart half Irishman who was calling himself king of both Dublin and York, was no friend of theirs. They wouldn't mind seeing him ousted. An agreement was reached. Thorfinn's two brothers would go raiding with Eirik, while Gunnhild and her people stayed with Thorfinn on Orkney. Perhaps Eirik Bloodaxe met Thorfinn Skull-Splitter at the great standing stone, destroyed in 1814, once known as Odin's Stone. They reached into the gap and clasped hands to seal their bargain. The key? Eirik's only daughter was to marry Thorfinn's eldest son.

Ragnhild had no say in the matter. That wasn't unusual. The boy was not consulted either. First marriages among the Vikings were arranged, for boys as well as for girls. Even in Christian times, as the sagas show, it was normal. In a scene set after the conversion, the hero of *Njal's Saga* took his foster son aside. "I would like to arrange a match for you," he said, "and find you a good wife."

"See to it, foster father," the boy replied. "I will agree to whatever match you make."

A marriage was an alliance. Its purpose was to produce children who would, physically, unite two kin groups. A marriage was a matter of politics, of economics, of avoiding the social chaos that ensued when husband and wife were not an equal match in wealth and status, when their families were not allies. It had nothing to do with love. If equality turned out not to be enough for the married couple, if love or at least respect did not follow—and, especially, if no children were produced—the couple could divorce. Love outside of marriage was also not out of the question, for either husband or wife, if the sagas can be trusted. Even for Christians, marriage throughout Europe was not a sacrament until the eleventh century; not until 1200 was divorce forbidden. In tenth-century Orkney, the idea of marriage as a life-long vow of sexual fidelity would have seemed absurd.

Ragnhild knew she must marry. She was Eirik and Gunnhild's only daughter. Descendant of kings, she was a valuable peace weaver. In the gift economy of the Viking Age, she was the ultimate prize her family could bestow on a friend. She might have been content with her betrothed, as Gunnhild was when she first met Eirik Bloodaxe. But, like her mother, Ragnhild grew disappointed with her spouse over time. Unlike her mother, Ragnhild acted. Queen of Orkney, after a dozen years of marriage she still had no children. She plotted her husband's death and married his brother. Havard the Fertile, they called him, but he gave Ragnhild no children either. She cast her eye on the men around her, played one nephew (greedy, gullible) against another (same), and when Havard was murdered by one and avenged by the other, Ragnhild called for the third son of Thorfinn Skull-Splitter and married him instead. He "became a mighty chieftain," says the *Saga of the Orkney Islanders*, yet Ragnhild remained childless. When he died fighting the Scots, he was succeeded by a married brother, and that brother by his half-Irish son. The Orkney line of Gunnhild Mother-of-Kings came to an end.

But Ragnhild's second marriage, and her third, were still years in the future. Now, in the early 940s, she was a young girl endeavoring to stand straight and look queenly while the Orkney wind grabbed the tails of all her garments and tried to rip them away, or whipped them against her legs and breast and face with the loud slap and crack of a banner in a gale.

The textile arts are often called "women's work." I think of them as "mothers' work." It may be true that the first spinsters and weavers and seamstresses were women, as myths portray them. Ancient societies were practical. Only women could breastfeed, and they did so for two or more years per child, both to improve the child's chance of survival and to space out births, as a breastfeeding woman is less fertile. For the society not to lose the mother's labor for those years, she needed a task compatible with caring for an infant. Spinning, weaving, and sewing fit the bill. They were not pastimes, either, but essential contributions to culture.

Like tattoos and body paint, clothes are symbols. They send a message. When Eirik Bloodaxe and Gunnhild Mother-of-Kings arrived on Orkney, they did not need to announce their royal status: Their clothes (and weapons) did it for them. They dressed in layers of fine, flowing cloth, an underlayer of crisp linen covered by two or more of wool. Depending on the time of year, their woolens were lined with silk or fur or quilted with goose down. Regardless of the season, they were trimmed with bright-colored ribbons and braids and strips of figured silk, their showy patterns picked out in gold and silver threads, and accessorized with bulky, ostentatious jewelry—the overall effect signaling power and success, provoking envy and desire.

Gunnhild, especially, shimmered and clattered with wealth. As a mother—and Mother-of-Kings—she wore a long-sleeved linen dress long enough to drag along the ground, showing her disdain for the time and effort put into its making. The whiter the linen, the better: Linen did not dye well, but it bleached beautifully. Gunnhild's white linen underdress had a low neck opening, low enough to free a nipple for breastfeeding when she unclasped the brooch at her throat. Otherwise the dress was tight-fitting, following her ample, motherly curves, with a wide, flowing hem to accommodate an easy walking stride and fine pleats for free arm movement.

Over this linen dress, Gunnhild wore a shorter one of the finest wool twill. It was made of the sheep's soft, short-haired undercoat, combed and spun into whisper-thin worsted thread, and woven with a dense warp of a hundred and fifty threads to the inch. Because the threads used for warp and weft were both spun clockwise (or, rather, sunwise; Vikings had no clocks), the fabric was light and stretchy, smooth and glossy, with a graceful drape. Depending on how the loom was strung, even a single-colored cloth could show a pattern of lozenges, diamonds, or rings. In Icelandic poetry, a "ring-woven shirt" meant either this luxurious fabric, the finest the Vikings made, or, metaphorically, a warrior's byrnie of linked metal rings.

The technique for making ring-woven cloth seems to have come from Western Norway, as had Gunnhild. The English and Irish spun their weft threads counter-sunwise, producing a markedly different fabric. The color of Gunnhild's dress also may have announced her origins. It was probably a rich, deep blue, a favorite color of the Vikings, archaeologists have found, just as the English preferred blood red and the Irish heather purple. The sagas, too, single out blue as special. Avengers often wear blue cloaks: By putting on their best clothes, the warriors show their pride in the deed, as well as preparing to meet their own possible deaths in style.

Gunnhild's wool overdress was cut as a tube or two rectangles and fell from her armpits to mid-calf. From the tiny remnants left in burials archaeologists can only guess at the style, so popular in the early Viking Age. But they agree that the dress must have hung, apron-like, from straps fastened above her breasts by a pair of brooches; these, with recessed pins that can only accommodate slender straps, are often found on female skeletons. Gaudy and heavy, the brooches are about four inches long, each one weighing nearly a quarter pound. Oval and domed, they looked like turtle shells to the archaeologists who first unearthed them; they named them "tortoise brooches." The finest, like Gunnhild's, were cast of bronze, their surface gilded and elaborately etched, with details enhanced by silver wire. Between their brooches, women hung strings of beads—glass, amber, jet, carnelian, silver, clay, rock crystal—sparkling with coins and gold or silver charms. One brooch might also anchor a chain of useful items: a knife, a needle case, a comb case, scissors, a purse, and even a key if the woman carried one. This apron-dress, too, was designed for easy breastfeeding. One brooch could be unhooked to quickly free a nipple. Long thought to symbolize her status as a free woman, a Viking woman's oval brooches may have a more precise meaning. Only a third to a half of Viking women were buried wearing oval brooches. I suspect they mark the role of a mother: In Gunnhild's case, the fineness of her costume marked her as Mother-of-Kings.

For this reason Ragnhild, though only a girl, would also have worn an apron-dress with oval brooches over a long linen shift: Ragnhild was being advertised to the Orkney islanders as a future mother-of-kings, though childbearing was not to be her fate.

Over her apron-dress Ragnhild, like her mother, wore a shawl or a cape, a long cloak or a showy backcloth. She may also have tied a braided fabric belt around her waist. Belts with metal buckles seem not to have been worn with this costume, but some way of controlling the flapping layers of fabric in the islands' stiff wind seems logical. For the same reason, Ragnhild and her mother covered their hair with fancy headcloths, knotted at the nape or under the chin, or at least kept their hair tidy with bands around their foreheads. If the weather was cold, beneath their dresses they wore linen leggings with feet, but no crotch; that way they could squat to urinate, the tent of their dresses providing privacy. Their feet were snug in soft leather ankle boots, with long laces that wrapped up their calves.

Did Hervor wear this elaborate costume? Probably not. I assume from her later career as a warrior that she was not expected to marry and have children; Viking warfare was a task that did not mesh well with pregnancy and childbirth. In poetry, marriage is a punishment for a valkyrie; it meant expulsion from the warrior band. In the sagas, even the most warlike of the shield-maids put their raiding on hold to have children. Rather than advertise her as a girl of high status available for marriage offers, then, Gunnhild dressed Hervor as she did the rest of her household: in a manner appropriate for her role.

What that role was, I can only guess. Captured in battle at Kaupang, Hervor may have been considered a slave. If so, she wore only a loose knee-length tunic of unbleached linen or coarse wool, with a square-cut neckhole and a slit for slipping it over the head, leaving her arms, legs, and feet bare. Both men and women of slave rank were dressed this way. But the size and chemistry of the bones recovered from the Birka grave tell us Hervor was well fed all her life; given that evidence, I suspect her status was somewhat higher than a slave's. A free servant girl would have worn the same long shirt in a finer fabric. She may have worn a long-sleeved linen underdress and a cloak or shawl but would still have had bare legs and feet. Ragnhild may also have worn a short dress to work in—when she wasn't being paraded as a marriage prospect. A long dress with a wide-enough hem to walk and work in required much more cloth.

If Hervor had already distinguished herself as a warrior in training, however, she wore a very different outfit. Her shirt was made of bright white linen, with the neck and hem decorated with colored braids or ribbons, or even with strips of imported silk. She wore it belted over wool or linen trousers. Unlike the leggings women wore, these trousers were closed at the crotch and had a wide seat gore to make them comfortable when riding a horse. They could be knee-length or longer. Hervor's status was shown by the fineness and quantity of the cloth in her trousers, baggy, pleated trousers being more expensive than slim-fitting ones. In cold weather, she wore a short rectangular cloak, pinned at one shoulder with a single ring-shaped iron brooch. She wore woolen strips wrapped around her calves, sometimes over linen hose or socks, and the kind of simple shoe that gave Olaf Cuaran, the king of Dublin and York, his Irish nickname. A *cuaran* was made of a large oval of untanned leather or seal-skin pierced with holes around the rim. Stepping in the center, you used laces to gather up the leather and tie it around your ankle. Hervor's fighting outfit was completed, perhaps, with a headband to keep her hair out of her eyes.

All of this clothing, and the impression Eirik Bloodaxe and his entourage made when they arrived on Orkney, was the responsibility of Gunnhild Mother-of-Kings.

Like queens in the Frankish Empire and noblewomen in England, like the Oseberg rulers and the lady of the Shining Hall, Gunnhild oversaw a textile workshop, producing both fine and practical clothing, bedding, tapestries, and even sails, work that was all possible with youngsters underfoot. With a few exceptions—timing a dye bath, warping a loom—most textile tasks did not require steady concentration. They could be interrupted by a needy child and returned to without loss. As the mother of nine children who survived infancy—making her continuously pregnant or nursing (or both) for perhaps twenty years—Gunnhild appreciated that fact.

Some work the queen did herself: Through the arts of embellishment, through line and color, she told stories, preserved lore, and enhanced status and reputation—including her own. Some work she considered beneath her: For the weaving of sailcloth or the shaggy pile weave used for sea cloaks, she used slave labor. But all of it she needed to understand to control its quality. These secrets she kept close. Cloth making generated wealth and gave her political clout. Without a sail, Eirik Bloodaxe went nowhere. Without a sea cloak, he got soaked and shivered. Without a fine tunic or an embroidered shirt, he was just another sword. Without a tapestry picturing his deeds, who would remember them?

Like the forging of iron into a sword, creating a deadly weapon out of fire and earth, cloth making magically transformed stalks, roots, leaves, and animal hair into wealth and standing. Gunnhild might not have been able to teach her daughter and Hervor to make a shirt like the Irish girl did in the saga: To ransom herself from Arrow-Odd, she sewed out of silk and gold threads a magic shirt that ensured he was never cold, never hungry, never tired when swimming, never burned by fire, and never wounded by an iron weapon unless he was running away. (It is this magic shirt that kept Arrow-Odd alive when he and his friends met Angantyr and his eleven brothers on the isle of Samsey in the *Saga of Hervor*; of the great battle, Arrow-Odd was the only survivor.)

But Gunnhild could teach the girls another magic trick: to turn stinging nettles into a shirt softer than linen, as Viking women often did. If you were careful to always run your hand up the stalk as you plucked the plant, the spines would lie flat and not hurt you. Then, like flax harvested from the field, the stalks were kept damp, spread out in the rain or dew or soaked in shallow pools, until they began to rot and the woody stem separated from the tough inner fibers. Dried and pounded with wooden beetles, then crushed between a board and a wooden blade, the fibers came free, ready for heckling, or drawing through finer and finer combs to straighten and separate them for spinning, which was itself a bit magical. As with linen, nettle thread made from young plants was soft and pliable (nice for shirts); that from old plants was sturdy and stiffer (good for socks).

Gunnhild could teach the girls to sort the wool of sheep, reserving the longer strands for strong warp threads and the fuzzy short hairs for the softer weft. She could teach them how long to card or comb the wool, brushing it between a pair of handheld rakes to fluff or align the fibers. She could teach them to heat the metal teeth of these rakes by the fire, to melt and distribute the lanolin, the natural wool fat, through the yarn. And she could teach them to amaze the youngsters—Ragnhild's little brothers, the children of her workers—by slowly pulling and twisting the dangling end of a hank of well-brushed wool to make it magically lengthen from a four-inch hair to a yard-long thread.

To lengthen and strengthen that thread further, Gunnhild taught them to spin. She taught her sons to spin as well: Spinning was an endless chore. The youngest boys—the nursling, the weanling, and possibly the five-year-old—were always with her in the weaving room, playing with a spindle like a top until they learned to use it properly. In the long winter nights, a boy or man without any other work to hand might have been set to spinning. It took a practiced spinster seven to ten hours to spin the thread a good weaver would use up in one hour. To make one set of clothes of coarse, practical cloth for a worker took at least thirteen *miles* (about 69,000 feet) of hand-spun thread.

The trick to spinning was to add a constant trickle of straight fibers (wool, flax, or nettle) as you pulled and twisted the thread. The task seemed to require four hands: one to hold the raw fibers, one to add them at a steady pace (too much and you'll get an ugly clot, too little and the thread will break), one to pull and twist (the critical step), and one to keep the finished thread from snarling. Having only two hands, ancient women invented tools: a distaff (literally, a "fuzz-stick") to hold the raw fibers; and a spindle to provide tension, twist, and a spool to hold the spun thread. The distaff, notched and carved to give the bound fibers purchase, could be tucked under one arm. The spindle, a slenderer stick, was weighted with a disc-shaped whorl of stone, clay, bone, amber, ivory, lead—the material didn't matter; the weight did. The lightest whorls made the finest thread; heavier whorls, depending on the spinster's skill, made either coarse or fine thread. The whorl could be wedged on the top or bottom of the spindle stick. A top-loaded spindle you roll off your hip (or thigh, if seated) and let spin to the floor. A bottom-loaded or drop spindle, you start twirling with a finger flick. Before either type strikes the floor give the thread a sharp tug and like a yo-yo the spindle will leap back to your hand. Coil the new thread around the spindle shaft, and start again. For a right-handed spinster, drop spinning gives a sunwise, or Z-spun, twist, while hip spinning gives a counter-sunwise, or S-spun, thread. It was important to keep track. If you start drop spinning and switch to hip spinning, your thread will untwist. Using one twist in the warp and the other in the weft made a cloth that was easily fulled—shrunk and made waterproof, good for a cloak or a sail. Using the same twist (usually Z) in both warp and weft was the way to add pattern and texture to plain-colored cloth.

But plain-colored cloth, even the finest ring-woven cloth, was not Gunnhild's ultimate goal. The height of the weaver's art was tapestry. Hung on the walls, tapestries did more than just liven up the living space or block out drafts. They were signs, symbols, messages meant to be read. They spoke of wealth and status, skill and fine taste, and the leisure to produce luxuries. More, they were "memory pegs": ways of passing down knowledge by fixing a tale in visual form.

In an oral culture like that of the Vikings, stories needed to be repeated to be remembered. Poets fixed them in verse, but even poets needed a nudge. In a scene from the *Saga of the Orkney Islanders* about a celebration well after Gunnhild's day, the women were hanging the tapestries in the feast hall when the earl turned to a visiting poet and said, "Make a verse about the man pictured there on the hanging." Was that man Eirik Bloodaxe? Or Sigurd the Dragon-Slayer? Before the Old Norse word *bók* meant "book," it meant "tapestry." Before the verb *skrífa* meant "to write with quill and ink," it meant "to weave." In another saga, a woman wove a tapestry "and wrote on it many and great deeds." She wrote, not with words, but with pictures. Tapestries were story cloths, carriers of tradition, time binders, tying the past to the present. Tapestries preserved—and shaped—history. The women who wove them were historians.

10

THE TRAGEDY OF
BRYNHILD

Ragnhild bends beneath a fish-oil lamp, squinting her eyes to count the fine threads of the tapestry loom. She has a deft hand and under her mother's praise has warmed to the task.

Hervor hates such fussy work, but today a new *skáld* is with them, telling a story while plucking a horsetail harp—the same story pictured in the tapestry they're weaving. It is Hervor's favorite story: the tragedy of Brynhild.

> *High on Hindarfell stood a hall,*
> *wrapped around in flame.*
> *Witches lit those fires*
> *of blazing river-light.*
> *There on the mountain*
> *slept a battle-wise warrior.*

The warrior, Hervor knows, was Brynhild. She was a shield-maid, a valkyrie. She fought in wars, killed kings. But now she was being forced to give up her weapons and marry.

The poet says it was Odin's punishment: Brynhild killed a king to whom the war god himself had promised victory.

Hervor thinks that's nonsense. She suspects Brynhild was badly wounded and could no longer fight well enough. Or she was a princess like Ragnhild, and her family needed her to marry to make an alliance.

Brynhild, however, resisted. She had no desire to be married or to become a mother. She cried:

> I am a shield-maid.
> I wear a helmet
> among the warrior kings,
> and I wish to remain
> in their warband.
> I was in battle
> with the King of Gardariki
> and our weapons were red
> with blood.
> This is what I desire.
> I want to fight.

Her kin would not hear of it. They said she must marry. They said it was Odin's will.

Where is Gardariki? Hervor interrupts.

On the East Way, answers Queen Gunnhild. As far from Orkney as you can imagine.

Remember that name: *Gardariki*, Hervor tells herself, the Kingdom of Fortresses. Someday she will go there.

Brynhild swore an oath, the *skáld* continues, his ringing voice demanding silence.

Brynhild swore to marry only a man who knew no fear. She called for the fiery wall to be kindled around her hall on high Hindarfell. Only a man without fear could make his horse jump the wall of flame—only that man would she marry. This oath she swore by a ship's strakes and the circle of a shield, by a mare's back and a blade's edge.

> If I break my oath,
> may I be cursed
> and slain
> by my own weapons.
> May my sword not bite
> unless it whistles
> above my own head.

Brynhild sealed her oath with a toast. But it was not to be.

Gunnar, it was, who wanted to marry Brynhild. He and his companions rode to her father's hall. Her father was agreeable, provided Brynhild did not refuse. She is so proud, he said, she will only marry a man of her own choosing.

They rode on to her foster father's hall, and he directed them to Brynhild's own hall on the mountaintop. The only man she will marry, he warned, is the one who rides through the wall of flames.

Gunnar could not make his horse leap the blazing fire. He took his brother-in-law Sigurd's stallion, but horses feel their rider's fear, and Gunnar's infected his mount: The stallion would not leap. Not until Sigurd took on Gunnar's likeness, by magic, and rode the stallion himself would the greathearted horse leap the fiery wall.

The fire flared up,
the earth quaked.
Flames leaped high
into the sky.
He rode as if
into oblivion.
The fire sank down.

Sigurd dismounted and went into the hall, the *skáld* continues. He had Gunnar's appearance and bearing, but his own eloquence and intellect. Brynhild sat on her throne with her sword in her hand, her helmet on her head, wearing a ringmail byrnie. Sigurd called himself Gunnar and asked for her hand. She refused him, until he charged her to remember her oath: She swore to marry the man who rode through the fire.

Her own oath had trapped her. It was binding and irrevocable.

Swear no oaths
you won't hold to.
Breaking faith
brings a terrible fate:
To be forever outcast,
cut off like a wolf.

She took the man who called himself Gunnar to her bed. And though he set between them a ring-hilted sword of sharp-edged iron, a wound-wand braided round with gold, its edges forged in fire and patterned inside with poison drops; though he did not kiss her nor take her into his arms, but lay with her like a sister—still in Brynhild's eyes it was her wedding night. She had married the man who had no fear. Her oath was fulfilled.

Her father held a wedding feast, where she clasped Gunnar's hand (the real Gunnar this time) and shared his wine. She followed him back to his home, where she lived happily, weaving a tapestry with golden threads, until his sister, Gudrun, revealed that it was not, in fact, Gunnar who rode through the wall of flame. It was Gudrun's own husband, Sigurd, who did so in disguise. It was Sigurd who had no fear.

Brynhild had been tricked. Her oath had been broken. Her husband had not braved the wall of flame but had sent another man in his stead. Brynhild was married to a fearful man after all, a man who'd gone white as a corpse when he'd faced her magic fire.

She struck her tapestry so hard it tore apart. She kicked open her chamber door so everyone could hear her anger. Her shouts echoed throughout the fortress. She took to her bed and would neither eat nor drink. Even Sigurd could not console her. She raged at him:

> *How dare you come see me!*
> *No one has behaved worse*
> *toward me in this trickery!*
> *What hurts most is I cannot*
> *find a way to redden*
> *a sharp blade with your blood.*

She was an oath breaker, an outcast, a wolf, cursed to be killed by her own sword. Gunnar and his brothers, on her orders, killed Sigurd. Then Brynhild turned her sword on herself: She knew her honor could not be repaired unless she and Sigurd, her true husband, shared the same fate.

And so, says the *skáld*, the tale of Brynhild comes to its tragic end.

In the sudden silence, as he wets his lips before launching into a new song, the lines of the poem swirl in Hervor's head: *I am a shield-maid. I wear a helmet among the warrior kings . . . I was in battle with the King of Gardariki and our weapons were red with blood. This is what I desire.*

This is what I desire.

This is what I desire.

I want to fight.

The legend of Brynhild was one of the most popular stories in the North, told and retold for hundreds of years. Episodes were woven into tapestries. They were carved on memorial stones and doorposts and cast as metal badges or amulets. They were alluded to in poetry and prose and worked into myths and genealogies. The later the version, the more romantic the story becomes. Brynhild's ambition becomes passion; a crisis of honor becomes a case of jealousy. The focus shifts from her internal struggle to honor her oath to the external demands of society.

At the same time, the hero who betrayed her in the original tale becomes fused with the famous Sigurd who killed the dragon Fafnir with a magic sword and won the dragon's hoard of gold. Sigurd roasted the dragon's heart and, tasting the blood, suddenly understood the speech of birds—thus learning of the treachery of his foster father, Regin, the smith who had made the magic sword. Regin was the dragon's brother. To him, Sigurd was only a tool for fratricide. He lusted after the dragon's hoard himself and was plotting Sigurd's death.

Sigurd killed his foster father and loaded the dragon's gold on his horse. He had ridden a long way from the dragon's lair, the story goes, when he saw on a hilltop ahead of him a brilliant light. He spurred his horse. Nearing the site, he saw that the roof and stockade of a hillfort were ablaze, the fire licking the sky, the banner a tongue of flame. Crossing the ramparts he saw an armed warrior spread-eagled on the ground. He rushed to see if the warrior was dead or alive and, unlacing the helmet, saw she was a woman. She barely breathed.

Drawing his sword, Sigurd sliced through the leather ties of her ringmail byrnie and slid it off her, then half lifted, half dragged her into the fresh air. She awoke as if from a deep sleep. Rising, she found a cup and a cask of beer. They shared the drink and talked of many things: how to carve victory runes on a sword, how to protect a ship with wave runes, how to heal wounds.

"I've never met anyone as wise as you," Sigurd said. "What advice can you give me?"

"Support your kin. Be patient with their failings. Don't be a flirt or quarrel with drunks. Control your temper. But don't let anyone call you a coward. And if you're caught traveling after nightfall, don't make your camp beside the road. You never know who might come by."

Though said to be a valkyrie, Brynhild here seems to be a practical and fully human woman. She falls in love with her rescuer and swears an oath to marry him, though he soon rides off and forgets her.

Some versions of the tale also give Brynhild a family: Her brother is Attila the Hun. Leaving her fire-damaged fortress, Brynhild is portrayed sewing alongside her sister, a model noblewoman admired not only for her skill at "stitching fine clothes with gold thread," but also for her intelligence and social graces. Such women were cheerful and made the feast hall a pleasant place. They played board games with their husbands, spoke affectionately to them, but also gave them good advice.

Brynhild, in this version of her story, was "more skillful with her hands than other women." She embroidered a tapestry with gold thread, picturing there the great deeds Sigurd had done: slaying the dragon and taking the treasure, as well as killing the treacherous smith. One day when Sigurd was hunting in the woods, his hawk landed on a tower near Brynhild's window. Climbing up to catch the bird, Sigurd peeked in the window and realized she was sewing his life's story. Though he failed to recognize the warrior woman he had met earlier on the mountaintop, "both her beauty and her work seemed of great worth."

As a poet used sound, a weaver used color. Before Hervor and Ragnhild began weaving the tapestry of Brynhild's tale, Gunnhild would have taught them the art of dyeing. They learned the phrase "dyed in the wool" and when to choose it over "dyed in the yarn" or "dyed in the cloth." On fine days, Gunnhild sent them out to scrape certain lichens off stones, to gather the leaves of silver birch and bog myrtle, and to harvest the yellow-flowering weed called woad. They learned what other dyestuffs to purchase, such as weld and madder root, which grew in England but not so far north as Orkney, to turn white wool into bright-colored cloth. They learned the tricks of drying and fermenting, of using lant (stale urine) versus lye (wood ash and water) to make acid versus alkaline baths, of when to add club moss and not iron oxide, if alum was unavailable to use as a mordant to make the dye colorfast. There was magic in pulling red, pink, yellow, or orange yarn from the same muddy-brown madder-root bath (the trick was in the timing). There was magic in drawing a white skein from colorless liquid, suffused with woad, and having it dry bright blue.

It was less magical and more mathematical to use those colors to create patterns and pictures. Like a poet counting syllables, knowing where to alliterate and where to place the stress, a weaver counted threads. A master of either art could wing it, knowing by instinct when the rhythm was right. A beginner, like Ragnhild or Hervor, had to concentrate and count. Weaving a tapestry was even more intellectually taxing than weaving cloth.

It took mathematical skill to warp a loom for a length of cloth, especially for a fancy ring weave: The amount of thread had to be calculated and cut to length. Then, once it was knitted onto the top beam of the loom and weighted at the bottom, each thread had to be tied to the correct one of four heddle rods to make the pattern. The warping process could take two weeks—even if you didn't make a mistake in your counting and had to start over. But after the loom was properly warped, the work of cloth making became more physical than mental.

The standard Viking Age loom was a vertical loom; its two upright posts, taller than a woman's head, leaned against a wall. The weaver wove from top to bottom, using a wooden or ivory tool called a weaving sword—and often carved with a hilt and a blade to look like an iron sword—to beat the weft firmly upward after every few lines. When the loom was full, she rolled her new cloth around the top beam, lengthened and reweighted her warp threads, and resumed weaving. A woman weaving alone all day might walk twenty-three miles, shuttling the weft back and forth, right to left, left to right, through the warp. Two women working together, passing the weft from hand to hand, could halve that distance. Two together also made lighter work lifting the heddle rods, to change the shed between each pass of the weft.

In the absence of a *skáld*, to make the time more enjoyable two weavers working together might sing a working song. One such song is preserved in *Njal's Saga*; there it introduces the Battle of Clontarf, when the Vikings were kicked out of Dublin in 1014. It may have been written, though, for a different battle, a Viking victory near Dublin in 919, in which case Hervor might have sung it. It is a song of weavers with magical power: Ones who weave not cloth, but battle. Their weft thread is crimson—blood. Their warp is made

> *of spilled intestines,*
> *the loom-weights*
> *are severed heads;*
> *the shafts are*
> *blood-drenched spears,*
> *the rods are*
> *iron-bound arrows;*
> *with swords we weave*
> *this victory-web.*

At the song's end, the weavers identify themselves as valkyries and ride off to join the battle:

> *Learn it well*
> *and tell the others,*
> *whoever hears*
> *the valkyries' song.*
> *Let's ride out hard,*
> *with naked swords*
> *held high,*
> *away from here.*

Again, anyone who thinks Viking women were not ruthless should listen to their working songs.

The loom described in *The Valkyries' Song*, a warp-weighted loom, could weave any kind of cloth, from sailcloth to tapestries. But the Vikings also had a smaller model, an example of which was found in the Oseberg ship burial. Its two uprights, rather than leaning against a wall, were held in a frame. Along with the upper beam, it had a fixed lower beam, replacing the loom weights to give the warp tension.

On this loom, you wove from the bottom up, not from the top down, beating the weft down with your weaving sword while sitting in comfort. It was a queen's loom, a loom of luxury. But weaving a tapestry with it was still hard work—hard mental work.

It was easier to embroider a tapestry (though it required more thread). The famous Bayeux Tapestry, made in England at the very end of the Viking Age, is an embroidery; the Oseberg tapestries, from ninth-century Vestfold, use a mix of embroidery and weaving techniques. In each case, the colors had to be placed precisely, the threads laid evenly and firmly fixed.

But when embroidering, you could at least see the picture take shape under your hands. You would outline a figure—a horse, say—with a stem stitch or backstitch before coloring it in, laying the colored threads densely and couching them with cross-threads to hold them in place. When weaving a tapestry, to create the same horse you must depend on your counting more than your eye, because the scene, from your point of view, is turned on its side. What you weave vertically will hang horizontally around the top of the hall, as a long, narrow frieze, each panel about fourteen inches wide and six feet long, like the Overhogdal tapestries, made in northern Sweden and carbon-dated to as early as the ninth century.

Nor do you start with a plain piece of cloth, as you do when embroidering, on which you can sketch a cartoon in charcoal. When weaving a tapestry, the picture, the story, is not *on* the cloth, but *in* the cloth. It took practice (and patience) to learn how to weave a simple figure like a person or a horse.

The technique is called snare weaving, or soumak. Instead of one spindle carrying your weft thread, you had the spindle of your base cloth (linen) and small skeins of eight or more different colors of wool, your pattern threads, to keep track of. Count six or nine warp threads, lay in a line of color, then snare it back to loop around two or three threads before continuing. When you've woven the colors into one line, lay down a line of plain linen thread to hold everything in place.

In one of the Overhogdal tapestries, experts can see that the weaver, at first, was not in command of the technique. The cloth is lumpy. After a few inches it smooths out: "Has the weaver learned the trick," they ask, "or has another person taken over the job?"

They also see signs of two or more weavers in how people on these tapestries are depicted. "It is almost as if they were arguing about how femininity, masculinity, and androgyny should be represented." Of the three hundred–some figures in these weavings, many more are women than men. There are also many more types of women, as revealed by their costumes and actions, while the men are more stereotyped.

The opposite is true on the famous stone carvings from the isle of

Gotland, thought to be the work of men: There the men are varied and the women are stereotyped. Unless, of course, we are reading the images wrong. A long gown and long hair in a twisted ponytail may not signify "woman" throughout the Viking world. Trousers may not signify "man." Some Viking Age images in silver and bronze seem to show armed, ponytailed people in trousers, as well as armed people in long gowns. One design found in several variations shows a horse and rider meeting a standing figure: Both may be armed. Both may be women. Are they mythological valkyries? Are they real women "transgressing gender boundaries"? Or are these boundaries mostly in modern (Victorian) minds?

What story the Overhogdal tapestries tell is debated as well. One reading is the legend of Brynhild. If so, the version woven in these pictures precedes the earliest manuscript of the tale by at least two hundred years. It is quite a bit different from the versions recorded in poetry and prose, as well. It focuses not on the male hero, Sigurd the Dragon-Slayer, but on the female heroes: Brynhild and Gudrun, both of whom were warrior women.

Like Brynhild, the hero of the *Saga of Hervor* was both "a beautiful girl" and "as strong as a man." She learned to wield weapons and she learned to weave cloth. She was brought up in an earl's house, but "as soon as she was able, she practised more with spear and shield and sword than at sewing or embroidery." She joined a Viking band and became its leader. She retrieved her father's sword from his barrow, joined a king's court, killed a king's man who unsheathed her sword without permission, and resumed the Viking life. She "was out raiding awhile," the saga says, "and when she grew tired of it," she went home to the earl's house "and set herself to learning needlework"—that is, she took up mothers' work. Soon, in the saga, she has a son.

Her decision to quit the Viking life, as told, had always seemed absurd to me. It was too abrupt, too out of character. But the more sagas I studied, the more I saw that settling down was a common path for Viking warriors, male or female. They aged out of the sea raider's role or were injured too badly to continue. In one saga, for example, Onund loses his lower leg in a sea battle against King Harald Fairhair. He fights on as "Tree-Foot" but admits, "I've not been glad since we stood in the shield-storm and that

Detail from a reconstruction of the Overhogdal tapestries.

witch-cursed axe wounded me." His friend advises him to find a wife and settle down. He does so, sailing (a bit morosely) to Iceland with his bride:

> *They used to call us useful*
> *in the storm of swords,*
> *when the blizzard of spears*
> *screamed, me and Sugandi.*
> *Now, one-legged and*
> *leaning on a stick,*
> *I'm off alone to Iceland.*
> *Life's gone downhill.*

He establishes a large farm beneath a great snowy mountain, with many servants. It prospers, and several quiet years pass before Onund Tree-Foot gets involved in Icelandic politics. (He'd lost his leg, not his fighting spirit.)

In another saga, young Ulf "went off on Viking raids, harrying and plundering" with his friend Kari. "He was a berserk," the saga says of Kari, but "when he gave up the Viking life, Kari went home to his farm on Berle

Island, a very wealthy man." He settled down and raised three children. Ulf, who was reputed to be a werewolf as well as a berserk, eventually decided to retire as well. He married Kari's daughter "and went home to his farm. He was a rich man, both in land and in goods. He claimed the rights his ancestors had held before him, and became a powerful figure. It is also said that he was an excellent farmer. He rose early in the mornings and went out to work in his smithy or look over his livestock and grain fields, sometimes meeting to talk with other farmers who came to consult him. He gave good advice."

Gunnhild Mother-of-Kings expected such a future for her foster daughter, Hervor, when she insisted she learn the textile arts. She could not know the girl wouldn't live long enough to retire from the Viking life. Hervor would never settle down to weave tapestries or run a farm and give her neighbors good advice. Instead, she would be buried as a war leader in Birka before she turned forty.

But to become Birka's war leader, Hervor first had to master the martial arts. When Eirik Bloodaxe left the Viking life in 946 to become king of York—or Jorvik, as he called it—sixteen-year-old Hervor had her chance, for Gunnhild Mother-of-Kings brought her household and all Eirik's children to York as well. There, Hervor and Ragnhild and her seven brothers lived in the midst of an army camp: Tenth-century York saw kings come and go with bewildering speed, as the English strove to reconquer the city, under Viking control since the 860s, and York's assembly of wealthy citizens, or *witan*, led by their defiant archbishop, sought to preserve their independence. Hearing of Eirik's exile, Archbishop Wulfstan offered the former king of Norway York's throne. Surely a man named Bloodaxe could keep the city free. Especially when he had so many sons.

11

SHIELD-MAIDS

*T*aut bowstrings make arrows sing. Tossed spears bite, and peace takes flight . . .

Hervor marches down the steep streets of Jorvik with her foster brothers, chanting the poem at the top of their lungs.

Bloody they lay where bright spears play. King Eirik that way wins fame each day . . .

Except for its ancient stone walls (some tumbling down) and a few odd free-standing pillars (the remnants of a Roman palace), Jorvik feels like home to Hervor: It is much like Vestfold, where she lived in the Shining Hall above the market town of Kaupang.

Out one of Jorvik's gates is a dense forest, home to deer, wild boar, and wolves, alive with birdsong, the oak and hazel coppiced to produce the slender bendable branches needed to weave wattle and daub walls. Ash, yew, and maple trees are managed as well, to produce wood of a certain size: The town's coopers specialize in lathe-turned bowls and drinking cups.

Another gate leads to the river, rich with oyster beds. Up the fish-filled tributary streams lie vast sheep meadows spangled with flowers, where skylarks pipe their lyric song. For the summer, the sheep have been herded to uplands of springy heather and squelchy bog, with limestone outcrops shining pale in the sun. Up there peat is cut and lead mined, under the shadow of circling sea eagles, while down below barley, oats, wheat, and rye are sown and apple trees blossom, filled with bees.

And, like a hive of bees, the city buzzes. Its tall timber houses and smaller thatched huts are crowded with people, ten thousand people, and their carts, horses, dogs, pigs, chickens, and geese. It reeks of pig shit and tanners' urine, of butchers' offal and river mud. It is raucous with the noise of hawkers' cries, the clang of blacksmiths' hammers, the whine of the cup makers' lathes, the clacking of looms. All that, as well, brings back Hervor's childhood, and if Jorvik is a bigger town than Kaupang—ten times bigger, they say—well, Hervor is bigger too.

At sixteen, she is taller than most people, and when she dresses as a warrior, in linen shirt and trousers and padded leather byrnie, her long hair twisted back, bow and quiver on her shoulder, shield and spear in her hands, and walks, loose-limbed, swaggering, down the street to the army's training ground by the riverside, men give way before her. Only when she speaks does she see the question dawn in their eyes, and she knows she'll be fistfighting or arm wrestling by evening to prove her courage.

Unless her foster brothers are at her side, like today.

Their swords will crack on shields stained black, chants Gamli.

Hone's Saddle! Battle Sun! Two swords beat as one, chants Guthorm.

Wound Dragon! Blood Dragon! Two swords bite as one, recites Ragnfrod.

Point and edge play when he enters the fray, says Harald, and Hervor jumps in with the refrain: *King Eirik that way wins fame each day.*

No one stands up to the sons of Eirik Bloodaxe.

They are thugs, complains Ragnhild. Why do you want to train with them instead of weaving our tapestry?

Hervor's foster sister doesn't understand. Her brothers are thuggish, true. They are proud and given to throwing their weight around, like their father, touchy when it comes to honor and rank, like their mother, but they are strong and skillful fighters—just the warriors you want in your warband.

Hervor especially likes Harald. He is more cheerful and kinder than the others. Though even Harald has a temper. Once, when drunk, he lit into one of his younger brothers for an imagined insult, and it took the rest of them combined to break up the fight. But, in general, Eirik's sons stick together—and stick up for their foster sister, Hervor, for she is a shield-maid in their Viking band.

"Bare is back without brother," the saying goes.

The best way to win a battle, the brothers teach her, is to break the enemy's line. The best way to break it is to taunt or trick individual warriors into rushing, enraged, alone, away from the shields of their comrades.

The shield-wall, a tactic used for both offense and defense when fighting on land against armed foes, depends on teamwork. Locked in formation, your shield overlapping your neighbors' on both sides, when signaled to push forward you must match strides—and courage—cutting down your enemy and stepping on their bloody corpses, or the wall will break. Likewise, when signaled to stand fast, you must hold steady, strong and stalwart, in the face of terror and brutal death.

For war is not pretty. It is mental as well as physical. It calls for a certain habit of mind, a fighting spirit that makes your grin as fearsome as your axe.

"Courage bests the sharpest sword," the saying goes. "Better to be keen than cowardly when the swordplay starts. Better to be glad than gloomy whatever happens."

That's why Hervor likes Harald best. He is always glad, never gloomy. He laughs even when she bloodies his nose. *Especially* when she bloodies his nose, for it is Harald, more than anyone, who has taught her to fight.

In war, he tells her, your fighting moves must be automatic. You'll become a warrior when your sword or axe is part of your arm. When your spears or arrows fly like your thoughts. When your shield and your shoulder work as one.

Her own shield bloodied her nose several times, before she learned to hold it properly, bracing it against her shoulder and elbow, not her hip. She learned, too, what weight and breadth of shield worked best. A two-ply shield, its two layers of thin boards set at right angles, covered with linen and rimmed with leather, is lighter but just as strong as a leather-covered shield made of one thickness of heavier boards. It is round, with a cut-out central hand grip; to be most maneuverable, it is just wide enough to cover her elbow. It is painted red, like those of her foster brothers, and the domed metal boss, which protects her hand on the grip, is low and rounded, like theirs, not conical like the shield bosses the Dubliners use.

Except in a shield-wall, when her shield is braced tight on either side by the shields next to her in the battle line, hiding behind it doesn't do much good. Nor does pushing it flat at an oncoming stroke. It's those moves that let her opponent's sword smash her own shield into her nose.

Instead, she has learned to use her shield fluidly, turning it at an angle to deflect the energy of an incoming stroke. She has drilled in the shield-wall formation since she was six years old, when she practiced with toy weapons alongside her foster brothers until they all reacted to the commands as a single fighting unit. But the shield-wall leaves your head and legs unprotected. It is good for a charge; but in a looser battle line, or fighting one-on-one, the shield comes into its own as an offensive as well as defensive weapon. Angled forward, Hervor's shield can both block blows and deliver them, knocking her attackers off-balance, injuring their weapon arms, even disarming them, before she punches the iron shield boss at their faces. Good shield work controls a fight.

Keep your weight low, your knees bent, your arms tucked close to your body. Use your hips and thighs, your power center, to swivel and shift your weight and add force to your stroke. Your footwork should be light; your blows should not. Cut all the way through your target, as if every swing of your sword will slice off a leg.

Grunt or squeal or yell—whatever suits you. It increases your power and, more important, distracts your opponent. Martial arts, after all, are mostly mind games. Raw strength is no match for the skill to read your opponent, to anticipate blows and outmaneuver them. Power matters, but so do speed, timing, suppleness, accuracy, daring, and force of will.

Marching down the steep streets of Jorvik with the elder sons of Eirik Bloodaxe, chanting the poem they heard in the king's hall the night before, Hervor feels her excitement growing. Soon they will reach the training grounds. Soon she will feel the battle joy, will feel herself come totally alive facing Harald's sword. Today, he promised, they'll start sparring with sharpened blades.

King Eirik that way wins fame—and he did, though not in battle. The poem that made Eirik Bloodaxe immortal as the last Viking king of York is so trite and generic in its battle scenes (though they sound wonderful when recited in Old Norse) that it could be describing any fight anywhere in the Viking world.

Snorri Sturluson recounts the story behind its creation in *Egil's Saga*. One night while Eirik and Gunnhild were holding court, he writes, they had an unexpected visitor: Egil the Poet, whose curse may have turned the land spirits of Norway against the royal pair. Egil had been shipwrecked off the English coast near York. (He blamed Gunnhild's witchcraft for that.)

Knowing it pointless to hide, he "gathered up his courage and determined, that very same night, to find himself a horse, and ride straight to the town."

"Why not just kill Egil at once," Gunnhild said to her husband, when the big ugly Icelander presented himself. "Or don't you recall what he has done, my king? He has killed your friends and your kin. On top of that, he has killed your own son! And slandered you yourself. Has anyone heard of royalty being treated like that?"

But Eirik Bloodaxe was in a bind. His second-in-command, Arinbjorn, who had given up his lands and titles in Norway to follow Eirik into exile, was Egil's staunch friend. "Egil and I stand together in this," Arinbjorn warned. "You will have bought Egil's life dearly, before we have both fallen. I expected more of you, my king, than to be struck down dead rather than be given a single man's life when I asked for it."

Arinbjorn claimed (falsely) that Egil had come to York expressly to recite a praise poem he had composed—a poem that would make Eirik's name immortal (and wipe out Egil's earlier slander). Eirik agreed to listen to the poem the next morning; he would then decide Egil's fate.

"We don't want to hear any poems of his," Gunnhild cried. "Have Egil taken out and cut off his head. I don't want to hear his words or see his face."

But Arinbjorn's plan won out—except that Egil had not composed any such poem. He sat in Arinbjorn's loft that night, struggling to fix praise for his enemy into the combination of rhyme, rhythm, and alliteration known as "court meter." Outside his window a swallow twittered, blocking his concentration—it was Gunnhild the Witch in bird form, he believed. Arinbjorn climbed to the roof and sat outside the window to ward her off.

The next morning, Egil faced Eirik again. Remembering the moment years later, he wrote:

> The king reigned
> with rigid mind,
> over rain-swept
> shores at Jorvik.
> That moonlight
> was not mild,
> that flashed
> from Eirik's eyes.

They gleamed,
dragon-like,
terrible
to look at.

To Eirik, Egil gave a battle in words:

Loud the swords sing,
on shield-rims they ring!
War follows the king,
cruel death does he bring.
First hear they all
the arrow-storm fall.
The king's battle-call
sounds loudest of all . . .

As the poem continued, the scenes of battle shifted to scenes of gener-osity (gold, gifts: generic again). The poem may be insincere and ironic. It could be about any king, except for the occasional mention of Eirik's name in the refrain. Its content is so stereotypical it seems almost a spoof, but its form is magnificent. Ignoring Gunnhild's advice, Eirik gave Egil a most generous reward: his head. And Egil, through his poem, intentionally or not, gave Eirik Bloodaxe, the last Viking king of York, immortality.

It must have been thrilling for Eirik's sons to hear that poem. They would have memorized its resounding lines at once—as Hervor did, too, despite Queen Gunnhild's contempt. As I imagine it, hearing Egil's praise poem in the militant city of York was the final push that sent Hervor on a different path from that of her foster sister, Ragnhild, who ended up as the bitter and childless Queen of Orkney.

Why did Hervor become a shield-maid when Ragnhild did not?

Because the two girls differed, it seems to me.

First, they differed by rank. Ragnhild, as the daughter of a king and queen, was a symbol of their power. She had two likely fates: to marry for politics or be captured by her parents' enemies and raped to spite them. Hervor, as the daughter of a mere raider, had more options.

Second, they differed in body type. Ragnhild was probably petite,

LEFT, *a Viking warrior, about an inch and a half tall, from Galgebakken, Denmark.*

RIGHT, *a very similar Viking warrior of the same size from Wickham Market, Suffolk, England.*

like her mother. Hervor, as I know from her bones, was unusually tall. The range of weapons she mastered, which were buried with her in Birka, show her strength, coordination, and keen eye.

Third, the two girls had different personalities, I think: Ragnhild expressed herself artistically, weaving and embroidering storytelling tapestries. Hervor had no patience for needlework, but she was willing to exhaust herself training with sword, shield, axe, spear, and bow, with riding, rowing, swimming, and sailing. On the practice field, her foster brothers cut her no slack. As a twelfth-century fighting master put it, "No athlete can fight tenaciously who has never received any blows: He must see his blood flow and hear his teeth crack under the fist of his adversary." If Hervor was to join the shield-wall, she—like anyone else—had to earn her place. And she did. Her joy was a joy of the body, a joy of pushing her physical and mental limits and breaking through to new levels of skill, regardless of the blood, aches, and bruises involved. Regardless of the pain. "It wasn't even accepting the pain, it was relishing it. Because pain is that connection to your body," says a modern female boxer.

Finally, the two girls differed in willpower: Ragnhild bowed to her forceful mother's wishes. Hervor held tight to her own ideas. Hervor was a fighter, and a fighter doesn't doubt: She may have "the open, inquisitive face of a child," like another modern female boxer, but in a fight, her childlike expression "hardens into terrifying purposefulness. . . . She has never lost, and it seems not to occur to her that she could."

Hervor's way was smoothed by her foster brothers. Any girl who grows up with seven brothers surrounding her in age—three older, four younger—may choose their rough-and-tumble sports, at least until biology catches up with her. Ragnhild may have played with the boys too, until the others outgrew her and she found herself the runt, always the loser in games of strength and speed.

Hervor, as a grown woman, was bigger than most men. Maturing early, as girls do, she may have enjoyed besting the littler boys. As her skills increased, her quickness and stamina and fighting spirit helped her best the big ones often enough as well—especially any who had not reached her level of training. As a strategist, her sex and size had no bearing on her ability. What mattered were her intellect and her instincts: her ability to outwit her opponents, to guess and defuse their attacks, to mentally juggle her options and quickly choose the best. You could call it luck.

It was luck, indeed, that she was born in the tenth century, when to be a warrior woman was merely unusual, and not two hundred years later, when it was deemed unnatural.

In Hervor's day, war was a family affair. An army was an impromptu collection of smaller warbands, each loyal to a leader like Eirik Bloodaxe. Eirik's warriors ate with him and slept in the same hall. They were clothed by Gunnhild's textile workers and armed by her smiths. They took part in the rituals Gunnhild led and shared in the feasts. They trained at home, in plain sight of youngsters of both sexes; their elders watched too, and criticized. To join Eirik's warband, Hervor had to prove herself, not to him, but to the men and women she would fight for and beside. Having trained her, they knew her skill. If they accepted her, it was not as a token, but as a warrior.

The people of York especially knew not to disrespect a warrior woman. In 918, a generation before Hervor arrived in northern England, the city surrendered to Aethelflaed, the warrior queen of Mercia. After the death of King Alfred the Great, it was she, his daughter, who led the effort to reconquer the Danelaw, the half of England controlled by Vikings. Continuing her father's strategy, Aethelflaed built and garrisoned ten fortresses, some along her border with Wales, the others facing—or even within—the

THE REAL VALKYRIE ✦ 145

Danelaw. Earthworks topped by formidable stockades, her fortresses gave the locals a refuge and her warriors a base from which to harass Viking raiders, picking off members of their foraging parties and burning any ships left poorly guarded.

Aethelflaed was a ruthless war leader. When a Mercian abbot traveling in Wales was killed, she leveled a Welsh town in revenge; among the thirty-four captives she took was a Welsh queen. When Vikings besieged her town of Chester, Aethelflaed "gathered a large army about her from the adjoining regions" and lifted the siege: "The pagans were slaughtered by the Queen like that, so that her fame spread in all directions," the English annals record. She captured the Viking fortress at Derby while her brother, King Edward of Wessex, engaged the main Viking army seventy miles south at Towcester. Hearing news of the savagery of her attack, two more Viking towns surrendered. Aethelflaed "peaceably got into her power, with God's help," the annalist wrote, "the fort at Leicester, and the greater part of the army that belonged thereto was subdued." The second city to surrender was York: "The people of York had promised her, and some had given pledges, some confirmed with oaths, that they would be under her rule. But very soon after they had agreed upon that, she died."

Aethelflaed was never crowned queen of York, but Hervor, living in the city, would have known her story in much the same form as it has come down to us today. In the early 900s, the Christian clerics in the English kingdom of Mercia recorded, without making any excuses for her sex, the military accomplishments of the warrior queen who ruled them "with just authority" and divine support. Their annals, listing the noteworthy events of each year, were later incorporated into some versions of the *Anglo-Saxon Chronicle*.

By 1200, however, when most accounts of the Viking Age were being written, army training camps had been removed from the domestic sphere—and officially closed to women. A woman's world, in general, had shrunk, thanks to the Christian Church's new focus on defining and enforcing social roles. Christian scholars now taught that the male form was "Godlike," making the female physically inferior. Mentally, she was weaker too. She was naturally more sinful and, when pregnant or menstruating, was considered "unclean"—to the extent that a woman who died while pregnant could be denied a Christian burial.

Beginning soon after the year 1000, when the world did not end as

146 ⊕ NANCY MARIE BROWN

church leaders predicted, and culminating in the Inquisition two hundred years later, the church turned in this new direction, finding for itself a new source of power in social control. As one historian notes, "The scale of the transformation of European society in the eleventh and twelfth centuries can hardly be exaggerated." The Mass was revised and new rituals were invented. Priests now, for the first time, were required to baptize infants and sanctify marriages (or refuse to do so, if those children and couplings did not follow the church's rules). They were required to hear sinners' confessions and intercede for the dead (though Purgatory, and the ways to escape it, was not invented until later in the 1200s). To enforce these changes, the concept of heresy was redefined: The fourteen heretics burned at the stake in France in 1022 were educated clerics who thought the church should keep its eyes on God, through study and prayer, not on man, through the arts of social control. Christians who wished to avoid their fate learned to root out deviance.

Gay and bisexual men soon began to be persecuted. As late as 1025, a homosexual act among consenting, unmarried men required no penance at all in Western Europe; if either was married, it was considered adultery. In 1179, homosexuality of any kind was redefined as a sin "against nature" and punished by excommunication.

Likewise, warrior women were declared abnormal, even wicked. Struggling to explain how Countess Richilde of Hainault could have been captured in battle in 1071, a priest writing around the year 1200 declared her a witch, not a war leader: She was on the battlefield to spew magic powder on her enemies, he said.

Saxo Grammaticus, assigned to write a *Gesta Danorum* (or *History of the Danes*) by the archbishop of Lund around the year 1200, struggled as well. Seeing no way to omit warrior women from his book, the good cleric cloaked his astonishment (or horror) in a believe-it-or-not voice, explaining:

> There were once women in Denmark who dressed themselves to look like men and spent almost every minute cultivating soldiers' skills; they did not want the sinews of their valor to lose tautness and be infected by self-indulgence. Loathing a dainty style of living, they would harden body and mind with toil and endurance, rejecting the fickle pliancy of girls and

compelling their womanish spirits to act with a virile ruthlessness. They courted military celebrity so earnestly that one might have guessed they had un-sexed themselves. Those especially who had forceful personalities or were tall and elegant embarked on this way of life. As they were forgetful of their true selves they put toughness before allure, aimed at conflicts instead of kisses, tasted blood, not lips, sought the clash of arms rather than the arm's embrace, fitted to weapons hands which should have been weaving, desired not the couch but the kill, and those they could have appeased with looks they attacked with lances.

To un-sex oneself was to go against nature. Shield-maids defied the churchman's idea of what it meant to be a woman. War is a man's game, his particular road to glory. For a woman to take part, to be ruthless and to cultivate soldiers' skills, to court "military celebrity," was to forget her true self, Saxo thought.

It's an idea that's still with us. Since the late 1800s, leaders of the women's movement have argued that if *we* ran the world there would be no more war. Some feminists still see "woman" and "warrior" as biologically opposed: Women are natural pacifists, they believe, because we give birth. This argument, writes a historian (and feminist) who has studied warrior women through time and across the map, "is based on a series of assumptions about the relative natures of men and women that is unflattering to both. It is also counterhistorical." Women have always fought, often professionally.

Some cultures, indeed, have forbidden women to join armies. These are often the same cultures, like that of ancient Rome, in which women are considered to be property owned by men. It was shameful for a Roman man to be beaten by a warrior woman, but beaten the Romans were—again and again, in Britain, Nubia, Arabia, Egypt, and what is now Turkey.

From China in 1200 BC to the United States today, archaeological and historical sources attest to thousands of women who have engaged in combat as warriors and war leaders. Yet routinely their witness, their histories and weapon-filled burials and battle-scarred bones, are dismissed. Scholars undercut (or ignore) them. Historians turn them into myths or allot their deeds to a convenient (or imagined) man. They're presented as anomalies.

Saxo, for his part, did his best to denigrate them. As one critic notes, "The mirror which Saxo holds up gives a distorted picture: It diminishes and distorts where it is not a downright laughing mirror." Yet despite his reservations, Saxo found he could not tell some stories from Danish history without praising women who acted with "virile ruthlessness," instead of being dainty, fickle, pliant, and alluring.

When recounting the Battle of Bravellir, fought circa 770 between the Danish king Harald Wartooth and his nephew, Sigurd Ring, who ruled in Sweden, Saxo begins "by reviewing the most eminent nobles on either side." Among those fighting for the Danes were Hetha, Visna, and Vebiorg, three warrior women "whose female bodies Nature had endowed with manly courage." Each woman led her own warband. Hetha, for example, was followed by the champion Haki Scarface and seven other named warriors, along with a hundred who go unnamed.

That the women's military skill was highly respected is revealed by King Harald Wartooth's battle line. The king's deputy, Saxo writes, "designed a wedge-shaped front, posting Hetha on the right flank, putting Haki in control of the left, and making Visna the standard-bearer," which meant Visna led the charge alongside the aging King Harald, who fought from a chariot. Bearing the king's standard was a key responsibility, assigned to the bravest warrior, for if the flag fell it signaled the king's death and the army would panic. It also meant the warrior could not carry a shield. Visna was up to the task. She "was a woman hard through and through and a highly expert warrior," Saxo admits. The Swedish champion Starkather targeted Visna. She did not drop the banner until he cut off her right hand. Starkather himself was forced to leave the field "with a lung protruding from his chest, his neck cut right to the middle, and a hand minus one finger." The shield-maid Vebiorg, meanwhile, killed another Swedish champion. Afterward, "while she was threatening more of Ring's warriors with slaughter," she was brought down by an arrow. Only Hetha leaves the battlefield unscathed; she is rewarded by being named the ruler of Jutland.

The story of the Battle of Bravellir, Saxo notes, "was handed down by word of mouth rather than in writing." If the tale lasted more than four hundred years before reaching Saxo's ears, it must have been told often— with the warrior women included. Did Hervor hear it in Gunnhild's court at York? We'll never know. But it's quite likely she heard the tale of another warrior woman Saxo names, Lagertha, since her story is entwined with that of the Vikings in England.

Lagertha's first husband was the famous Danish Viking Ragnar Lodbrok, who, the story goes, was captured and killed in a snake pit by none other than the king of York. It was to avenge their father's death, his saga says, that the sons of Ragnar amassed the Great Heathen Army that invaded England in 865. After taking York and killing its king, Ragnar's sons "dominated the military scene in the British Isles as a whole for close to twenty years," says a modern historian, and "shaped the whole later history of England and Scotland."

As Saxo tells her tale in the 1200s, none of these heroic sons were Lagertha's; her story belongs to Ragnar's youth. When young Ragnar set out to avenge the death of his grandfather, a king in Norway, Lagertha was one of many warrior women who joined his warband. She was "a skilled female fighter, who bore a man's temper in a girl's body," Saxo writes. "With locks flowing loose over her shoulders she would do battle in the forefront of the most valiant warriors. Everyone marvelled at her matchless feats."

Ragnar himself was impressed, swearing "he had gained the victory by the might of one woman."

After the battle, he asked around. Whose daughter was she? Whose wife?

Lagertha heard the whispers. "She ordered a bear and a hound to be fastened up in the porch of her house so that these animals might act as a defense," Saxo writes.

I can imagine how it went: Lagertha looked Ragnar over and was not impressed. She would rather return to her farm in Norway's fjords and live life her own way than be shackled to a minor Danish king's son. Tell him if he's serious, she said, he should follow me home. Him alone. She was surprised when one day her scouts said he was coming.

When he entered the courtyard, she stood on her balcony. Release the dog, she said.

An enormous bearhound burst from a pen; Ragnar grabbed it by the throat and throttled it.

Is that the best way you know to welcome me? Ragnar shouted.

Release the bear, said Lagertha.

An enormous bear burst from a pen.

You are an exceedingly perverse woman, Ragnar yelled as he held the bear at bay at the end of his spear.

Lagertha laughed. She raised one hand, and a volley of arrows flew from all sides of the courtyard. The bear fell dead.

And you are an exceedingly persistent man, Lagertha said—in my imagination, at least—and agreed to marry him.

Saxo says only, curtly, that Ragnar killed the hound and the bear "by piercing one with his spear and catching hold of the other's throat." He and Lagertha stayed together for three years. Long after he had left her and both had remarried, Lagertha learned that Ragnar was losing his grip on his Danish kingdom. He'd armed the young, he'd armed the old, but still the rebels were winning. Lagertha—now a middle-aged mother of three—sailed south to his aid, gathering forces along the way until she led a fleet of a hundred and twenty ships. Her ships flew behind the enemy's lines. Outmatched by her forces, the rebels fled in panic toward Ragnar, whose warriors, rallying, let few escape.

Lagertha is the most famous Viking shield-maid today, thanks to her fictionalized portrayal by Katheryn Winnick on the History Channel TV series *Vikings*. But another warrior woman Saxo mentions, Rusila—or as the Irish called her, Inghen Ruaidh, the Red Girl—may have been better known in Hervor's time, for she was even then leading a fleet of Vikings in the Irish Sea.

THE RED GIRL

N ews of Eirik's defeat arrives late at night, as such news always does, but the queen is prepared for it. The queen is always prepared, Hervor is aware—she's learned more than embroidery in Gunnhild's *skemma*. She's learned that a leader makes her own luck.

Study your allies as well as your enemies, Gunnhild always says.

York's *witan* is fickle. Rich merchants all, York's leaders fear the English will fire the town. They'll surrender their king before chancing that fate—they've done it before—or their queen. So when Hervor hears that Archbishop Wulfstan, the *witan*'s spokesman, has been captured and forced to pledge allegiance to the English, she knows Gunnhild will flee the city before anyone looks on her or her children as battle prizes.

And before they discover her ships are ballasted with English silver—both the plunder from Eirik's successful raids and the taxes paid to the town.

I've been called to join King Eirik, Gunnhild tells the dignitaries who see them off at the quay.

It's not really a lie. Everyone knows where Eirik, defeated, is likely to turn up.

Reaching Orkney, Gunnhild settles once more at Stone Ness, where Thorfinn Skull-Splitter makes them welcome. Eirik Bloodaxe arrives soon after, in convoy with Arinbjorn, their disagreement over Egil the Poet's ugly head behind them. The Orkney earl's brothers, still Eirik's allies, captain a third fleet in their wake.

They stop ashore only long enough to drop off their wounded, recruit, and restock before sailing south; it's still raiding season, after all. His older sons will sail with him on this raid, Eirik decides, along with their warband—which means Hervor can claim an oar too.

Where are you heading this time? Queen Gunnhild asks.

Dublin, King Eirik replies: That's where everyone's going these days.

They coast along the Headland of Cats, cruise past the Southlands to the Turning Point, cross west to Big Bay to gather more warriors, then follow the Southern Isles, like a giant's stepping-stones, south to Ireland.

Dublin is where the previous Viking king of York, Olaf Cuaran, now reigns. Are they sailing there to kill him or to join him? Hervor isn't sure. Most likely Eirik himself hasn't decided.

No matter. From what she's heard—from what Eirik is telling the warbands—there is loot enough in the Irish Sea for all.

It's two weeks of easy coastal sailing from Orkney to Dublin. Easy, that is, for an experienced sailor like Eirik, attuned to the dance of wind and sea, of sea and sand. For Hervor, crewing a warship for the first time, there's much to learn. To ignore her stiff muscles and blistered hands, she learns to read the water as well as the weather: There are maelstroms—"sea holes"—known to swallow ships on the ebb and cast up their fragments at flood tide. Mists that hide whole islands. Narrow necks to portage across, rather than risk the tide race at the cape. Channels that close twice a day, turning an island into mainland and the reverse. Submerged rocks blocking bays and inlets; sandbanks shifting from storm to storm. From deep water to dry land, the passage crosses marshes and mudflats, through intricate networks of turbulent shallow channels. Disembarking? Watch out for the quicksand.

At length they reach the river Liffey: wide and shallow and swift running. They row upstream on the incoming tide, past the great standing stone that marks the entrance to the harbor, past the burial mounds of illustrious dead ranged along the riverside. Where the Liffey meets the river Poddle is a haven for dragonships, a tidal basin called by the Irish Dubh Linn, or the Black Pool. The town named for that pool occupies the tongue of land between the two rivers, rising from the waterfront to a low ridge with long views over the countryside.

To Hervor, once she's had some days to look around, Dublin seems like a bigger Kaupang, with superior defenses. Its busy lanes are paved with planks, logs, or woven wattle. Its thatch-roofed houses are set gable end to the streets, which wind up from the riverbanks to a royal feast hall on the height of land overlooking the Black Pool. Though densely packed inside the town's earthen ramparts and wooden stockades, each Dubliner's house plot has room, inside its fence, for storage huts and workshops, a garden, a byre, and a cesspit. Unlike those in York, the dwellings seem to be all the same: long, rectangular houses with central longfires flanked by sleeping benches. They are so uniform there must be professional housebuilders in town—and house owners who care little for the residents' comfort. All but the best houses are damp, even waterlogged; some in the lower plots, where Eirik has found lodging for the warbands, flood when the tide is high. The posts and thin branches of the wattle house walls are rotting and need to be replaced. The bones woven into the lowest sections of wattle fail to keep out the rats. Fleas and lice infest the dirt floors; Hervor's feet sink into mud despite the layers of sawdust and straw Eirik has ordered spread.

But the Dubliners she sees seem not to know they live in squalor: They act rich. They wear caps and scarves of figured silk imported, she learns, from far-off Byzantium and beyond. They wear jewelry fashioned in the town itself, out of amber, ivory, and exotic gemstones, their arms brilliant with silver bangles. They build warships and pay extra to have them gaily painted bright yellow and black, blue, red, or green.

Where does their wealth come from? It doesn't take Hervor long to find out. As she wanders through town with Eirik's sons, armed and swaggering and watching one another's backs, Hervor sees signs of slave dealing everywhere. Though Dublin is half the size of York, it seems to have twice as many people roped and chained and penned up for sale. Young women like herself, strong and healthy—and stripped to their linen shirts—are being bought and sold in merchants' yards and houses, in the streets, and on the quay. Young men are treated the same way. By the river, in a pen she thought was a cattle yard, a crowd of dirty, half-dressed people of all ages huddle, peering listlessly at passersby and scratching their flea bites. Some captives are sold right off the ships: These newest arrivals are, in general, better dressed, their clothes being part of the purchase.

Hervor and Harald, Eirik's son, are sparring with staves on the riverbank one day when another slave ship runs its prow onto the sand. They break off and watch as the slave-dealers swarm it—several richly dressed people on the ship are bought, or perhaps ransomed, right away. Then the rest are led, roped, down the gangplank by a well-armed warband, its leader a tall warrior with bright red hair.

They've resumed their sparring match when something about the leader catches Hervor's eye—long enough for Harald to get past her guard and give her a stiff crack across the ribs.

She hears the wild, high laugh of a girl ring out as she hits the dirt, rolls, and is up again before Harald can follow up his advantage. Backing out of range, she stops the fight to stare at the red-haired slave-dealer, who has stopped too and is staring back at Hervor, grinning.

When you learn how to fight, the newcomer says, come see me. I'd like another girl on my ship. Ask for the Red Girl, she says. Everyone in Dublin knows who I am.

According to Saxo Grammaticus, writing his *History of the Danes* around the year 1200, there once was a woman named Alvild who "changed into a man's clothing and from being a highly virtuous maiden began to lead the life of a savage pirate. Many girls of the same persuasion had enrolled in her company by the time she chanced to arrive at a spot where a band of pirates were mourning the loss of their leader, who had been killed fighting. Because of her beauty she was elected the pirate chief and performed feats beyond a woman's courage."

Peeling off two hundred–some years of clerical misogyny, I can hear in my mind's ear the version of this tale Hervor heard: In it, virtue and piracy were not at odds, and Alvild's peers elected her their leader for her feats and courage, not her beauty.

Saxo also writes of a Viking chieftain known as Rusila, or the Red Girl. According to his account, she was raiding in the Irish Sea when she learned her brother had allied with the Danes and proclaimed himself king over the Trondheim region of Norway. Sailing east to challenge her brother's right to rule, she met his Danish allies and overcame them. She then took her victorious fleet south and attacked Denmark itself. On the Danish king's home ground, however, Rusila was outmatched. "Defeated, she ran from the fight, withdrew to her fleet, and made away over the water with only thirty ships, the rest having been seized by the enemy."

Her brother attacked her in this weakened state but still couldn't best her. He "was robbed of his whole army, so that he only escaped by traveling on foot" over the mountains of central Norway back to Trondheim. "So Rusila turned her flight into triumph," Saxo writes.

The Danish king, however, persisted, and Rusila was not allowed to enjoy her victory. "When the Danes appeared among the islands where she had expected safe refuge, she turned tail without offering resistance. The king hotly pursued her, intercepted her fleet at sea and utterly destroyed it." Even so, Rusila "slipped away with a small number of other vessels, her boat, rowed at high speed, furrowing the waves" until she ran into her brother again: His new, Danish-backed fleet "cut her to pieces." For killing his sister, he was allowed to govern Trondheim as a puppet of Denmark.

Two of Rusila's friends, Saxo writes, had remained with the Vikings in Ireland. Hearing of her death, the two men set off to avenge her. They challenged the Danish king to single combat. Two of the king's champions fought in his stead, and one of Rusila's friends was killed. The other, when he was healed of his wounds, swore fealty to the Danes—for no Viking wanted to be a lone wolf.

Historians relegate Saxo's Rusila to the "misty world" of legend. The only datable name in the Danish cleric's Book Eight, in which he writes of the Red Girl, is that of King Godfrid, who founded Kaupang around the year 800.

But these same scholars also connect Saxo's legend to Irish reports of the Inghen Ruaidh, the Red Girl, who harassed Munster in the mid-tenth century.

Did Saxo get his dates wrong? Quite possibly. Like Snorri Sturluson, he was creating history from poems and folklore, along with the writings of his contemporaries, who included Snorri's friends and family members. In his *History of the Danes*, Saxo praises these Icelanders; he admits to having "scrutinized" their "store of historical treasures and composed a considerable part of this present work by copying their narratives." One of the Icelanders Saxo met was Pall Jonsson, Snorri Sturluson's much older foster brother. Pall was consecrated bishop of Iceland by Saxo's boss, the archbishop of Lund, in 1195. He is thought to have written the *Saga of the Orkney Islanders*. He also wrote a history of Denmark (now lost), which he may have shared with

Saxo. Unlike Snorri, Bishop Pall was not a misogynist. He's a likely source of legends of strong women.

But to assume that Saxo's Rusila is the same woman as the Irish Inghen Ruaidh is sexist: What's more likely? That Saxo flubbed his dates, or that there were two famous female Vikings known for their red hair (or their bloody swords) in a hundred-year span?

I understand the urge to conflate the two women. I'm susceptible too. It's the same urge that makes me conflate the revenge of Queen Asa, from Snorri's *Heimskringla*, with the Oseberg grave mound. It's the urge to apply a good story to a historical or archaeological fact.

For there's no story of the Inghen Ruaidh: This Red Girl is just a name in a list of Vikings roving the Irish Sea in the years leading up to 949.

The whole of Munster "was plundered by them, on all sides, and devastated," says the twelfth-century Irish chronicle called *The War of the Irish with the Foreigners*. Ireland's southwest corner was "filled with immense floods and countless sea-vomitings of ships and boats and fleets" of sea raiders. There was "the fleet of Oiberd, and the fleet of Oduinn, and the fleet of Griffin, and the fleet of Snuatgar, and the fleet of Lagmann, and the fleet of Erolf, and the fleet of Sitriuc, and the fleet of Buidnin, and the fleet of Birndin, and the fleet of Liagrislach, and the fleet of Toirberdach, and the fleet of Eoan Barun, and the fleet of Milid Buu, and the fleet of Siumin, and the fleet of Suainin, and lastly the fleet of the Inghen Ruaidh," the Red Girl.

Despite their Irish spelling, several of these names are Norse. Erolf is Herjolf. Sitriuc is Sigtrygg. (None of them translates into "Eirik Bloodaxe.") But by the mid-900s, the Vikings had been in Ireland well over a hundred years. So many Norse had taken local spouses that the nationality of names cannot distinguish raiders from defenders. In the tenth century, the Norse fought on both sides in most battles in the British Isles. Their warbands included not only Irish, English, Scottish, and Welsh fighters, but those from the far reaches of the Baltic Sea, from Russia, Saxony, and France, even from Spain and Africa, for captured warriors were invited to switch sides, and the enslaved could win their freedom by fighting at their masters' sides.

Nor did a masculine-sounding name mean the warrior was male: In the *Saga of Hervor*, Angantyr's daughter called herself Hervard while leading her Viking band. The Red Girl may have used a male name as well, but her gender was clearly no secret to her enemies. Still, other than listing her last, the Irish chronicler makes no distinction between her and the other Viking captains. Male or female, these "furious, ferocious, pagan, ruthless, wrathful" raiders showed no mercy. "The evil which Erinn had hitherto suffered was as nothing compared to the evil inflicted by these parties," he wrote of the Red Girl and her companions.

"In short," he concluded in *The War of the Irish with the Foreigners*, unlocking his ample word hoard,

> until the sand of the sea or the grass of the field or the stars of heaven are counted, it will not be easy to recount or to enumerate or to relate what the Irish all, without distinction, suffered from them: whether men or women, boys or girls, laics or clerics, freemen or serfs, old or young—indignity, outrage, injury, and oppression. In a word, they killed the kings and chieftains. . . . They killed the brave and the valiant . . . and they brought them under tribute and servitude; they reduced them to bondage and slavery. Many were the blooming, lively women; and the modest, mild, comely maidens; and the pleasant, noble, stately, blue-eyed young women; and the gentle, well brought up youths, and the intelligent, valiant champions whom they carried off into oppression and bondage over the broad green sea.

Or, as a Viking king's praise poet put it more succinctly, recalling a different raid in a different land, "Bright fire burned their houses." Many lay fallen; many fled to the woods; many were captured:

> *A lock held the girl's body,*
> *fetters bit into her flesh.*
> *For you, many women*
> *were led to the warships.*

I've always thought of the Vikings as raiders and traders. I knew there was slavery in the Viking Age, though romanticized accounts gloss over that sordid fact. The history of Dublin makes it brutally plain: Raiding and trading and enslaving were all one to Viking warriors. Vikings raided to gather wealth. Like most warriors of their time, they went to war to make a profit. They traded to turn one kind of wealth into another. Captured people were a kind of wealth. They were loot. If Hervor was a Viking warrior, then she was a slaver.

Viking Dublin was the largest slave market in the British Isles. In Dublin, thousands of men, women, and children caught in Viking raids were sold into slavery. Shiploads of captives came to Dublin from as far as Africa. After a battle near the Strait of Gibraltar, an Irish chronicle reports, Vikings brought "a great host of Moors in captivity with them to Ireland," adding, "Long were these blue men in Ireland." An island just south of Dublin was a human warehouse site. What initially looked to archaeologists like a livestock pen on Dublin's waterfront was found to have a hearth and human fleas.

When Hervor arrived, the town was about a hundred years old. Vikings first raided Ireland, the annals say, in 795 and settled in Dublin around 841. They chose the site for several reasons: The Black Pool made a safe harbor; the ridge rising between the rivers Liffey and Poddle provided good lookout posts. But more important was the famous hurdle-work ford a little upstream, where the Irish had laid down mats of woven branches, or hurdles, with posts fixing them to the bottom of the Liffey. At low tide, people and animals could cross on this sunken bridge without sinking into the mud. Nearby stood a monastery, a way station for travelers, for at the hurdle-work ford four of Ireland's five great highways met. These roads, wide enough for two horse carts to pass, led to Limerick, Annagassan, Waterford, and Tara. The Vikings seized the monastery by the ford in their first attack. Limerick, Annagassan, and Waterford soon sprouted Viking forts, and their trade roads proved to be fine funnels for bringing coins, cattle, church ornaments, jewelry, weapons, horses, and, most of all, human captives to the market the Vikings established on the river Liffey's beach.

Along with raiding, Dublin's Vikings hired themselves out as mercenaries. The Liffey valley was one of the three most fertile river plains in Ireland; it marked the boundary between the Irish kingdom of Leinster, to the south, and that of Meath, to the north. In 853 the Viking king of Dublin sided with his northern neighbors, marrying a princess from Meath. In 902, the king of Leinster burned Dublin to the ground. To avoid becoming slaves themselves, Dublin's Vikings "abandoned a good number of their ships and escaped half dead after they had been wounded and broken," an Irish annalist crows.

Some of these Dubliners regrouped on the island in Dublin Bay called Ireland's Eye. Some fled across the Irish Sea to Wales, from which they were pushed into English Mercia. There the Lady Aethelflaed decided it might be useful to have a force of Viking mercenaries near at hand and granted them land near Chester, but they soon grew greedy and attacked the city. Aethelflaed famously fought them off. As the Vikings tried to scale the walls, her people pelted them with rocks, doused them with boiling beer, and even, legend says, threw beehives into their midst, loosing swarms of angry bees.

A third group of Dublin refugees landed near Cuerdale and headed overland, through the Pennine Hills, for York, first burying their war chest by a riverbank. They never came back for it. In 1840, workers unearthed it: The hoard contained seventy-five hundred coins and thirteen hundred silver ingots, rings, and hacksilver bits—eighty-eight pounds of silver in all. Most of the coins had been minted in the Danelaw; others were English, French, Italian, or Byzantine. Fifty coins are Arab dirhams, minted in Spain, Baghdad, Afghanistan, and the Himalayas. The cash had been bundled into bags, sealed with bone pins, and buried in a lead-lined chest.

The biggest Viking hoard found in Western Europe, the Cuerdale Hoard equaled the purchase price of about five hundred captured and enslaved people. Yet, in one monastery-raiding spree in the 950s, Dublin's Vikings brought home three thousand captives.

What did a town of fewer than five thousand citizens do with three thousand captives? They shipped them abroad as soon as they could.

Slavery, of course, was not a new concept to the Irish. Long before the Vikings arrived, every wealthy Irish household used slave labor to milk the cows and make the butter, grind the grain, chop the wood, and herd the pigs. Soldiers captured in war and the families of the defeated, merchants unable to pay their debts, farmers' children in a famine year—all might be reduced to slave status. Before the Vikings introduced a cash economy, the Irish used the price of an enslaved girl, or *cumal*, as a standard of value. But they don't seem to have sold people abroad—that was the Vikings' innovation, hinging upon their extensive trade network connecting Dublin to Iceland, in one direction, and Baghdad, in the other.

In Viking Dublin, a *cumal*—a young female captive—was worth eight to ten cows or three ounces of silver. Originally pegged to the weight of a barleycorn, the Viking ounce by the tenth century had been recalibrated to the weight of a standard silver coin—the Arab dirham. Ten dirhams equaled one ounce. Rather than carry around jingling coins, however, the Dubliners melted them down and cast thin silver bangles, each one weighing an ounce. It was more convenient—and impressive—to wear your wealth on your sleeve. Each girl captured in a raid, then, was worth three bangles—in Dublin, that is.

The farther these girls were sold from their homes, the more valuable they became (they were less likely to run off or to be ransomed or rescued). In one saga, a group of captive Irish girls in Norway are priced at eight ounces each—eight bangles, or eighty dirhams—though one girl is sold to an Icelandic chieftain for three times that amount. Viking traders sold girls on the Volga River, according to Arab sources, for a hundred dirhams. Conveyed as far as Baghdad, however, captives with certain sought-after qualities could be sold for five thousand, ten thousand, even a hundred thousand dirhams.

The Vikings were no more nor less brutal than their contemporaries when it came to trafficking in humans. As one historian notes, "Early medieval narratives make it plain that wars were slave hunts."

Gudrod, the Viking king of Dublin, staged such a hunt in 921. His target was the rich Irish town of Armagh, and he timed his raid for the festival of Saint Martin—the Christian version of the Winter Nights feast, held on November 11—when everyone would be wearing their best clothes. The town being well inland, Gudrod could not call on the swiftness of his ships for surprise, but otherwise his battle plan was that of Vikings elsewhere: Gather intelligence and choose the best time to attack. Sneak up on your target without being seen. Fan out, blocking all exits. At the sound of the ox-horn trumpet, attack: running, shouting, beating your shields. Going berserk is a great way to unnerve your opponents. Slaughter anyone who stands fast—not because you are by nature bloodthirsty, but because terror-stricken people do not think well. Herd them into a trap, like the church, from which they cannot escape. Eliminate anyone who acts like a leader. If you planned well, the town was yours. You could ransack it for valuables at your leisure, before burning it down.

At Armagh, Gudrod left the last step a little too late. He had captured a massive booty of well-dressed soon-to-be-enslaved locals, but he was not content. Settling in to Armagh, Gudrod divided his army into three and sent them out to pillage the hinterlands. But word of the town's troubles

Image of a Viking woman, from Tisso, Denmark.

had gotten out. The Irish attacked one of Gudrod's contingents and wiped it out. The Vikings might have been, as that wordy chronicler of *The War of the Irish with the Foreigners* wrote, "shouting, hateful, powerful," and thirty-three other adjectives, including "without mercy" and, strangely, "blue-green" (for the color of their clothing?), but meeting an Irish army, he said, was like "swimming against a stream; it was pummeling an oak with fists."

The Irish, on this occasion, did not bother to take captives, to enslave or ransom. They slaughtered. But when they sacked the Viking towns of Dublin in 944 and Limerick in 968, they listed among their booty not only gold, silver, jewels, and beautifully woven cloth (including silks and satins), but people as well: The Irish raiders led away the Vikings' "soft, youthful, bright, matchless, girls; their blooming silk-clad young women; and their active, large, and well-formed boys" to be sold as slaves. "Every one of them that was fit for war was killed, and every one that was fit for a slave was enslaved."

Nor were the Irish particularly gentle with their captives. At the sack of Limerick the Irish led out "a great line of the women of the foreigners." The Vikings' "soft, youthful, bright, matchless, girls" were "placed on the hills of Saingel in a circle, and they were stooped with their hands on the ground." In that position, they were approached en masse "by the horseboys of the army" and raped from behind, "for the good of the souls of the foreigners who were killed in the battle."

What woman wouldn't choose, if given the opportunity, to be the raider, not the violated captive? What woman, once violated, wouldn't yearn for revenge? It was revenge that brought the valkyrie Lagertha to Ragnar Lodbrok's army, writes Saxo Grammaticus. The Swedish king who killed Ragnar's grandfather had taken Ragnar's kinswomen and "exposed them to public prostitution," in Saxo's polite phrase—likely what the Irish did to the women of Limerick. When Ragnar invaded, "Many women of quality, who had lately suffered abuse to their bodies . . . began to dress themselves as men and flock in eagerness to his camp, vowing that they would put death before dishonor."

According to the Icelandic sagas, when Eirik Bloodaxe was ousted from the kingdom of York (for the first time, in 948), he and Gunnhild took their court back to Orkney and there celebrated the marriage of their daughter Ragnhild to the son of Thorfinn Skull-Splitter. Then Eirik took up the Viking life again, perhaps turning his ships south to Dublin—no one knows exactly where he spent the next four years. "Go south to Dublin: That's where everyone's going these days," was the advice of a Norwegian chieftain to his troublesome son in *Egil's Saga*.

If Dublin was Eirik's destination and Hervor went with him, she would have fought alongside the Red Girl, who was then among the Vikings harassing Munster, enslaving the Irish and selling them abroad. Was Hervor herself captured, raped, and enslaved? That's one possible story. If so, she managed to escape.

Whatever happened, she did not stay in the west. She did not return to York with Queen Gunnhild, when Eirik Bloodaxe regained the throne there in 952. She was not in the warband of Eirik's sons when they challenged their uncle, Hakon the Good, for the kingship of Norway after Eirik's death in 954. Given no facts, I can only imagine how Hervor made her way from Dublin to Birka, from the far western node on the Viking slave route to a node in its center, on the doorstep of the East Way to Byzantium, Baghdad, and beyond. I can imagine Hervor left her foster brothers' warband and joined the Red Girl's, for as Saxo points out in his story of Alvild, women "of the same persuasion" liked to keep company. I can imagine that she sailed east with a shipload of captive girls to sell in the slave markets at Birka.

13

SLAVE GIRLS

Hervor is bored. The sea is fair, the wind steady, and there is nothing to do but blister under the sun and be dizzied by its bright sparkle on the waves. She leans down from her rowing bench and lazily traces her left foot on the floorboard with her eating knife. Shifting her weight, she cuts the footprint deeper, then starts on her right foot. She is just squiggling in toenails when a shadow blanks the fine lines out.

What are you doing?

The bailing scoop lands by her feet with a hollow clap. She sheaths her knife and picks up the tool.

Cutting my toenails, she says. What's it look like?

She is still smiling at the sly double meaning when she reaches the bilge to take her turn at bailing. What had she been doing? Carving *I was here* into the ship, as the ship has carved its presence into the calluses on her hands and the cramp in her calves and the creak in her back.

And this is a dry ship, a seaworthy ship that needs only one person to bail.

It is much preferable to the first ship the Red Girl put her on in the Irish Sea. Caught in a contrary wind in that old, leaky vessel, they bailed day and night—warriors and captives together—their hands cramped with cold, their shirts soaked through, until they were exhausted, and still they bailed. They needed two buckets, one going down while the other came up, over and over, taking turns, dipping and dumping until the danger passed.

Today, on a sunny day under sail, bailing is almost a pleasure—at least it breaks up the monotony. The bilgewater is cold on her toes; the wooden bailing scoop, like a dough trough with a handle, is perfectly curved to match the hull of the boat. No hurry to hoist the full bucket to the deck, haul herself after it, and cross between two sea chests—themselves well designed for their double task as rowing benches and trunks for clothing, food, and loot. Each chest is wider at its base and tapers up to a rounded lid carved from a hollowed half tree trunk, stable in a tossing sea and sturdy enough to sit on. There is just enough room between the benches: When the oars are out, each rower can tap the shoulder of the one in front. At anchor or under sail, the floorspace between the benches makes a snug sleeping berth or, as now, an aisle linking the bilge to the gunwale.

Before she bends for the next bucketful, she lets her eyes slip over the slave girls, huddled aft of the mast in the little shade cast by the sail. She wonders who they were before they were caught.

But for battle luck, she could be in their place, she knows.

Though perhaps not. This set of girls was carefully picked. They are buxom and big-hipped with silken hair and good teeth, none too tall or too small, too young or too old, the best of the hundreds of women the Red Girl has captured—the ones destined for the East Way.

They've made themselves a nest in the midst of the cargo, among bales wrapped watertight in sailcloth tarps, and lie at their ease like queens, not slaves—though it is easy to see who was born noble and who was not. The nobles' limbs are sunburned and peeling. At night the Red Girl rubs them with grease to keep their skin soft—and their sale value high. For the same reason, she has a handsome dress packed away for each girl—a dress to parade in through the marketplace, not one to soil on the voyage. On the ship, they are stripped to their linen shirts.

Treat them like horses, the Red Girl told Hervor. High-bred young fillies worth ferrying overseas. Speak calmly to them. Feed them well. Keep them clean.

And if they complain of the cold?

The Red Girl grinned. You can share your sea cloak. But don't get attached. They're not your fillies; they're mine.

Some cold nights Hervor shares more than her sea cloak: The skin sleeping bags the warriors use are sized for two. No fighting, no forcing, is the Red Girl's rule. There are not enough slave girls for every warrior to have a bedwarmer, so the men double up in their sleeping bags. Occasionally one asks Hervor to share her bag with him, but she always declines. Pregnancy is too much of a risk to indulge herself that way. Sometimes she sleeps with the Red Girl. Mostly she sleeps alone, and cold.

She shrugs. Men have another advantage on board ship: The gunwale is low enough they can piss over the side. She drops her trousers where she stands and pisses into the bilgewater, then continues her work, lazily scooping it into the bucket and tipping it into the sea.

Some years before Hervor became a slave-dealer in the Red Girl's crew, a noble young Irishman named Findan was sent to Dublin to ransom his sister, captured in a Viking raid. He traveled with an interpreter, a bodyguard, and a bag of cash. He never made it to town. Along the way Findan was set upon by a Viking band, tied up, and taken to their ship. After a cold, hungry, uncomfortable night in fetters, he convinced the Vikings his capture dishonored them. Says the *Life of Saint Findan*, "The foreigners held a conference and some, whose attitude was more reasonable and in whom God had inspired, as we believe, humane feelings, argued that people coming from Ireland for the purpose of ransoming others ought not to be forcibly detained." Findan was set free.

His luck did not last long. His family got caught up in a feud between two Irish chieftains, one of whom attacked Findan's farmstead. "They came at night, surrounded the house with their forces and threw firebrands onto the roofs." They killed his brother at his side, but Findan escaped—for a time. The two clans called a truce. Findan was paid blood money for his losses. His enemies invited him to a feast—only to betray him. Vikings "seized him from the midst of the guests, as they had contracted with his enemies to do, bound him in the closest bonds and carried him off." He was sold—once, twice, three times—before finding himself on a ship headed for Orkney.

On the way, they met another Viking fleet. One of the ships' captains came on board, peacefully, to gather intelligence about Ireland, he said, but he was recognized by a man whose brother he had killed. A fight broke out. Findan, though tied to his oar, fought as well as he could on his master's behalf. Other Vikings in the two fleets broke up the fight, and when Findan's ship sailed on, his master rewarded him for his efforts. He untied him and promised to treat him well.

When they reached Orkney, Findan was allowed to go ashore with the Viking crew "to rest, to roam about exploring, and to wait for a favorable wind." Rather than cast his lot with the Vikings, though, Findan looked for a way to escape. He hid in a sea cave until the Vikings gave up searching and left without him—even though it was freezing cold and he almost drowned each time the tide came in. Saved from slavery and the cold sea, Findan pledged the rest of his life to God, which is why his story was written down.

It could have had quite a different ending.

In the mid-900s, an Arab traveler named Ibn Hawqal visited Islamic Spain. Al-Andalus was a fertile land, he wrote, and its people—even its artisans—were wealthy. They wove beautiful linen and silk cloth. They made marvelous musical instruments. They bred the best mules: Each one sold for three thousand dirhams, twice as much as a horse. "A well-known export," he continued, "is slaves, boys and girls captured in France and Galicia, as well as eunuchs." Ibn Hawqal believed that "all the *Saqaliba* eunuchs in the world" came from Spain. These eunuchs were worth even more than mules. In Baghdad, a girl pretty enough for the harem might sell for five thousand dirhams. But a fine eunuch could fetch twenty times as much.

The Arabic term Saqaliba, often translated as "Slavic," may have applied to any fair-skinned Northerner. According to the Italian chronicler Liudprand of Cremona, the boys were brought to Spain not by Vikings, but by merchants from the north of France. Writing in about 949, Liudprand listed the gifts he presented to the emperor of Byzantium: "nine excellent cuirasses, seven excellent shields with gilded bosses, two silver gilt cauldrons, some swords, spears, and spits, and what was more precious to the emperor than anything, four *carzimasia*, that being the Greek name for young eunuchs who have had both their testicles and their penis removed. This operation is performed by traders at Verdun, who take the boys into Spain and make a huge profit."

Eunuchs in the Arab world were not expected to chop wood or herd pigs. Some were recruited into the army. Others became house servants or were trained as bureaucrats and court officials—posts with significant power. Castration, as the ninth-century writer Al-Jahiz of Basra explained, focused the mind. Take two brothers, even twins, he said:

When one of them is castrated, he becomes a better servant and smarter in all kinds of activity and manual work. . . . You will also find him more intelligent in conversation—these are all his qualities. His brother will remain in his innate ignorance, natural stupidity, and Saqaliba simple-mindedness; he will also be unable to understand foreign languages. His hand will be clumsy and he will not become skillful.

The result of a boy's castration, Al-Jahiz concluded, "is the purification of his intelligence, sharpening of his acumen, strengthening of his nature and stimulation of his mind."

Such was the future Findan feared, perhaps, when he braved the high tide in an Orkney sea cave to elude his Viking captors. But what happened to the sister he had been sent to ransom? The *Life of Saint Findan* says nothing more about her.

Some women captured by Vikings, though sexually violated, though lacking any way of fighting back, still preserved their honor and self-respect. Yrsa was "swept up along with the cattle" when Vikings raided her estate in Saxony, Snorri Sturluson writes in *Heimskringla*. She was "a young woman of amazing beauty," he says, and the raiders soon found out she was also intelligent, well educated, well spoken, and of royal blood. "People thought a lot of her; the king most of all." Yrsa became a queen in Sweden and "was considered an excellent leader."

Astrid was a queen in Vestfold, Norway, when Gunnhild and her sons came to power there in the 960s, killing Astrid's husband, King Tryggvi. Pregnant, Astrid escaped. By the time Gunnhild's spies hunted her down, in Sweden, her son was a toddler. Gunnhild offered to foster the boy; Astrid refused. She did not want him raised in the house of his enemies—or worse, killed. She did not trust Gunnhild. She fled again, this time in a merchant ship sailing across the Baltic to Russia, where her brother served the king of Gardariki.

She never made it. Vikings from Estonia captured her ship. When they divvied up their loot, they separated three-year-old Olaf from his mother. The boy would be traded for half a goat, then a good cloak, and would suffer six years as a farmer's field slave before being recognized and redeemed by his uncle. He grew up to become King Olaf Tryggvason of Norway.

His mother became the booty of a different warrior and went home with her captor to Estonia. In a slave market there, Queen Astrid was recognized by a trader from Viken—"though she looked a bit different than the last time he saw her. She was pale and thin and poorly dressed." When he called her by name, she recognized him too. She asked him to buy her and return her to her kin. "I will on one condition," he said: "that you marry me." Knowing he came from a good family, was accomplished and well-off—a worthy match—she agreed. According to Snorri, she did not enter his bed until they reached Norway and her kin had consented to the marriage.

The most famous captive in the sagas is Melkorka, an Irishwoman of exceptional self-control. We meet her on Burnt Island (near modern-day Gothenburg, Sweden) around 940, at an assembly to which "people came from nearly every country we've ever heard of," the saga says. Among them was an Icelander, Hoskuld, whose wife, Jorunn, was well educated, capable, and proud of it—or as one translator puts it, "headstrong." She and their four children, however, were back home, and Hoskuld was on Burnt Island enjoying himself: meeting distant relatives, drinking and indulging in festival food, betting on horse races or wrestling matches, and perusing the foreign goods for sale. In one splendid tent set off by itself, he met Gilli Gerzkr, a well-dressed merchant on his way east to Gardariki.

Hoskuld glanced at Gilli's fine wares. When nothing seemed to satisfy the Icelander, Gilli asked if he was looking for something special. "Yes," said Hoskuld. "I want to buy a slave girl, if you have any for sale."

Gilli lifted the curtain that closed off the back of the tent: Twelve women sat there in a row. "Go in and see if any of these girls suit you," Gilli said. Hoskuld looked them over thoroughly. He liked the looks of the one sitting on the end of the bench, though she was poorly dressed. He asked how much she cost.

Gilli named an exorbitant price: twenty-four ounces of silver. Hoskuld untied his money pouch and told Gilli to bring out his scales; his ready cash weighed exactly twenty-four ounces. Hoskuld took it for an omen and purchased the girl, even when Gilli told him of her defect: She could not speak. "I've tried everything I could think of, but I've never gotten a word out of her," Gilli said. To Hoskuld, the man with a headstrong wife, that may have seemed a bonus. Hoskuld took the girl back to his tent and raped her. The next day he dressed her in finer clothes. "Gilli Gerzkr didn't spend much on your clothing," Hoskuld said, "but it's true he had twelve to dress, and I have only one."

Back home in Iceland, Jorunn obeyed her husband's order to treat the girl well. But she gave some orders of her own: After returning home, the saga says, Hoskuld "slept with his wife every night." That winter the girl gave birth to a son, without making a sound. Hoskuld acknowledged the baby as his own—which made the boy free, not of slave status. "Like everyone else, Hoskuld thought he'd never seen a prettier or more noble-looking child." He named the boy Olaf (it was a very popular name).

When Olaf was six months old, Jorunn said the girl must start working around the farm or leave. Hoskuld made her a house servant, causing her to be in Jorunn's presence day and night. Jorunn never heard her speak.

Two years later, Hoskuld was out early one morning when he heard a strange voice by the stream. He walked down the hill and came upon the girl teaching her son Irish. She had never been mute. By refusing to speak, she kept her innermost person—and so her honor—safe; she remained a noblewoman, not a slave. Pressed to reveal her lineage, she announced that her father was King Myrkjartan of Ireland and she was the Princess Melkorka, captured by Vikings at age fifteen.

Hoskuld was impressed. Returning to the house, he bragged to Jorunn of his concubine's noble kin. Jorunn was less pleased. That night as Melkorka helped Jorunn off with her shoes and stockings as usual, "Jorunn snatched up the stockings and whipped Melkorka on the head." Rather than slavishly cringing, Melkorka punched her mistress, giving Jorunn a bloody nose. Hoskuld had to physically separate the two women.

Instead of punishing Melkorka, he set her up on her own farm and let Olaf grow up there until he was seven, when he was sent away to be fostered by a rich man who was childless. He came to be known as Olaf Peacock for how well he dressed.

When he was eighteen, Olaf Peacock arranged for his mother to marry—behind Hoskuld's back, though with the connivance of another of Hoskuld's sons. Olaf then set off to find King Myrkjartan of Ireland, carrying a gold ring Melkorka had been wearing when she was captured. (Don't ask how she managed to keep a gold ring during her years as a slave: Sagas don't always make sense.)

Olaf first went to Norway, which was ruled by Queen Gunnhild Mother-of-Kings and her sons, according to the saga's somewhat flexible chronology. The queen took a fancy to the handsome young Peacock. When he could find no passage to Ireland, Gunnhild stepped in to help. "I will give you everything you need for this voyage," she said. She requisitioned a ship, hired and equipped a crew of sixty warriors, and sent him on his way in style.

Despite a near shipwreck, Olaf made harbor in King Myrkjartan's realm. Because he spoke fluent Irish and was versed in Irish law, Olaf was allowed to land and make his case to the king, who recognized the ring and acknowledged Olaf as his grandson. Olaf Peacock stayed the winter in Dublin, the saga says, helping to fight off attacks by Vikings. Yet when offered the kingdom, he declined: His mother would not be happy, he explained, if he did not return to Iceland. Once back home, he married the daughter of Egil the Poet and became one of Iceland's leading chieftains.

Romanticized as it is, Melkorka's tale is reinforced somewhat by other sources, including the accounts of Arab travelers who met slave-dealing Vikings, or Rus, as they called them, along the East Way. According to Ibn Rustah of Isfahan, who wrote a seven-volume encyclopedia between 903 and 913, the Rus "treat their slaves well and dress them suitably, because for them they are an article of trade."

Like Melkorka, some of them were sex slaves. Ibn Fadlan, who met the Rus along the Volga River in 922, noted that "with them there are beautiful slave girls, for sale to the merchants. Each of the men has sex with his slave," he added, though unlike Hoskuld they didn't retire to a private tent: "Sometimes a group of them comes together to do this, each in front of the other. Sometimes the merchant comes into their presence to buy a slave girl from one of them and he will chance upon him having intercourse with her, but the Rus will not leave her alone until he has satisfied his urge."

The sex slaves also had light household duties, like Melkorka. In a famous passage illustrating his disgust at the Northerners' filthy habits, Ibn Fadlan notes that a slave girl brings in a large basin of water every morning. Her master "washes his hands and his face and the hair on his head in

THE REAL VALKYRIE ✛ 171

the water, then he dips his comb in the water and brushes his hair, blows his nose and spits in the basin." Then comes the disgusting part. Without changing the water, the girl "takes the basin to the man beside him and he goes through the same routine as his comrade. She continues to carry it from one man to the next until she has gone round everyone in the house, with each of them blowing his nose and spitting, washing his face and hair in the basin."

Unlike Melkorka's relatively happy old age, with a successful son, her own farm, and a tolerable marriage, other women captured and enslaved by Vikings faced a bleak future. Recounting the funeral rites of the Rus, Ibn Fadlan notes that a poor man was placed inside a small boat and cremated. For a rich man, his possessions were divided in three: one third was for his household, one third provided his grave goods, and one third was spent on "alcohol which they drink on the day when his slave girl kills herself and is burned together with her master." Later, in what appears to be an eyewitness account of such a funeral, Ibn Fadlan makes it clear that the girl (or sometimes boy, he notes) does not kill herself but is intoxicated, raped, and ritually murdered.

Archaeologists have found Viking burials that somewhat fit Ibn Fadlan's description, including one on the Isle of Man in the Irish Sea of a rich man buried with a young woman's bludgeoned body laid on top of him, alongside the remains of slaughtered animals. Other graves containing apparent human sacrifices have been found in Sweden and Ukraine. When those graves contain weapons and both male and female skeletons, the researchers routinely describe them as male warriors and female sacrifices.

Some scholars have even argued that Birka grave Bj581—the grave of our Hervor—is in fact the grave of a male warrior whose body was either never buried or has since gone missing; they view the dead woman as simply one of the invisible man's possessions, equal to the dead horses. Dismissing that interpretation, the 2017 analysis of Bj581 reports: "The distribution of the grave goods within the grave, their spatial relation to the female individual, and the total lack of any typically female attributed grave artefacts disputes this possibility." They add, "Male individuals in burials with a similar material record are not questioned in the same way."

To be sacrificed to accompany a slave owner to the otherworld was not a fate exclusive to girls, Ibn Fadlan noted, and at least one Viking Age burial backs him up: On the Danish isle of Zealand, a woman laid to rest with a spear by her side was buried with a man whose wrists and ankles had been tied, as if he were a slave in fetters.

Writing about the route the Rus slavers took from Kyiv to Byzantium in the mid-tenth century, the emperor Constantine VII paints a dark picture of slave trading in action: To negotiate the largest of the river rapids, he wrote, the Rus first put ashore sentries to guard against attacks by the nomads. Then, while some of the Rus portage the ships, "the rest of them, picking up the things they have on board the ships, conduct the wretched slaves in chains six miles by dry land until they are past the barrier."

The Icelandic sagas mention slaves in chains or fetters as well—in stories of heroic escapes. When his guards fell asleep, one saga hero, captured in battle, "rolled over to where an axe lay, and was able to cut the rope off his hands. Next he knocked off his fetters, though it required taking off both heel bones too. Then he killed all the guards. He dove into the sea and swam to land." Given the damage to his feet, these fetters seem to be iron rings or shackles clasped around his ankles, joined by a chain. (A page later we read that his heel bones "healed so well that nothing stood in his way.")

The same plan works for two brothers in a more realistic saga: "There was an axe on the ground with its edge turned up. Grim crawled over to it; he succeeded in cutting the bowstring off himself with the axe, though he wounded his hands badly." Then he freed his brother and they slipped overboard. They made it to land, managed to break off their fetters, and walked some distance, before being rescued by Vikings they knew.

If slavery was the economic driver of the Viking Age, I'd expect as many iron ankle shackles to turn up in excavations as swords, but they do not. A set of iron chains was found in Ireland, attached to a heavy iron neck collar. Iron shackles were found in Dublin too, as well as in Birka, Hedeby, and along the East Way, but the finds are few.

Were Vikings not buried with these tools of their trade? Or did slavery not require shackles and chains? Rope works just as well to bind a captive (unless you leave axes lying around), and spare rope was always available on a Viking ship. In a pinch, it seems, a bowstring will do.

The Vikings also invoked magic to bind or loose a captive. In Norse myth, the evil wolf Fenrir, who will eat the god Odin in the last battle, was bound by fetters made from "the noise of a stalking cat, a woman's beard, a mountain's roots, a bear's sinews, the breath of a fish, and the spit of a bird." All but the bear sinews are impossibilities, but fear might work as well to psychologically bind a captive. Valkyries in battle were said to be able to cast "war-fetters" to paralyze their foes with shock. They could also use charms or runes to break the fetters that bound them or their friends. A tenth-century German charm speaks of these warrior women, calling upon their aid to escape:

> Once sat women
> They sat here, then there
> Some fastened bonds,
> Some impeded an army,
> Some unraveled fetters:
> Escape the bonds,
> Flee the enemy!

Likewise, *The Words of the High One*, when listing the runes the god Odin could carve, says:

> If my enemies
> bind me in bonds,
> I chant a charm
> that frees me:
> Fetters spring from my ankles,
> locks fall from my wrists.

Better than iron shackles for keeping captives from escaping, better than charms, better than rope, was the open sea. No one would escape on those long summer days when the wind was fair, the sun was shining, the shore was a hairline of blue in the offing, not an enemy sail was in sight, and even slave-dealers like Hervor could grow bored. On the deck boards of the famous ship buried in the Oseberg grave mound, a bored Viking carved several scenes: the prow of a ship, a herd of horses, an elk with an arrow in its throat, and a hunting dog. On the deck boards of the Gokstad ship, also buried in Vestfold, Norway, the graffiti is more personal: the outlines of two feet, left and right, complete with toenails.

No captive would think of escaping in the kind of storm described in *Grettir's Saga*, when the bailers "needed two buckets, one going down while the other came up." No, enslaved or free, everyone on that ship would be grabbing up a long-handled bailing scoop, like the one buried with the Oseberg ship, and pitching in to save the ship from sinking and themselves from drowning.

But on the main slave routes from Dublin to Orkney, and then again from Kaupang in Norway south through the Danish straits and past the island of Samsey to the town of Hedeby—or, alternatively, hugging the coast of Sweden, swinging east to the isle of Gotland or north to Lake Malaren and the town of Birka—on these routes that Hervor sailed, a captive could dream of escaping nearly every night.

The Vikings not only preferred to sail within sight of land; they preferred to sleep ashore in tents—though several sagas reveal how risky that could be, when enemies sneak up on a sleeping camp, cut the tent ropes to drop the heavy fabric on the sleepers, and beat them with cudgels. Along hostile shores, Vikings slept onboard, anchored in a harbor, using the tent fabric to rig awnings over their sleeping berths to hold off the rain. This, the sagas show, was only slightly less risky: Those tent ropes, too, were cut.

The Vikings went ashore, as well, to cook their meals. One saga includes a camp scene that would be funny, if it did not lead to an ugly feud. Thorleif Kimbi, an Icelander traveling with Norwegian traders, drew the short straw and had to cook for the captain and crew, but another Icelander was hogging the porridge pot. His porridge "wasn't thick enough, and he kept stirring it while Thorleif stood over him." The Norwegians "shouted from the ship that Thorleif better get going with his cooking, or was he as slow and lazy as every other Icelander?" Thorleif Kimbi lost his temper. He grabbed the pot off the fire and dumped the porridge on the ground. The other man whacked him with the hot porridge ladle, burning his neck—at which point they glared at each other and vowed to meet again with proper weapons.

While all the camp bustle was going on, setting up tents, fetching water and firewood, cooking and eating (or arguing about it), someone had to keep an eye on the cargo—especially the human cargo. All night, while the rest of the crew delighted in a stationary bed, someone had to guard the captives left on the ship, anchored offshore, while someone else watched over the camp.

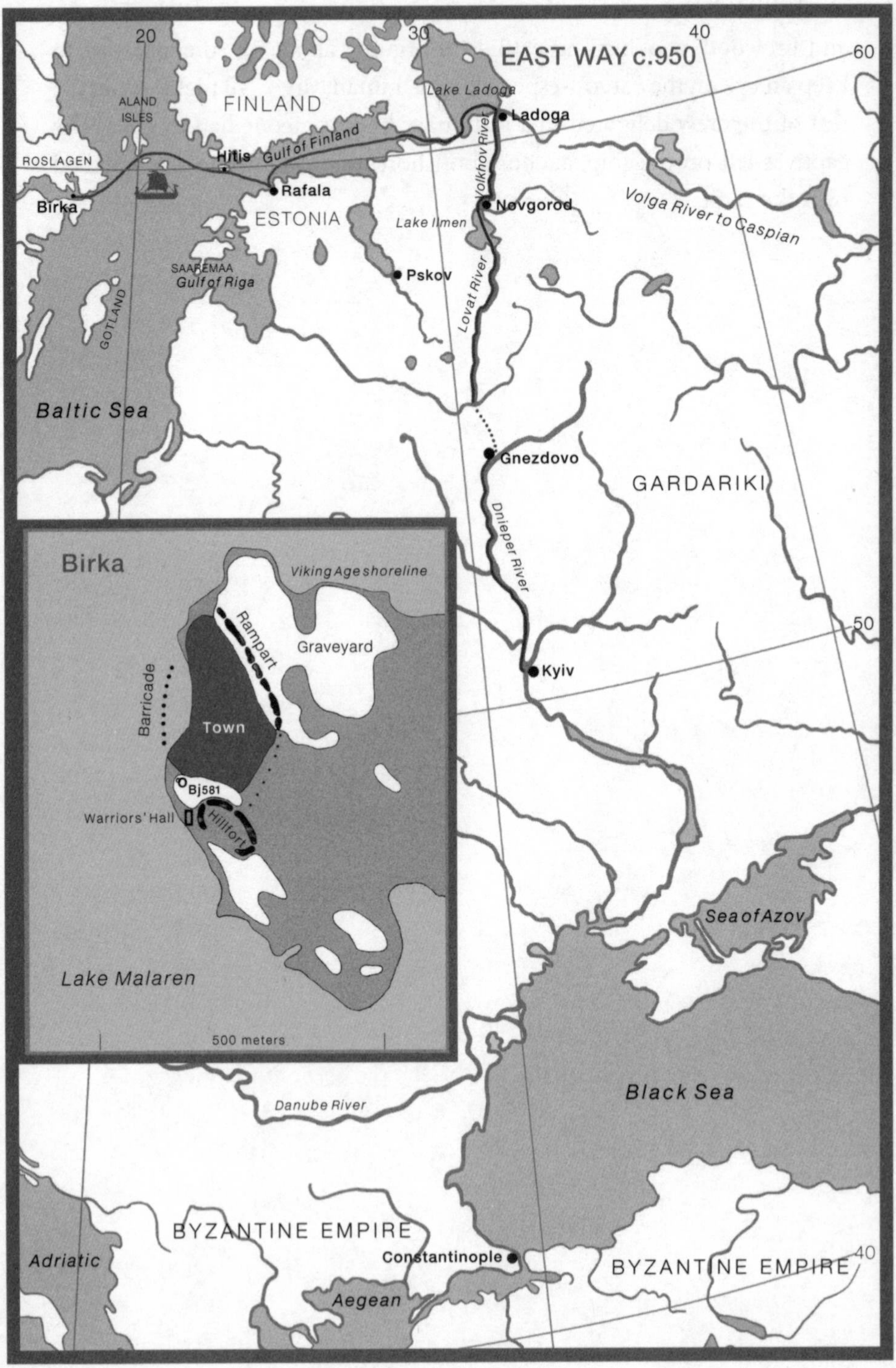
EAST WAY c.950
20
30
40
60
50
40
FINLAND
ALAND
ISLES
ROSLAGEN
Hitis
Gulf of Finland
Birka
Rafala
ESTONIA
Lake Ladoga
Ladoga
Volkhov River
Novgorod
Lake Ilmen
Volga River to Caspian
SAAREMAA
Gulf of Riga
Pskov
GOTLAND
Lovat River
Baltic Sea
Gnezdovo
GARDARIKI
Dnieper River
Kyiv
Birka
Viking Age shoreline
Rampart
Graveyard
Barricade
Town
Bj581
Warriors' Hall
Hillfort
Lake Malaren
500 meters
Sea of Azov
Black Sea
Danube River
BYZANTINE EMPIRE
Adriatic
Constantinople
BYZANTINE EMPIRE
Aegean

14

THE SLAVE ROUTE
TO BIRKA

O ne night, a stranger shows up while Hervor is on watch. She has news
for the Inghen Ruaidh. Hearing the Irish, Hervor lets her in to the camp.

Your brother's Danish friends are lying in wait for you at Burnt Island,
the stranger says.

Is Trond with them? the Red Girl asks.

No. The stranger grins. Your brother's right here, anchored not far off,
with only two ships. He took tribute off my father last night. He tried to
take me, as well.

Would you like to join us when we pay him a visit?

I'll fetch my weapons. I left them in the woods with my brother.

Fetch him too, if he's a fighter, the Red Girl says.

They rouse the crews and clear two ships of loot. They reload them
with round beach stones for throwing. With the sails lowered and the oars
double manned, they slip silently toward the harbor the stranger spoke of.

It is well before dawn, still pitch-dark, and the fog thick, but the stranger
and her brother know the waters well. Trond's two longships lie abreast, anchored in the lee of an island, though some distance offshore. Their awnings
are up, their crews fast asleep on board.

Silently, the Red Girl's ships flank their prey. Her warriors chop the
awning ropes with axes and drop the heavy fabric. As the sleepers star-
tle awake, they find themselves pelted with stones and pierced by arrows.
Many, naked but for their shirts, leap overboard and swim for the island.

The Red Girl's archers and stone throwers target their splashes, but some make it to safety.

Less than half manage to grab up their weapons and roll free of the awnings. Few have time to unhook a shield from the rails on the ship's gunwales before the Red Girl's warriors grapple to the enemy ships and board them. The shouts and cries and battle yells, the clash of steel on steel, grow deafening.

Trond's warriors are as tough and unflinching as his sister's, but they are outnumbered, and they know it—and there is no sign of Trond himself on either ship.

A great black-bearded brute rushes the Red Girl. He strikes her shield and splits it in two—but at that moment a stone hits his hand and he drops his sword. The Red Girl seizes her advantage and hamstrings him, then deals him his death blow as he falls. With that, the rest of Trond's warriors lose heart. It is easy to surround them with shields and disarm them.

Some of you I recognize, says the Red Girl. And I think you know me, too. I'll give you a choice. You can swim to shore and hunt out my straw-hearted brother, or you can switch sides and fight for me.

They look at one another. There are eight of them. The smallest—and keenest—speaks up. You'll lay no load of shame on us?

None, says the Red Girl. You fought well. You can keep your weapons, and you'll take equal shares in the loot.

They share glances again, and he nods. We'll join you, Rusila.

Then let's clear the bodies off these ships and get out of here, the Red Girl says.

They have just enough hands to manage four ships on the return, two of them heavy with the weapons and clothes and loot of Trond's warband, the other two hampered with their own dead and wounded.

Rejoining the other ships in their fleet, they find the camp quiet. The stranger slips off for home—her brother has been killed—and returns with salves and a healer for the wounded, horses laden with food and drink, and her father, who gravely accepts the return of the tribute that Trond took, or at least most of it.

Stay here as long as you like, he says, and accept our thanks. He cradles his son's body before him on the saddlebow as he rides away.

They take two days to bury their dead, bind up their wounds, and reorganize the fleet—now seven ships, not five.

Who cast that stone? the Red Girl asks.

I did, says Hervor.

You will captain my brother's dragonship, she says, and take a captain's share of the loot.

On the Viking slave route from Dublin to Birka, the greatest peril was meeting rival Vikings. Kings were valued to the extent that they kept trade safe. But in the mid-tenth century, when Hervor joined the Red Girl's fleet, in my reconstruction of her life, the kings bordering the Irish Sea were weak; the kings of Norway, Denmark, and Gautland were at war; and the king of Sweden was eyeing Birka itself.

Sailing from Ireland to Orkney in convoy with Eirik Bloodaxe, at the close of the raiding season, Hervor would not have feared attack: Their fleet was too large. But the next stages on her voyage were perilous. Denmark had been trying to take control of Viken ever since Eirik Bloodaxe was exiled from Norway ten or more years before. While Hervor was growing up in Orkney and York, and raiding in the Irish Sea, the Oslo Fjord was filled with Danish Vikings. About the time she sailed east, King Hakon the Good reclaimed Viken for Norway.

The bustling town of Kaupang, by then, was gone. No Shining Hall gleamed from the hilltop, no high-pitched roof of golden pine broke from the trees. No pilots would have met the Red Girl's ships at the harbor's mouth to guide them past the stakes and barricades. The busy harborside of Hervor's childhood had dwindled to a few wattle huts, a few hammers ringing on anvils, a few shipwrights making repairs. Slave-dealers from Gardariki no longer visited the town, sourcing potential harem girls.

Perhaps the Red Girl's fleet sailed on to the mouth of the Gaut Elf River (near the modern Swedish city of Gothenburg), where the borders of Norway, Denmark, and Gautland met. The kings of Scandinavia held assemblies there on Burnt Island every three years, and such assemblies included well-attended markets. At one, the Icelandic chieftain bought the Irish princess Melkorka from the slave-dealer Gilli Gerzkr, who was on his way to Gardariki.

But when Hervor passed Burnt Island, the kings were at war; there'd be no peaceful assembly that summer.

From Burnt Island, the slave-dealers had two choices. They could cross the Kattegat west to Danish Jutland, the peninsula that pokes like a thumb into the Oslo Fjord, and head south to the great market town of Hedeby, on the border of Otto the Great's Saxony. This route took them past the isle of Samsey—where I like to think Hervor stopped to break open her father's barrow and retrieve his sword. To reach Hedeby required navigating the narrows of the Little Belt along Jutland's coast or the Great Belt between the islands of Funen and Zealand; both routes were controlled by the Danish king Gorm the Old and his son Harald Bluetooth from their royal estates at Lejre and Jelling.

Or the slave-dealers could head southeast from Burnt Island, hazarding the Oresund, the strait that today divides Sweden from Denmark (in the tenth century, both banks were Danish), toward the markets on Gotland, a big island in the Baltic Sea, and at Birka in Lake Malaren.

The Oresund was an excellent place for an ambush, according to *Njal's Saga* (from which I borrowed some details in the scene at the beginning of this chapter). Sailing the Oresund in the early 960s, the saga hero Hrut found his four ships blocked by eight. Their commander was Atli the Outlaw, a Viking based in Lake Malaren. Atli had been banished from both Sweden and Denmark, the saga says, for plundering and killing. His father had angered Norway's king as well, by refusing to pay him tribute, and had holed up on Gotland. Viking hoards on Gotland hold massive amounts of Arab silver—some sixty-seven thousand dirhams have been dug up so far—proving the island was a key node on the East Way, along which Vikings exchanged furs, walrus ivory, iron, and other northern resources, including human captives, for silk and silver coins.

Atli preyed on ships like Hervor's going to Birka, which competed with Gotland for the Eastern trade. But Hrut was not trading—he was pursuing a fugitive. His ships were not crowded with cargo, but in fighting trim. He formed a battle line and braved Atli's trap.

"Here comes wealth for the winning," said Atli to his warriors. "Take down the awnings and clear the ships as quick as you can!"

He closed with Hrut's fleet and called out a challenge. "Where are your lookouts? Didn't you see the warships in the sound?"

Learning Hrut sailed for the sons of Gunnhild, Atli quipped, "My father and I have never been fond of your Norwegian kings."

He ended the conversation abruptly, casting a spear at Hrut's ship. "The warrior in its way fell dead. Then the battle began," the saga says. Grappling hooks drew the ships close to make two fighting platforms, butting head-to-head. Sword fighters and axe wielders leaped over their own ships' prows onto their enemies' decks. Archers and spear throwers shot from beside the masts, over their comrades' heads. Heroes on both sides were wounded or killed. Then the leaders came face-to-face: "Atli struck Hrut's shield and split it in two. At that very moment, a stone hit his hand and he dropped his sword. Hrut snatched up the sword and cut off Atli's leg, then dealt him a death-blow." The rest of Atli's forces disengaged. "Hrut and his warriors took a lot of loot off them, along with their best two ships," but let their enemies slink away in the other six vessels.

In the early 950s, when Hervor sailed to Birka, the warships to be wary of were those of King Hakon of Norway. After sweeping the Danes out of Viken, Hakon chased them south to Jutland, where he won a great battle, according to Snorri Sturluson in *Heimskringla*. He chased them farther, into the Oresund, where again Hakon "was victorious, disabling all the Vikings' ships," writes Snorri. "After that, King Hakon raided throughout Zealand, robbing the people, killing some and taking some captive." The Norwegian king raided throughout Danish Skania, then sailed into the Baltic Sea, raiding north in Gautland and south in Wendland (now part of Germany). "He accepted ransom-money and tribute on land, but killed every Viking at sea, wherever he found them."

King Harald Bluetooth of Denmark vowed revenge, and Gunnhild Mother-of-Kings was the one who gave it to him. After Hervor left Orkney on her way to Birka, saying goodbye to her foster mother for the last time, Eirik Bloodaxe was called back to York to be its king again. He lasted two years. In 954, he and his captains, including the faithful Arinbjorn, were killed in battle.

Gunnhild led her sons and the rest of Eirik's army east and offered their services to Harald Bluetooth. In 961, after several attempts and the deaths of two of her sons, they defeated King Hakon. Harald Graycloak (as Gunnhild's son came to be known to distinguish him from the many other Haralds of the time) was crowned king of Norway, though he shared the throne with his brothers and his mother. As Snorri notes, from 961 to 975, Gunnhild "had a large share in ruling the country"; she and her sons "often met to talk things over together and to decide how to rule." It was the "Age of Gunnhild."

Hervor may never have heard of Gunnhild's triumph. By 961, she may already have been dead and buried in Birka, a war leader herself. Or word may have reached her as she traveled the East Way, before returning to Birka to be buried, at the very latest, by 970. If so, she may have shared the story of Gunnhild Mother-of-Kings with another reigning queen, Olga of Kyiv.

I don't know how or when Hervor arrived in Birka. All I know is that she did arrive sometime in the mid-900s and was buried there as a warrior when she was between thirty and forty years old.

Did she arrive in Birka a victor, with news of the death of a notorious outlaw like Atli? No one knows.

Did she sneak up on sleeping Vikings and steal their ships and loot? Perhaps. That's one of Egil the Poet's deeds in *Egil's Saga*. It's also ascribed to the young Hrolf Gautreksson, husband of the warrior woman Thornbjorg, in the saga that bears his name.

Did Hervor sail with the Red Girl and earn her own ship in a battle like that? Or were her companions instead well-known traders like Gilli Gerzkr, regulars on the route past Birka to the royal Swedish city of Uppsala or, on the East Way, to the kingdom of Gardariki?

It was hard to reach the fortified town of Birka, in any case, without proving oneself a friend. Cruising north along the coast of Gautland, keeping the isle of Gotland to starboard (far to starboard if, like Hrut, she'd just killed the son of a chieftain there), Hervor left the Baltic Sea where Sweden's landmass bulges to the east. Threading through a maze of islands, with side inlets blocked by pile barricades and other defenses, her ship was funneled north into the narrow Himmer Fjord to the site of the modern town of Sodertalje. What is now a canal was, in the mid-900s, a short but heavily defended portage into Lake Malaren, Sweden's third-largest lake, which stretches almost a hundred miles east to west. Once past the portage, the tiny island on which Birka sat lay dead ahead.

Approaching from the south, the first thing Hervor saw was Borgberget, the Fortress Rock, rising sheer nearly a hundred feet from the water and capped by a stone rampart and wooden stockades behind which archers lurked. As she rounded the western shore of the island, Hervor passed below a steep hillside bounded by rocky cliffs and buttressed by more ramparts. Its five stone-built terraces held a great hall, its high shingled roof shining in the sun, and some smaller buildings, four of which seemed, from the smoke and ringing of hammers on anvils, to be smithies. This, Birka's garrison with its Warriors' Hall, would become Hervor's home—and here she would eventually be buried, on the westernmost promontory. Above her grave a prominent stone would be raised as a landmark, to be the first thing the next generation of warriors noticed as they approached the island.

The town itself lay to the north, under the shoulder of the Fortress Rock, in a shoreline depression shaped like a fan. Hervor noticed—and dismissed—its beach, bristling with jetties. Lines of reed-roofed wooden houses and workshops, gable ends to the water. Fenced plots crowded with pigs and chickens and reeking cesspits. Muddy lanes and wooden walkways leading up a slight slope to where a few larger longhouses sat on stone terraces. To Hervor's eyes, Birka was just another smoky, noisy, damp little market town like Dublin or Kaupang—except for its magnificent defenses. A barricade of pilings, studded with sunken boats, blocked the harbor, leaving only a slender, twisting channel. An earth-and-stone rampart more than twenty feet wide wrapped around the town's seventeen acres and linked it to the fortress. Above the town's ramparts rose wooden stockades, with archers' walks and battlements and towers overlooking each gate. Outside the walls lay vast graveyards. Nearly two thousand barrows and boat-shaped stone settings, along with thousands of flat graves not so easily seen, testified to the might of Birka's ancestors.

All in all, Birka's defenses proclaimed the town's power and strength, defying anyone who saw it as prey. Combining control of the waterways with armed patrols on horseback and archers on every wall, these defenses were designed to defeat the usual Viking strategy of surprise, siege, threat, and extortion. Nor were the town's fortifications merely defensive. The walls and barricades were bases from which to launch an attack. They were designed to provoke an enemy into making unwise moves. They were traps.

"I'll burn down this town and kill everyone in it, or else die in the attempt," swore the hero of *Hrolf's Saga*, facing a fortified Swedish town that could have been Birka itself.

Replied the town's king and war leader, the warrior woman Thornbjorg, "You'll be goat-herds in Gautland before you get control of this town." Then she began beating her shield and drowned out the rest of his threats. She had prepared for his coming by hiring smiths to build a rampart around the town, as strong and sturdy as they could make it, and to equip it with devices "so that no one could breach it, either with fire or iron."

Hrolf urged his warriors on, but their every assault was repulsed. "They attacked with fire, but water ran from pipes set into the walls. They attacked with weapons and by digging under the walls, but the townsfolk poured burning pitch and boiling water on them, along with huge stones." When they retreated, "some wounded, the others exhausted," the towns-folk came out "onto the wall, laughing and mocking them and questioning their courage. They paraded around in silks and furs and other treasures, showing them off, and dared them to try and take them." Said Hrolf's second-in-command, "It seems to me this Swedish king pisses rather hot."

When they finally did break in, by building wooden platforms to shield the diggers burrowing under the town's walls, they found no one there, though "food and drink was laid out in every house; clothes and treasures were all bundled up, ready to go." Said Hrolf's second-in-command, "Let's have a drink and something to eat, and then we can divvy up the loot."

Answered Hrolf, "Now you're taking the bait, just as they wanted." Quickly searching the town, he found the escape tunnel and chased King Thornbjorg into the woods, coming upon her and her warriors before they could regroup for the counterattack. So Hrolf did take the town, in spite of its traps and tricks—though he did not kill its occupants or burn it to the ground, as he had threatened. Instead, he chose to govern it himself, as Birka's enemies most likely would have done as well.

Some of the enemies Birka's defenses were aimed at, Hervor soon learned to her surprise, were the royals in the manor across the strait, on the neigh-boring island of Adelso. When Hervor arrived Birka was ruled, not by the king of Sweden, but by companies of free traders who paid professional warriors like Hervor to protect them, both in the town and along their major trade route: the East Way.

When Birka was founded in about 750, it was oriented toward the west; its trade partners were the towns of Ribe and Hedeby in Denmark, Norway's Kaupang, and Frisia's Dorestad. The king on Adelso may have been the king of the Swedes, whose main seat was at Uppsala, or "The High Halls," north of Lake Malaren. North of the Swedish kingdom stretched the lands of the Finns and Sami; to the south was the kingdom of the Gauts (also known as Geats or Goths). From the eastern end of Lake Malaren, a well-traveled trade route across the mountains connected Sweden with the Trondheim district of Norway.

At Uppsala, legend said, the fertility god Freyr established the Yngling dynasty. The kings buried under the great mounds at Borre in Norway's

Vestfold were said to be Ynglings; Harald Fairhair and his son Eirik Bloodaxe claimed descent from them. At Uppsala, pagan rituals, including sacrifices to the *dísir*, were held at a temple described by the monk Adam of Bremen in the 1070s as "entirely decked out in gold": "Of every living thing that is male, they offer nine heads, with the blood of which it is customary to placate deities of this sort," he wrote. "The bodies they hang in the sacred grove that adjoins the temple," humans alongside dogs and horses and even bears. Music was part of the ritual, too, but Adam could not bring himself to speak of it: "The incantations customarily chanted," he said, "are manifold and unseemly; therefore, it is better to keep silence about them." (An Andalusian traveler visiting the Viking town of Hedeby around 950, when Hervor was passing through, had a similar reaction: "I have not heard an uglier singing," he said. "It is a humming coming from their throats that's worse than dogs barking.")

On the way to Uppsala, wrote Adam, you pass Birka, "a desirable, but to the unwary and those unacquainted with places of this kind a very dangerous, port." The danger came not only from the Vikings cruising Lake Malaren, but from Birka's own defenses against such sea raiders: "They have blocked that bight of the restless sea for a hundred or more stadia" (at least twelve miles) "by masses of hidden rocks," Adam claimed, making the passage perilous but the harbor "the most secure in the maritime regions of Sweden."

Birka was desirable to a cleric like Adam for its trade in "strange furs, the odor of which has inoculated our world with the deadly poison of pride." He added, "We hanker after a martenskin robe as much as for supreme happiness." Archaeologists have found thousands of pine marten paw bones in Birka's soil; the animal's fur was known as "sable." The paws of squirrels—their fur marketed as "miniver"—along with bones of bears and foxes prove many skins were prepared for sale in the town. These and other furs, such as beaver and otter, came from the dense coniferous forests at the far reaches of Lake Malaren and through the town's trade with Finn and Sami fur trappers farther north and east.

But Adam did not mention Birka in his *History of the Archbishops of Hamburg-Bremen* solely for its trade goods: Birka was the site of Sweden's first church. In 829, the Frankish emperor Louis the Pious sent a Christian missionary named Anskar there. Anskar set off from Denmark in a convoy of merchant ships, following much the same route as Hervor. He did not have a safe passage. As his student Rimbert wrote in the *Life of Saint Anskar*, "While they were in the midst of their journey they fell into the hands of pirates. The merchants with whom they were traveling defended themselves vigorously and for a time successfully, but eventually they were conquered and overcome." The pirates—Vikings—took the merchants' ships and trade goods. They took the royal gifts intended for Birka's king and Anskar's "nearly forty books." But the Vikings did not, strangely, take the missionaries themselves to hold for ransom or sell into slavery. Instead, they put them ashore. "With great difficulty they accomplished their long journey on foot," Rimbert wrote, "traversing also the intervening seas, where it was possible, by ship." A trip that should have taken five days took an entire month.

At Birka they were "kindly received" by the Swedish king. After he "had discussed the matter with his friends" at an assembly and received the townspeople's consent, the king permitted Anskar to preach. The Word of God was especially welcomed by the Christians held as slaves in Birka, though there were Christian merchants in the town as well. One, a wealthy old woman named Frideburg of Dorestad, was known to keep a flask of wine by her bedside, in case she felt death approaching before a priest came to Birka; dying with wine on her lips, she could pretend she had received the sacraments. Wishing to bequeath her wealth to the needy, she told her daughter to take it back to Dorestad because in Birka "there are here but few poor," Rimbert reports. Did she mean deserving Christian poor? Or were the people of Birka really so well-off?

Anskar was able to convert only one important pagan. Herigar, called the "prefect" of Birka, built a church on his estate outside the city walls, by the sheltered bay he named Cross Haven. But Herigar's influence was not enough to protect the monks who replaced Anskar, when he was called back south to become archbishop of Hamburg. The people of Birka attacked the Christians' house "with the object of destroying it." They killed one of the monks; the others "they bound, and after plundering everything that they could find in their house, they drove them from their territory with insults and abuse." There was no priest in Birka until Anskar himself came back in 852 and again received permission to set up "a place of prayer."

Anskar's efforts had little effect. Of Birka's thousands of graves, only a few hundred are simple enough to be Christian: While pagans were buried with weapons, food, clothing, tools, furniture, and sacrificed animals or human companions to make their afterlives more pleasant, Christians were buried in simple linen shifts or winding sheets, or at most wearing their Sunday best. Yet in some Christian-looking graves in Birka, both a cross and a Thor's hammer can be found. Likewise, a woman buried with a witch's staff wears, among her many beads and amulets, a silver crucifix.

A hundred years after Anskar's first mission, when the Warriors' Hall was built, Birka remained decidedly, even aggressively, pagan. Spearheads were buried at several sites in the hall's foundation and under its protective rampart. These dedicate the area to Odin, god of war, whose weapon of choice was the spear. Beneath the central roof-bearing posts of the hall, along with more spearheads, were buried an intriguing set of objects: forty comb cases made of deer antler; a Thor's hammer amulet, also carved from antler; a bronze sword-chape (the decorative metal tip on the end of a sword's sheath) bearing an image of Christ; and two silver dirhams with their Islamic inscriptions, "Mohammed is the messenger of Allah." The comb cases—personal objects of no great worth—represent each warrior in the garrison, archaeologists think, imbuing the building with each individual's spirit and strength. The coins in the mix help date the ritual and the building of the hall: The later coin was struck sometime between 922 and 932.

Were the warriors dedicating the building to Christ and Allah, through the sword-chape and the coins, as well as to Odin and Thor? The archaeologist who unearthed the deposits thinks not. The number of spearheads smothers the other religious offerings. The design of the hall itself is demonstrably pagan: Its boat-shaped walls and pairs of roof-bearing posts hark back to the chieftains' halls of an earlier age. The litter of cattle bones, including skulls and jaws, found on its floor speaks of animal sacrifices and ritual feasts.

The Warriors' Hall was "a statement of identity," "a sign of defiance," and "a response to an external threat." In the mid-900s, King Hakon of Norway, raised in England, was preaching Christianity and refusing to take part in pagan rituals. King Harald Bluetooth, who controlled the trade routes south and west of the Baltic, bragged of making the Danes Christian. The runestone he raised at Jelling on Jutland in 965 to mark his parents' grave mounds bears the same image of Christ found on the Birka sword-chape—buried, overwhelmed by Odin's spears, in the foundation of the Warriors' Hall. The warriors of Birka were taking sides, turning their backs on the increasingly Christianized Viking West, and reaffirming their ties to their pagan trading partners to the east.

15

RED EARTH

Hervor wanders through Birka's marketplace, wondering what to spend her earnings on. With a captain's share of the Red Girl's loot, she is richer than she's ever been before—though not as rich, it seems, as all the women around her. For every two men in the marketplace, Hervor notices a woman weighing silver with her folding scales, buying or selling. Their wealth is obvious: They wear it.

One woman especially catches Hervor's eye. Edging her silk cap is a showy ribbon woven in several colors, its pattern picked out in silver thread. On this cool day, she has tossed a light shawl across one shoulder, clasping it at her hip with a ring-shaped pin. Her long-sleeved coat is a richly textured weave of wool and linen, trimmed with elaborate silk braids in a style Hervor has never seen before. A large gilded-bronze disc brooch at the woman's breastbone holds her coat partly closed, while revealing glimpses, as she walks, of a long wool dress in a supple weave, decorated with row upon row of bright silk bands sewn with silver thread. Her pleated linen underdress, the only ordinary garment she wears, peeks out at hem and neck, where it is clasped by a smaller gilded round brooch that is nearly invisible beneath her showy necklace of blue, green, and white glass beads, beads of amber and of silver, silver filigree pendants, mounted silver coins, and lozenges made of gold foil. A leather-sheathed knife, a small pair of scissors, a bronze needle case, and a silver-mounted purse complete her outfit.

As she notices Hervor staring, this splendidly dressed woman approaches. She tips a small bag to pour raw amber stones and carved amulets into the palm of her hand, including an amber Thor's hammer.

Would you care to have one made? she asks.

They have just agreed on a price when a little girl runs up, a fat little girl wearing another extraordinary necklace of beads—so many beads of blue and yellow glass and gold and silver foil that the string wraps twice around the girl's neck. She, too, carries a knife and a needle case and wears a coat clasped with a gilded disc brooch at her breastbone.

Greeting the child, Hervor realizes with surprise that, though so many women walk and work in the town, this is the first child she's seen.

Where are the other girls and boys? she asks the amber carver.

Home with their families, she replies. Birka is not a place to raise children. Here, we work.

I am an embroiderer, the little girl says proudly, pointing to her needle case.

And the amber carver is not only an artisan but the manager of a textile workshop, her fine clothes advertising her company's products.

Though spread throughout the town, rather than concentrated in a royal hall, Birka's textile workers are organized into businesses, Hervor learns, with managers who arrange for a steady supply of materials—raw wool and flax, imported silk thread, dyestuffs, and gold and silver wire—and who handle sales to the many traders who come to the island to buy cloth.

I specialize in silk, as you can see, the woman says. Especially Byzantine silk. When you pick up your Thor's hammer, I'll show you what we can do with a warrior's riding coat.

She is clearly not Birka's only silk merchant. As Hervor walks on through the town, she sees so many coats, caps, tunics, and dresses decorated with those dazzling bands of colored silk and metal threads that she soon accepts it as simply the local fashion.

And not only are the women of Birka exotically dressed. Many of them parade through town with exotic and well-dressed men on their arms—like the couple now approaching. The woman, carrying a belled hunting falcon on her wrist, is dressed in the old-fashioned style Queen Gunnhild wore, with large box-shaped brooches clasping the narrow straps of her apron-dress. But the Birka woman's brooches shine like bright gold, as do the gilded round brooch at her throat, the golden bands on her dress front, the golden braids on her sleeve ends and hems, and the gold-foil beads that dominate her necklace. The overall impression she gives is of a slender tree draped with gold. But as lovely as she looks, the silver-mounted purse and the folded set of scales at her belt proclaim her a tradeswoman—not a queen.

Her husband's profession is equally apparent to Hervor: He is extremely well armed, carrying sword, shield, spear, and axe, as well as a bow and quiver of arrows. He leads a fine saddle horse; its bridle has gilded cheek pieces. But what most intrigues Hervor is the man's elegant cap: Shaped like a helmet, it is sewn of stiff silk, trimmed with gold and silver braids, and topped by a filigreed silver cone sticking up like a spike.

Where did your cap come from? Hervor asks the man.

Kyiv, he replies, along the East Way. He looks her over and nods. She, too, is well armed, with her sword at her waist, her quiver and bow, her axe and shield and spear. You could get one, he says, if you agree to guard the next group of merchants traveling east through Gardariki. Go up to the Warriors' Hall. They're always looking for good fighters.

Gardariki. Hervor nods. That's where she'll go next. She has always wanted to go to Gardariki.

And she'll get a cap like his.

Before she dies, she will. The filigreed silver cone in her grave in Birka, numbered Bj581, exactly matches one in the double grave numbered Bj644, on whose occupants I've patterned the couple Hervor met. A third matching cone was found in a grave near Kyiv, where such Slavic-style filigree work is common.

This double grave, Bj644, is the only grave in Birka, other than Hervor's own, to contain a full set of Viking weapons. The warrior was older than his wife and not from Sweden—chemical analyses of the bones and teeth in Birka's graves show, in fact, that more than half of the town's thousand inhabitants, both men and women, had, like Hervor, come from away. The warrior's wife, with her falcon and folding set of scales and silver-mounted purse, so splendidly dressed in gold, may also have been the owner of an iron mine, for when she and her husband were buried, a hammer—not a Thor's hammer amulet but a full-sized worker's tool—was included among their grave goods: the symbol of a mine proprietor.

Where the rivers run red and the water tastes rusty, where a rainbow film forms on stagnant ponds—here is where the making of a warrior's weapons begins. Nodules of bog ore, like peas, lie in layers under the peat. Crusts of iron collect on pebbles in lake bottoms, easily raked up. Groundwater percolating through some types of rock dissolves out iron molecules that, reaching the surface, react with oxygen—they rust—and with the help of bacteria solidify into reddish sludge. This sludge accumulates, year by year, in floodplains and riverbanks, drying into layers of iron-rich umber or limonite, commonly called "red earth."

Much of Middle Sweden sits on red earth. The land's vast forests provided ample charcoal to smelt the earth into iron bars, the raw material for weaponsmiths. Sweden's network of waterways made it easy to ship those bars to Lake Malaren, where the town of Birka was ready to receive them and market Swedish iron throughout the Viking world.

That iron, in fact, helped create the Viking world. Swedish iron production increased dramatically in the 700s. By midcentury, Viking raiders were harassing the shores of the Baltic—what they knew as the East Sea—as is proven by an archaeological find on the Estonian island of Saaremaa: two Viking ships filled with dead Swedish warriors, buried before 750. Birka was founded about 770. By the early 800s, when Vikings were raiding throughout Western Europe, Swedish ironworking was at its peak. Irish annalists insist the superior Irish warriors would have routed the raiders were it not for the Vikings' "hard, strong, and durable" steel swords. Modern historians surmise the kings of Sweden came to power by controlling access to that iron and, therefore, those swords.

Turning red earth into steel swords was not easy. The technology had many points of possible failure. The skill and effort it took to make a sword explains why so many legendary Viking swords like Tyrfing, the Flaming Sword in the poem *Hervor's Song*, were said to have been made by the dwarfs in their halls of stone. It's understandable that smiths were connected with the earth, the source of their raw materials, and with mythical beings like dwarfs—there's something magical about metallurgy, about making a weapon of death out of dirt.

First the red earth was roasted to drive out moisture and crack the ore surface, making it more porous. Then it was mixed with charcoal bits and fed into a furnace, a simple cylinder with walls made of sand, clay, and manure, as small as thirty-two inches tall and twelve wide, banked by earth and stones, with a small hole for a bellows mouth and a larger opening at the bottom for the slag, or waste, to run out. Each firing lasted six hours or more and required constant attention—and a trained ear—to optimize the airflow, add fuel or ore, and tap out the glass-like slag based on the sounds issuing from within the furnace.

The end result was a "bloom," a spongy mass of iron like a cauliflower head. Depending on the furnace size it weighed ten to ninety pounds, but only half the bloom was iron. In its pores and pockets hid unmelted slag that had to be pounded out, or the iron would be brittle. While still hot, the bloom was beaten with heavy hammers. It was reheated, pounded thin, folded, pounded thin again, folded again, the process repeated four or five times—it took hours of sweat and a lot of charcoal. Heated, the slag melted and ran out. Pounded, the remaining slag inclusions grew smaller, flatter, and more evenly distributed. The quality of the iron rose; its weight dropped. It took time and patience, muscle and skill, to make good iron. Even a large bloomery could make only enough iron to produce three thousand rivets in a year; a large Viking ship required up to seven thousand rivets.

The quality of the iron is not only a function of slag. Iron alloyed with a little phosphorus (less than 1 percent) is more resistant to rust; it makes good wire, knives, hooks, and locks and was sold in Viking times in sword-shaped bars. Iron alloyed with carbon, however, becomes steel. Phosphorus content varies with the ore: Bog ore has more phosphorus than red earth. Carbon content varies with temperature: At higher heats, iron incorporates more of the carbon emitted as the charcoal burns. A skillful ironworker can control the heat, and so the carbon uptake, to some extent by adjusting the airflow. Less work with the bellows makes a low-carbon steel easy to shape and good for tools and cooking pots; this iron was sold in spade-shaped bars. More bellows work makes a high-carbon steel excellent for the edges of weapons; it was sold in ring-shaped bars.

To forge a special sword, like Tyrfing, the Flaming Sword, the smith may have sought a different source of carbon: bone coal. Those bluish chunks of bone left over when a funeral pyre dies out, whether human or animal, become bone coal. Collected from the cooled pyre, bone coal was mixed with the charcoal in the furnace to endow a sword with the strength and spirit of the animal or ancestor whose bones lent their carbon to the steel.

A good sword is both flexible and strong. Well-balanced, it leaps to the hand. It becomes an extension of the warrior's arm. It dances around the enemy's weapon, cutting more quickly and with more control, even in a less experienced hand. In the sagas, a superior sword like this can bend in half, tip to hilt, and the blade will spring back without breaking. A useless sword, by contrast, bends and stays bent: Two saga heroes, in the midst of battle, try to stamp such swords straight again underfoot.

Low-carbon steel gave the sword its flexibility; high-carbon steel gave it its strength. Bars of each were lengthened into rods, twisted, and welded together, a final layer of high-carbon steel wrapping the twisted bundles to make the cutting edge. The process could result in exquisite patterns— herringbone, star-and-wave—on the surface of the blade, depending on the smith's art. The dark and light bands of the different alloys were enhanced by etching.

Shaping a sword takes a trained smith many days of labor—seventy to a hundred hours just hammering. But all can be lost when the sword is quenched, plunged into liquid to quickly cool it, magically fixing the microstructure of the metal so no ordinary pounding—of sword against shield or battle-axe—will break it. Choosing the time to quench is crucial. The steel must glow a steady deep orange. Too soon or too late and the metal will crack. The sword is worthless, the smith's work wasted. A sword can be quenched in a barrel of water, milk, oil, urine, or blood. Quench it in oil, though, and the blade will ignite as you draw it out: a Flaming Sword. Perhaps that's how Hervor's Tyrfing got its name.

Coming upon *Hervor's Song* for the first time, as a college student new to Old Norse literature, I wondered not *should* Hervor wield her father's Flaming Sword, cursed as it was to destroy her family line, but why would she want to? Wouldn't a woman rather fight with a bow, standing out of the fray and picking off her targets?

Now I realize my young imagination was cramped by those Victorian stereotypes that say women lack the ruthlessness to fight. That they are, by nature, too dainty to wield a heavy Viking sword. It took one evening with a group of Viking reenactors to disabuse me of that nonsense: Their best fighter happened to be female.

Still, the axe that splits kindling can split skulls. The knife that guts a pig can gut a warrior. The spear that fends off a wild boar or bear can fend off a berserk. The arrows that bring down flying geese or fleeing deer can bring down an enemy fighter. Sword fighting mimics no household task. To learn to fight with a sword, the warrior must practice with a sword.

And a Viking sword *is* heavy. The blade is two inches wide, two to three feet long, and rounded to a point, both edges sharp. As it was forged, a long, shallow groove called the fuller was formed down the center of both sides to lessen the weight, but a Viking sword with pommel and grip still weighs a bit over two pounds—a little more than a modern baseball bat, a little less than the heaviest golf club, but unlike these it is wielded with one hand. It takes long and careful training to wield a sword well—even longer to wield it in either hand, as some saga heroes could.

Meanwhile, the warrior was handicapped. A sword wielded poorly is worse than no weapon at all. No one can pick up a sword for the first time, on a battlefield, say, and outface a trained sword fighter. Sword fighting requires balance and timing, as well as strength; the hardest thing to learn is to lead with the strike, not to first step within striking range, plant one's feet, and then swing.

Could Hervor have fought well with a sword? Indeed, she could have. She was taller than most people of her day and well nourished. Because of the way Viking armies were organized in the tenth century, she had ample opportunity to spar with other warriors. Many Viking women may have trained in sword fighting in their youth. When Gudrun in one Viking poem "took up a sword and defended her brothers," she reveals her valkyrie training: "The fight was not gentle where she set her hand," the poem says. She felled two warriors. She struck one "such a blow, she cut his leg clean off. She struck another so he never got up again; she sent him to Hel, and her hands never shook." Though a wife and a mother, Gudrun remained a warrior woman, the poet asserts, with the skill and reflexes needed to target a weak spot (the legs) and to strike hard.

A sword was not the most useful weapon in a pitched battle. It was held in reserve until the enemies had closed and stones, arrows, and throwing spears had all been exhausted. In hand-to-hand fighting, a spear could keep a sword busy, a battle-axe could match it, and both spear and axe could be used two-handed.

But like most Viking warriors, Hervor longed for a sword. Swords were special. They were jewelry, in a way, decoration, an extension of the warrior's soul. Recall the dapper warrior Geirmund, who lost his sword, Leg-

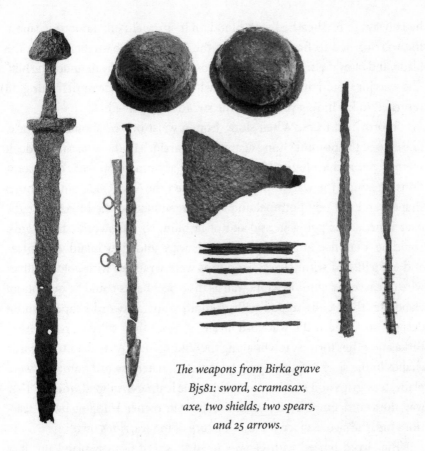

The weapons from Birka grave Bj581: sword, scramasax, axe, two shields, two spears, and 25 arrows.

Biter, to his deserted wife: "He went around in a gray sea-cloak over a fine red tunic, with a bearskin hat on his head and a sword in his hand. It was a good, well-made weapon, with a walrus-ivory hilt. There was nothing fancy about it, but its edge was sharp and it never showed a spot of rust."

Swords had names: Friend-in-War, Night-Bringer, Long-Tooth, Blood-letter, Wound-Wand, Helmet-Dog, Walrus, Snake. The name Tyrfing, the Flaming One, might be a metaphor too, rather than the result of its being quenched in oil. To Viking poets, if a battle was a "spear clash," a sword was the "fire of the spear clash," flickering like a tongue of flame as the warrior fought.

Swords had personalities. In battle they bickered and sang. They formed friendships, coming alive in certain hands, refusing to fight for others. They were finicky, stubborn, and untrustworthy if not handled right. One sword known to be always victorious broke when borne against its rightful owner. Hervor's Tyrfing could never be drawn without killing; it had always to be sheathed with blood on it. To wield one famous weapon, the warrior had to first sit alone on the edge of the battlefield, draw the blade, and blow on it: "Then a little dragon will crawl out from under the hilt." The warrior would turn the sword slowly from side to side until the dragon returned to his hiding place, and the sword was primed.

Swords had faces. When slung from a waist belt or shoulder baldric, one side of the pommel hung against the warrior's body—the same side, it seems from archaeological finds that show asymmetrical wear or decorations, meaning the warrior habitually turned the "face" side out. Pommel shapes, and the way pommel and hilt were affixed to the blade, changed over time, styles going in and out of fashion, so old swords, heirlooms, could be identified at a glance. Pommels were gilded or inlaid with silver and embellished with jewels; handgrips were wrapped with gold or silver wire or carved of shining white walrus tusk. Scabbards could be even more elaborate, their ends tipped with decorative metal sword-chapes, whose designs announced the warrior's loyalties. More than sixty warriors from Birka and other fortress towns along the Vikings' East Way flaunted sword-chapes in the shape of a stooping falcon. Alternately, sword pommels were plain steel, grips and scabbards a serviceable leather-wrapped wood. Either way, the sword announced something about its owner. Hanging by the warrior's hip, the sword's face was a miniature of the warrior's own.

The sword buried with Hervor in Birka grave Bj581 is plain. But it is somewhat uncommon. According to the typology devised in 1919 to sort Viking swords by pommel and hilt, it falls into Type E. Only 3 percent of the swords found in Norway and 6 percent of those from Sweden are of this type, and none have been recovered from Denmark. But 13 percent of the Viking swords found in Russia and Ukraine are Type E.

This fact and the Eastern look of some of the other weapons and items of dress buried with her imply that Hervor did not stay in Birka until she died, nor did she likely return west (with the Red Girl or her own warband). Instead, it seems, she followed the plan the silk-capped warrior suggested in the scene I reconstructed earlier: She went to the Warriors' Hall and arranged to join a trading run along the East Way.

16

A BIRKA WARRIOR

The butchers' lane is blocked. She saw the herd of cattle ferried over that morning, but she hadn't considered where they'd end up, until now, when she finds herself facing a lane mired in blood and manure and offal, headless carcasses on hooks being efficiently jointed, raw skins rolled for tanning, brains in some buckets, blood and tallow and intestines in others, hooves piled for glue, dogs and pigs swarming underfoot snatching whatever they can, and a pen full of bellowing beef on the hoof blocking her way. Rather than backtrack, she slips through the gate in the town wall.

She can cut through the fields and come back in at the next town gate, she thinks. Or maybe she'll skip the town altogether and head for the hillfort's outer gate, reaching the garrison that way. It isn't far, and the sudden peace and quiet outside of town is refreshing. She has just determined to walk the long way up to the Warriors' Hall when a horse archer appears, galloping toward her, an arrow on his bow.

She raises her hands, palm out, and waits.

He brings his horse to a sharp stop but doesn't lower his bow. New here? he asks.

A few days, she replies.

He is handsome in his silk-trimmed riding coat—she will have to get one, she thinks—though what really intrigues her is his bow. It isn't bent right. And it is very small.

Does that thing shoot? she asks.

He laughs. See that goose?

The bird is flying low toward the lake. The archer spurs his horse underneath it, shoots, spins, picks the dead goose up off the grass, and returns to where Hervor waits, amazed.

Where can I get one? she shouts.

He laughs again. You are new here, aren't you? He holsters his bow—still strung, she notices—dismounts, and ties the goose to his saddle. First things first, he says. If you leave the town, you leave the town's law. So don't leave the town without an escort. If I'd felt like it, I could have shot you, not the goose, and there's nothing your people could have done to me. Second, where do you think you're going?

Warriors' Hall, she says. I want to join the garrison. And go east.

Then you'll need a horn bow, he says. Come on.

He sets off walking, leading his horse, and since it is the way she wants to go anyway, she follows. Along the way, she quizzes him about his bow—it can shoot any kind of arrow, he says, so long as they are sized right: blunt-tipped for fox hunting, armor-piercing for battle, basket-headed for shooting burning rags.

His bow case and quiver both hang from his belt, clattering as he walks, and not only does he leave his bow strung, his arrows sit in the quiver pointed end up.

Don't you jab your hand? she asks.

I did when I was a boy. Once or twice.

The gate guard at the white stone lets them through with a nod.

We just passed the witch, the archer says.

The guard? Hervor looks back over her shoulder.

No, under the stone. He was buried here before the fortress was built, and now he keeps the walls safe for us.

They are impressive walls, making a wide semicircle around the top of the hill, from cliff to cliff, and rising almost three times her height. Crossing under the gate tower she can see there are two stone walls, inner and outer, tied together with rubble and earth, and topped by wooden stockades with walkways and battlements. A watchful witch is always a plus, of course, but she doesn't think Birka's fortress walls need much magical help to stay standing.

The walls enclose a vast grassy slope, most of it open but for a few storehouses and stables, where they leave the archer's horse. A great whaleback

THE REAL VALKYRIE ✠ 199

of gray rock breaks from the hilltop. It gives a commanding view over the lake and the nearby islands and all the waterways leading up to the town. From here, Birka's houses and boats look like ants, the people like lice.

The Warriors' Hall, on a terrace backing right up to the cliff edge, outside the main fortress walls, looks little from here as well—and when they reach it, Hervor realizes it is, indeed, small for a Viking feast hall. It is only half as long as the Shining Hall at Kaupang, where she lived as a child, though it fills every bit of level space available. It has two doors, to left and right on its south face.

The archer leads her through the nearest one into a high-ceilinged room with a central hearth. It is a weapons store: Shields and spears hang on the walls. Beneath them sit forty locked chests, each like a sailor's rowing bench. He unlocks one and puts away his weapons; she sees other valuables stored there as well, wrapped in cloth. Then he carefully locks everything back up again—but his padlock, and those locking the other chests, is puny. It is a miniature bronze lock, technically elaborate and decorated with concentric circles—but puny.

What's the point of a lock so easy to break? she asks.

You ask a lot of questions, he says. They are *seals*, not locks. Breaking someone's seal is a clear sign of robbery. In an emergency, though, it's good to have quick access without having to fumble with a key. Now, he says, it's your turn to answer some questions.

The door on the left leads to the feast hall itself, with a seat of honor for the war leader in its northwest corner, bench space for the garrison's forty warriors flanking the central hearth, and more weapons hanging on the walls. Taking her arm, the archer leads Hervor through the crowd.

I found this one wandering outside the town walls, he tells the war leader. She wants to join the garrison and go east.

How was Hervor received when she walked into the Warriors' Hall? Did she impress the Birka warriors with the quality of her sword, like her namesake in the *Saga of Hervor*?

In the saga, Hervor's warband abandoned her on Samsey island. Seeing the fires rise from her father's grave and hearing the thunder of his ghostly voice, they took fright and sailed away. After she retrieved her father's sword, the saga simply says that Hervor "stayed on Samsey until she got a passage

away, and nothing is said of her travels" until she came to the hall of a king
named Gudmund, where she "behaved like any warrior." Among other
things, she hung out in the king's hall with the other warriors, checking
out one another's weapons. Of her Flaming Sword, one warrior remarked
that "he'd never seen a better blade." When Hervor abruptly killed him for
unsheathing the sword to look at it, the king forbade the man's friends from
seeking revenge: "With the weapon she has, I think it would cost each of
you dearly to take her life," he said.

Another of the warriors' pastimes, in the saga, was watching King
Gudmund play chess. Once, when the game was not going his way, the
king asked if any of the onlookers could give him advice. Hervor "stepped
up and studied the board, and after a little while Gudmund was winning."
Chess was the board game of choice when the *Saga of Hervor* was written. But chess, while ancient, was not known in the North until after our
Hervor's time. The first proof of it being played in Europe is a Latin poem,
penned in a Swiss abbey in 997, introducing the rules of this new game.

Viking chess—Hervor's game—is *hnefatafl*. *Tafl* means "board" or "table." *Hnefi* means "fist" or, by analogy, the captain of a warband. Unlike
chess, with its even ranks of soldiers lined up on either side, *hnefatafl* is
a peculiarly Viking-style game: The members of a small warband, surrounding their captain as if with a shield-wall, are attacked by a leaderless
mob that outnumbers them two to one. It's practice for the Viking raiding
party cut off from its ship. The Vikings win—that is, the "fist" reaches the
edge of the board—not by strength, but by strategy.

Luck is also involved: The answer to a riddle in the *Saga of Hervor* is
"a die in *hnefatafl*," and dice are almost always found with the *hnefatafl*
pieces in Viking warriors' graves. Hervor's grave in Birka held a complete
hnefatafl set: Twenty-eight whalebone game pieces, the "fist" marked by an
iron nail, and three dice carved of walrus ivory. These were found clumped
together as if contained in an invisible bag on her lap; bits of an ironbound
gameboard lay beside her knees.

Another Birka grave contained *hnefatafl* pieces of clear and green-
striped glass. The sagas mention pieces made of walrus ivory, gold, or
wood—the game could even be played with nuts. On shipboard it was
played with pieces set on spikes, to hold them steady when stuck into a
gameboard with holes. One Icelander regretted playing with his travel
set at home—his stepmother, when he was too caught up in the game to

answer her question, grabbed a piece and struck him with it. The spike caught him in the eye and ripped it out. (After that, the saga says, "he was very difficult to get along with.")

When violence breaks out, it's not usually instigated by the onlookers. In another saga, when two boys quarreled over a game, Thorgils "swept the pieces off the table, and let them fall into their pouch," then swung the full pouch at Sam, striking him so hard his ear bled. When a king and an earl had the same sort of quarrel—whether a player should be allowed to take back a move—the earl grew so angry he dumped the gameboard on the floor and stalked out of the room. (The king had him followed and killed.) Sometimes it seems *hnefatafl* boards were balanced on the players' knees: One board was upset when a boy farted and the player laughed. In a scene matching the one in the *Saga of Hervor*, a Norwegian merchant losing a match in Iceland asked a friend for advice. Rather than improving the merchant's strategy, as Hervor did the king's, however, the friend noticed the Icelandic player "had a sore foot, with a toe that was swollen and oozing matter." Using a straw, he teased a kitten into coming near and pouncing on the man's injured toe. "He jumped up with an exclamation, and the board was upset. They now quarreled about who had won."

Like chess, *hnefatafl* is played on a checkerboard, but the size of *hnefatafl*'s grid is not fixed. While a modern chessboard is always eight squares wide by eight squares tall, *hnefatafl* boards range in size. From Viking Age Ireland comes a small board, only seven by seven squares. The number of pieces in Hervor's grave suggests her preferred board was nine by nine. Two boards found in the Gokstad ship burial in Vestfold, Norway, are eleven by eleven and thirteen by thirteen, while a board found in tenth-century York is huge: fifteen by fifteen. The larger the board, the more pieces involved, and the more complicated the game. Regardless of the board size, though, the rules of the game change to match the skill of the players.

A beginner plays with the simplest rules. The captain, or *hnefi*—distinguished by a nail in Hervor's set—begins in the center square, surrounded by the few dark pieces (the defenders). The white attackers (always twice as many as the defenders) are ranked on the board's outermost squares. All pieces move like the rook in chess—as many spaces as the players want in a vertical or horizontal line. A piece is captured if sandwiched between two enemies, except for the captain, which must be surrounded on all four sides in the beginner's game. If your captain is surrounded, you lose. If it reaches any square on an edge, you—playing defense, as a beginner would do—win.

In this beginner's setup, the captain's side has a distinct advantage. The game gets harder if the attackers only need to flank the captain, not surround it, to win. It gets harder still if the captain's safe squares are limited to the four corners of the board—at this point, the advantage switches to the attacking side. Where the attackers are placed at the beginning of the game can change the odds back. Or some squares can be made off-limits to either attackers or defenders (or both). Or the captain can be weaponless—that is, not permitted to help capture an opposing piece. Or such restrictions can be determined by rolls of the dice. No one knows all the rules by which Vikings played *hnefatafl*. The game changed from place to place and player to player, making it crucial to agree on your rules before engaging in (or betting on) a game. Did Hervor offer to take on any challengers, play by their rules—and win every match? Was that why she was accepted into Birka's garrison when she came to the Warriors' Hall?

For *hnefatafl* was not simply a way to pass the time. Mastery of *hnefatafl*, like that of chess today, was seen as a sign of mathematical intelligence. The game was part of a warrior's education. It developed your ability to strategize—and to foresee your enemy's tactics. To play defense, you learned when sacrificing a piece meant victory and when it made you too weak. To attack, you learned where to build your walls and when to begin picking off defenders and closing the trap. When played with dice, it taught you how to deal with the unexpected—how to adapt your plan on the run. To have been buried with a game of *hnefatafl* on her lap, Hervor must have been an exceptional player and, by analogy, a war leader known for her clever strategies and consistent good luck.

Before being accepted into Birka's Warriors' Hall, Hervor was likely tested in other ways. A warrior could excel, not only at board games, but at impromptu poetry contests as well, the sagas say. Teams played tug-of-war and rough ball games similar to hockey or rugby. In one colorful tale, we read about a game in which "everyone suddenly ganged up on Bosi, but he fought back hard and pulled the arm of one of the king's men out of joint. The next day, he broke the leg of another one. The third day, two men at a time came after him, and many others got in his way. He hit one with the ball and knocked his eye out, and he threw the other down and broke his neck."

Sagas tell of warriors competing in wrestling, running, jumping, archery, spear throwing, lifting or tossing stones, walking on the oars of a moving ship, and swimming—which mostly meant who could last the longest underwater. Arrow-Odd brags,

> I never shot
> the shorter arrow,
> the linden shaft
> light in my hands.
> When we tried our skill
> at swimming,
> I left them blowing
> bloody snot.

Apparently he held his opponents underwater so long the vessels in their nostrils burst.

Two Vikings in the *Saga of Egil One-Hand* competed in sword fighting: "They went ashore and tested each other's skill, and they were nearly an equal match"—despite one of the fighters having only one hand. "In the evening, they all sat down and drank together, before going to sleep for the night. In the morning, the two took up their weapons again and fought strongly, each of them destroying three shields. By then the sun was due south. Then Egil One-Hand said, 'Do you want to play this game any longer?'" When neither won after a third round, they dropped their swords and wrestled, ending up fast friends.

As the final step to becoming a Birka warrior, Hervor likely swore to a set of rules like that of the legendary Jomsvikings. Based at Jomsborg, a fortress town founded around 950 by the Danish king Harald Bluetooth, on the Baltic Sea in present-day Poland, the Jomsvikings were a professional fighting unit. Members had to be older than eighteen and younger than fifty. Each was individually tested: No one was admitted simply for being kin. In fact, kinship—the cause of so many feuds in the Icelandic sagas—was made meaningless. To be a Jomsviking meant casting aside the family honor. If a new member was later found to have killed the close relative of an existing Jomsviking, the saga says, the two warriors were forbidden to fight it out. Instead they must bring their disagreement to the war leader, whose judgment was final.

Likewise, no Jomsviking was allowed to marry. Scholars of a Victorian mindset have long translated this law as "No man should have a woman in the town" and interpreted it to mean that women were barred from the premises. One calls the warband "a monastic-type existence." But the words translated as "man" and "woman" can also mean "person" and "wife," rendering the law "No one should keep a wife in the fortress." The next law clarifies the situation: "No one should stay away longer than three nights," making it impossible to carry on any kind of family life. The Jomsvikings may, in fact, have been an all-male warband during the time of the saga. But their law says nothing against warrior women. As elsewhere in the Viking world, members of the warband were *drengir* ("lads" who followed a leader) or shield-maids of unmarried status, with no conflicting loyalties.

They were a team: They had one another's backs. Each would avenge the others. None would run from an enemy of equal strength or weaponry. All loot they won in battle, big or small, they would bring to a central spot to be shared out by their leader. None would speak a word of fear or complaint, no matter how bleak things looked. None would stir up trouble. None would spread rumors but would take any news to the war leader at once.

Because of their tight discipline, they were the fiercest Vikings of all.

As a Birka warrior, Hervor would have been assigned a weapons chest with a padlock and a key bearing the garrison's symbol: a falcon. By the mid-tenth century, towns like Birka, based on trade and protected by hill-forts, had sprouted from Sweden to the Silk Roads. They dotted the Baltic coastline and punctuated the Russian rivers. These eastern towns were founded, or at least frequented, by the Birka warriors, for all along the trade routes Birka's falcon motif is found.

Styled like a stooping raptor, the falcon symbol was forged into the keys' shafts: Ten falcon keys were found near the padlocked weapons chests of Birka's garrison; others were found in Finland and Gotland. The Birka falcon decorates brooches and equipment mounts and graces sword-chapes—the decorative metal tips of a weapon's sheath. Three of Birka's richest graves (though not Hervor's) contained falcon sword-chapes. Matching copies have been found in graves of similarly rich armed merchants in nearly every fortified town between Birka and Kyiv.

A mold for casting falcon sword-chapes was found in Birka's town cen-

A key, sword-chape, and brooch displaying the falcon symbol, found in Birka, Sweden.

ter, though they were made elsewhere as well, for sixty-seven falcon sword-chapes are known altogether, with some small variations in design. One was found in the west of France, a few were scattered in Norway and Denmark, but the vast majority come from Sweden, Finland, the Baltic States, Russia, and Ukraine. They are immediately recognizable. They proclaimed that the sword's bearer belonged to an elite group of warriors. They may have proclaimed, too, an allegiance to Freyja, in her guise as goddess of war. As well as claiming half the slain, Freyja could take on the shape of a falcon.

To fill her weapons chest, if she did not already have everything she needed, Hervor would have been issued weapons. Those that archaeologists found buried in the remains of the Warriors' Hall, which was burned down and abandoned sometime between 965 and 985, were "plain and functional, without ornament or inlays," meant for battle, not display. There were at least five different kinds of axes, and every type of spear-head imaginable, some meant for javelins (throwing spears), others for the larger lances (thrusting spears).

Hervor might have been issued a ring-woven shirt, or ringmail byrnie: A great variety of iron rings, in various shapes and sizes, were found in the burned-down hall. Or she might have been given lamellar armor, made of small, thin plates of iron stitched onto a leather backing. On the hall floor, archaeologists found hundreds of lamellae in eight different designs. These match no other armor designs known from the Viking Age. They may have come from Byzantium or from the steppes of Central Asia, whose nomads wore similar armor. Helmet fittings were also found, though no complete helmets. Viking helmets are surprisingly rare archaeological finds, with only two known worldwide. The Birka helmet fittings, of gilded bronze, are decorated with lines of birds flanking a tree. The pattern looks Byzantine, though it does not match any helmet mounts from the emperor's own workshops.

The type of scramasax found in Birka, a "rare and prestigious" single-edged knife about twenty inches long, was also of Eastern origin. It was quite showy, hanging horizontally, via metal rings, from an elaborate belt that was studded with bronze or silver mounts; the knife's leather sheath was decorated with matching ornaments. The scramasax was likely not a weapon every Birka warrior was issued, but instead a status symbol to be won or earned.

The most important weapon of the Birka warrior, however—as well as the most unusual—was the bow. Birka's defenses were designed for the bow. Archers on horseback policed the barricades blocking the water approaches to the island, sending intelligence back to the town. Archers on ships drove the enemy into the town's harbor, from which stakes and pilings made it hard for them to flee. Archers on the wall walks could shoot facing both outside and inside the ramparts of town and fortress—turning both enclosures into death traps. Archers in every situation were trained to shoot continuous showers of deadly—sometimes flaming—arrows to make the enemy panic. Hervor was buried with twenty-five spike-headed, armor-piercing arrows. Quivers of the kind buried in other Birka warriors' graves could hold sixty arrows. If each member of Birka's garrison was an archer, and each archer had a quiver of sixty arrows, an attacker would face well over two thousand projectiles—and who's to say each Birka warrior had only one quiver?

An attacker might not expect the range, accuracy, or speed of Birka's archers, for they were not using the plain wooden bows common in the North. At least 10 to 20 percent of the town's garrison used Magyar bows, the signature weapon of the steppe nomads who populated lands from the Danube east to the Caucasus. These horn bows, or composite bows, have been called "the most effective weapon in existence before the advent of the gun." They are not the simple shaped sticks of a northern bow, a weapon anyone with a knife can make in a day and use, after the wood dries, in a week. A Magyar bow can take a full week to fashion and months to dry. It is a laminate of wood, bone, horn (preferably from a Hungarian gray cow, though goat or sheep will do), sinew (the shredded tendons of a horse or deer), glue (made from those same tendons, boiled, or from the gas bladders of fish), and leather or bark. It has a core of hard maple wood, steamed into shape; a grip and ear-tips of bone; plates of horn glued to its belly (the side nearest the archer) for stiffness and strength; and sinews glued to its back (the side facing the target) for elasticity. Leather or bark is used to waterproof critical parts. At least one of Birka's artisans knew how to fashion a Magyar bow, for a replacement bone ear-tip was found when archaeologists excavated the town.

A Magyar bow is a recurve bow. Looking at one at rest, unstrung, a neophyte might see a clumsy arc, like an ordinary bow made inexpertly, and try to string it backward—breaking it. Stringing it properly is tricky as well. "If a person who is unskillful or weak attempts to recurve and string one of these bows," wrote an archer in 1831, "if he take not great heed, it will spring back, and regain its quiescent position; and, perhaps, break his arm." According to a modern archer, to string one requires "arms and shoulders strong enough to do a one-arm pull-up." But stringing the bow was not a daily task: A recurve bow is not weakened by storing it strung. The standard bow case was a stiff leather holster, letting a warrior on horseback keep a strung bow looped to her belt, ready for battle.

Hervor, if she was already a fine archer before arriving at Birka, as I suspect, may have understood at a glance the mechanical advantage of the Magyar bow's complex curves; if not, one demonstration by an Eastern-trained archer would be enough to convince her. A large Magyar bow, about four feet long, is two-thirds the size of an English longbow, considered the best of the Western wooden bows. Yet this Magyar bow can kill at 800 feet— twice the killing range of the longbow. An Eastern archer can hit a bull's-eye, repeatedly, at 250 feet out, and can wield the bow from the back of a galloping horse or the rolling deck of a ship as easily as from a hillfort's arrow loop.

A skilled Western archer, like Hervor, could pick up and shoot a Magyar bow with no special training. She could even use her own arrows. But she wouldn't match the Eastern archer's accuracy, range, or firing rate unless she learned a new way to shoot. Releasing the bowstring with a thumb—protected by a ring of horn, bone, or bronze—instead of using two or three fingers, as Westerners do, makes the arrow fly faster, resulting in quicker and smoother firing. Thumb-ring archery lengthens the archer's draw, giving the arrow more force and allowing it to fly farther or penetrate a close target more deeply.

Then there was the Eastern archer's closed quiver. A metal-reinforced box of stiffened leather, it hung by two straps from the archer's belt, slanted forward, with the arrowheads—seeming so completely wrong to a Western archer—pointing up. It took practice to learn to grasp an arrow without jabbing your hand. But once you'd mastered the motion, you could much more quickly reload your bow. Expert archers could grab a handful of arrows at a time and feed them smoothly onto the bowstring.

Some Birka warriors were buried with closed quivers—the metal loops used to fix these quivers to a belt were found. More such fittings were found, as well, in the burned-down Warriors' Hall, along with a well-used copper-alloy thumb ring. The wear on the ring shows the archer was right-handed. Hervor's grave shows no signs of either thumb ring or closed quiver. The bow Hervor was buried with could have been a Magyar bow. But, if so, she did not shoot it in full Eastern style. To switch from grasping arrows over the shoulder, feather end up, to at the hip, tip end up, required years of retraining—years Hervor apparently did not have.

17

THE KAFTAN

From the back, it looks like wings. She can't see it on herself, of course, but she's seen it on enough others around town: broad-shouldered, narrow-waisted, tight at the wrist. When she raises her arms the long sleeves burst from her back like the wings of a falcon. It is an elegant look—but also functional, allowing her upper body a complete range of motion, perfect for an archer.

Wrap-style and double-breasted, her new riding coat, or kaftan, as they call it, is tailored with tiny stitches from twelve pieces of fine, bleached linen. The women who did the work, she notices, have hands differently shaped from her own, their small, slender fingers padded with needle calluses.

Some kaftans have a row of bronze buttons down the front; Hervor chose a less-expensive fastening of twisted-fabric frogs. All are also meant to be belted: Stuffed humps or lumps are sewn in where the jacket meets the skirt, for her swordbelt to rest on.

Some are completely lined with fur, but Hervor chose a lining of padded linen. She'd rather keep her woven wool cloak clasped at her shoulder for warmth.

Some kaftans are high-necked, some have wide, folded lapels. Hers is the most distinctive, she thinks: asymmetrical, with one side standing high, the other folded down.

Some kaftans have skirts that fall to midcalf; others graze the ankles.

Hers barely reaches her knees and, like all the others, is slit to make mount-ing a horse easy.

And, like all the other kaftans from this workshop, her coat's every edge, inside and out, is adorned with two-inch-wide strips of glossy silk woven with silver threads in brilliant patterns. For added shine, the Birka tailors stitched on tiny sequins of mirrored glass to catch the light.

With a wool tunic or a loose linen shirt beneath it, slim or baggy trousers, and boots, the kaftan was the uniform of the Magyars and other horse archers from the Asian steppes. In its basic design, this nomadic style had remained unchanged for centuries: The kaftan's long sleeves, wide at the shoulder, slim at the wrist, were set in with triangular side pieces that gave the garment its distinctive winged shape.

Many Birka residents—not only the town's Eastern archers—were buried in this style of dress. Of fifty male burials with costume remnants, only ten show no traces of Oriental style. Archaeologists uncovered rows of small bronze buttons. Elaborate silver- and gold-wire braids and twisted knots. Ornate belts festooned with bronze or silver ornaments—often one belt for a blade and another for bow and quiver. Fancy purses with distinc-tive bronze frames and closures.

Sixty-three graves excavated in Birka contained fragments of silk, most of it datable to Hervor's time. Despite the poor state of preservation of these scraps, the town is to Viking Age archaeologists "the queen of silk sites." They can trace Birka's silks to the Caucasus Mountains and the Caspian Sea, to the Eastern Islamic caliphate with its capital in Baghdad, to Byzantium, and even to China.

Since cloth did not last well in Birka's acidic soil, archaeologists look to the East to imagine how these silk garments were styled. They find match-ing buttons, braids, and belts in eighth- to tenth-century burials in the Caucasus Mountains, particularly at a high-altitude site known as Mosh-chevaja Balka, or Ravine of the Mummies, where textile preservation is spectacular. The riding coat worn by Hervor, as the bits of silk found in grave Bj581 suggest, may have looked like one found in this ravine and now on display at the Metropolitan Museum of Art in New York City. This particular kaftan, with the asymmetrical neckline I've described in the scene above, was completely lined with squirrel fur, the silk strips edging its every seam in a mixture of patterns in brilliant reds and blues.

The same sewing technique used in the Caucasus and in Birka was found in the Oseberg ship burial in Vestfold, Norway. Across the Viking world, silk fabric was cut into strips and stitched back together, like piecing a quilt, to make an explosion of color and contrasting designs—and a declaration of its wearer's wealth and status. Silk strips were used for collars, cuffs, hems, ribbons, and trimmings: One linen sleeve found in Moshchevaja Balka is trimmed with horizontal stripes of contrasting silk bands from cuff to shoulder.

In the town of Pskov, on the border of Estonia and Russia, a complete woman's outfit in the traditional Viking style was found, rolled up around two oval tortoise brooches and stuffed into a birch-bark container. It consists of an underdress and an apron, both of blue linen, beautifully decorated with silk. When the archaeologists cleaned and laid out the silk strips, they were surprised to recognize the pattern: It was a popular design, a hunting scene said to represent Prince Bahram Gur, who ruled Persia in the fifth century. The same silk pattern is found on the throne of Saint Ambrose in Milan, in the tomb of Saint Kunibert in Cologne, in the binding of a gospel in Prague, and in the Viking Age graves in the Caucasus.

The silk strips sewn on the Pskov costume contained two repetitions of Prince Bahram Gur's hunt. The piece of cloth was originally about forty inches long and eighteen inches wide. The fabric was cut into strips a little under two inches wide and used to trim the hems and cuffs of the long-sleeved underdress. Clearly the tailor who made the outfit couldn't care less about the prince or his story: Sometimes the scene was sewn on upside down. What was important were color and shine. Combined with two other types of silk, the prince's pattern formed a brilliant panel along the apron top, with the shiny red-violet silk of the hunt scene flanked by bands of bright blue-green.

In the first book I wrote about Vikings, I described the queen buried in the Oseberg ship as dressed in "wool and silk and linen. Light, supple fabrics that clung to her form and draped elegantly." A critic scoffed. "How would Vikings get silk?" And, indeed, colorful silk does not fit the image modern media give us of Viking couture. Nor does it fit the image given us by the Icelandic sagas.

For two hundred years, from about 750 to 950, the trade routes from Birka down the Baltic Sea to Russia, then along the rivers and through the steppes to the Silk Roads, were well traveled. By the time the sagas were written, in the 1200s, they had been forgotten—as had the Vikings' taste for gaudy silk fabrics in clashing colors. Only a few silk garments in the stories stand out. At a Yule feast in Norway in the mid-900s, Arinbjorn gave his friend Egil the Poet a long silk gown; it was called a "slider" because its hem touched the ground. It was a kingly gift: The equivalent gift Egil gave in return was a ship's sail. "Arinbjorn had had this slider made to fit Egil's size," says the saga. It was "sewn all over with gold thread and had gold buttons all the way down the front." We get a sense of just how much silk was involved later on, when Egil's son borrowed the coat to make a grand entrance at the yearly assembly in Iceland. It was so long on him that "it dragged along the ground and got all covered with mud when he took part in the procession to the Law Rock." When Egil saw the damage, he considered his slider ruined.

Another silk slider exacerbates a feud. To atone for the brutal killing of their foster brother, Njal's sons were fined an enormous amount of blood money. They heaped up the coins and hacksilver—thirty-seven and a half pounds of it—at the Law Rock. Then "Njal took a silk slider and a pair of boots and laid them on top of the heap." In the saga, the coat is thought quite unusual: It sparks a series of sexual insults over whether it was meant to be worn by a man or a woman—or by a beardless man easily mistaken for a woman, or a bearded man whom a troll used as a woman every ninth night.

Could this inflammatory "slider" have been a silk-trimmed kaftan like the one Hervor wore? In the 1200s, when these sagas were being written, the Christian Scandinavian kings were waging crusades against the pagan warriors along the Baltic shores who still dressed in this style. The North's once-active trade networks through their East Sea to Byzantium, Baghdad, and beyond were mere memories. Unisex fashions were not the only things long forgotten: Land and sea routes had become confused. When the sagas mention the East Way, their geography is horribly skewed. Depending on the saga, voyagers on the East Way end up in what is now northern Finland, northeast Poland, northwest Russia, or Ukraine. They camp on islands before well-known towns that are near no islands—and never were. They reach recognizable coastlines or rivers to which they give impossible names. Places once routinely visited become the homes of fabulous beasts: In one saga, a man nicknamed Braggart claimed to have killed a flying dragon in a place well known to the Birka warriors—a place where Birka falcon emblems have been found. Uniformly, these stories reveal their medieval authors' unfamiliarity with that corner of the world.

Most of all, the sagas mistakenly make the East Way sound like a single route, analogous to the North Way, which follows the coast of Norway from the Oslo Fjord to the arctic. But journeying from Birka to Baghdad or Byzantium was not as straightforward as hugging a coastline. It required negotiating various rivers and overland portages, each with distinct political and geographical dangers. The favored "East Way" in 750 or 850 was not the same way most traders traveled in 950 or 1050. In the earlier years, they headed to Baghdad or other nodes on the Silk Roads; in the later period, their goal was Miklagard, the Great City: Constantinople. Even in 950, however, to reach Byzantium the Birka warriors chose a different East Way from that taken by Vikings from Gotland.

Their route was determined by the traders' alliances. Trade requires trust. Both buyer and seller must feel physically safe. They must agree on rules of exchange. When trade routes cross cultural and language boundaries, symbols must signal intent. Traders along the various East Ways, for instance, used standardized scales to weigh silver. Their weights, based on the weight of an Arab dirham, were made of bronze (not easily tampered-with lead) and shaped like cubes with the corners sliced off. This same shape decorates the metal rods they used to measure cloth. It also decorates their jewelry: Traders on the East Way wore C-shaped cloak pins with terminals shaped as tiny weights. These distinctive cloak pins signaled that the traders were trustworthy. They knew how to properly weigh silver. Pins like these were found in Finland and Gotland dating from the late 800s; by 950, they were common in Birka.

The traders' armed guards, likewise, had to signal they were not simply Vikings, out on a raid. Hence the eclectic, urban style of dress worn in the fortresses and trading posts from Birka to Kyiv. Hervor, like the other Birka warriors, sported a silk-trimmed kaftan not because she herself came from the East, but because she had allies there. Her Western connections were also announced. Alongside the silk bands, the palmettos, hearts, and

Eastern scrollwork, the Birka warriors' gear is embellished with the last Viking style of art uncorrupted by Christian influences: the Borre style. Named for the royal estate north of Kaupang (where such designs were first found by modern archaeologists), Borre art, with its fat ribbons and pretzel knots and round-eared cats with gripping feet, was popular from Dublin to Kyiv until the mid-tenth century.

Mixing Norse and Magyar, Byzantine, Bulgar, Persian, Arabic, Finnic, Sami, and Slavic motifs, the clothing and ornaments of the Birka warriors spoke of power, success, and access to the exotic. Like her cohort, Hervor wore a costume that declared her differentness. As a Birka warrior, she belonged everywhere and nowhere: She was a far-traveler, a hired sword in a merchant's employ, embodying the polyethnic culture of the trade routes known to the Vikings as the East Way. She was one of the Rus.

In June 860, a fleet of two hundred ships sailed beneath the walls of Constantinople, "their crews with swords raised, as if threatening the city with death." The Byzantine emperor and his army were away. "Why has this dreadful bolt fallen on us out of the farthest north?" asked Patriarch Photius, head of the Eastern Church.

Like his coreligionists in the West, when faced with a whirlwind Viking raid, the patriarch deduced that these merciless warriors "holding bow and spear," their voice "as the roaring sea," were sent by God. The Byzantines had grown contemptuous, sinful. They "forgot to be grateful." They were fat, foolish, and insolent. "We enjoyed ourselves, and grieved others." These warriors from the North, "surpassing all others with cruelty and bloodthirst," were the weapons of God's anger, said the patriarch: "I am talking about the *Rhos*."

The name for these Northerners—Rus, as we spell it—may come from the Old Norse verb "to row"; as the Arab encyclopedist Ibn Rustah noted in the early 900s, "They fight best on shipboard, not horseback." It may come from the place-name Roslagen (itself derived from "to row"), which describes a stretch of the coast of Sweden just north of Lake Malaren; the Finns called people from Roslagen "Ruotsi." According to Bishop Liudprand of Cremona, writing in the mid-tenth century, Constantinople was menaced from the north by four barbarous tribes: "Magyars, Pechenegs, Khazars, and Rus, whom we call also by the other name of Northmen."

The warrior in Birka grave Bj581, as imagined by artist
Tancredi Valeri, based on archaeologists' interpretations.

Liudprand thought "Rus" meant "red," as in the name "Rusila." The Rus, he said, are so named "because of their look": They had red hair or, suggests another translator, ruddy skin.

The Arab geographer Ibn Khurradadhbih, writing his *Book of Roads and Kingdoms* in about 840, seems to have agreed. To him, the Rus were Saqaliba, the Arabic term for fair-skinned Northerners: The "look" was what mattered, not precisely where they came from. Yet Ibn Khurradadhbih was impressed by how far the Rus traveled to sell their "beavers and black fox pelts, as well as swords." They journey, he wrote, "from the farthest reaches of the land of the Saqaliba" down the Dniepr River to the Black Sea, crossing it to reach Constantinople, or down the Volga to the capital of the Khazars. From there they "embark upon the Caspian Sea, heading for a point they know. This sea is 500 *farsakhs* long"—each Persian *farsakh* being equal to four miles. At the southeast corner of the Caspian Sea is the city of Jurjan (Gorgan in modern Iran), a node on the Silk Roads.

"Sometimes," continued Ibn Khurradadhbih, "they transport their merchandise on camel back from the city of Jurjan to Baghdad. There, Saqaliba eunuchs serve them as interpreters." Some of these eunuchs likely traveled into slavery along those same routes down Russian rivers, despite the claim by Ibn Hawqal, the tenth-century Arab geographer, that "all the Saqaliba eunuchs in the world" come from Islamic Spain. Slavery was central to the Rus economy, as it was throughout the Viking world. As Ibn Rustah wrote, the Rus "treat their slaves well and dress them suitably, because for them they are an article of trade."

Trading along the East Way was the practice of the people of the North long before the Rus reached recorded history. On the Swedish island of Helgo, a little east of Birka in Lake Malaren, archaeologists found a silver Byzantine dish, a hoard of seventy Byzantine gold coins, a Coptic ladle from Egypt, and—spectacularly—a little bronze Buddha, serene on his lotus flower, embellished with silver and blue gems. It was made in the sixth century on the eastern border of Pakistan. How it got to Sweden, sometime in the 700s, no one knows. But it may have been brought west by a Buddhist merchant. In Moshchevaja Balka, the graveyard in the Caucasus where the pattern for Hervor's silk kaftan was found, a merchant was buried in the eighth or ninth century with a Buddhist sutra, sacred Buddhist images painted on silk, and bits of a Buddhist votive banner.

Direct contact between Birka and the Islamic world is also attested. Quantities of silver, in the form of dirhams, began flowing north to Sweden in the 750s, when the Umayyad caliphate collapsed. The Abbasid caliphs established a new capital, Baghdad, in 762, and made peace with the Khazars, who commanded the mouth of the Volga. As Baghdad grew, the demand for fair-skinned Saqaliba slaves increased. At the same time, northern furs—marten, beaver, ermine, fox, rabbit, and squirrel—became fashionable in elite Arab circles. Among the people who supplied those furs and slaves were the Rus, with their westernmost outpost being the town of Birka. A rich woman buried in Birka a hundred years later may have come from the Arab world herself. She wore a silver finger ring with a "stone" of violet-colored glass; an inscription on the glass, in Kufic script, reads "For Allah," or maybe the more familiar "inshallah," "God willing." The lack of wear on the ring implies the woman bought it directly from an Arab silversmith.

In 860, when they brandished their swords before the high-walled city of Constantinople (whose half a million people outnumbered them seventy to one), the Rus were not, as Patriarch Photius claimed, "obscure, insignificant, and not even known until the incursion against us"—though when he adds that they were "armed with arrogance," his description was likely accurate.

Envoys from the Rus had met with the previous Byzantine emperor in 839. They seem to have made a trade deal, for they parted on excellent terms. Rather than returning north via the Russian rivers, the Rus envoys joined a Byzantine embassy to the court of the Frankish emperor Louis the Pious—a decision that literally made history. *The Annals of St-Bertin* note the Byzantines brought Louis "gifts worthy for an emperor, and a letter." In it, Emperor Theophilos asked Louis to help the envoys—"who said they, meaning their whole people, were called *Rhos*"—return home. It is the first mention of the Rus in the West.

Louis was suspicious. He had never heard of the Rus. He was certain the envoys were Swedes—and spies. Was it the language they spoke to one another? No matter what their ethnicity, a dialect of Swedish seems to have been the Rus lingua franca along the East Way. Or was it how they described their homeland? No one knows. But Louis certainly knew Swedes. It was he who had sent Anskar to Birka, ten years before, to convert the Swedes to Christianity. Anskar was now archbishop of Hamburg, his companions in Birka had become martyrs, and the Swedes were still aggressively pagan. Louis decided to detain these so-called Rus "until he could find out for certain whether or not they had come in good faith." He sent a letter back to Constantinople. "If they were found to be genuine," he would grant the Rus safe conduct through his empire; if not, he would send them back to Byzantium for Emperor Theophilos "to deal with as he might think fit."

I don't know how this story ends—no letters tell whether the Rus envoys made it home or not. And where was home? Were they from Birka? If so, they may have been Swedes who did not consider themselves "Swedish." That is, like Hervor and the other Birka warriors, they did not identify as subjects of the Swedish king. Instead they belonged to a multiethnic trading society that spread from Birka east along the Baltic coasts of Finland and Estonia to the town of Ladoga, in modern Russia near St. Petersburg,

then south through Kyiv to Constantinople or east down the Volga to inter-
sect with the Silk Roads and the caravan-way to Baghdad. All along these
routes, archaeologists find similar hillforts, houses, graves, clothing, jewelry, insignia, weapons, money, and boats. The settlements all date from
around 750 and disappear in the late 900s.

The Rus who ransacked the suburbs of Constantinople in 860 were indeed
rowers from the North. But they were not the tools of Patriarch Photius's
angry God. They were not at all interested in the Byzantines' sins. They
had come to the Great City, their Miklagard, for Byzantine silk.

According to the *Russian Primary Chronicle*, compiled between the
twelfth and fourteenth centuries, when they returned there in 907, with
allies, their intention was unmistakable. This time, the Northern fleet was
said to number two thousand ships. They beached their boats before the
city walls. Then their leader, Oleg (in Swedish, Helgi), "commanded his
warriors to make wheels which they attached to the ships, and when the
wind was favorable, they spread the sails and bore down upon the city
from the open country. When the Greeks beheld this, they were afraid,
and sending messengers to Oleg they implored him not to destroy the city
and offered to submit to such tribute as he should desire."

The peace treaty was signed by Emperors Leo and Alexander and, representing Oleg, king of Gardariki, by "we of the Rus nation: Karl, Ingjald,
Farulf, Vermund, Hrollaf, Gunnar, Harald, Karni, Fridleif, Hroarr, Angantyr,
Throand, Leidulf, Fast, and Steinvid"—all common Norse names. It covered the usual clauses: how to deal with the murder of a Rus by a Byzantine
and vice versa, assault, theft, inheritance, escaped criminals or slaves, the
transfer of prisoners, army service, shipwrecks, and ships seeking shelter
from the storm. But at its heart was trade. Rus merchants, who swore to
"do no violence" and to live only in the St. Mamas quarter outside the city
walls, could enter by one gate, unarmed, in parties of fifty, with an imperial
escort. They paid no taxes and were supplied with bread, wine, meat, fish,
fruit, and baths for six months. More food was provided for their journey
home, along with ropes, anchors, sails, "and whatever else is needed."

They were also, in 907, paid tribute: gold, "every sort of adornment,"
and, most of all, silk. "Oleg gave orders that sails of *pavolochity* should be
made for the Rus and of *kropin'nyya* for the Slavs." *Pavolochity*, often translated as "brocade," was a heavy silk fabric with a geometrical pattern. *Kro-*

pin'nyya described a lighter silk fabric. The Rus hung their shields upon the gates of Constantinople as a sign of victory, the chronicle concludes. Then they "unfurled their sails of brocade and the Slavs their sails of silk, but the wind tore them. Then the Slavs said, 'Let us keep our canvas ones.'" Enough silk to make a sail was an enormous treasure, not something to let the wind shred even to make a statement.

Not all Viking silk came from Byzantium. Some came from China, like the two-colored star-and-dot-patterned damask, made from unspun raw silk, found in Birka. Some came from Baghdad, where, according to tenth-century tax rolls, four thousand people produced silk or cotton fabrics. Some silk found in Birka and in Moshchevaja Balka is Sogdian silk, woven near Samarkand and Bukhara in modern Uzbekistan and Tajikistan. Some may have come from the Persian city of Jurjan, on the shore of the Caspian Sea, where the Arabic writer Ibn Khurradadhbih says the Rus traded; in the mid-900s, adds Ibn Hawqal, no better silk was to be found anywhere.

But we know most about Byzantine silk thanks to the *Book of the Eparch*, a handbook on commerce written in tenth-century Constantinople. The eparchs, among their official duties, set standards and prices. All the various silk guilds reported to them, and they ensured the guilds followed the rules. These were intricate (or should I say, Byzantine?); the penalties for flouting them ranged from confiscation to flogging to death. Raw silk, for example, could be sold only in public markets, not in private shops and not outside the city walls. Silk fabric from Baghdad could be sold only in specialty shops—and those shopkeepers could deal in no other goods. Certain patterns—yellow medallions, peacocks, lions—could be worn only by employees of the Great Office, servants in the imperial chamber, and the chief eunuchs, respectively. Silk dyed royal purple, using an extract from murex snails, was reserved for the emperor's family; the trim on a single garment could require twelve thousand crushed snails. Ordinary mortals could wear only pseudo-purple, dyed with lichens. Silk dyed scarlet red, using crushed kermes insects, was expensive, though not impossible for a foreigner to buy—if the purchase was approved by the eparch. That it did reach the Viking world is proved by the discovery of kermes-dyed silk in the Oseberg ship burial in Vestfold, Norway. Foreigners like the Rus, before they brandished their swords before Constantinople's walls and negotiated a better trade deal, were also limited by how much silk they could buy: up to the value of ten bezants. The bezant was a Byzantine gold coin equal, at that time, to one Arab gold dinar or fifteen silver dirhams. A good horse cost twelve bezants.

In 944, the Rus leader Igor (Swedish, Ingvar) negotiated a new treaty with the Byzantines, increasing the amount of silk the Rus could buy to fifty bezants' worth. It was a concession hard won. Three years earlier, when Igor's fleet of a thousand ships threatened the city, Emperor Romanos sent out against them "fifteen old battered galleys" with "fire-throwers not only at the bows but at the stern and both sides as well." His sailors allowed themselves to be surrounded, then "began to fling their fire all around." This was the famous Greek fire, a sticky mixture of sulfur, saltpeter, naphtha oil, and possibly quicklime or pine tar, that was shot flaming from a pressurized tube and could not be quenched by water; rather, it burned on top of the waves. The Rus "threw themselves in haste from their ships, preferring to be drowned in the water rather than burned alive in the fire." Some sank under the weight of their armor. Some caught fire as they swam. Those who reached the shore were captured and later "beheaded in the presence of King Hugh's envoy, namely my stepfather, by order of Romanos," writes Liudprand of Cremona. "As the result of this," he continues, "Igor returned to his own country completely demoralised."

Liudprand did not know the Rus very well. Three years later, Igor was back. His "innumerable ships . . . covered the sea." Says the *Russian Primary Chronicle*, "When the Emperor heard this news, he sent to Igor his best boyars to entreat him to come no nearer, but rather to accept the tribute which Oleg had received, and to the amount of which something should even be added." Part of the "something" added in the new treaty was the permission to buy five times more silk.

It was to bring back some of this silk treasure, perhaps, that Hervor set off from Birka one late spring morning, sometime in the 950s or 960s, with a merchant fleet traveling the East Way.

THE EAST WAY

Hers is a lapstrake boat built of oak and riveted with iron, but otherwise it has little in common with the one she captained to Birka. Boats on the East Way have to be light enough to lift and drag overland, round-bottomed to float and maneuver in shallow streams, flexible and strong to endure the rough handling of high seas. They must be swift to row and sail, quick to change course.

Birka's shipwrights waste no weight on comforts for the crew: no flat decks, no sea chests to sit on. Just thwarts for the six rowers, the captain, and lookout, the pared-thin shell of the boat bending and flexing under their bare feet.

They were laughably little boats, Hervor thought when she first saw one. Less than half the length of Queen Gunnhild's ship, with its fifteen pairs of oars and crew of thirty-two. Smaller, even, than the smallest of the warships in the Red Girl's fleet.

Hervor had scoffed at the idea of these eastern skiffs as warships. Then she tested one—and spent the rest of her loot from the Red Girl to buy it.

With a breeze bellying out the light little sail in its forward-stepped mast, her boat races over the lake with the speed of a falcon. With a flick of the oars, it flies up the rivers that flow into Lake Malaren from all parts of Middle Sweden. It floats up their tributaries to where furs are sold and iron manufactured, bouncing off the rocks and rapids. With a covering of birch protecting its keel, it slides across the portage-ways the local people have prepared (and charge a fee to use) of grassy lanes or bogs firmed up with twig basketry or V-shaped ditches lined with sturdy logs sunk into the mud. Hervor has learned when to cut a new false keel of birch, and how best to hammer it on.

The only boats that can best hers on these routes are the Sami's dugout canoes, their round bottoms carved from a single trunk of aspen, steamed and spread wide, their sides built up with thin, overlapping strakes sewn on with reindeer sinews or spruce roots, both lighter than iron rivets, their pointed prows tipped with a beak or a knob that makes a good handle, with a hole for a drag rope.

Hervor learns the hard way not to increase her boat's sail. The light sails of linen or hemp sold in Birka's market, taller than they are wide, look absurd to her Western eyes. So she borrows a good woolen sail, wider than it is high—and capsizes her boat before it leaves Birka's harbor.

She should have looked more carefully at the silver coins struck in the town. On one side is a lapstrake boat with a little sail stuck high on its mast, to catch the breezes on a river journey.

A good East Way boat is so light it's tippy. With only five strakes up to the gunwale, the height of Hervor's boat above the keel is little more than an ell—when the boat is at rest, a rower can dabble her hand in the sea. Heeled over, under sail, the gunwale nearly kisses the water's surface. To keep afloat, not only does the boat's sail have to be sized and balanced correctly; its crew themselves must act as ballast, shifting their weight toward starboard or port, stem or stern, depending on the wind and the weather.

But with a fair wind and a fine crew, Hervor's boat sails perfectly dry. Narrow and elegantly raised at stem and stern, it has a slightly asymmetrical shape: Its hull is wider and higher toward the prow, providing a shield against waves and spray, while its narrower stern releases the water easily.

There is only one thing lacking in such a boat: elbow room. In quiet waters, Hervor can fit fifteen people into it, even seventeen, if they don't need to be comfortable. But for sailing night and day, cooking and sleeping on board, eight feels tight.

And their trade goods? No iron bars in this ship. Only the lightest and most luxurious goods make sense: To the east Hervor's ship will carry walrus ivory, feathers and down, musk from beavers for making perfume, sable and miniver and other fine furs, amber and hazelnuts, knife blades and swords, trained hunting falcons, and a girl or two to be sold into slavery. Returning west, their cargo will be carnelian beads, color pigments, jewelry and precious stones, exotic spices, silver coins, and all kinds of silk.

In the midst of World War II, with the Nazis extolling their Viking heritage, the Swedish writer Frans G. Bengtsson began writing "a story that people could enjoy reading, like *The Three Musketeers* or the *Odyssey*." Bengtsson had made his literary reputation with the biography of an eighteenth-century king. But for this story he tried a new genre, the historical novel, and a new period of time. His Vikings are common men, smart, witty, and open-minded. "When encountering a Jew who allies with the Vikings and leads them to treasure beyond their dreams, they are duly grateful," notes one critic. "Bengtsson in effect throws the Viking heritage back in the Nazis' face."

His effect on that Viking heritage, however, was not benign. His story, *Rode Orm*, is one of the most-read and most-loved books in Swedish and has been translated into more than twenty languages; in English it's *The Long Ships*. Part of the story takes place on the East Way, which the red-haired Orm travels in a lapstrake ship with twenty-four pairs of oars. Based on the Oseberg ship's fifteen pairs of oars or the Gokstad ship's sixteen, such a mighty vessel would stretch nearly a hundred feet long and weigh sixteen to eighteen tons, empty. To cross the many portages between the Baltic Sea and the Black Sea, Red Orm's "cheerful crew" threw great logs in front of the prow and hauled the boat along these rollers "in exchange for swigs of 'dragging beer,'" Bengtsson wrote.

This, say experimental archaeologists, is "unproven," "improbable," and—after several tries with replica ships—"not possible."

But Bengtsson's fiction burned itself into popular memory. Early scholars were convinced, too: A drawing of dozens of men attempting to roll a mighty ship on loose logs illustrates the eastern voyages in the classic compendium *The Viking* from 1966. "Seldom has anything been surrounded by so much myth and fantasy" as the Viking ship, notes an expert on the boats of Middle Sweden. Like the myth of the Viking housewife with her keys, the myth of the mighty Viking ship is so common it's taken to be true. But the facts do not back it up.

In the 1990s, archaeologists attempted several times to take replica Viking ships between rivers or across isthmuses using the log-rolling method. They failed. They scaled down their ships. They still failed. Their ships were a half to a third the length of Red Orm's mighty ship. They weighed only one to two tons, not sixteen tons. Yet they could not be cheerfully hauled by their crews, no matter how much beer was provided. The task was inefficient even when horses—or wheels or winches or wagons—were added.

We think bigger is better, but it's not.

The beautiful Oseberg ship with its spiral prow and the sleek Gokstad ship, praised as an "ideal form" and "a poem carved in wood," have been considered the classic Viking ships from the time they were first unearthed. Images of these Norwegian ships grace uncountable books on Viking Age history, uncountable museum exhibitions, uncountable souvenirs in Scandinavian gift shops.

But a third ship of equal importance for understanding the Viking Age was discovered in 1898, after Gokstad (1880) and before Oseberg (1903), by a Swedish farmer digging a ditch to dry out a boggy meadow. He axed through the wreck and laid his drain pipes. The landowner, a bit of an antiquarian, decided to rescue the boat and pulled the pieces of old wood out of the ground. His collection founded a local museum, but the boat pieces lay ignored in the attic—unmarked, unnumbered, with no drawings to say how they had lain in the earth when found—until 1980, when a radiocarbon survey of the museum's contents dated them to the eleventh century. Their great age was confirmed by tree-ring data, which found the wood for the boat had been cut before 1070.

In the 1990s, an archaeologist took on the task of puzzling the pieces back into a boat. She had bits of much of the hull: of the keel, the stem and stern and five wide strakes, even some of the wooden rail attached to the gunwale. She had most of the frames, one bite, and two knees. About two feet in the middle of the boat was missing: where the ditch went through. The iron rivets had rusted away, but the rivet holes in the wood were easy to see and, since the distance between them varied, the parts could only go together one way. The wood itself had been flattened by time, but it was still sturdy enough to be soaked in hot water and bent into shape—the same technique the original boatbuilder had used.

When she had solved this 3D jigsaw puzzle, she engaged the National

Maritime Museum in Stockholm to help her mount the pieces on an iron frame; the Viks Boat went on display in 1996. Then she created a replica, *Talja*, and tested it by sailing, rowing, and portaging around Lake Malaren. *Talja* glided up shallow streams, its pliable planks bending and sliding over rocks. With only the power of its crew, it was easily portaged from one watershed to the next, from Lake Malaren to Lake Vanern in the west, itself draining into the Kattegat.

She knew not to use a too-large sail. For an earlier replica of a similar round-bottomed, lapstrake boat, she had borrowed a woolen sail of the kind used for Norwegian Viking ship replicas—and capsized. A smaller, lighter sail of hemp proved a better fit. Cannabis was grown in central Sweden from the seventh century on; according to pollen data, its popularity grew when the use of sails became widespread. Hemp fiber is procured from the cannabis plant in the same way as linen from flax: soaked, slightly rotted, beaten, dried, and spun. The long hemp fibers were twisted into rope, good for rigging. The short fibers were woven into sailcloth. The technology may have come from the East: The word *canvas* comes from the Arabic for "cannabis."

With a suitable sail on her forward-stepped mast, the replica ship *Talja* sailed out of Lake Malaren, up Sweden's coast, and across the Baltic Sea to the Aland Islands of Finland. A second replica, *Fornkare*, was built in 2012 and taken on the East Way from Lake Malaren to Novgorod the first year, then south, by rivers and lakes, some 250 miles through Russia the second year. There the expedition "paused"—as the Vikings would have, to wait out the winter—intending to continue south to Kyiv the next spring, though for unexplained reasons (money? politics?) that didn't happen. Still, *Fornkare*'s captain concludes, "The vessel proved itself capable of traveling this ancient route" from Birka to Byzantium.

It is the Viks Boat on which I've based Hervor's boat in the scene at the beginning of this chapter. It is thirty-one feet long—longer than two earlier replicas that failed the East Way portage test—and about seven feet wide. The Viks Boat replicas passed the portage test for two reasons. First, they were built, like the original, with strakes that were radially split, not sawn. A large oak log—its diameter more than twice the width of each plank—is notched lengthwise with an axe; then wooden wedges are pounded into the crack until the log splits in two. The halves are turned round side up and split again and again until they are as thin as possible, then the strake is shaved with a plane until it is smooth and perfectly even. Unlike sawing a log into planks, tangentially, this radial splitting technique does not cut the wood fibers. The resulting strake is easy to bend and hard to break—at less than half an inch thick. The resulting boat is equally seaworthy at almost half the weight of the same size boat built with the same lapstrake technique, but using sawn boards. Empty, the Viks Boat replicas weigh only half a ton—about as much as a horse.

The second reason the Viks Boat replicas proved adequate for the East Way was that archaeologists had set aside Frans Bengtsson's fantastical log-rolling technique for crossing from stream to stream. By studying the ways the Sami had portaged their light dugout canoes through the waterways of Sweden and Finland throughout history, the archaeologists began to see signs of similar portage-ways around Lake Malaren. They built some themselves and had teams race replica ships through an obstacle course of portage types: smooth grassy paths, log-lined roads or ditches (with the logs aligned in the direction of travel), and bogs layered with branches. A team of two adults and seven seventeen-year-olds finished the winding half-mile course with *Talja* in an hour—including several stops when someone stumbled into stinging nettles or got a cramp or the boat slipped off the logs on a curve. When the portage was straight over four-inch-thick logs sunk into the mud so they didn't shift, the boat raced at 150 feet a minute. As an ethnographer wrote about a journey with a Sami couple in 1939, "the boat got speed over the rollers so it whistled through the bushes."

Along with mighty boats and beer-fueled, rolling-log portages, *The Long Ships* perpetuated another myth about the Vikings' East Way: that no women went on the voyages.

When Red Orm set off on his expedition to the East, writes Bengtsson, his wife and daughters were left at home; they "wept loudly," while the men leaving "were glad at the prospect of adventure." Among these "men" was Orm's young son: "The obstinacy of his desire to go drove Ylva" (Orm's wife) "more than once to weep tears of grief and rage. She asked him what he thought a thirteen-year-old boy could do in a company of full-grown fighting-men." Yet the boy got his way.

His older sister, Ludmilla, stayed home, though clearly Bengtsson had modeled her character on the warrior woman in the *Saga of Hervor*.

Silver coin found in a grave north of the Warriors' Hall in Birka, Sweden.

Ludmilla "disliked working at the butter-churns or on the weaving-stools, preferring to shoot with a bow, at which sport she soon became as skillful as her teacher." She "played truant in the forest." Her "obstinacy and boldness" pleased her father, prompting him to remark, "She will be a difficult filly to tame." But he quickly married her off so a chieftain would agree to accompany him east, and the last we hear, Ludmilla ruled the chieftain's household and enjoyed bossing him around, her archery skills unneeded.

Bengtsson, writing in the 1940s, ascribed to the Victorian ideal: Men had adventures; women stayed home. Archaeologists in the 1990s agreed. The sketches of ships found throughout the Viking world on sticks and boards, or scrawled like graffiti on memorial stones, one archaeologist averred, were "the work of men." Like the cars and planes modern boys doodle in their schoolbooks, ship graffiti depicts "a male field of interest," he said, which prompted him to muse, "One important task for future research is to identify female graffiti, if they exist, and to explain why, if they cannot be found"—though he had an answer in hand: "Probably women were simply too busy."

There is, of course, no way to tell if the hand holding the graffitist's knife was male or female.

But there is ample evidence that Viking women owned and appreciated ships: They wove them into tapestries. They were buried in them.

"According to the myth of the powerful Viking," writes the Viks Boat expert, we ought to find "a well-armed male" in every burial ship. "When men are found in the graves, everything seems to be in order," she writes, "but when women were found in wealthy boat burials, the picture was broken." It did not fit archaeologists' preconceived notions and so was explained away: Since a Viking woman "could not have had any power of her own," archaeologists reasoned, the boat and other precious artifacts found in her grave must instead "reflect the power and wealth of her husband."

Yet as more and more Viking Age burials are excavated or reanalyzed, our picture of the past is evolving. Today, the likelihood of finding "a well-armed male" in a boat burial in Sweden has plummeted. The mightiest boats have women in them. The same is true for a graveyard in Russia. At the same time, in some parts of Sweden the richest men are buried, not in boats, but in wagons or sleighs—long thought to be a feminine way for a Viking to travel.

The preponderance of rich female boat burials in Vastmanland, on the western edge of Lake Malaren, suggests the province had not only rich women merchants, as at Birka, but women rulers as well. Tacitus deplored these neighbors of the Swedes in Roman times. Writing in the first century AD, he noted: "So notoriously do they degenerate not only from a state of liberty, but even below a state of bondage." Their crime? "Here the sovereignty is exercised by a woman." Some of the Viking Age boats in Vastmanland's graves display Sami techniques: a stretched dugout bottom to which strakes were stitched on with sinews or roots. Along with boatbuilding, the people of Vastmanland may have shared other aspects of Sami culture, such as equality of the sexes. To Tacitus, this fact made the Sami "astoundingly savage." He wrote: "The same hunt feeds men and women alike, for the latter are with them everywhere, and seek their share of the kill." In the 1500s, long after the Viking Age, the encyclopedist Olaus Magnus described Sami men and women still hunting together and sharing the kill equally.

When not Sami-style, the burial boats of Middle Sweden, male or female, are much like the Viks Boat: The keel is wide and low, and the boat has a rounded bottom amidships. The burial boats can be larger or smaller than the Viks Boat—one had sixteen pairs of oars, equal to the Oseberg and Gokstad ships. But their shape is entirely unlike these Norwegian burial ships. The beauty of the Gokstad ship, its poetic quality, comes from its curves, the hull swelling out from the gunwale, then closing tightly back in, making a distinctive V-shape down to the deep, straight keel. These concave curves improve the ship's sailing ability at sea. But the keel cuts too deep to float a shallow, stony stream. Over a portage, even the minimal keel of the Viks Boat replicas needed to be protected with an easily replaceable covering of birch, as had been found on the original. The Old Norse name for this false keel was *drag*. To "set a *drag* under someone's pride" was to encourage arrogance.

Historians and archaeologists of the Viking Age have long benefited from an ideological false keel. With the Viks Boat taking its rightful place as an exemplar of the Viking ship, and the number of Viking women buried in boats proving they are not exceptions to some arbitrary rule, it's time to knock off that damaged *drag* and replace it. Says the restorer of the Viks Boat, "We should get used to a completely different picture of the Scandinavian traveling eastward in the Viking Age, one that is far from the traditional image of the male Viking warrior in the prow of a big warship."

The Baltic sailing season was confined by sea ice to the six months between May and October. All winter, goods came in to Birka on the ice roads. Bars of iron and tubs of black pine tar came from the west, dragged across the frozen lake on sledges by reindeer or by horses with ice nails pounded into their hooves; the traders themselves wore iron crampons or ice skates made of polished bone. Furs came from the north, traded for salt and other goods at the Sami winter villages, where the solitary hunters came together for the season. Seal products came from the east, from hunters who haunted the edge of the sea ice, as late winter melted into spring. Seal oil was used to light lamps or, mixed with pigments, to make paint; sealskin was made into shoes, sacks, and sailors' foul-weather gear.

Birka lay at the crossroads of these trade routes, its markets busy all year. And as summer arrived, the Birka merchants' fleets set off along the East Way, in search of silver and silk. Bengtsson's fictional crew, in their unlikely forty-eight-oared ship, numbered about the same as the groups of Rus allowed to enter Constantinople, according to the treaty Oleg negotiated in 907: fifty, with an imperial escort. Given vessels the size of the Viks Boat, fifty Rus would require a fleet of six to eight ships. In June, the weather in Middle Sweden is balmy: seventy degrees and sunny, the meadow flowers blooming, butterflies fluttering, the hay ready to cut, ducks and geese rafting on the glassy surface of the lake, a solitary swan, a sea eagle circling overhead. It was hot, thirsty work rowing even a light, streamlined ship.

According to Adam of Bremen, writing in the 1070s, it took five days to travel from Birka to Russia. But the Viks Boat replica *Fornkare* took sixteen days in 2012, rowing when necessary, sailing continuously by day and by night when the wind held, and making as few landfalls as possible.

The first stage of the voyage, to today's Stockholm, took *Fornkare* one day, rowing half the time. Weaving eighteen miles through a shallow-water maze of islands and peninsulas, the travelers passed the island of Helgo, where the sixth-century bronze Buddha was found. They passed several places now named Ekeby, or Oak Village, where in the Viking Age groves of oaks were protected and allowed to grow tall enough for ship timbers; to make the Viks Boat's strakes took a straight oak tree more than 230 years old.

Traveling that route in the tenth century, Hervor and her crew passed fishing boats casting small nets for roach, whitefish, and perch. They passed farms growing peas, beans, flax, hemp, and oilseed crops. They saw dogs, cats, chickens, pigs, goats, sheep, horses, and cows, which some farmers were ferrying over to a small island to graze on the spring grass, having set loose planking into their thin-shelled boat to give the beasts better footing. Some four thousand small farms, each home to ten people or so, lay scattered about the lake's edges, some solitary, others clustered in small villages: The Malaren valley was the most densely populated part of Sweden in the Viking Age. It was a rich area, and its riches were well protected. The routes leading into the lake were narrowed with pilings and barricaded with poles, as so many modern place-names reflect by incorporating the word *stek* or *stok* or *steg* or *stig*, all cognates of the English *stick*. At Stoksund (Barrier Sound), where the city of Stockholm (Barrier Island) now lies, the lake joined the East (now Baltic) Sea.

Stakes and stockades were not the lake's only protections: On prominent cliff tops along the route were watchfires, pyres ready to be lit if an enemy were sighted. This line of beacons, each within sight of the next, stretched from Birka east, across an arm of the Baltic, to the Kokar hills in the Aland Islands, once the easternmost point in Sweden, 125 miles away. From Kokar, a warning could reach Birka, by beacon, in one night, while the enemy ships were still some two days away.

Each pile barricade, each cliff-top beacon, was likely guarded, as well, by a company of Birka warriors outfitted with horses and Magyar bows, excellent for patrolling the waterways and picking off targets while staying

out of range. It was a challenge to creep up on Birka. Yet, as Snorri Sturluson relates in *Heimskringla*, Vikings loved a challenge.

Snorri calls Malaren "Logrinn," meaning the great lake, or the inland
sea. From all over central Sweden, "the water runs into Logrinn," he writes,
"but it has only one mouth out to the sea, and that outlet is narrower than
many rivers. Thus, when the rain and snow-melt are heavy, the water rises
so high and flows so furiously there are rapids through Stoksund and the
land is flooded all around." A small fleet of Norwegian raiders trapped in
Lake Malaren by the Swedes, who had drawn chains across the strait and
brought an army to its bank, escaped over the flooded fields by lifting their
rudders clear, hoisting their sails to the tops of the masts, and steering with
their oars. When the Swedish warriors sought to bar their passage, the
waterlogged banks of the strait collapsed, Snorri writes, and the warriors
drowned. "But the Swedes say otherwise," he judiciously adds, "and call
it nonsense to think people died there." The Swedes, after all, knew their
straits.

When Hervor set off on the East Way in the 950s or 960s, her convoy would have caught the spring runoff at Stoksund as well, running its
rapids into the Baltic Sea, where a further maze of thirty miles through
islands, skerries, and shoals awaited them off Sweden's east coast. Then
the Birka merchants turned north—for the southerly route to Russia was
controlled by their rivals on the Baltic islands of Gotland and Saaremaa.

19

AT LINDA'S STONE

The waves keep growing. Her ship slows, struggling to sail against the wind. Suddenly a gust spins them side-on to the swell and nearly pitches them over. Hervor, flush as if under attack in battle, is about to yell Strike the sail! when she glances over at her steersman. He is the oldest in her crew of eight, the one whose sea skills she trusts most. He is unconcerned, even though his steering oar is all the way underwater.

Douse the fire! she shouts instead. The cook is making the midday meal, feeding reeds and twigs into the larger cauldron, over which the porridge pot swings on its frame. At Hervor's shout, he slips the small pot off its hook and sets it into the cauldron, where it nests tightly, extinguishing the flames. They'll wait to eat until the sea is calmer.

The waves are a handspan from lapping over the gunwale on one side. Without being told, her crew shifts their weight to rebalance the boat. It bobs over the swells like a duck, its pliable hull undulating under their bare feet, and, once the portside oars can again reach the water, it swivels to catch the wind. The sail bellies out again and the boat darts through the high sea, only a little spray splashing in to wet their faces.

It is truly an exceptional little boat. Any of the big ships Hervor has sailed on, along the North Way or in the Irish Sea, would have sunk if caught crossways like that to the waves, sail up in a storm wind.

But, thanks to the contrary wind, they are no longer heading for the night's harbor they planned, and which she can see ahead, its stone-built cairn a knob on the horizon. All around, she sees the other boats in the Birka convoy adjusting course as well. They are angling farther north, toward Oak Island, instead of toward the main market on Aland. It will take them a bit out of their way, adding a day's journey to their sail to Arrow Sound, but it's unavoidable with this wind.

Hervor hopes the merchant leading their fleet has friends on Oak Island. If not, she and her warriors will find themselves sleeping on board tonight, slumped against the sides of the ship, the sail flung over the yard and pitched with poles to make a tent, porridge again to eat, lookouts waking in shifts. Or, if the Oak Islanders are the merchant's enemies, they'll be raiding that night, not resting. She glances at the spears propped in the boat's stern. Either way, she'll be ready.

Once past Stockholm's barricades and out in the Baltic, if Birka's merchants had been on good terms with the people of Saaremaa, Hervor's convoy might have turned south and entered the Gulf of Riga, which is guarded by this big Estonian island. Saaremaa means "Land of Islands"; its name in Swedish, Osel, derives from its name in the sagas, Eysysla, or "Island District." To the saga writers, it was a nest of sea raiders (and flying dragons).

Saaremaa was where Queen Astrid of Vestfold was sold into slavery. In *Heimskringla*, Astrid sailed east from Sweden with a party of merchants headed for Russia. She was trying to keep her young son out of the clutches of Queen Gunnhild Mother-of-Kings, but instead delivered him to slave-dealers from Saaremaa. "They took the people as well as the trade goods, killing some, but some they kept to divvy up as slaves." Astrid's son, Olaf Tryggvason, the future king of Norway, fell to the lot of a Viking named Klerkon, along with Olaf's old foster father and young foster brother. Klerkon didn't see the old man as much of a prize: "He didn't think he had much hard work left in him, so he killed him." Klerkon took three-year-old Olaf and the older boy to market and traded the pair for "a rather good goat." Olaf's new owner sold the littler boy on (for "a rain cloak") to an Estonian farmer, who treated Olaf well and became very fond of him, the saga says.

The royal slave boy's new family may have farmed on Saaremaa, but the island is heavily forested and its little arable land did not support its large population in the tenth century. The island's economy relied, instead, on raiding and trading—to the extent that another name for Saaremaa was Kuresaar: *Kura* in Estonian means "something wicked, evil." In usage, Kura parallels the words Viking or Rus.

Culturally, too, the three groups blur; already by Hervor's day, they'd been entwined for centuries. The earliest archaeological record of a Viking raid is two lapstrake ships unearthed on Saaremaa between 2008 and 2012. Buried in about 750, the smaller ship was a rowing boat, thirty-eight feet long, fast and narrow and light. The larger one, fifty-five feet long, had a sail, marking the beginning of the design we call the Viking ship.

The smaller ship held the bodies of seven warriors with their weapons, placed rather haphazardly and covered with their shields. The thirty-four warriors in the larger ship, however, were buried in a way that seems to combine the kind of ship burial elsewhere reserved for a Viking leader (as at Oseberg and Gokstad) with the communal graves favored by Estonians. These warriors were stacked three deep inside the ship, each with a sword (or two) and some with game pieces, their layers separated by sand. Their shields and the ship's sail made a roof over their grave, weighted down with stones. The ninety-one arrows found in the ship, some embedded in the wood, seem to show how the warriors died; many of their bones also exhibit battle trauma. Isotope tests tell us the warriors came from Sweden, near Birka; four of them were brothers. One skull—of the war leader?—was found with a *hnefatafl* king piece in the mouth. By his hand was a handsome ring-hilted sword.

Despite the warrior culture they shared with Saaremaa (or because of it), Hervor's convoy from Birka risked ending up like Queen Astrid's merchants or these buried warriors if they chose the southern route east. Without guarantees from Saaremaa's chieftains—obtained via friend-ship, family ties, taxes, or bribes—no one could pass the narrow straits into the Gulf of Riga. They were barred from what later became known as the Great Route East: This route followed the Daugava River past the mighty hillfort of Daugmale. Each of the river's hundred rapids forced the merchants to unload their cargo and portage past the barrier—and pay a toll. After another long portage, they'd reach the Dniepr River a little north of Kyiv. South of the city, the Dniepr offered its own hazards, in the form of rapids and raiding tribes of nomads, before it reached the Black Sea and Byzantium.

The Great Route from the Gulf of Riga was the most popular East Way in the eleventh and twelfth centuries—after Birka had disappeared. In Hervor's time, though, the Great Route was dominated by the Vikings of Saaremaa and their allies on Gotland. Merchants from Birka in the mid-tenth century had to find another way.

That way sent Hervor north along the Swedish coast to Roslagen, home of the Ruotsi, or "rowers," as the Finns named them, then east some twenty-four miles to the main island in the Aland archipelago.

Aland means "Land of Water": Its sixty-five hundred islands include big Aland itself, with its golden beaches and shallow harbors, another three hundred inhabitable isles, including hilly Kokar, where the watch-fires burned, and thousands of rocky islets, skerries, sea stacks, and shoals rising above the waves like the backs of sleeping whales. Aland has bays full of fish and seals, swans and seabirds; hayfields, orchards, and excellent pasturage; and shadowy forests of rowans, hazelnuts, junipers, birches, firs, and pines, home to deer and other game. Locked in by ice through the long, dark winters, the islands are within easy reach of the Swedish coast for capable rowers on a sunny day. To sail there in June can be a pleasure cruise: the Aland Sea glassy smooth, water and sky both vivid blues, the breezes soft and hardly salty. As one sailor said in 2009, "We experienced a substantial stillness."

But the Aland Sea is not always still. In June 2000, the Viks Boat replica *Talja* encountered sudden high winds—what the restorer of the boat termed "an opportunity to study [its] capacity to deal with a very high sea." *Talja* "proved excellent for the purpose," even somewhat over-loaded with a crew of ten. As in the scene I've created at the beginning of this chapter, the Viks Boat replica "was so light that she was floating like a cork on, not in, the waves," which reached ten feet. The boat's freeboard—the distance between the gunwale and the waves—was ten inches. Yet *Talja* was not swamped; the only water taken in was spray.

The wind did require a change in plans. Reaching their intended harbor on Aland proved impossible. Sailing against the wind, *Talja* lost speed, becoming so slow its side-mounted steering oar could not engage the water. The boat swiveled parallel to the waves—a dangerous position. "Then the very worst can happen," writes one Viking ship expert. "The ship can plunge sideways from a wavetop down into the valley in front, and then be filled with water by the wave from which it has fallen." Previous Viking ship replicas in such a fix have sunk.

"This was never a problem for this light boat," wrote *Talja's* builder. The only difficulty was turning the ship to refill the sail, for the oars on one side were completely submerged while the others waggled in the air. Finally the ship caught enough wind to sail to a different inlet, some distance north. After nine hours at sea, *Talja* reached the shallow, sandy harbor at Eckero (Oak Island), where the crew learned two modern fishing boats that day had called for emergency help. Their stiff hulls were in danger of cracking in the rough seas, while *Talja's* lapstrake hull, built of radially split planks, bent and flexed with the waves.

From the Aland Isles, Hervor's convoy continued along Finland's island-studded southwestern coast, with its sheltered bays and narrow sounds, stopping each night at one of the many scattered coastal hamlets. Near deserted in the wintertime, these settlements became busy summer trading posts to which the inland Finns brought, among other things, excellent pottery—thin walled, dark, and smooth—and bronze-handled fire starters, their handles depicting horses and riders.

Archaeologists have found these Finnic pots and fire starters in Birka, along with the characteristic Finnic cloak pin, the terminals of its open ring sporting knobs shaped like the standard weights for weighing hacksilver. Identical scales and weights appear in Birka as in this part of Finland too. The Finns were also paid in coin. Archaeologists often find Arab silver dirhams in tenth-century sites in southwestern Finland; after Birka died, around 975, however, they become scarce. Falcon keys are found in Finland as well, speaking to a trade network connecting the two places.

Family ties likely connected them as well, for the culture of coastal Finland in the tenth century looks, to archaeologists, much more like central Sweden than like Finland's interior. A smart Swede sailing Finland's complicated coast would want a local pilot; a smart trader would arrange for safe harbors on the way. A logical way to do both was to marry into a local family.

Orsund (Arrow Sound) on Hitis is one of the harbors in which Hervor may have spent the night. The island derives its name from the Finns' god of the hunt, Hiisi, and in a holy grove there archaeologists found offerings buried in the sand or set under stones: a sword, a spear, a broken chain, a pin with a bull's head, and a round brooch bound with thread.

There were no jetties: Arrow Sound was a lagoon harbor, where traders simply beached their boats—easy for a round-bottomed Swedish boat—or anchored them offshore, if they were deep-keeled Norwegian ships. Near the shore archaeologists found signs of fortifications and the remains of a workshop: iron ship rivets, a spindle whorl, beads, bits of amber and raw glass, whetstones, and fragments of silver coins. Some of those coins were Arab dirhams.

In the sagas, this part of Finland is called "the watchfire coast" for the beacons lit on rocks and cliff tops to warn of Viking raiders. Those Norwegian marauders nearly trapped in Lake Malaren, Snorri writes in *Heimskringla*, later landed in southwest Finland and raided there, but the locals had been warned. They had "fled into the woods, leaving their houses empty of all valuables." The Vikings "found little loot, and no people at all."

When evening drew on, the raiders turned to go back to their ships. "But as they entered the woods," Snorri writes, "enemies came at them on all sides, shooting at them and attacking hard. The Norwegian king told everyone to take cover and try to fight back if they could. But that wasn't easy, because the Finns used the woods to protect themselves." Like a real-life game of *hnefatafl*, the surrounded Norwegians lost many warriors before the king broke free and reached his ships.

Nor was that the end of their difficulties: "That night the Finns raised a storm at sea and other furious weather by their magic. But the king had the anchors taken up and the sails set, and all night they beat along the coast." The Finns followed their progress along the shore, watchful in case they tried again to land.

Leaving Arrow Sound, Hervor's convoy entered the Gulf of Finland, a 250-mile-long arm of the Baltic, pointing east. The gulf's northern shore offered complicated sailing, through rocks and reefs and shallows. Nor was that part of Finland's coast well populated. Few harbors offered fresh water, firewood, and food or shelter from "furious weather"—which was common, no magic required.

Hardened sailors likely amused themselves telling newcomers like Hervor tales of such terrible storms. One story is preserved in the *Kalevipoeg*, the Estonian national epic, reconstructed from folklore in the 1800s. The hero "was sitting on top of a cliff watching the clouds and waves," the story begins, when "suddenly the sky became overcast, and a terrific storm arose, which lashed the breakers into foam." The Thunder-God was out hunting. "He hurled down flash after flash of lightning from his strong right hand against a company of wicked demons of the air, who plunged from the rocks into the sea, dodged the thunderbolts among the waves, and mocked and insulted the god." The demons he hit littered the shore, burned into "a disgusting mass that even the wolves would not touch."

Wary of meeting such weather without a harbor in sight, Hervor's convoy of Birka merchants crossed the gulf at its narrowest spot, forty-three miles, and headed for Tallinn Bay. The town there was shielded from winds and storms by two jutting peninsulas and two offshore islands, which offered ample room for the crew of a merchant fleet to camp. The harbor was marked by a sheer-sided tableland, its white limestone cliffs rising 150 feet. The Rus called this landmark Rafala, from the Swedish for "cliff"; later it became Toompea, or "Cathedral Hill," in the center of the city of Reval, now Tallinn. In Estonian mythology, the hill was the burial mound of the giant Kalev, erected by his grieving wife, Linda. Perhaps, camped in sight of this striking white cliff, Hervor heard Linda's tale.

It begins when Kalev, the "father of heroes," came to Estonia riding an eagle. He had two brothers: one was a merchant traveling the East Way into Russia, the other a warrior in Finland. Kalev married Linda, who had already rejected marriage proposals from the Sun and the Moon, as well as from the sorcerers of the Waters and the Winds. Kalev and Linda had three sons, but while Linda was still pregnant with the youngest one, Kalev fell sick.

Linda took her round brooch and bound it with a thread—like the thread-wrapped brooch archaeologists found in the holy grove at Hitis. She spun the brooch like a top, sending forth a spirit beetle to ask for help from the Sun and the Moon and the Evening Star and even from the Wind-Sorcerer. But they gave no help. By the time her spirit beetle returned, Kalev the Eagle-Rider was dead.

Linda fasted and wept. She bathed his corpse four times. She brushed his hair and dressed him in silk. "She herself dug his grave thirty ells below the sod" (forty-five feet deep, according to Viking Age measures). She mourned for four months; then "she heaped a cairn of stones over his tomb, which formed the hill on which the Cathedral of Reval now stands." Only then did Linda retire to the house and give birth to her youngest son, the hero of the epic.

As Linda is the shaper of Estonia's landscape, her sons are its fertility gods. One day they went hunting with their dogs, killing bear, elk, wild ox, wolves, foxes, and hares. They hunted in forests of pine, oak, birch, and alder and through fields of rye. They walked on well-trodden paths; they waded through deep sand and mossy bogs. They "sang till the leaves of the trees shone brighter than ever . . . the golden ears of corn swelled, and the apples reddened, the kernels formed in the nuts, the cherries ripened, red berries grew on the hills and blue berries in the marshes." The birds "joined the concert"; the waves beat time on the rocks. When they came home, their mother was gone—the Wind-Sorcerer had stolen her away. The epic follows Kalevipoeg, which means "Kalev's son," as he goes in search of her.

Unbeknownst to the hero, who wanders into adventures but never finds his beloved mother, the Thunder-God had already come to Linda's aid. He turned her into a huge stone and set her on top of Mount Iru, site of the hillfort that guards the rich farming settlements in the river valley a few miles upstream from the harbor at Rafala. From Linda's stone, lookouts on Mount Iru could spot ships as far away as the Finnic archipelago; the beacons they lit would spread the alarm. As at Birka, with a garrison constantly on watch, no one could approach the harbor of Rafala unseen.

Linda's lookout post is not the only prominent stone near Tallinn Bay. More than a hundred house-sized boulders stand nearby, allowing us to locate another folktale. According to Snorri Sturluson's *Heimskringla*, King Sveigdir of Uppsala once swore an oath to find the war god Odin. He sailed far to the east to an estate called At Steini (At the Stone), where, Snorri explains, "There's a stone as big as a house." One evening, as Sveigdir made his way to bed, dead drunk, he looked over at the stone. A "dwarf stood in the doorway and called to Sveigdir, inviting him to come in if he wanted to meet Odin. Sveigdir ran into the stone, and the doorway closed behind him. Sveigdir never came out."

It's probable that no dwarf, no magic, was involved. Another Uppsala king, Yngvar, attacked At Steini in a Viking raid, Snorri tells us. Archaeologists note that the hillfort at Iru was burned down at least four times during the Viking Age, so Yngvar's attack was not unique. Hoards of silver dirhams have been found near Tallinn Bay, and Rafala's slave market was well known. It was at Rafala that Queen Astrid, captured by Vikings from Saaremaa, was put up for sale again and bought by her Norwegian countryman, after she had agreed to marry him. And it was at Rafala that her brother, in service to the king of Gardariki, discovered and freed his young nephew, who would grow up to become Norway's King Olaf Tryggvason.

Like the Shining Hall at Kaupang in Norway, or the royal manor at Adelso near Birka, At Steini housed the chieftain or war leader whose might, at least in the early days, protected the trading post—as King Yngvar of Uppsala learned. When he attacked At Steini in the seventh or eighth century, his forces were overpowered, and he was killed. He was buried under a mound, close by the sea, Snorri writes. A Latin chronicle says his grave lies on Saaremaa. Is he among the thirty-four warriors buried together in their ship and unearthed in 2012? Is he their war leader, with the ring-hilted sword and the *hnefatafl* king piece in his mouth? "One wonders," says a prominent archaeologist.

The myth of Linda reveals something else Hervor might have noticed about Rafala: As at Birka, women were not second class.

Estonian folklore revolves around women, and while its pagan culture was warlike, women were not excluded from that facet of life. In ancient Estonian burials, bodies were buried in communal tombs, marked, as Linda did Kalev's, by cairns, or coverings of stone. The bodies were allowed to rot before burial; then parts of skeletons of all ages and sexes were so intermingled that archaeologists cannot distinguish individuals, much less determine their gender.

The Estonian language makes the same statement. Like all Finnic languages, it uses only one personal pronoun—no she, he, or it, just *tema*. Even today, an Estonian trying to learn Russian or another Indo-European language will stumble over which pronoun to use; says one, "it sounds irrelevant."

Estonia's communal burials held few or no grave goods, but in the middle of the tenth century—Hervor's time—individual burials like those found throughout the Rus world became popular. Yet even in these individual graves, filled with weapons and jewelry and a skeleton capable of being sexed, gender remains irrelevant. Estonian women and men wore identical jewelry—unlike in neighboring lands, where men, though gaudily bedecked, had their own jewelry styles. Likewise, weapons are found in up to 30 percent of female graves in tenth-century Estonia, along with nongendered objects like tools, implying that women had equal access to power.

In Estonian society, power was corporate. It resided not in one individual, but in a council. The power of a single council member was limited—even if that councilor was the king or war leader. A charismatic war leader from a strong clan could persuade and encourage, but the decision to go to war rested with the council.

Nor could the council be co-opted by the men. Property, in Estonian society, was also collective; clan-based, it was passed down through the female line. According to a law recorded in the thirteenth century, when a man marries, "he shall then let all his goods follow his woman. If he wishes to leave her, he will lose arable land and goods." A man joined his wife's family, which made daughters as valuable as sons—or more valuable. In folklore, the mother of an only son is derided as nearly childless. To raise her status, she must bear a daughter.

This clan-based society, where power was shared and women were esteemed, was confusing to the Christians like Snorri Sturluson and Saxo Grammaticus who wrote about it in the thirteenth century. The church disapproved of—and had worked hard to eradicate—such societies for hundreds of years. Man was meant to rule woman, Christianity taught. A single, God-anointed king was meant to rule society. An elected council at which power was shared by men and women was unworkable—if not evil. With whom should a Christian king negotiate? With whom could he make a treaty?

Yet before Christianity conquered the North, it's likely the Estonian way was more common. Throughout the Rus world in Hervor's time, from Birka to Kyiv, a single warrior culture applied. Men and women all along the East Way, on its various routes, no matter their ethnicity, wore the same silk costumes, animal-patterned jewelry, and elaborate belts. They carried the same weapons and sported the same insignia, including the Birka falcon. They buried their dead in similar ways. Would it be surprising if they also shared myths, songs, and values?

20

"GERZKR" CAPS

L and and water merge at the sea's eastern edge. Past Rafala the margins
grow increasingly boggy, impossible to farm, impassable except when
iced over. Few people inhabit these shores, Hervor learns. There are no
friendly harbors for Birka merchants.

They press on, rowing up the wide river Neva, its waters cold and clear,
past reefs and shoals to a great inland sea much larger, even, than their
own Lake Malaren. They skirt the lake's southern shore and row a few
short miles up the Volkhov River, its high banks, hemmed by dark forests,
growing nearer and nearer as the waterway narrows. Hervor watches for
archers among the trees but spots none; nor are they attacked, though
surely they have been seen.

They float a difficult set of rapids, overlooked by the ruined stone walls
of an abandoned hillfort, and reach the Rus town of Ladoga, its earthen
ramparts and wooden stockades an exact match to those at Birka. Here,
where the Low River branches off from the Volkhov, it seems to Hervor,
Birka rises again. She laughs: Has she traveled for days only to return to
her starting point?

It's no accident, her companions say. Ladoga was founded by Birka
merchants. Our people have traded here for generations.

Hervor wonders if the Ladogans would claim, instead, that they were
the ones to found Birka.

The warrior who leads them up to the warehouse is a Birka warrior:

His sword's scabbard is capped by a falcon sword-chape. A horse archer like her friend from Birka's Warriors' Hall, he sports a silk-trimmed kaftan and a Byzantine bronze buckle on his belt. On his head is a tight-fitting, silk *gerzkr* cap like the one she admired in Birka, though its peak bears no silver filigreed spike. Instead, the earflaps of his cap are fastened up with buttons of intricately coiled silver wire.

Passing through the marketplace, her mind on silver cap fittings, Hervor sees numerous examples of fine metalwork. Among the charms in their bead necklaces, the women hang small filigreed crescents, like little moons encrusted with twisted silver wire and sprinkled with silver dots. Merchants bear gilded Finnic cloak pins with faceted heads. A large, portly man in a dark brown kaftan, splendidly finished with twenty-four bronze buttons down its front—Hervor stops to count—wears a large pendant cross with a pattern of dots punched into the silver. He sits in his doorway cracking hazelnuts and glowers at her as she stares. On a rug at his feet fine birch-bark boxes are displayed for sale—but he'll hardly sell any looking at people like that, Hervor thinks.

The windows and doors of the workshops are thrown wide in the fine weather. Peeking in as she passes, she sees a potter making fine jewelry molds out of clay, great lumps of it in a basket at his feet. As she watches, he scores in the tail of a Birka falcon. Farther down the lane, a glassmaker turns a glowing rod over a fire, pinching off glass beads. A leatherworker sews a shoe. A combmaker picks through a pile of antler discards, hoping he's overlooked a usable length. A candlemaker rolls beeswax strips into tall tapers. A pair of weavers, their linen shirts sweated through, pause for a drink of whey before returning to their length of fine ring-woven cloth.

The knife maker, like the horse archer, might have come straight from Birka. Hervor bought a new knife there of an identical design, made from three layers of iron, the blade etched in beautiful patterns, the cutting edge polished steel.

And, as in Birka, the slave-dealers in Ladoga's center display their wares under colorful awnings, the girls well dressed, the boys bare chested and made to flex their muscles as the newcomers walk by. Fur dealers, too, flaunt their offerings, inviting Hervor and her companions to feel the softness of their samples: sable and miniver, fox and otter. Her newly trained eye is surprised to see so much beaver for sale, and at good prices too; in Birka beaver is rare.

But when they reach the compound where they will stay, Hervor's confident sense of familiarity flees. Ladoga's dwellings are like none she's used to. There are two types of houses: large and small. Their walls are mere piles of logs, roughly hewn to connect at the corners. The small houses are square, the large ones oblong, more like a normal longhouse, yet they are all linked together, large and small, in clusters around courtyards, with covered galleries connecting each house to the others.

As Hervor approaches the main house in the compound, intent on the architecture, a small girl dressed as a warrior, with a Magyar bow and closed quiver on her hip, comes rushing out and slams into her.

Out of my way, filthy merchant scum, the girl shouts and, pushing her way past, flees out the door.

A servant slips through the crowd after her. Hervor grabs the woman's arm. Who is that?

The servant shrugs her off angrily. Hervor, the swineherd's bastard, she says, and rushes after the girl.

Hervor is dumbfounded. The other Birka warriors burst out laughing. Yes, says her steersman, that's your namesake. Hervor of Ladoga, daughter of the earl's daughter and whoever herds the pigs in this place.

The city of St. Petersburg, founded in 1703, now occupies the drained swampland at the Gulf of Finland's eastern end, but the Neva is still navigable between the Baltic Sea and Europe's largest lake, Ladoga. In the mid-700s, at the same time Birka was founded, a town protected by a hillfort grew up along a tributary south of the lake. Birka and this town, now known as Staraja Ladoga, or Old Ladoga, had been trading for two hundred years by the time Hervor's convoy of merchants arrived. Scandinavian objects are found in the very deepest archaeological layers of the settlement, while isotope studies of Ladoga burials show that a third of the town's people were born by Lake Malaren.

Ladoga was a major transportation hub on the Vikings' East Way. Several routes lay south and east from the town. From here the Rus merchants described in Arabic texts navigated the Volga River and the Caspian Sea, then traveled by camelback to Baghdad or beyond it on the Silk Roads. Another route led from Ladoga south to Kyiv, then down the Dniepr River to the Black Sea and, across it, to Constantinople. But past

Ladoga, a deep-keeled Norwegian-style Viking ship like the Gokstad ship, seventy-six feet long, carrying eight tons of cargo and thirty-five people—or Frans Bengtsson's fictional longship of even greater size—could neither sail nor row. The Viking ships that opened up the East Way were the light Swedish boats like the Viks Boat, carrying crews of eight to ten and a cargo of up to a ton.

The name Ladoga, first used for the tributary, then the town, then the lake, comes from Alode-joki, Finnic for "Low River." Aldeigjuborg (Low River Fort) is mentioned several times in the Icelandic sagas—not as a destination, only a point of transit. Travelers going east left their ships there in dry dock, transferring their cargo to riverboats or horse-drawn sleds. Those going west waited out the winter there, readying their seagoing ships for when the Baltic ice broke up. Ladoga was the gateway to Gardariki, the Kingdom of Fortresses, from which traders nicknamed Gerzkr brought back "exceptionally fine cloth" and "precious furs," says Snorri Sturluson in *Heimskringla*. Traveling east, these merchants trafficked in humans: On Burnt Island in the Kattegat, Gilli Gerzkr sold the Irish princess Melkorka, who kept her dignity by refusing to speak, to the Icelandic chieftain; the other eleven girls for sale in Gilli's tent may have traveled on to Gardariki.

Like Gilli, several Gerzkr-named merchants in the sagas wear distinctive *gerzkr* hats. Translators call these "Russian hats," and reenactors generally make them out of fur, which is a good guess; but they could also be gaudy silk caps topped with filigreed silver cones, like the one Hervor and another Birka warrior were buried in.

The *Saga of Hervor* is one of the few to set a scene or two in Ladoga itself. The story begins in Estonia, where the king of Ladoga seized two dwarfs before they could slip inside their house-sized stone. To ransom their lives the dwarfs were forced to make the king a sword "that would never rust. It was to cut iron and stone as easily as cloth, and bring its bearer victory in all battles and duels." This was the famous Flaming Sword, Tyrfing, which Hervor later took from her father's grave on the isle of Samsey.

When he grew old, the king of Ladoga gave the sword Tyrfing—and his daughter—to the Swedish warrior who captained his garrison. (Another version of the saga says the warrior stole the sword and ran off with the princess.) The pair set up house in Sweden and had twelve sons. The eldest, Angantyr, returned to Ladoga to marry Svava, the daughter of the earl who then ruled the town. After the wedding feast, Angantyr left her, pregnant, to go fight and die on Samsey.

The widowed Svava gave birth to a beautiful girl, the saga says, and named her Hervor, "Aware of Battle." The girl grew up in the earl's household and became "as strong as a man." She was also as strong willed as a man, as we have seen: "As soon as she was able, she practised more with a bow and a sword and shield than at sewing or embroidery," even though, the saga adds, "she did more harm than good."

Perhaps, like the hero Arrow-Odd, she left her arrows lying around on the benches for people to sit on in the dark, or, like the hero Egil the Poet, she murdered her opponents in the ball games. Was she as annoying as the hero Grettir, who broke the wings of his family's geese, I wonder, or the hero Olaf, who saddled a billy goat when asked to ready his foster father's horse? "One time, when Hervor was outside," the saga says, "she was standing near some slaves; she was abusive to them, as she was to everyone." One of them—no deferring servant this—lashed back at her: "It's only to be expected that you would behave so badly. That's why the earl forbids us to mention your father. He's ashamed for you to know that the lowest of his slaves lay with his daughter and you are their child."

Outraged, Hervor confronted the earl, who said the rumor was wrong. Her father was not the swineherd; he was a Viking raider, a hero held in high esteem. He had died in battle and was buried with his brothers on the isle of Samsey.

Instantly Hervor decided to seek out their grave and retrieve the treasure buried with them. She told her mother, "Prepare for me, as quickly as you can, everything you would give to a son." Then, "taking a warrior's gear and weapons, she went alone to a place where there were some Vikings." She joined their band, calling herself by the masculine name Hervard. "After a little while," the saga says, "this Hervard became the leader of the band."

Our Hervor is not this Hervard-Hervor. Her bones say the warrior woman buried in Birka grave Bj581 grew up in the west of the Viking world, not here in Ladoga, in the east. It's unlikely they met each other, either, as in the scene I've imagined at the beginning of this chapter. But the archaeological and the literary sources inform each other. The saga brings the skeleton to imaginative life; the burial gives a foundation of reality to the tale: There were warrior women in the Viking Age. They did carry "a warrior's gear and weapons." They did become the captains of their bands.

In addition to proving the saga is not fantasy—though it may be fiction—archaeology can reconstruct the town where the saga's Hervor grew up, even depicting for us the house in which she was rebuked by the enslaved woman.

The small, square buildings archaeologists have unearthed in Ladoga, built out of horizontal logs with dovetailed corners like log cabins, are a classic Slavic style of house. They generally have only one room, about ten feet square, with the hearth in one corner. Some have attached porches. Objects found inside them show that some of these small houses were used as workshops, others as dwellings.

Ladoga's larger, more oblong houses, though also built log-cabin-style, incorporate Swedish architectural features. They have central long-fires and broad sleeping benches along the side walls. Their roofs are held up by rows of internal posts, and they have wooden floors. Most have a storeroom attached. The biggest of these Swedish-style houses were built as a house within a house: The longhouse, with its longfire and benches, was surrounded on three sides by a covered gallery; on the fourth side a long storeroom was attached. These big houses were often surrounded by a group of the small square houses; each cluster may have been the compound of a different trading company.

The largest of the big houses, set a bit apart from the others, was built just before 900 using wood from a dismantled ship, then rebuilt, bigger, in the 930s. It might have been the earl's hall, where the Hervor in the saga grew up; some archaeologists call it "the prince's palace." More than eighteen hundred square feet in size, it housed ten to twenty people. Lost or discarded within it, for archaeologists to find a thousand years later, were weights from a trader's scales, spindle whorls, combs, game pieces, beads and bits of amber, broken glass drinking cups and pottery, an iron Thor's hammer, and a gold finger ring. Whoever lived there was quite well-off.

Like Birka, Ladoga was home to many religions and ethnic groups. Its graveyards include high, conical mounds with many people buried together; low, round individual barrows; and wood-lined chamber graves. Some of its people were cremated, others buried whole, with extensive grave goods or without any.

Many of Ladoga's residents were artisans, like those in Birka, and shared common practices: The method of making knives in Ladoga, from a sandwich of different kinds of iron, for example, was a Swedish technique, not known elsewhere in Eastern Europe before 900.

Like Birka, Ladoga drew visitors from the cold, coniferous taiga region to the north. Lured by the market's jewelry, weapons, tools, cloth, and pots, they paid with high-quality furs. From the south, visitors seeking fur and weapons paid in silver: Archaeologists estimate that 90 to 95 percent of all Arab silver dirhams found in Sweden passed through Ladoga.

Both townspeople and visitors were guaranteed a fair market by Ladoga's warriors, who mirror those of Birka: A tenth-century chamber grave in Ladoga held a warrior (thought to be a man) buried like the woman in Birka grave Bj581—though not quite so richly. With him in his grave were two horses, riding tack, arrowheads, a knife, a bucket, a bone pin, and a Byzantine bronze buckle—but no sword, spears, shields, or scramasax. A falcon sword-chape was found elsewhere in Ladoga.

While only three spears and no swords have been unearthed so far in the town (nothing like the abundance of weapons found in Birka), it's clear that Ladoga, too, was a martial society. A rune stick with an inscription of fifty-two runes, written in the short-twig Swedish style, seems to praise a dead warrior (though some scholars read the runes as a description of an arrow or a shield, and still others say it's a magical inscription, invoking the aid of an elf). Finally, lending more credence to the *Saga of Hervor*, archaeologists found seven wooden practice swords or toys in the town—implying children were trained in martial arts.

At Ladoga, lapstrake Viking ships were repaired—near the waterfront archaeologists found a smithy that made iron rivets. But shipwrights were also busy making local boats, to sell or rent to travelers arriving in deep-keeled Norwegian ships unsuitable for the shallow Russian rivers.

The Russian *chëln* was an expanded dugout canoe, similar to those the Sami used in Lake Malaren. Keelless and double-ended like a modern canoe, and steered with a paddle at each end, they were very light and maneuverable boats. Empty, a thirty-foot *chëln* could weigh half as much as the oak Viks Boat of the same length, but it could seat the same number of rowers and carry the same amount of cargo.

Adopting the local boats may have simplified the traders' logistics. The route south from Ladoga to the Black Sea was well mapped by the

time Hervor arrived in the mid-tenth century, and the land was called
Gardariki, or Kingdom of Fortresses, for good reason. With no roads
through the dense forests, trade followed the rivers. Where rapids were
impassable, or the route crossed between watersheds, there were portage
paths guarded by warriors and staffed by porters. For their use, merchants
paid a toll to the Rus captain in the nearby hillfort. Possibly only the load
was carried. Boats suitable for each river, or for each stretch of a river,
might have been provided as well. A perk of belonging to a Rus merchant company in the tenth century, it seems, was gaining access to such
services—for a price, of course.

For that price the Rus also, in theory, promised peace along the waterways. They did so by suppressing the surrounding population of Slavic
farmers and fur trappers, forcing them to pay a tribute of one squirrel skin
and one rabbit skin per hearth. In the 860s, the Slavs of Gardariki rose in
rebellion, says the *Russian Primary Chronicle*. Refusing to pay tribute, they
drove the Rus warbands "back beyond the sea" and began to rule themselves. The attempt failed; the region fell into chaos. "One clan fought another, and they warred and captured, and there was endless bloodshed."
Ladoga was burned to the ground. It was soon rebuilt, with the same mix
of house styles, most likely by the very same people. But the conflagra-
tion marks the time of the Slavic rebellion and the subsequent founding—
according to this tradition, at least—of the Russian state.

After years of war, reports the chronicle, the Slavs held an assembly:
"Let us seek a prince who may rule over us and judge us according to
the law." They sent envoys west to the Rus—whom the chronicler explains
were not Swedes, Norwegians, English, or Gotlanders—to recruit three
brothers, Rurik, Sineus, and Truvor. They brought their families and warbands and took control of three fortress towns along the trade routes.

Generations of scholars—and demagogues—have argued that Rurik
and his brothers were Scandinavian or German Vikings and that, as one
haughty German opined in the eighteenth century, "Wild, boorish, and
isolated Slavs began to be socially acceptable only thanks to the Germans,
whose mission, decreed by fate, was to sow the first seeds of civilization
among them."

Yet the trade routes through Slavic lands to Byzantium, Baghdad, and
beyond were traveled long before Rurik arrived. Some hillforts and portages were then a hundred years old; other towns, like Kyiv, were much

older. The Rus were merely the next wave of warriors seeking control over the long-standing exchange of northern furs for southern silks.

Nor were the Rus a race: The distinguishing trait of every Rus town is its mix of peoples. Rus, like Viking, was an occupation, a way of life, not a nation or ethnic group. It's more likely the three brothers were Slavic, or half-Slavic, than Scandinavian or German. Sineus is Slavic for "Bluebeard"; Truvor means "Hornblower." Rurik has no apparent Slavic meaning, but in one source he goes by the Slavic name Yeryek. The Rus, of course, included Slavs in their multiethnic mix. There's no contradiction in Rurik being both Slavic and Rus—and a Viking.

Rurik's fortress, now called Gorodishche, or Little Fortress, lies a few miles upstream from the town of Novgorod (New Fortress), known in the sagas as Holmgard, or Island Fortress. Founded in about 930, Holmgard would become the seat of Queen Allogia, under whose protection the young Olaf Tryggvason, redeemed from slavery, learned to be a king. Novgorod was famous for law and order: Killings were punishable by death. One day while he was wandering in the marketplace, nine-year-old Olaf met the man who had enslaved him—and who had killed Olaf's foster father for being too old to be a useful worker. "Olaf had a little axe in his hand," writes Snorri in *Heimskringla*. "He hit Klerkon in the head, so the axe sank into his brain." Olaf outran the immediate hue and cry, and his uncle took him to the queen.

Queen Allogia ruled Novgorod alongside her husband, King Valdamar (or Vladimir), and it was their custom, Snorri writes, that "the queen should keep half of the warband, providing for the warriors at her own expense, and assessing whatever taxes and tribute she needed to cover it." Queen Allogia's "warband was no smaller than the king's, and they were often in competition for the best warriors." The queen took a liking to the courageous boy. When she learned he was a king's son in exile, she paid blood money for the killing and kept Olaf by her side—until he turned a handsome eighteen and slanderers wondered aloud "what he and the queen were always talking about together." Then she sent Olaf away to become, after many adventures, king of Norway in 995.

In Hervor's day, Novgorod was still a rough frontier town. To reach it from Ladoga, Hervor's convoy of Birka merchants in their riverboats and canoes rowed 130-some miles up the Volkhov River and crossed shallow Lake Ilmen. At the lake's southern end the river braided through a maze

The filigreed silver cone found next to the skull in Birka grave Bj581.

of islands. On one stood the town, on another Rurik's fortress, their situation memorably described by the Persian geographer Ibn Rustah in 903, after his visit to the Rus: "The island where they live takes three days to walk across and is covered with forests and wetlands, unhealthy and so waterlogged that if a man only steps on the soil, it quivers." In Novgorod, archaeologists have noted, all the streets were boardwalks.

Once the soil iced up, however, it made a good sledge road. For the next segment of the journey, south of Holmgard, it was better for the Birka convoy to wait until winter. Gnezdovo, their destination, was three hundred miles south, near the modern city of Smolensk. Though the Lovat River flowed from the right general direction, it was not easy navigating upstream. Journeying by boat, the traders could expect a month of constant unpacking and repacking, and an extra-long portage near the end, crossing from the river's headwaters into the next watershed. With horse-drawn sledges over ice and snow, the trip could be accomplished in half the time. Again, it was a perk of a Rus merchant company to easily trade boats for horse transport and to know new boats awaited at Gnezdovo, for sailing down the Dniepr River to Kyiv.

Gnezdovo, though it's gone now, was a crowded and powerful town in the tenth century. With its hillfort and garrison of warriors—some displaying the Birka warrior's falcon sword-chape—its busy workshops and bustling river harbor, its apparent disdain for agriculture, its litter of lost (or hoarded) Arab and Byzantine coins, its waterlogged wooden houses and muddy streets, and its Swedish welded-steel blades, Gnezdovo was a twin to the other Rus towns Hervor had visited. Like them, it was a travelers' service station.

Its vast graveyards, now hidden beneath dense pine forests and tall grass, present an eclectic mix of Slavic, Baltic, Swedish, Byzantine, Magyar, and Khazar costumes and rites. Archaeologists have found warriors buried with arrows, spears, swords, and horses. They've found couples cremated in lapstrake Viking-style boats. And they found a fabulously rich woman buried with a birch-bark box in which were folded a blue linen dress, a silk shawl, and two luxurious Chinese silk dresses, one light brown, the other a warm orange-red with a dramatic pattern of a griffin and dragon worked out in gold threads.

A jeweler in Gnezdovo, not in Kyiv, may have made the fancy silver cone for the top of Hervor's silk *gerzkr* cap. Its filigree technique is typically Slavic, and Gnezdovo is well known to Viking Age archaeologists for its many crescent-moon-shaped lunula pendants, made of sheet metal and decorated with the same filigree-work.

Hervor's cone, too, was made of sheet metal, in this case a sheet of silver, cut, curled, and soldered into a cone two and a half inches tall. Its flared bottom was snipped into four deep, rounded lobes, each with a hole punched for sewing it onto the cap. Its pointed top was embellished with a knob. Then came the filigree work: The knob is encrusted with diamond patterns made up of tiny silver dots. On each of the cone's four sides, silver wires surround twenty-two nested Vs of dots. More dots edge the wires and circle the sewing holes. It's a rigidly geometric design—not at all like the looping, dizzying interlace of most Viking jewelry—but still dazzling in its complexity. Shining in the sun, it must have sparkled like a dewy spider's web.

21

QUEEN OLGA'S REVENGE

She sewed it to the peak of her silk *gerzkr* cap as soon as she returned to her lodgings, and this morning she expected to turn heads. But instead of staying another day in Gnezdovo, they caught a fair wind and are now sailing down the Deep River, wide and smooth and pleasant on a fine spring day, and there is no one to notice her headgear but her own few shipmates. They barely give her a raised eyebrow before the weather grows too warm to wear any hat at all.

Stripped to their linen shirts and trousers, she and her crew sail day and night and sleep by turns. It is the easiest stage of their voyage since they left Lake Malaren, with wind and current both speeding them along.

Before she knows it, they've turned a bend in the river, and there, where a stream flows in from the west and the ferries make their crossing, she sees a fortress on a hilltop shining high above a town: King's Fort, or Kyiv.

They round the tip of a great sand spit and row into the well-protected harbor, beaching their boats before a busy trading town backed by a forested bluff. The fortifications that circle Kyiv's hilltops, though built in the same style as those at Birka, with earthen ramparts and a wooden stockade topped by guard towers, dwarf any she has ever seen before.

In cap and kaftan, to make an impression, and fully armed, Hervor leads her crew up the long, tree-lined road through the town toward the massive fortress. She tries not to look like a newcomer. She notes the buildings' straw-thatched roofs—a fire hazard, she thinks, though the houses are rather far apart and their yards are large. Each one seems to contain a turf-roofed sauna and a tall dovecote.

The air is filled with a constant humming and buzzing, now loud, now soft. She tries not to crane her neck to find the source of the noise. Finally she locates it: In the kitchen garden of a simple house sits a strange wooden box, riddled with holes through which bees swarm in and out. Honey and wax will be cheap in Kyiv's market, she reckons, if ordinary housewives keep bees like chickens. And the mead will flow freely in the hall.

A shout draws her attention back to the road. Her steersman shoves her into a doorway just in time to keep them both from getting jostled by a great herd of pigs being chased by a boy and a dog down the lane. Once she has dusted herself off, Hervor lingers a bit longer in the doorway— from deep within the house comes the sweet sound of an eight-stringed lute and a set of panpipes.

At the main gate of the fortress they are met—as Hervor has come to expect by now—by a Birka warrior, with a falcon sword-chape on the tip of his sword's scabbard. And here, at last, her *gerzkr* cap with its silver fili- greed cone gets an appreciative glance—the same she gives to his Magyar closed quiver, its bronze lid beautifully decorated with a floral motif.

Escorting them past a temple and several sizable wooden houses to their lodgings within the garrison, the warrior politely asks Hervor where she comes from.

Birka, most recently, she replies. Before that Dublin, Orkney, York, Kaupang—you could say I've been around.

Queen Olga will want to speak with you of your travels, he says.

The queen's palace is the great wooden house at the crest of the hill, it- self walled within the fortress's walls, and surrounded by burial mounds— one of which, the warrior points out, contains the twenty noble Derevlians who were buried alive in revenge for the murder of Olga's husband, King Igor.

He says it nonchalantly, as if sure Hervor knows the story. Only her warrior training keeps the shock from showing on her face. Inwardly she thanks him for alerting her to the character of the queen she is about to meet. Queen Olga and Queen Gunnhild would make excellent allies, she thinks—if not deadly enemies instead. And each would, no doubt, be grat- ified to know of the other's existence as a ruling queen in a Viking king- dom. Hervor certainly has a tale she can tell to the queen of Gardariki.

Her opportunity comes a few days later, when she is among the Birka merchants invited to the palace for an archery demonstration. The archers ride from one end of the small courtyard to the other at full gallop, shooting at targets to left and right, above and below, and if any of them miss what they are aiming at, she doesn't notice it. Then the whole troop attacks an army of straw dummies, circling them like a whirlwind, shooting constantly—Hervor swears some of them are shooting an arrow from each finger. It is a marvelous display.

As their leader approaches the queen's viewing stand, Hervor leaps in front of him. Where did you learn that? she cries. Can you teach me? Can I join you?

Let me guess, he says. You're the Dubliner my mother wants to speak with?

She should have recognized him: It's Prince Sviatoslav. But he is so ordinary looking to have such a reputation for bravery and daring— though he does, as they say, step light as a leopard. He is an inch or two shorter than she and has shaved his head, all but one long lock that hangs down on one side. He has bristly eyebrows over bright gray eyes, a snub nose, and splendid long mustaches. In one ear he wears a gold hoop, set with jewels.

I'll take you to her, he offers with a grin.

The queen is taller and more substantial than her son, with extremely broad shoulders. She wears a long-sleeved green dress, decorated with bands of silk thickly embroidered with gold thread. A light cloak lined in golden silk is tossed over her shoulders; a silk band studded with gold ornaments holds back her braided hair; a necklace of beads and golden discs lies like a bright collar around her neck. The wide belt at her waist is cinched with a gilded bronze buckle shaped like a griffin, and from it hangs a small bag of dark leather with silver edgings. On the bag's flap is a cross intricately worked in silver filigree.

Here's the Dubliner, Mother, Sviatoslav says. She's joining my warband.

Queen Olga glances at him, then turns back to Hervor. She can't, she says. She shoots with her fingers, not her thumb. Look at her hands. Really, Son, you need to learn to look before you act.

Queen Olga had obviously examined Hervor as carefully as Hervor examined her.

I can learn, Hervor insists.

I'm sure you can. And when you do, then you can apply to join my son's warband. Now, come with me into the palace and tell me about Dublin and the West. Who was your father?

I never knew my father, Hervor answers. I was raised by Queen Gunnhild Mother-of-Kings. Let me tell you about her.

Exotic and eye-catching in Birka, outlandish in Kaupang, Dublin, or York, Hervor's silver-spiked silk *gerzkr* cap would not have drawn much attention in cosmopolitan Kyiv.

As big as York—some eight to fifteen thousand people—Kyiv was first settled in the 600s by the Khazars, whose name derives from "wanderer." Nomads who dominated a vast territory of forests and steppes from Kyiv east into the Caucasus, the Khazars then dominated every route that later became known as the Vikings' East Way. Known for their horses, their wine, their wax and honey, the silver or bronze ornaments on their belts, their kaftans and balloon-legged trousers, and the silks, spices, pigments, precious stones, incense, and perfumes traded through their territory from the Silk Roads, the Khazars had, by the 900s, given up their shamanistic religion (their totem ancestor being the wolf) and become, variously, Muslim, Christian, and Jewish.

Their King Joseph was Jewish and carried on a correspondence with Hasdai Ibn Shaprut, the Jewish vizier of the caliph of Islamic Spain. As King Joseph wrote in about 950:

I live at the mouth of the Volga River, and with God's help I guard its entrance and prevent the Rus who arrive in ships from entering into the Caspian Sea for the purpose of making their way to the Muslims. . . . Were I to let them pass through even one time, they would destroy the whole land of the Muslims as far as Baghdad.

Like the Rus, the Khazars were not only multireligious; they were multiethnic. One Arab traveler described them as having black hair. Another found them to be fair-skinned and blue-eyed, with reddish hair. To the Rus, what was of most interest were their weapons. The Khazars fought with morning stars: heavy balls of iron, bronze, lead, bone, or stone attached by a chain or leather strap to a long handle. Some of the balls were round, some oblong, some spiked. The Khazars fought, as well, with two-headed axes: These had a long, narrow blade on one side and a hammer, a second blade, or a spike on the other. They fought with straight, single-edged broadswords and with sabers: curved and single-edged until the tip, which was sharp on both sides.

None of these weapons was apparently the equal of the Vikings' two-edged swords. Before he died in 1030, Persian writer Miskawayh wrote about a Rus raid on the shores of the Caspian Sea in 943. After the Rus victors had buried their dead and left, he said, "the Muslims dug up the graves and found a number of swords, which are in great demand to this day for their sharpness and excellence."

By the time Hervor reached Kyiv, Khazaria had shrunk and its westernmost lands had been taken over, first by the Magyars, with their excellent horn bows, and then by the Rus, who were harassed themselves by a new nomadic tribe moving in from the east, the Pechenegs, from whom the Rus bought horses, cattle, and sheep, and with whom they contested for the rights to tribute along the Dniepr, or Deep River, south to the Black Sea and the silk sellers of Constantinople.

Kyiv, in the Turkic language spoken by the Khazars, means "the settlement on the river bank." The Rus knew it as Konugard, or King's Fort. It lay at the confluence of the Dniepr and a tributary stream, the Pochaina (now under the city), and was backed by a steep escarpment, on top of which sat a small fortress. In about the year 900, the fortress began to grow; by 950 it was enormous. But it and the houses it protected were still built out of wood. Not until the time of Queen Allogia did the Kyivans begin building with stone and decorating their stone churches and palaces with frescoes, carved marble, and slate tiles. In Hervor's day, Kyiv looked like a much bigger Birka.

The similarity was more than coincidental: Birka warriors were members of Kyiv's garrison at the time, as I've suggested in the scene at the beginning of this chapter. Sometime before 950, a warrior about two inches taller than Hervor, at five foot nine, was buried beside Kyiv's fortress in a chamber grave very much like Bj581 in Birka. When archaeologists unearthed this warrior—he is assumed to be male—in the 1970s, they found him lying on a leather-covered wooden bier. His belt was buckled with a Byzantine bronze griffin; his kaftan or cap was decorated with silver filigreed buttons. His leather purse held four Byzantine copper coins, the oldest from 867, the youngest minted in 920. Beside him were the remains of a Magyar bow and twenty-six arrows in a closed quiver, its lid decorated with a bronze floral motif. His sword, in its wood-and-leather scabbard, lay at his hip. At the tip of the scabbard was a falcon sword-chape identical to those found at Birka.

When Hervor visited, Queen Olga had ruled Kyiv for about ten years; her son would take control around 957. Olga (in Swedish, Helga) had been widowed in 945 when her husband, King Igor (or Ingvar), let his greed outweigh his battle sense.

It was Igor who watched his warriors writhe and twist and leap overboard to drown, while simultaneously burning to death, when his ships were set alight by unquenchable Greek fire. It was Igor who made a pact with his enemies, the nomadic Pechenegs, and returned to Constantinople for revenge—earning significant trade concessions from the Byzantine emperor, including the right to buy five times as much silk as anyone else.

Igor funded his wars by exacting tribute from the Slavic tribes that lived in the vicinity of Kyiv, including the Derevlians. Returning from one tax-collecting trip, Igor made the mistake of sending his main force home with the loot—furs, mostly, but also honey, wax, and mead. King Igor took only a few Rus warriors with him to the town of Iskorosten, intending to collect an additional tax, and the Derevlians in the city slaughtered him.

Too late did they ponder the repercussions of killing the Rus king. "So they sent their best men, twenty in number, to Olga by boat," says the *Russian Primary Chronicle*. She welcomed them and inquired politely "as to the reason of their coming." They formally took responsibility for the killing of her husband and offered her blood money. They invited her to marry their own prince instead.

Olga, who is always presented in the chronicle in a courtly manner, replied, "Your proposal is pleasing to me; indeed, my husband cannot rise again from the dead." She said she would consider the matter, and told them to send word to Iskorosten to increase the size of their embassy, so she would know they were serious about their offer.

The first ambassadors should return to their ship, Olga said, for she wished to honor them in an appropriate way. "I shall send for you on the morrow," she told them, "and you shall say, 'We will not ride on horses nor go on foot; carry us in our boat.' And you shall be carried in your boat."

That night, she had a great pit dug in the center of Kyiv's fortress. In the morning, the Derevlians arrived, in their boat, sitting on the thwarts "in great robes, puffed up with pride." Olga's people ceremoniously carried the boat to the pit and dropped it in. Olga walked to the edge of the pit. She "bent over and inquired whether they found the honor to be to their taste," records the chronicle. Despite the Derevlians' screams for mercy, she "commanded that they should be buried alive," in a parody of a royal Viking ship burial.

Somehow their fate remained a secret, and when the Derevlians' second delegation came to Kyiv, they did not question Olga's courteous offer to refresh themselves before dinner by bathing in the royal sauna. Olga sealed it and set it on fire.

She sent word to the people of Iskorosten: "I am now coming to you, so prepare great quantities of mead in the city where you killed my husband, that I may weep over his grave and hold a funeral feast for him." Weep she did, feast she did, and "when the Derevlians were drunk, she bade her followers fall upon them, and went about herself egging on her retinue."

Then Olga went to war. Returning to Kyiv, she gathered an army and attacked the Derevlian lands.

Queen Olga was not, herself, a shield-maid. Her army was led, ostensibly, by her little son, Sviatoslav, who cast the first spear. Though it "barely cleared the horse's ears," his captain cried out: "The prince has already begun battle; press on, vassals, after the prince."

Olga's army routed the Derevlian troops and ravaged the Derevlian lands until only Iskorosten remained unconquered. She besieged the city for a year, says the chronicle, without success, until Olga "thought out this plan. She sent into the town the following message: 'Why do you persist in holding out? All your cities have now surrendered to me and submitted to tribute, so that the inhabitants now cultivate their fields and their lands in peace. But you had rather die of hunger.'"

The Derevlians asked what tribute was required to buy peace. Olga scoffed. A city under siege could not be expected to have honey or furs at hand. She would accept a mere token: three pigeons and three sparrows per house. The townspeople agreed. They captured the required number of birds (it's surprising they had not yet eaten them) and turned them over. "Olga gave to each soldier in her army a pigeon or sparrow, and ordered them to attach by a thread . . . a piece of sulfur bound with small pieces of cloth." When night fell, the birds were released to fly home to their nests, and the army's fire arrows ignited the whole town. "Thus the dovecotes, the coops, the porches, and the haymows were set on fire. There was not a house that was not consumed, and it was impossible to extinguish the flames, because all the houses caught fire at once. The people fled from the city, and Olga ordered her soldiers to catch them." Some she killed; some she enslaved; the rest she left to pay tribute. Olga may not have been a shield-maid, but she was certainly a war leader—and a ruthless one.

The *Russian Primary Chronicle* is not a history book in the modern sense. It is a "tale of bygone years," according to its subtitle. Like an Icelandic saga, it was written down in the twelfth to fourteenth centuries, hundreds of years after the fact, and mingles truth with fiction, history with fantasy. Generations of scholars have pointed out that the "incendiary bird" motif is a common one. Snorri Sturluson credits a future king of Norway with just such a strategy in Sicily, where he fought as a mercenary; Saxo Grammaticus says the Vikings played a similar trick on Dublin. Each writer took the motif from a folktale, historians assume; so, by extension, Queen Olga's revenge is labeled "picturesque" and "largely legendary." In fact, to one translator of the chronicle, Olga's entire reign consists of "empty years": Faced with "scanty data," the chroniclers filled their pages with "tradition."

We have long underestimated the queen of Gardariki. According to a modern archaeologist, "Even such a fabulous description as Olga's attack on Iskorosten, the city of the Derevlians, contains a core of historical truth." Excavations in Iskorosten, the oldest part of modern Korosten, have revealed that a rich hillfort, littered with Scandinavian, Byzantine, and Slavic objects, was indeed burned down in Olga's days.

Like Queen Asa in Norway's Vestfold, Queen Olga ruled her kingdom until her son Sviatoslav came of age, at least ten years later. Like the sons of Gunnhild Mother-of-Kings, Sviatoslav valued his mother's advice and kept her by his side, deferring to most of her wishes until her death in 969, for she was known to be wise and politically astute.

The chronicle gives several examples of her intelligence and ability to rule. Queen Olga marked her boundaries and established fortified towns throughout her newly conquered province. She moved its political center from ruined Iskorosten to the hill town of Ovruc and began industrial-scale quarrying of the schist found there; spindle whorls of this light red stone became very popular in late-tenth-century Sweden. Olga sectioned off hunting grounds and honeying grounds, beekeeping being a particular Derevlian specialty, and controlled access to them. She established marketplaces and trading posts, set new levels of taxes and tributes, and standardized the laws.

Her influence was long lasting: As the chronicle's medieval author noted several hundred years later, "Her hunting-grounds, boundary posts, towns, and trading posts still exist throughout the whole region."

Sometime between 946 and 957—the date is disputed—Queen Olga visited Constantinople. The *Russian Primary Chronicle* provides the fullest account, but her visit is also described by the Byzantine emperor Constantine VII, who charts the rigors of the trip.

Thirty miles past Kyiv, the Dniepr River (before it was dammed in modern times) cut through crystalline cliffs and seethed around slabs of stone. "There are sheer high rocks, which look like islands; when the water reaches them and dashes against them it causes a loud and terrifying tumult as it crashes down," wrote the emperor.

The next forty-five-mile stretch was a nightmare of whitewater. Seven or nine or twelve rapids are listed in various sources. Seven have Swedish names. Translated, they mean Racer, Laughing, Steep Cliff Falls, Ever Dangerous, Roaring, Island Falls, and Don't Sleep. Along the banks of these rapids, Viking objects have been found, lost by accident or left as sacrifices, including a tenth-century bronze pin decorated in the Borre style, several Viking swords, and a runestone bearing two Vikings' names.

Traders from Birka and elsewhere would wait until June to brave the rapids, when the water was high but not rushing with spring runoff. In the right boats, some of the rapids could be run. Others were mandatory portages. The Rus, wrote the emperor,

lay their boats alongside the bank before this point and make the people go up on shore, though they leave the cargo on board. Then they walk into the water naked, testing the bottom with their feet so as not to stumble over stones; at the same time they thrust the boat forward with poles, many of them at the bows, many amidships, and others at the stern. With all these precautions they wade through the edge of these first rapids, close along the bank; as soon as they have passed them, they take the rest of the crew back on board, and go on their way by boat.

Nor were the rocks the only hazard of these portages. Among the people put ashore, he points out, were "all those who are appointed to keep watch. Ashore they go, and unsleeping they keep sentry against the Pechenegs."

When Queen Olga reached Constantinople after this harrowing journey, the emperor treated her like a head of state. According to his own account, Olga only "nodded her head slightly" upon meeting him, whereas her companions were expected to prostrate themselves full length upon the ground.

Olga was then invited to share dessert with the emperor. While there's no record of her impressions, his extravagant banquet hall and after-dinner entertainments must have astonished Olga of Kyiv as much as they did Liudprand of Cremona, who came as an envoy from the Franks in the 940s. Fruit was brought to the table in "golden bowls, which are too heavy for men to lift and come in on carriers covered over with purple cloth," Liudprand writes. "Through openings in the ceiling hang three ropes covered with gilded leather and furnished with golden rings. These rings are attached to the handles projecting from the bowls, and with four or five men helping from below, they are swung on to the table by means of a moveable device in the ceiling." As for the entertainment, Liudprand writes,

A man came in carrying on his head, without using his hands, a wooden pole twenty-four feet or more long, which a foot and a half from the top had a cross piece three feet wide. Then two boys appeared, naked except for loin cloths round their middle, who went up the pole, did various tricks on it, and then came down head first, keeping the pole all the time as steady as though it were rooted in the earth. When one had come down, the other remained on the pole and performed by himself. . . . I was so bewildered that the emperor himself noticed my astonishment.

When Olga dined with the emperor, the room's attention remained on the Rus queen herself. The emperor "wondered at her intellect," according to the *Russian Primary Chronicle*. "He conversed with her and remarked that she was worthy to reign with him in his city." Though she was middle-aged and he was already married, Olga interpreted his comment—correctly, it seems—as a marriage proposal. Protective of her independence—and her kingdom's sovereignty—she pointed out that she was still pagan. She was willing to be instructed in the Christian faith and to convert, she said, but only if the emperor himself sponsored her.

He agreed to do so, and eventually Olga and her companions, including thirty-four Rus women, were baptized. The emperor then repeated his marriage proposal. "But she replied, 'How can you marry me, after yourself baptizing me and calling me your daughter? For among Christians that is unlawful, as you yourself must know.' Then the emperor said, 'Olga, you have outwitted me.'"

In 1547 Olga was declared a saint for her efforts to bring Christianity to the Rus, but she is not known to have proselytized. During her reign, says the *Russian Primary Chronicle*, "when any man wished to be baptized, he was not hindered, but only mocked."

Cross pendants do show up more frequently in Kyivan graves from that period, especially in women's graves, but they may simply be souvenirs: expressions of fashion, not faith. As one scholar points out, in the emperor's register of gifts, Olga's thirty-four "handmaidens" are treated as merchants. Trade, as it had been for her husband, Igor, was the primary reason Olga traveled to the Great City—and the reason she converted.

Queen Olga may have been sincere in her new faith: She retained a priest until her death and requested a Christian burial, with no funeral feast and no elaborate grave mound.

But Olga was also a clear-eyed politician. Like her peers Harald Bluetooth of Denmark and Gunnhild Mother-of-Kings and her sons, Olga perceived how the world was shifting. The Christian Church, which did not yet emphasize intolerance and social control, was nevertheless closing down some options, while opening others. The church stymied trade with pagans on principle. But its bureaucracy—with common values, accounting standards, and language—made the logistics of trade run smoother within the Christian world.

As Christian kings came to power in Viking lands, they readily found new trading partners in their fellow religionists. Coins minted in Western Europe began to outnumber Arab dirhams in Viking hoards. The importance of the East Way was fading.

Olga's son, Sviatoslav, was not so politically astute. When she urged him to convert to Christianity, he replied, "How shall I alone accept another faith? My followers will laugh at that."

Sviatoslav treated with the Byzantines as his father had: with swords. Wrote the Byzantine historian Leo the Deacon, who met Sviatoslav once, "He was hot-headed and bold, and a brave and active man."

As the *Russian Primary Chronicle* puts it, he "stepped light as a leopard." Identifying less with his Swedish ancestors than with his Eastern steppe-nomadic enemies, on campaign he "carried with him neither wagons nor kettles, and boiled no meat, but cut off small strips of horseflesh, game, or beef, and ate it after roasting it on the coals. Nor did he have a tent, but he spread out a horse-blanket under him, and set his saddle under his head; and all his retinue did likewise."

He inspired loyalty, and his warriors proudly followed him. He defeated the Khazars; he defeated the Pechenegs; he defeated the Bulgars. He brought under his control all the routes of the East Way, from the Danube to the Volga, and consolidated the Rus kingdom. He was the Rus equivalent of Norway's Harald Fairhair. Then, like his father and grandfather before him, he led his forces against the Byzantine Empire—and there his luck ran out.

Trapped in a town on the Danube, having lost his best warriors, Sviatoslav called his remaining captains together and debated what to do. They were overwhelmed by the Byzantines' armored cavalry. They were unable to escape by water, since the Byzantines' triremes, bearing Greek fire, blocked the river.

But Sviatoslav was not yet ready to sue for terms. He urged his army "to be victorious and live, or to die gloriously," reported Leo the Deacon. According to the *Russian Primary Chronicle*, Sviatoslav declared, "We must not take to flight, but we will resist boldly, and I will march before you. If my head falls, then look to yourselves." And his warriors replied, "Wherever your head falls, there we too will lay down our own."

So the battle began, "and the carnage was great." Who won depends on whose account you read.

The Rus "spiritedly drew up to oppose the Roman forces," writes Leo the Deacon, who like other Byzantines considered himself the heir to the Roman Empire. The Rus killed the Roman champion. They "shouted loudly and fiercely, and pushed back the Romans." But just as it seemed the Rus would win the field, "there appeared a man on a white horse" who broke through the Rus lines "in a wondrous fashion, and threw them into disarray." It was the great martyr Theodore, come from beyond the grave to save Constantinople. At least, that is the story Leo the Deacon tells. He also mentions that "at the same time a wind and rainstorm broke out, pouring down heavily from the sky, and struck the enemy, and the dust that was stirred up irritated their eyes."

That night, Sviatoslav "was distraught and seething with rage" at the destruction of his army. But he knew, Leo reports, that "it was the task of an intelligent general not to fall into despair when caught in dire straits, but to endeavor to save his army in any way possible. And so at dawn he sent envoys to the emperor."

Once the terms of the peace treaty had been agreed upon, Sviatoslav demanded to meet the emperor in person. Leo the Deacon himself attended their meeting on the banks of the river. Emperor John Tzimiskes, he reports, arrived on horseback, "clad in armor ornamented in gold, accompanied by a vast squadron of armed horsemen adorned with gold."

Sviatoslav arrived by boat, "grasping an oar and rowing with his companions as if he were one of them." Leo notes his shaved head, except for the lock that hung down on one side, and his long mustaches. His "rather angry and savage appearance," Leo says, was somewhat ameliorated by the gold earring, "adorned with two pearls and a red gemstone," that he wore in one ear. His clothing was white, a simple shirt and trousers of linen, and "no different from that of his companions," Leo writes, "except in cleanliness," which means Sviatoslav had brought an extra set of clothes in his saddlebags, for in the battle he had just lost, Leo reports, Sviatoslav had been struck on the collarbone and knocked flat, then stricken with many arrows, causing him to lose a lot of blood. He was not the same kind of war leader as the emperor, who stayed behind his lines.

According to the *Russian Primary Chronicle*, the emperor agreed to pay Sviatoslav a vast tribute, and the Rus returned north with "great riches and immense booty."

According to Leo the Deacon, the Rus gave up the town and released their captives in return for food for the journey home (a measure of grain for each warrior) and free passage through the fire ships. Sviatoslav asked the emperor to guarantee, as well, that the Pechenegs would not attack on his way back, but the Pechenegs refused to be bound.

At a difficult portage on the Dniepr rapids, the Pechenegs surrounded and killed Sviatoslav. They took his distinctive head, stripped it of its hair and flesh, and turned his polished skull into a gold-plated drinking cup. He was about Hervor's age when he died.

22

DEATH OF A VALKYRIE

Hervor is patrolling the busy waterfront at Birka, taking a turn at the oar, so to speak, as a good leader should. She recognizes the ship as Irish as soon as it rounds Borgberget: A deep-keeled Western ship of oak, it is gaily painted bright yellow, with its gunwale and waterline strake both a jaunty green, like the Dublin shipwrights favor.

Its crew rows through the keyhole slot in the harbor wall. They'll have picked up a Birka pilot in the outer harbor, so they know where to berth. Hervor dismounts and leads her horse toward the dock, squinting to see if she can spot a familiar red head among the crew, but there is none. Instead a dark-haired man with skin burned black by the sun seems to be in charge. He organizes the securing of the ship and the off-loading of its cargo, summoning porters and carters with an air of long experience.

He is quite a striking man. Hervor wonders if he is not sunburned at all, but rather one of those men born that color, the ones the Dubliners call Blue Men, who come from the southern shores of the Inland Sea. If so, he is probably a follower of Muhammed.

As he and his people approach the end of the crowded wharf, Hervor racks her brain for the few words of Arabic she learned along the East Way, so as to greet him properly.

She is so focused on this interesting man that she overreacts when a slave in his party suddenly drops and rolls, rises, spins away, and slams into Hervor's side. Her scramasax is out and has slit the slave's throat before

Hervor notices she herself is bleeding—the slave somehow snatched her own eating knife and stabbed her in the groin.

The Blue Man is shouting at her—everyone is shouting. Hervor carefully wipes clean her weapon and resheathes it, waiting for the hubbub to die down.

I seem to have bought myself a slave, she says to the enraged man. And I suspect, since she obviously had warrior training, she will cost a bit more than usual.

She mounts her horse—she hopes no one notices how much that motion costs her—and signals to her partner down the beach to take control of the area.

If you send someone up to the Warriors' Hall, she says over her shoulder, I'm sure we can agree on a price. Though we'll need to take into account the scratch she gave me, you understand.

Her saddle is dyed red by the time she reaches the Warriors' Hall. In spite of the healer's best treatment, the bleeding cannot be stopped. By midnight, Birka is without a war leader: Hervor is dead.

At the battle on the Danube in 971, before Sviatoslav sued for peace, there came a black day of defeat for the Rus, when the Byzantine emperor's cavalry drove the Rus warriors back against the walls of the town and many were "trodden underfoot by others in the narrow defile and slain by the Romans when they were trapped there." As the victors were "robbing the corpses of their spoils," wrote John Skylitzes in his *Synopsis of Byzantine History* a hundred years later, "they found women lying among the fallen, equipped like men; women who had fought against the Romans together with the men."

Hervor was not among them.

Years before Sviatoslav's disastrous campaign, Hervor had returned to Birka. With her skill at arms and flair for strategy, she rose to a position of esteem among the Birka warriors and was buried with ceremony beside its garrison, overlooking the town.

Did she die of a wound received in Birka's marketplace, victim of a vindictive slave? Probably not. That story is told by Snorri Sturluson in *Heimskringla*, about the vengeance taken on a slave-dealer by the future king of Norway, young Olaf Tryggvason.

I don't know how Hervor died—no one does—though experts in the language of bones can often tell the cause of death from a skeleton. Swords leave long, straight cuts on the bone, with few secondary stress fractures. Axes both cut and crush. Spears and arrows cause characteristic puncture wounds. Stones, clubs, and morning stars shatter bone. Cuts on the left side of the body or head mean the warrior died fighting face-to-face (most people are right-handed). Cuts on the lower legs, angled from below, mean the warrior was on horseback—or had already fallen. Wounds to the crown of the head mean the warrior was attacked by mounted enemies and likely had no helmet. Punctures to the hands and cuts on the wrist or forearm mean the warrior parried without a weapon.

Battle wounds need not be fatal: The sagas mention several Vikings, like Onund Tree-Foot and Egil One-Hand, named for their battle scars, while in Norse mythology, the god Tyr had only one hand. Amputations—whether by enemy weapons or a healer's axe—were cauterized with fire-hot tongs or knives and treated with pine tar or pitch, which have antiseptic properties. If the warrior did not die of blood loss, gangrene, or sepsis, he or she would find some place in Viking society. As *The Words of the High One* reminds us, "The lame ride horses, the handless herd cattle, the deaf fight bravely. The blind are better than burning corpses. The dead do nothing."

Many illnesses also leave their mark on bones, as pits or deformities. Leprosy, syphilis, cancer, and tuberculosis can be diagnosed, for example, as can nonfatal sinus infections, arthritis, and diet-related diseases like anemia, scurvy, and rickets.

But we do not have all of Hervor's bones, and the surfaces of those retrieved from grave Bj581 are too degraded to tell us what injuries or illnesses she suffered.

Most Viking skeletons, in fact, reveal no trauma. Many that do are open to conflicting interpretations, like the warrior buried in the Gokstad ship, who was first thought to have died as a bedridden, spoon-fed, arthritic old man, and later deemed to have been killed in battle by "at least two persons with different weapons."

The bones of a Viking buried in Repton, England, are better preserved. Believed to be a leader of the Great Heathen Army, he was killed "by a massive cut into the head of the left femur," archaeologists assert. The blow hit an artery, causing him to bleed to death. It also seems to have gelded him: Those burying him carefully set the curved tusk of a wild boar between his thighs, as if to replace his lost penis.

King Hakon the Good, in the story told by Snorri Sturluson, also bled to death, struck in the brachial artery by an arrow shot by Gunnhild Mother-of-Kings or her errand runner. Snorri also writes of warriors dying (bravely, with a quip on their lips) of deep internal wounds. A healer after one battle brought a wounded warrior a special dish of porridge; she had mixed in "crushed leeks and other herbs and boiled it together and was giving it to the wounded to eat," Snorri writes. "With it she could learn if they had internal wounds, for, if so, the wound would begin to smell of leeks." The warrior refused to eat the leek porridge, for a diagnosis of an internal wound was a death sentence. He urged the healer, instead, to pull the arrowhead out of his wound. "She took tongs and tried to pull the arrow out, but it held fast and did not move; there was only a little of it sticking out, for the wound had swollen." Her patient told her to cut into the wound to free the arrow and he would pull it out himself. He "took the tongs and yanked out the arrowhead. But it had barbs on it, and caught on them were strings of his flesh, some red, some white, and when he saw them, he said: 'The king has fed us well. I'm still fat around my heart's roots.' Then he fell back and was dead."

Other Vikings' deaths were not so heroic—though equally memorable. Among those who besieged cities in France in the ninth century, many died of dysentery. Writes one French cleric, they "discharged their guts with a watery flow through their arses: and so they died." The great Ragnar Lodbrok himself might have so succumbed. Rather than dying in a snake pit in York, Ragnar was stricken with diarrhea while attacking Paris in 845, claims a French account. Soon after he returned to the Danish court, "all his entrails spilled onto the ground." Ragnar's death from dysentery may explain his famous nickname. Lodbrok means "shaggy trousers," and both modern and medieval readers have struggled to explain exactly what these are. A thirteenth-century saga says Ragnar wore pants of heavy cloth boiled in pitch and rolled in sand to protect against dragons' breath. "Garments boiled in pitch comes startlingly close," one scholar writes, to garments soiled by dysentery. Like her, I can imagine someone at court witnessing Ragnar's collapse and relating later that his breeches "looked black and sticky, as though they had been boiled in pitch."

Heroes in the sagas die from a fall off a horse. They die after stepping on a horse's skull in which a poisonous adder lies. They are struck overboard by a sail yard—loosed by a storm or a sorcerer—and drown. They tumble off a balcony, dead drunk, and drown in a mead vat. They are swept away by an avalanche. They are skewered by the horns of an escaped bull. They are struck by a pitchfork thrown by a slave. They are burned to death in a feast hall. They die from a spear thrust in the dark. And they die of old age, bemoaning their weakened state, as did Egil the Poet, Queen Gunnhild's nemesis, in verse:

> *My bald head bobbles,*
> *my balance is gone,*
> *my dick is soft; it drips,*
> *my hearing's dried up.*
> *My feet are cold,*
> *frigid as widows . . .*

When Egil died, his stepdaughter and her husband dressed him in fine clothes, the saga says. They laid him to rest on a headland, his weapons by his side, and raised a burial mound over him. When Iceland became Christian and a church was built on the farm, Egil's bones were dug up and reburied beneath the altar. They were dug up again some years later, when a new church was built. They were "much bigger than other human bones," the saga reports. The skull was huge and heavy and covered all over with wavy ridges: It looked like a scallop shell. The priest picked it up and placed it on the churchyard wall. Curious to see just how thick it was, he took up a heavy axe and struck it as hard as he could with the hammer side. The skull didn't crack. "It wasn't even dented, where he had whacked it, only a little whiter in color."

Egil the Poet may not have suffered merely from old age. A scallop-ridged skull of exceptional hardness, a bobbing head on a swaying neck, blindness, deafness, loss of balance, cold feet—all of Egil's symptoms, including his celebrated ugliness—could be the result of Paget's disease, in which bone cells grow out of control; it is the second-most common bone disease after osteoporosis, which is also seen in Viking Age skeletons. In his last years, Egil must have suffered from excruciating headaches. It might have been some consolation to him, if the rumor reached Iceland, that Queen Gunnhild had been lured back to Denmark and there drowned in a bog. A well-preserved corpse fished from a Danish bog in 1835 was known as Queen Gunnhild Mother-of-Kings until 1977, when carbon dating placed the drowned woman's death in the fifth century BC.

The 1889 drawing of Birka grave Bj581 by Evald Hansen, based on Hjalmar Stolpe's site plans.

All I know about how Hervor died is that she did not die of old age. Examining her teeth and bones, osteologists estimate she was thirty or forty. But, if I know nothing about her death, I know a great deal about how she was buried.

One piece of advice the valkyrie Brynhild gives to Sigurd the Dragon-Slayer concerns the dead: "Care for their corpses," she says, "wherever you find them, whether they died of sickness, or drowned, or were killed in battle. Bathe them, wash their hands and faces, dry and comb their hair, lay them in a coffin, and bid them sleep well."

For a Christian burial, that was about it. Sometimes the bodies were buried naked, wrapped in a linen shroud; sometimes there wasn't even a coffin.

For an elaborate pagan burial like Hervor's, however, the washed body rested first in a temporary grave. Was it pickled? Frozen? Rubbed with oil and herbs? No one knows, but archaeologists routinely find the animal bones in Viking graves to be better preserved than the human ones. In one ninth-century boat grave from Uppsala, for example, the fragile skeleton of a chicken was intact, while the buried woman's bones were "in remarkably poor condition." She had started to decay while the time-consuming arrangements for her funeral were made.

Special clothing might be sewn for the dead to wear. Funeral ale might be brewed and food gathered for a feast. Someone might be chosen to accompany the dead—or someone might volunteer, if what Ibn Fadlan says is true. Traveling from Baghdad on a mission for the caliph in 922, Ibn Fadlan witnessed a Rus funeral on the banks of the Volga River that included all these things. It lasted ten days—ten days of feasting and heavy drinking—and culminated in the gang rape and strangulation of a girl (the volunteer), the killing of horses, cows, chickens, and a dog, and the setting ablaze of the ship in which the dead man sat, all accompanied by the frenzied beating of spears on shields and the spine-tingling chants of the woman Ibn Fadlan called Malak al-Maut, usually translated as "Angel of Death," though "Valkyrie"—"Chooser of the Slain"—might be a better fit. It is a dramatic send-off much like that given the Oseberg queens in 834, though their ship was not burned.

The Persian writer Ibn Rustah, who completed his seven-volume encyclopedia in 913, recorded a different burial rite among the Rus. Instead of in a boat, fired or not, this dead man was buried in "a hole as big as a house." He was "dressed in his clothes and wearing his gold bracelet"—his best clothes, but not specially made funeral garments. Food, wine, and coins were placed in his grave, along with "his favorite woman," who was shut inside the tomb alive.

Ibn Rustah believed she died there, but she might have been just visiting, as the valkyrie Sigrun did her dead husband, according to one poem: "Sigrun went into Helgi's burial mound and said, 'I am as happy to see you again as Odin's greedy ravens are to find a still-warm corpse. . . . I want to kiss you, my dead king, before you take off your bloody ringmail byrnie.'" Likewise, two friends in a saga made a pact "that whichever lived longer would build a grave mound for his friend, placing in it as much wealth as he thought honorable. Then he, the living, would enter the mound with the dead and sit there three nights, after which he could leave if he wanted to."

Hervor crossed to the otherworld with no slave or companion by her side. While her body (perhaps pickled) lay in a temporary resting place, they dug her a hole as big as a small house. From the door of the Warriors' Hall, they marched down the lane between the two graveyards on the terrace north of Borgberget, the Fortress Rock. Reaching the cliff, they turned west, out to the end of the promontory. There, above Birka's harbor, in plain sight of the royal manor across the strait at Adelso, they lit a bonfire beside another warrior's grave. Did they drink and feast to her memory? Did they dance and chant or compete at games? I don't know. I can't even be sure of the bonfire, though such fires were standard in similar burials along the East Way.

Once the fire burned out, they began to dig. When the pit was big enough—nearly twelve feet long, six feet wide, and up to six feet deep—they lined the hole with walls of wood and stamped its bottom into a floor. Did they erect a dovetailed log structure, as was done elsewhere, or build a plank house with corner posts? I can't be sure; only traces of the walls remained. Was the floor, as elsewhere, of beaten clay or solid planking? Nothing so fancy, it seems.

At one end, where they had not dug quite so deep, they boxed off a cramped stall, less than four feet wide. Into this they coaxed her two horses, a stallion and a mare, and slit their throats (their skulls show no marks of an axe between the eyes). As their blood drained, their knees buckled and they slowly crumpled, as dying horses do. Their heads were turned facing each other, their necks intertwined; one horse was bridled, the other was not.

Then they carried Hervor into her death house and arranged her, sitting on her saddle: Iron stirrups were found by her now-vanished seat. She was dressed in her riding coat, a splendid kaftan rich with bands of silk embroidered with silver and sparkling with mirrored sequins. On her head they set her *gerzkr* silk cap, topped by its fancy filigreed silver cone. They fastened a wool cloak at her shoulder with a simple ring-shaped pin of iron.

At her head and her feet, propped against the walls, they set her two round shields, their bosses facing away so she could jump up and grab a shield's handgrip. Her long spear was angled into the ground, the spearhead lodged in the horses' stall wall, as if she were holding the shaft in her hand.

At her left side, where she would have worn it, assuming she was right-handed, they laid her sword, a serviceable steel-edged weapon with a leather-wrapped hilt, nothing fancy about it, in its sheath. Beside it they placed a whetstone and her sheathed eating knife.

To her right, within easy reach, they laid her twenty-inch scramasax, its sheath elaborately decorated in shining bronze. Her horn bow was set there too, strung, in its bow case, with twenty-five armor-piercing arrows, their hafts glittering with silver wire, gathered into a quiver feather side up: She had never mastered the point-up technique of the Magyar closed quiver.

By her right foot they set her battle-axe, along with a comb and a simple bronze washing bowl, much repaired.

Against her knee they leaned her gameboard, a handsome one with an iron frame. They placed her pouch of game pieces in her lap: twenty-eight whalebone warriors and three walrus-ivory dice, for playing *hnefa-tafl*. There, too, or in a second pouch, were three trader's weights, a sliver of a silver dirham (dated 913 to 933), and a miniature spearhead amulet.

When all was arranged to everyone's satisfaction, a warrior standing on the lip of the grave cast a short spear over Hervor's shoulders into the pit.

One archaeologist interprets this act, seen in another Birka burial as well, as dedicating the dead to Odin, god of battle. Whether such was its meaning in Hervor's case, I will never know. But that there was *some* meaning in the flight of this spear—and in the placement of everything in her grave—I have no doubt: "Note the detail, the precision, the deliberate choice and positioning of objects," this expert says. Nothing is accidental about Hervor's grave or about any of the elite Viking graves that have been excavated. Each one is different. Each one tells a story, or many stories, all mysteries to us now.

Well-furnished chamber graves like Hervor's—called "houses of the dead" in Danish—are unusual in Sweden, though they are more common in Kyiv and Gnezdovo, along the East Way. Of the eleven hundred burials excavated at Birka, more than half are cremations, most of them marked by mounds. Throughout Sweden, most people in the Viking Age were buried this way, their bodies and grave goods burned and then crushed. Sometimes all that's left to study are flakes of bone and bits of metal.

Another four hundred of Birka's dead were buried simply, some in coffins, some without, with no grave goods other than items of clothing. They might have been Christians, or they might have been poor. Their graves tell us very little about their lives.

Only a hundred and eleven of Birka's dead rated a death house like Hervor's. Some were warriors. Some were traders. Forty percent were women—a number that might rise, since the graves at Birka were sexed by metal: male for weapons, female for jewelry.

Now that we know Bj581, long touted as the classic Viking warrior's grave, housed a warrior woman, we might want to rethink our assumptions about the gender of similar graves with weapons and horses.

> She was a valkyrie and rode on the wind and the sea.
> She practised more with spear and shield and sword than at
>   sewing or embroidery.
> She was a woman hard through and through and a highly
>   expert warrior.
> She would do battle in the forefront of the most valiant
>   warriors. Everyone marvelled at her matchless feats.
> I am a shield-maid. I was in battle with the King of
>   Gardariki and our weapons were red with blood.
> As heroes we were widely known—with keen spears we cut
>   blood from bone.
> Let's ride out hard, with naked swords held high, away from
>   here.

After the spear was tossed over her shoulder, Hervor's death house was roofed with wooden timbers—probably covered with charcoal, tar, and birchbark to delay their rotting, as in other chamber graves—and sealed under a layer of turf.

With teams of horses they dragged over a granite boulder and wedged it upright. At thirteen feet high, Hervor's standing stone was as tall as her grave was long, and the largest monument capping any burial at Birka. Rising from the western edge of the promontory beneath the Fortress Rock, it would be the first thing a traveler noticed when approaching the town: A sign of safety under the watchful eyes of the Birka warriors.

And so it was the first thing Birka's unknown conquerors saw when they attacked. They came from the lakeside, scaling the cliff and swarming past Hervor's grave. With hundreds of flaming arrows, they set the Warriors' Hall ablaze, trapping the Birka warriors within. They set fire to the smithies and the garrison's stores. They burned down the stockades, the gate and battlements, and took control of the hillfort. By then, they owned the town.

Did Hervor's companions break down the walls of the burning hall, as Thorolf and his friends did when trapped by King Harald Fairhair? Did the Birka warriors make a heroic last stand, as Bjorn the Merchant did when Eirik Bloodaxe set fire to the Shining Hall at Kaupang? From the weapons and articles of dress that archaeologists saw littering the hall when they excavated it in the late 1990s, it appears the warriors did not. They died, terribly, in the flames. The victors removed the bodies and the salvageable weapons but left the rest on the floor, to tell the gruesome tale. It's here the archaeologists found signs of the Birka warriors' Eastern dress and Magyar bows, of ringmail and lamellar armor both, of shields on the walls and practical weapons stored under (puny) lock and (falcon) key, of a close-knit cohort of some forty warriors who dedicated their hall to the old ways of Odin, in defiance of Christ.

Birka's Warriors' Hall was never rebuilt, its garrison never re-formed. The hillfort remained in use for a few more years, but after the attack the town fell into a decline from which it never recovered. By 975 Birka ceased to function as a node on the East Way. Its artisans and traders found new homes, perhaps on the isle of Gotland, which became the Baltic Sea's trading center, or in Sigtuna, about twenty miles up Lake Malaren, where the first Christian king of the Swedes established his official residence before the year 1000. Laid out in a planned grid punctuated by churches, Sigtuna was a new-style town, firmly facing the Christian West and turning its back on the still-pagan eastern shores of the Baltic Sea. It was a town built to service the bureaucracy of Christian kingship, not as a free marketplace of goods and ideas. Sigtuna was a Swedish town, a political center in which trade was regulated by the king and his ministers, not the multicultural, multiethnic mosaic of Birka. In this, Sigtuna mirrored Smolensk, which replaced Gnezdovo, and Schleswig, which replaced Hedeby at about the same time. At Sigtuna, new silver coins were minted. None have been discovered in Birka.

When Hjalmar Stolpe arrived on Bjorko, or Birch Island, in 1871, the Viking Age town of Birka and its thousand-plus residents were long forgotten. The island was a sleepy place, home to only five or six farm families. An entomologist with the Royal Swedish Academy of Sciences, Stolpe was drawn to Bjorko by reports of the farmers' plows turning up quantities of amber; he wondered if some of that amber preserved ants. "His finds," noted Stolpe's obituary, "inspired him with a desire for archaeological investigation."

By the time he began working on grave Bj581, Hervor's grave, Stolpe had excavated more than five hundred burials in and around Birka. Trained in stratigraphy, he produced "meticulous" scientific reports; his field drawings on graph paper—a technique he introduced to archaeology—were "exceptional."

He had also developed his instincts, learning to recognize hidden graves by the shallow depression left when a chamber collapsed, or simply by the thickness of the grass that grew there. "I have located many graves by striking the ground with a stick and listening for the duller sound made by the somewhat looser soil in the grave filling," he wrote.

The dip and the grass both identified Hervor's grave, but Stolpe was stymied in his first efforts to excavate. The great standing stone marking her burial had toppled over and sunk into the chamber, as the roof beams rotted and the ceiling caved in, capping it nearly completely. But by 1878, Stolpe had mastered a brand-new excavation technique—dynamite. He lit a match and blew the lid off the valkyrie's grave. We are still hearing echoes of that blast.

ACKNOWLEDGMENTS

In 2012 Neil Price, distinguished professor of archaeology at the University of Uppsala, Sweden, gave a series of lectures at Cornell University in Ithaca, New York; these were subsequently published on the university's YouTube channel. His focus, he said, was "stories, the power of stories, and the role that narrative played in the life of the Vikings, its influence on their perception of the world."

Price's ideas influenced my discussion of valkyries in *Ivory Vikings* (St. Martin's, 2015), though we continue to disagree on a key issue: To Price, a valkyrie is a goddess or demon, a shield-maid is "semi-human," and Bj581 was the burial of a possible "real" warrior woman. To me, the three ideas are synonymous. In the first of his Cornell lectures, "Children of Ash: Cosmology and the Viking Universe" (www.youtube.com/watch?v =nJZBqmGLHQ8), Price noted about valkyries: "We don't know whether we have any Viking Age depictions of them. These things don't come with labels; we have to try and interpret them." I would add that we don't know what the Vikings meant by the words "valkyrie" and "shield-maid" either; we can only try to interpret them.

When I met Price in 2016, at the Society for American Archaeology's conference in Orlando, Florida, I told him I planned to write a book on the concept of the valkyrie in the Viking Age, and I was looking for a warrior burial to study in depth. From the 2013 survey by Price's former student, Leszek Gardeła, "'Warrior-Women' in Viking Age Scandinavia?," I knew of a handful of graves that would suffice for my purposes. The questions I wanted to answer were, I thought, simple: How do we know a buried warrior was male or female? What stories influence our perception?

I asked Price if he could refer me to an archaeologist, preferably a woman, who was an expert on a Viking Age weapons grave, preferably the burial of a woman.

He looked at me funny. "I can't talk about that—yet."

He suggested, very casually, that I meet Charlotte Hedenstierna-Jonson, who was also attending the conference in Florida. I listened to her paper, on a topic I wasn't then interested in, and didn't make the connection—until September 2017, when "A Female Viking Warrior Confirmed by Genomics" was published in the *American Journal of Physical Anthropology*, with Hedenstierna-Jonson as first author.

I am extremely grateful to Price for that early warning and to Hedenstierna-Jonson, senior curator at the Swedish History Museum, for graciously agreeing to be interviewed twice, once in Stockholm and once during her lecture tour of the United States after the team's second paper on the Bj581 burial was published in 2019. Without their work, I would have no story to tell. Hedenstierna-Jonson, particularly, paints an entirely new picture of Viking life in her 2006 doctoral thesis, *The Birka Warrior*, and the many articles she has published since then. Her vision, more than anyone else's, has shaped this book. I have endeavored to remain true to her and her colleagues' scientific conclusions, though I may have taken my interpretations further than they believe the data warrant. In our correspondence, Price wrote, "On balance of probability—and our own subjective impressions—we all feel that the most likely reading of the burial is that this was a warrior woman, but there are many reasonable alternatives, both as to gender and role." He warned me against ruling out those alternatives. I'm afraid I didn't comply. He added that "this question of whether it is even possible to read the lives of the dead from the things that accompany them in the grave is a massive one in archaeology." I side with those archaeologists who assume it is possible. All speculations are my own.

I was equally inspired by Stacy Schiff's *Cleopatra: A Life* (Little, Brown, 2010). Writes Schiff, "The holes in the record present one hazard, what we have constructed around them another." She sees it as the biographer's job, and I agree, to "peel away the encrusted myth and the hoary propaganda." Yet myths die hard, as Ulrich Raulff notes in *Farewell to the Horse*

(Liveright, 2018): "History is written in the indicative mood, but lived and remembered in the optative—the grammatical mood of wishful thinking. This is why historical myths are so tenacious. It's as though the truth, even when it's there for everyone to see, is powerless—it can't lay a finger on the all-powerful myth." *The Real Valkyrie* is my attempt to lay a powerful myth to rest: The myth that Viking women stayed at home, keys on their belts, while Viking men, carrying swords, raided and traded from North America to Byzantium, Baghdad, and beyond.

Many other scholars and institutions helped shape this book. The Birka Portal on the website of the Swedish History Museum (http://historiska.se /birka/) is an extraordinary research tool; I'm indebted to the scholars who created it and grateful for their generosity in sharing both information and images. Thanks also to the University of Oslo's Viking Ship Museum; the National Museum of Denmark; the Jamtli Museum in Östersund, Sweden; the UK Portable Antiquities Scheme; and the British Museum for digitizing their Viking Age holdings and sharing their databases. Researching the Viking world from the United States, especially during a pandemic, would not have been possible without these online resources.

Both when they agreed with me and when they challenged my views, I enjoyed discussing the questions in this book with Guðný Zöega (Skagafjörður, Iceland, August 12, 2015), Leszek Gardeła (Reykjavík, Iceland, July 30, 2016), Judith Jesch (Reykjavík, Iceland, August 13, 2018), Marianne Moen (Oslo, Norway, August 20, 2018, and by correspondence), and Jóhanna Katrín Friðriksdóttir (York, England, February 23, 2019). They are in no way responsible for my assumptions and interpretations.

Bill Short and his colleagues at Hurstwic Viking Combat Training Center in Southborough, Massachusetts, allowed me to handle Viking weapons at a training session on March 12, 2019, and shared their experiences and experiments with me (for details, see the Hurstwic Facebook page). Thanks to Bill also for his correspondence. Kudos to Barbara Wechter of Wechter Arms, for living the life of a Viking warrior woman.

Two lectures presented by musician Einar Selvik at the 2018 Midgardsblot in Borre, Norway, were more inspiring than I could have imagined: Long parts of this book were composed with Wardruna on infinite loop. What Selvik said about Viking music and magic applies also to the rest of Viking culture: "What it is, how it was done, the gritty details: We don't know any of that. We can only hypothesize or assume." And we must not underestimate the difficulty of our task: "Their way of thinking is a more complex way than ours."

Thanks, too, to fantasy novelist Sofia Samatar for letting me live inside the mind of a warrior woman. Her novel *The Winged Histories* (Small Beer Press, 2016) was one of the highlights of my reading year. In the words of her sword-maiden, Tavis, "At times we were seized by a sudden and absolute happiness. It happened most often when we were beating back an attack and then we howled and dismembered the bodies, choking with joy."

For practical assistance, Gísli Pálsson of the University of Iceland came through as always, supplying me with a flat while I made use of Iceland's extraordinary National Library in Reykjavík. For their hospitality, I also thank Melanie Saunders and William Fergus in Boston, Bill Short in Massachusetts, Kristín Vogfjörð and Guðbjörg Sigurðardóttir in Reykjavík, and Trina Andersen in Tønsberg.

Elise Skalwold opened my eyes to the richness of Vestfold, Katrín Driscoll was a superb tour guide to Viking Dublin, Kristrún Heimisdóttir's sensitive intervention was much appreciated at the Saga Conference in Reykholt, Lance Lazar was a fine host at Assumption College, and Alice Klingener came through with a tricky translation from Swedish. As my research assistant in Norway, Gabriel Dunsmith's dependability and poetic eye added much to my first experience of a Viking Metal festival. In notes he shared with me, he wrote: "The energy at the shows is almost pensive—we are waiting for something to happen. We are waiting to be transformed. The music, when it comes, has a spiritual force because it relates to the land and our bodies. You can feel the throat-singing in your own body; it stirs up an emotional response. The sweetness of the mead, the raucous atmosphere of the place—it all creates an inner state that allows you to see the world differently, and perhaps with more clarity."

Thanks to Claire Van Vliet for urging me to think differently about art and illustrations, for enhancing the photographs I finally chose, and for providing the maps of the valkyries' world. Thanks to my agent, Michelle Tessler, for encouraging me to jump on the Bj581 idea before I knew where the story would take me. And thanks to my editor, Elisabeth Dyssegaard, for challenging me to let that story take me as far as it could.

Finally, thanks to my husband, Charles Fergus, for keeping my spirits up while hard at work on his own books, and to Sigrún Brynjarsdóttir for getting me back on the horse.

LIST OF ILLUSTRATIONS

FURTHER READING

The books, articles, and dissertations that influenced me the most are listed here; in the notes they are referenced by author's last name and date. Medieval texts appear only in the notes.

Androshchuk, Fedir. *Vikings in the East: Essays on Contacts Along the Road to Byzantium (800–1100).* Uppsala University, 2013.

Back Danielsson, Ing-Marie. *Masking Moments: The Transitions of Bodies and Beings in Late Iron Age Scandinavia.* Doctoral thesis. Stockholm University, 2007.

Brink, Stefan, and Neil Price, eds. *The Viking World.* Routledge, 2008.

Callmer, John, Ingrid Gustin, and Mats Roslund, eds. *Identity Formation and Diversity in the Early Medieval Baltic and Beyond.* Brill, 2017.

Clarke, Howard B., Sheila Dooley, and Ruth Johnson. *Dublin and the Viking World.* O'Brien Press, 2018.

Downham, Clare. *Viking Kings of Britain and Ireland: The Dynasty of Ívarr to A.D. 1014.* Dunedin Academic Press, 2007.

Duczko, Wladyslaw. *Viking Rus: Studies on the Presence of Scandinavians in Eastern Europe.* Brill, 2004.

Eriksen, Marianne Hem, U. Pedersen, B. Rundberget, I. Axelsen, and H. Berg, eds. *Viking Worlds: Things, Spaces and Movement.* Oxbow Books, 2015 (especially the chapters by Heidi Lund Berg, Lydia Carstens, and Charlotte Hedenstierna-Jonson).

Friðriksdóttir, Jóhanna Katrín. *Women in Old Norse Literature.* Palgrave Macmillan, 2013.

Friðriksdóttir, Jóhanna Katrín. *Valkyrie: The Women of the Viking World.* Bloomsbury Academic, 2020.

Gardeła, Leszek. "'Warrior-Women' in Viking Age Scandinavia?" *Analecta Archaeologica Ressoviensia* 8 (2013): 273–340.

Gardeła, Leszek. "Amazons of the North?" In *Hvanndalir: Festschrift für Wilhelm Heizmann*, pp. 391–428. Ed. A. Bauer and A. Pesch. De Gruyter, 2018.

Griffiths, David. *Vikings of the Irish Sea: Conflict and Assimilation, AD 790–1050.* History Press, 2010; rpt., 2012.

Hedenstierna-Jonson, Charlotte. *The Birka Warrior.* Doctoral thesis. Stockholm University, 2006.

Hedenstierna-Jonson, Charlotte. "To Own and Be Owned: The Warriors of Birka's Garrison." In *Own and Be Owned: Archaeological Approaches to the Concept of Possession*, pp. 73–91. Stockholm Studies in Archaeology 62. Ed. Alison Klevnäs and C. Hedenstierna-Jonson. Stockholm University, 2015.

Hedenstierna-Jonson, Charlotte. "Foreigner and Local: Identities and Cultural Expression Among the Urban People of Birka—A Matter of Identity." In *Shetland and the Viking World: Proceedings of the Seventeenth Viking Congress*, pp. 189–96. Ed. V. E. Turner, O. A. Owen, and D. J. Waugh. Shetland Heritage Publications, 2016.

Hedenstierna-Jonson, Charlotte, and Anna Kjellström. "The Urban Woman: On the Role and Identity of Women in Birka." In *Kvinner i Vikingtid*, pp. 183–204. Ed. N. L. Coleman and N. Løkka. Makadam förlag, 2015.

Hedenstierna-Jonson, Charlotte, Anna Kjellström, Torun Zachrisson, Maja Krzewinska, Veronica Sobrado, Neil Price, Torsten Günther, Mattias Jakobsson, Anders Götherström, and Jan Storå. "A Female Viking Warrior Confirmed by Genomics." *American Journal of Physical Anthropology* (2017): 1–8.

Hjardar, Kim, and Vegard Vike. *Vikings at War.* Casemate, 2016.

Holck, Per. "The Oseberg Ship Burial, Norway: New Thoughts on the Skeletons from the Grave Mound." *European Journal of Archaeology* 9 (2006): 185–210.

Holck, Per. "The Skeleton from the Gokstad Ship: New Evaluation of an Old Find." *Norwegian Archaeological Review* 42.1 (2009): 40–49.

Holmquist, Lena. "Birka's Defence Works and Harbour." In *New Aspects on Viking-Age Urbanism*, pp. 35–46. Ed. L. Holmquist, S. Kalmring, and C. Hedenstierna-Jonson. Stockholm University Archaeological Research Laboratory, 2016.

Hraundal, Þórir Jónsson. *The Rus in Arabic Sources: Cultural Contacts and Identity.* Doctoral thesis. University of Bergen, 2013.

Larsson, Gunilla. *Ship and Society: Maritime Ideology in Late Iron Age Sweden.* Doctoral thesis. Uppsala University, 2007.

Larsson, Gunilla. "Early Contacts Between Scandinavia and the Orient." *The Silk Road* 9 (2011): 122–42.

Mägi, Marika. *In Austrvegr: The Role of the Eastern Baltic in Viking Age Communication Across the Baltic Sea.* Brill, 2018.

Moen, Marianne. *The Gendered Landscape.* Master's thesis. University of Oslo, 2010, published with different pagination as BAR International Series 2207 (2011).

Moen, Marianne. *Challenging Gender: A Reconsideration of Gender in the Viking Age Using the Mortuary Landscape.* Doctoral thesis. University of Oslo, 2019.

Normann, Lena. *Viking Women: The Narrative Voice in Woven Tapestries.* Cambria Press, 2008.

Olausson, Lena Holmquist, and Michael Olausson, eds. *The Martial Society: As-*

pects of Warriors, Fortifications, and Social Change in Scandinavia. Archaeological Research Laboratory Stockholm University, 2009 (especially the chapters by Fedir Androshchuk; Charlotte Hedenstierna-Jonson; Eva Hjärthner-Holdar; Judith Jesch; Anna Kjellström; Fredrik Lundström, Hedenstierna-Jonson, and Lena Holmquist Olausson; and Elisabeth Piltz).

Price, Neil. *The Viking Way: Magic and Mind in Late Iron Age Scandinavia*. 2nd ed. Oxbow Books, 2019.

Price, Neil. *Children of Ash and Elm: A History of the Vikings*. Basic Books, 2020.

Price, Neil, Charlotte Hedenstierna-Jonson, Torun Zachrisson, Anna Kjellström, Jan Storå, Maja Krzewinska, Torsten Günther, Veronica Sobrado, Mattias Jakobsson, and Anders Götherström. "Viking Warrior Women? Reassessing Birka Chamber Grave Bj.581." *Antiquity* 93 (2019): 181–98.

Short, William R. *Viking Weapons and Combat Techniques*. Westholme Publishing, 2014.

Skre, Dagfinn, ed. *Kaupang in Skiringssal*. Kaupang Excavation Project Publication Series, vol. 1. Aarhus University Press, 2007.

Skre, Dagfinn, ed. *Means of Exchange*. Kaupang Excavation Project Publication Series, vol. 2. Aarhus University Press, 2008.

Skre, Dagfinn, ed. *Things from the Town*. Kaupang Excavation Project Publication Series, vol. 3. Aarhus University Press, 2011.

Skre, Dagfinn, and Frans-Arne Stylegar. *Kaupang, the Viking Town: The Kaupang Exhibition at UKM, Oslo, 2004–2005*. University of Oslo, 2004.

Vedeler, Marianne. *Silk for the Vikings*. Ancient Textiles Series, vol. 15. Oxbow Books, 2014.

Williams, Gareth. *Weapons of the Viking Warrior*. Osprey Publishing, 2019.

NOTES

The sources listed under "Further Reading" are here referenced by author's last name and date of publication. Other sources, if cited more than once per chapter, are listed by author's last name and a short title. Names are given here in the authors' original spellings. Although modern Icelanders prefer to be called by their first names, for the sake of consistency I use their last names on second reference, following English practice. Translations from Old Norse / Icelandic sources are my own, unless otherwise noted here. I used the following editions:

Edda, by Snorri Sturluson, ed. Anthony Faulkes, 2nd ed. (Viking Society for Northern Research, 2005), vols. 1–2.
Eddukvæði (The Poetic Edda), ed. Gísli Sigurðsson (Íslensku bókaklúbbarnir, 2001), containing the poems *Atlamál in grænlensku, Fáfnismál, Hávamál, Helgakviða Hjörvarðssonar, Helgakviða Hundingsbana II, Helreið Brynhildar, Hymiskviða, Lokasenna, Sigurdrífumál, Sigurðarkviða in skamma, Völundarkviða,* and *Þrymskviða.*
Egils saga, ed. Sigurður Nordal (Íslenzkt fornrit II. Hið íslenzka fornritafélag, 1933).
Eiríks saga rauða, ed. Einar Ól. Sveinsson and Matthías Þórðarson (Íslenzkt fornrit IV. Hið íslenzka fornritafélag, 1935).
Eyrbyggja saga, ed. Einar Ól. Sveinsson and Matthías Þórðarson (Íslenzkt fornrit IV. Hið íslenzka fornritafélag, 1935).
Fornaldarsögur Norðurlanda, vols. 1–3, ed. Guðni Jónsson and Bjarni Vilhjálmsson (Reykjavík, 1943–44), containing *Bósa saga ok Herrauðs, Egils saga einhenda ok Ásmundar berserkjabana,* and *Hrólfssaga Gautrekssonar.*
Gísla saga Súrssonar, ed. Björn K. Þórólfsson and Guðni Jónsson, in *Vestfirðinga Sögur* (Íslenzkt fornrit VI. Hið íslenzka fornritafélag, 1958).
Grettis saga Ásmundarsonar, ed. Guðni Jónsson (Íslenzkt fornrit VII. Hið íslenzka fornritafélag, 1936).
Grottasöngr, ed. Clive Tolley (Viking Society for Northern Research, 2008).
Harðar saga ok Hólmverja, ed. Þórleifr Jónsson (Sigurður Kristjánsson, 1908).
Heimskringla, by Snorri Sturluson, vol. 1, ed. Bjarni Aðalbjarnarson (Íslenzkt fornrit XXVI.

Hið íslenzka fornritafélag, 1941), containing *Prologus* (Prologue), *Ynglinga saga, Hálf-dana saga svarta* (Saga of Halfdan the Black), *Haralds saga hárfagra* (Saga of Harald Fairhair), *Hákonar saga góða* (Saga of Hakon the Good), *Haralds saga gráfeldar* (Saga of Harald Graycloak), and *Ólafs saga Tryggvasonar* (Saga of Olaf Tryggvason).

Heimskringla, by Snorri Sturluson, vol. 2, ed. Bjarni Aðalbjarnarson (Íslenzkt fornrit XX-VII. Hið íslenzka fornritafélag, 1945), containing *Ólafs saga helga*.

Hervararkviða (The Waking of Angantyr), ed. E. V. Gordon, in *Introduction to Old Norse* (Oxford University Press, 1927; rpt., 1980), 142–47.

Hervarar saga: Saga Heiðreks Konungs ins Vitra: The Saga of King Heidrek the Wise, ed. and trans. Christopher Tolkien (Thomas Nelson and Sons, 1960).

Jómsvikinga saga: The Saga of the Jomsvikings, ed. N. F. Blake (Thomas Nelson and Sons, 1962).

Kormáks saga, ed. Einar Ól. Sveinsson (Íslenzkt fornrit VIII. Hið íslenzka fornritafélag, 1939).

Landnámabók (Book of Settlements), ed. Jakob Benediktsson (Íslenzkt fornrit I. Hið íslenzka fornritafélag, 1968).

Laxdæla saga, ed. Einar Ól. Sveinsson (Íslenzkt fornrit V. Hið íslenzka fornritafélag, 1934).

Njáls saga: Brennu-Njáls saga, ed. Einar Ól. Sveinsson (Íslenzkt fornrit XII. Hið íslenzka fornritafélag, 1954), containing the poem *Darraðarljóð*.

Nóregs konunga tal in *Ágrip Fagrskinna*, ed. Bjarni Einarsson (Íslenzkt fornrit XXIX. Hið íslenzka fornritafélag, 1985).

Orkneyinga saga, ed. Finnbogi Guðmundsson (Íslenzkt fornrit XXXIV. Hið íslenzka forn-ritafélag, 1965).

Poetry from the Kings' Sagas, vol. 1, *From Mythical Times to c. 1035*, ed. Diana Whaley (Bre-pols, 2012), containing the poems *Eiríksmál* and *Haraldskvæði (Hrafnsmál)*.

Poetry from the Kings' Sagas, vol. 2, *From c. 1035 to c. 1300*, ed. Kari Ellen Gade (Brepols, 2009), containing the *Poem About Haraldr harðraði* by Valgarðr á Velli.

Völsunga saga, ed. R. G. Finch (Thomas Nelson and Sons, 1965).

Örvar-Odds saga, ed. R. C. Boer (E. J. Brill, 1888).

INTRODUCTION: THE VALKYRIE'S GRAVE

1–2 **Bj581:** Hedenstierna-Jonson et al. (2017). Price et al. (2019) ("very surprised"); they list a dozen scholars who label Bj581 a warrior's grave. "Bj" stands for Björkø, the island on which the town of Birka lies. The contents of the grave are curated by the Swedish History Museum in Stockholm; see http://historiska.se/upptack-historien/context/786 -grav-kammargrav-bj-581/. Hjalmar Stolpe's notebooks and field drawings from 1878 are online at http://historiska.se/birka/digitala-resurser/. Bertil Almgren, *The Viking* (Tre Tryckare, Cagner, 1966), 44 ("position"). The coin is dated 913–33; 980 is the latest assumed date of the destruction of Birka. Dawn Hadley ("unquestionably masculine"), quoted by Shane McLeod, "Warriors and Women," *Early Medieval Europe* 19 (2011): 339.

2–3 **pirates:** Price (2020), 357–58. Magnus Magnusson, *Vikings!* (Elsevier-Dutton, 1980), 61 ("fury," "Bitter"). Nirmal Dass, *Viking Attacks on Paris* (Peeters, 2007), 39 ("ran-sacked"). Anne Stalsberg and Oddmunn Farbbregd, "Why So Many Viking Age Swords in Norway?" *Studia Universitas Cibiniensis* (2011): 47–52. Robert Wernick, *The Vikings* (Time-Life Books, 1979), 6 ("brawny").

3 **"sexing by metal":** Neil Price, interviewed April 8, 2016, credits the term to Ing-Marie Back Danielsson, who traced the practice to 1837 and reveals the uncertainty surround-ing robustness and pelvic structure; see Back Danielsson (2007), 26, 60–67. On Viking graves with female-looking bones, see Leszek Gardeła, "Warriors, Warlocks, Widows,"

Medievalists.net (December 2019). Martin Rundkvist, "Shield Maidens!" *Aardvarchae-ology* blog, July 29, 2019 ("noise"). In 2019, for a television special, *National Geographic* reconstructed the face of a warrior woman buried with her weapons in Nordre Kjølen, Solør, Norway. Identified as a female weapons burial when it was discovered in 1900, the grave came to new prominence after Birka grave Bj581 was confirmed to be female; DNA studies have been launched to learn about her "diet, age, disease history, possible injuries, genetic sex determination, and more," according to a November 18, 2019, press release from the University of Oslo.

3 **elite burials:** Moen (2019), 236–38, 260–63.

3 **know the Vikings:** Friðriksdóttir (2020) argues the opposing view, that Bj581 requires no rethinking of our understanding of the Viking world, 58–64; she warns, "We can't simply equate chromosomes with social gender." See also Price (2020) on the debate surrounding Bj581, 177–78, 328–29.

3 **Harby:** The National Museum of Denmark catalogues the figurine as "Valkyriefigur fra Tjørnehøj, Hårby"; see https://samlinger.natmus.dk/DO/asset/12789. On other images, see Gardeła (2018), 402–4.

4–5 **dismissed as a "valkyrie":** Snorri Sturluson describes valkyries in his *Edda*, 1:30; on Snorri being untrustworthy, see my biography of him, *Song of the Vikings* (Palgrave Macmillan, 2012). Judith Jesch, "Valkyries Revisited," *Norse and Viking Ramblings* blog, July 29, 2013 ("mythological," "warriors were men"). Friðriksdóttir (2020), 67 ("firmly supernatural"). Price (2019), 274 ("semi-human"). Christopher Abram, *Myths of the Pagan North* (Continuum, 2011), 68 ("perfectly ordinary"). Neil Price, "The Way of the Warrior," in G. Williams, P. Pentz, and M. Wemhoff, eds., *Viking* (National Museum of Denmark, 2013), 116.

5 **gender lines:** I discuss the household duties of Viking women in *The Far Traveler* (Harcourt, 2007), chs. 6 and 9, and *Ivory Vikings* (St. Martin's Press, 2015), ch. 3. Ben Raffield, Neil Price, and Mark Collard, "Polygyny, Concubinage, and the Social Lives of Women in Viking-Age Scandinavia," *Viking and Medieval Scandinavia* 13 (2017): 187 ("dominant role"). Preben M. Sørensen, *The Unmanly Man* (Odense University Press, 1983), 20 ("decisions"). Price (2020), 155–58.

5 **keys:** Jenny Jochens, *Women in Old Norse Society* (Cornell University Press, 1995), 132. Anne-Sofie Gräslund, "The Position of Iron Age Scandinavian Women," in B. Arnold and N. L. Wicker, eds., *Gender and the Archaeology of Death* (Altamira Press, 2001), 84 ("for honor"). The bawdy *Þrymskviða* is the mythological poem "most often mentioned" as having been composed after Iceland's conversion to Christianity; see John Lindow, *Norse Mythology* (Oxford University Press, 2001), 14.

5–6 **Women with weapons:** Gardeła (2018) names eighteen in histories, sagas, and myths. Friðriksdóttir (2013) adds four saga women. Price (2019) names fifty-one valkyries and adds one historical woman, 275, 280. I add three giant women mentioned in poems. On the laws, see Carol Clover, "Regardless of Sex," *Speculum* 68 (1993): 363–87.

6 **Victorian society:** Moen (2010 [2011]), 29–30; (2019), 11, 14, 72, 74–77, 87–88, 106. Elizabeth Arwill-Nordbladh, "The Swedish Image of Viking Age Women," and Liv Helga Dommasnes, "Women, Kinship, and the Basis of Power in the Norwegian Viking Age," in R. Samson, ed., *Social Approaches to Viking Studies* (Cruithne Press, 1991), 53–58, 65–73.

6 **Calling keys the symbol:** Heidi Lund Berg, "'Truth' and Reproduction of Knowledge," in Eriksen et al. (2015), 124–43. Pernille Pantmann, "The Symbolism of Keys in Female Graves on Zealand During the Viking Age," in L. Boye, ed., *The Iron Age on Zealand* (Royal Society of Northern Antiquities, 2011), 75 ("misinterpretation," "mistake," "myth").

6–9 **martial society:** Hedenstierna-Jonson (2006), 26; (2015), 83. Hjardar and Vike (2016), 31, 180. Moen (2019), 282. Judith Jesch, "Constructing the Warrior Ideal in the Late Viking Age," in Olausson and Olausson (2009), 73 ("fled not"). Clover, "Regardless of Sex," 367 ("any more decisive"), 368 ("like a son"), 370 (*drengr*). Tom Shippey, *Laughing Shall I Die* (Reaktion Books, 2018), 230 ("led by a leader"). John Gillingham, "Women, Children, and the Profits of War," in J. L. Nelson, S. Reynolds, and S. M. Johns, eds., *Gender and Historiography* (Institute of Historical Research, 2012), 68 (*manna*). Saxo Grammaticus, trans. P. Fisher, *The History of the Danes, Books I–IX* (D. S. Brewer, 1970–80; rpt., 2008), 280 (spelled Lathgertha, "battle in the forefront"). The valkyrie names are trans. Price (2019), 280. *Grottasöngr*, st. 15 ("As heroes"). *Hervarar saga*, ch. 4 ("*kvennmann*").

9–10 **bones can be eloquent:** Hedenstierna-Jonson et al. (2017); Charlotte Hedenstierna-Jonson, interviewed June 14, 2018 (on the skull). Holck (2009), 45–46 ("splintery," average height). Holck (2006) notes that bodies in modern Norwegian graveyards disintegrate in fifteen to twenty-five years, 190. Anna Kjellström, "People in Transition," in V. Turner, ed., *Shetland and the Viking World* (Shetland Amenity Trust, 2016), 198 (loose teeth).

10–12 **surrounded by weapons:** Price et al. (2019). Hedenstierna-Jonson (2006), 55–57; "Women at War?" *SAA Archaeological Record* 18 (May 2018): 28–31; "Traces of Contacts," in B. Tobias, ed., *Die Archäologie der Frühen Ungarn* (Verlag des Römisch-Germanischen Zentralmuseums, 2012), 29–48; and "Close Encounters with the Byzantine Border Zones," in O. Minaeva and L. Holmquist, eds., *Scandinavia and the Balkans* (Cambridge Scholars Publishing, 2015), 139–52. Fedir Androshchuk (2013), 222; "Vikings and Farmers," in Olausson and Olausson (2009), 93–104. Holmquist (2016). Short (2014), 14 (61 percent).

12–13 **location:** Charlotte Hedenstierna-Jonson, interviewed June 14, 2018. See also the online Supporting Information for Hedenstierna-Jonson et al. (2017) and the online Supplementary Material for Price et al. (2019).

13 **game pieces:** Gavin K. E. Davies, *From Rules to Experience* (doctoral thesis, Swansea University, 2015), 26, 43–61 (luck). Mads Ravn, "The Use of Symbols in Burials in Migration Age Europe," in D. S. Olausson and H. Vandkilde, eds., *Form, Function & Context* (Almqvist & Wiksell International, 2000), 289 ("strategic thinking"). Helene Whittaker, "Game Boards and Gaming Pieces in Funerary Contexts in the Northern European Iron Age," *Nordlit Tidskrift for Kultur og Litteratur* 20 (2006): 107 ("success in warfare").

14 **date their finds:** Aina Margrethe Heen-Pettersen, "The Earliest Wave of Viking Activity?" *European Journal of Archaeology* 22 (2019): 523–41.

1: HERVOR'S SONG

20 **Hervor's Song:** *Hervararkviða*, also known as *The Waking of Angantyr*, is contained in *Hervarar saga ok Heiðreks*, literally, *Hervor's Saga and Heidrek's*. In his edition, Christopher Tolkien changed the name of the saga to *The Saga of King Heidrek the Wise*, giving all agency to Hervor's son. I've taken the opposite approach, and refer to it as *Hervarar saga*, or the *Saga of Hervor*.

20 **translated into English:** Heather O'Donoghue, *From Asgard to Valhalla* (I. B. Tauris, 2007), 109.

20 **Gothic novel:** Anthony Faulkes, "The Viking Mind, or In Pursuit of the Viking," *Saga-Book* 31 (2007): 59.

21–22 **composed around 1120:** Maria Mundt, "*Hervarar Saga ok Heiðreks Konungs* Revisited," in T. Paroli, ed., *Poetry in the Scandinavian Middle Ages* (Spoleto Centro Italiano de Studi sull'Alto Medioevo, 1988), 263–74. Tolkien, *Saga of King Heidrek*, vii ("historical authenticity"), in G. Turville-Petre, ed., *Hervarar saga ok Heiðreks* (VSNR, 1956), xi–xx ("ruthless rewriting," "remote antiquity"). Back Danielsson (2007), 59 ("sorting frenzy").

22 **poems:** Snorri Sturluson, *Heimskringla Prologus* ("still know," "mockery"); *Separate Saga of St Olaf*, quoted by Guðrún Nordal, *Skaldic Versifying and Social Discrimination in Medieval Iceland* (VSNR, 2003), 12 ("composed correctly").

23–24 **hnefatafl:** *Hervarar saga*, ch. 9 ("what women"). Gavin K. E. Davies, *From Rules to Experience* (doctoral thesis, Swansea University, 2015), 26, 33–40, 43–61 (luck). Elisabeth Piltz, "Byzantium and *He taktike episteme* as a Cognitive Reference for Varangian Military Tactics," in Olausson and Olausson (2009), 152. Hjardar and Vike (2016), 24, 93–94. Elsa Roesdahl, quoted in Kristian Sjøgren, "What Made the Vikings So Superior in Warfare?" *Science Nordic* (December 20, 2017).

24 **Battle of the Goths:** *Hervarar saga*, ch. 10. Tolkien, *Saga of King Heidrek*, viii ("oldest of all").

25 **"not like other people":** *Hervararkviða (The Waking of Angantyr)*, line 94 in Gordon's edition; the line does not appear in all manuscripts of the poem. Sandra Ballif Straubhaar, *Old Norse Women's Poetry* (D. S. Brewer, 2011), 65 ("hardly human").

25 **Viking band:** Charlotte Hedenstierna-Jonson, "A Brotherhood of Feasting and Campaigning," in E. Regner et al., eds., *From Ephesos to Dalecarlia* (Stockholm Museum of National Antiquities, 2009), 43–53. Ben Raffield, Claire Greenlow, Neil Price, and Mark Collard, "Ingroup Identification, Identity Fusion, and the Formation of Viking War Bands," *World Archaeology* 48 (2016): 35–50. Ashot Margaryan et al., "Population Genomics of the Viking World," *Nature* 585 (September 17, 2020): 390–96.

26 **amulets:** Shane McLeod, "The Acculturation of Scandinavians in England," *Journal of the Australian Early Medieval Association* 9 (2013): 83. Peter Pentz, "Viking Art, Snorri Sturluson, and Some Recent Metal Detector Finds," *Fornvännen* 113 (2018): 17–33. Williams (2019), 27, 29. Pamela D. Toler, *Women Warriors* (Beacon, 2019), 35n (challenge coins).

26–27 **sword buried:** Fedir Androschchuk, "Vikings and Farmers," in Olausson and Olausson (2009), 93–95. Miskawayh, trans. P. Lunde and C. Stone, *Ibn Fadlan and the Land of Darkness* (Penguin, 2012), 151 ("sharpness"). *Hervarar saga*, ch. 1–3 (Tyrfing). One manuscript contains more detail on the sword's creation; see Tolkien, *Saga of King Heidrek*, 68. *Grettis saga*, ch. 17 (Jokul's Gift). *Egils saga*, ch. 61 (Slicer).

27–28 **web of friendship:** Viðar Pálsson, *Power and Political Communication* (doctoral thesis, University of California, Berkeley, 2010). *Hávamál*, st. 41 ("Long friendships"), 42 ("be a friend"). *Haraldskvæði (Hrafnsmál)*, st. 19 ("By their gear").

29 **"rule all Norway":** *Hervarar saga*, ch. 3.

2: GUNNHILD MOTHER-OF-KINGS

32 **Shining Hall:** Skre (2007), 223–42.

32–33 **Snorri:** Sigurðar Nordal, *Snorri Sturluson* (Helgafell, 1920; rpt., 1973), 76. On his character, see my biography of him, *Song of the Vikings* (Palgrave Macmillan, 2012).

33–34 **Gunnhild:** *Haralds saga hárfagra*, ch. 35–39, ch. 43 ("never seen"). *Haralds saga gráfeldar*, ch. 1, 3 ("how to rule"). *Nóregs konunga tal* ("Age of Gunnhild"), 202. M. J. Driscoll, ed., *Ágrip af Nóregskonungasögum* (VSNR, 1995), 87–91 ("smear campaign"). Devra Kunin, trans., *A History of Norway and the Passion and Miracles of the Blessed Óláfr* (VSNR, 2001), 15 (princess). Jóna Guðbjörg Torfadóttir, "Gunnhildur and the Male Whores," *Sagas & Societies Conference* (Universität Tübingen, 2002).

35 **Eirik Bloodaxe:** *Haralds saga hárfagra*, ch. 43 ("blessed"). *Egils saga*, ch. 78 ("gleamed").

35 **Harald Fairhair:** *Haraldskvæði* (*Hrafnsmál*), st. 19 ("silver-clad swords"). *Egils saga*, ch. 4 ("harshest terms").

36 **Bjorn, king of Vestfold:** *Haralds saga hárfagra*, ch. 35. On Tunsberg (modern Tønsberg), see Skre (2007), 469.

38 **Feast halls:** *Egils saga*, ch. 22. Lydia Carstens, "Powerful Space," in Eriksen et al. (2015), 12–27. Price (2020), 98–99.

3: THE TOWN BENEATH THE SHINING HALL

41–43 **Kaupang:** Skre and Stylegar (2004), 26, 29–33, 42–43 ("modesty"). Skre (2007), 223–42, 467–69. Skre and Lars Pilø, "Introduction to the Site," in Skre (2008), 24. Skre, "Kaupang—'Skiringssalr,'" in Brink and Price (2008). Skre (2011), 446. Janet Bately and Anton Englert, *Ohthere's Voyages* (Roskilde Viking Ship Museum, 2007), 44–47; I use the Old Norse spelling, "Ottar." Moen (2019), 190 ("burials speak").

43 **"strong, healthy":** Laura Maravall Buckwalter and Joerg Baten, "Valkyries," *Economics & Human Biology* 34 (August 2019): 181–93. For a contradictory study, see Price (2020), 159.

43 **stewed:** Daniel Serra and Hanna Tunberg, *An Early Meal* (ChronoCopia Publishing, 2013), 143, 155, 157.

44 **Vestfold:** Moen (2010 [2011]), 32.

44 **Hedeby:** Michael Müller-Wille, "Hedeby in Ohthere's Time," in Bately and Englert, *Ohthere's Voyages*, 165. Volker Hilberg, "Hedeby in Wulfstan's Days," in A. Englert and A. Trakadas, *Wulfstan's Voyage* (Roskilde Viking Ship Museum, 2009), 92.

45 **Lindisfarne:** Gwyn Jones, *History of the Vikings* (Oxford University Press, 1968), 194 ("from the blue"). *Anglo-Saxon Chronicle*, trans. Benjamin Thorpe (Longman, Greene, Longman, and Roberts, 1861), 48 ("forewarnings").

46–47 **trade route:** Bjørn Myhre, "The Early Viking Age in Norway," *Acta Archaeologica* 71 (2000): 43–44. Tenaya Jorgensen, *The Scandinavian Trade Network in the Early Viking Age* (master's thesis, University of Oslo, 2017), 7, 21, 26–29. Aina Margrethe Heen-Pettersen, "The Earliest Wave of Viking Activity?" *European Journal of Archaeology* (2019): 523–41. *Haralds saga hárfagra*, ch. 34 (Jaeren). J. R. L. Anderson, *Vinland Voyage* (Funk and Wagnalls, 1967), 67 ("vicious tumble"). *Frankish Annals*, quoted by Skre (2011), 445 ("set out for Vestfold").

47 **Artisans:** *Völundarkviða*. Johann Callmer, "Wayland," *Uppåkra Studies* 7 (2002): 337–61. Skre and Stylegar (2004), 47, 50, 58. Skre (2011), 411, 417, 426–33.

48 **slavery:** Jorgensen, *Scandinavian Trade Network*, 21. Ben Raffield, "The Slave Markets of the Viking World," *Slavery & Abolition* 40 (2019): 682–704. Price (2020), 141–54.

49 **dirhams:** Christoph Kilger in Skre (2008), 239 (fake), 246.

49 **risk of trade:** Skre and Stylegar (2004), 59. Frans-Arne Stylegar, "The Kaupang Cemeteries Revisited," in Skre (2007), 83. Skre (2007), 446–52. Ingrid Gustin, "Trade and Trust in the Baltic Sea Area During the Viking Age," in J. H. Barrett and S. J. Gibbon, eds., *Maritime Societies of the Viking and Medieval World* (Maney Publishing, 2015), 25–40.

4: LITTLE "HEL-SKINS"

51 **Arrow-Odd:** retold from *Örvar-Odds saga*, ch. 35.

52 **Olaf and Sigrod:** Snorri Sturluson, in *Haralds saga hárfagra*, ch. 35, is unclear about how long after the killing of Bjorn the Merchant Eirik Bloodaxe killed his brothers Olaf and Sigrod.

53 **bow chisels:** The lines of verse are translated by: H. Pálsson and P. Edwards, trans., *Egil's Saga* (Penguin, 1976), 148 ("bow chisels"). A. Faulkes, trans., *Snorri Sturluson: Edda*

(Everyman, 1987; rpt., 1995), 139, 141 ("sea thuds," "froth piles," slightly revised). A. W. Brøgger and H. Shetelig, *Viking Ships* (Twayne, 1951; rpt., 1971), 113 ("mane").

54–57 **childhood:** *Hervarar saga*, ch. 3 (Hervor). *Landnámabók*, ch. 112 ("Hel-skins"); trans. H. Pálsson and P. Edwards (University of Manitoba, 1972), 57 ("puny-looking"). On loving mothers, see Friðriksdóttir (2013), 129. *Egils saga*, ch. 31 (feast), ch. 40 (foster mother, ball game). *Njáls saga*, ch. 11, 12, 17 (Hallgerd). *Laxdæla saga*, ch. 28 ("We both lie abed"). *Landnámabók*, ch. 68 (fishing). *Laxdæla saga*, ch. 29 (Leg-Biter). *Njáls saga*, ch. 95 (Hildigunn). *Óláfs saga helga*, ch. 2 (Olaf). *Grettis saga*, ch. 14 (geese).

57 **Irish legal text:** Bronagh Ni Chonaill, "Child-Centred Law in Medieval Ireland," in R. Davis and T. Dunne, eds., *The Empty Throne* (Cambridge University Press, 2008), 14–15. Bronagh Ni Chonaill, "Flying a Kite with the Children of Hiberno-Norse Dublin," in J. Bradley, A. J. Fletcher, and A. Simms, eds., *Dublin in the Medieval World* (Four Courts Press, 2009), 17.

58 **"make the bread":** *Völsunga saga*, ch. 6–7.

59 **Tools:** Moen (2019), 97, 190. See also my *Ivory Vikings* (St. Martin's Press, 2015), 135, 144.

59–60 **rough games:** Ni Chonaill, "Flying a Kite." Leszek Gardeła, "What the Vikings Did for Fun," *World Archaeology* 42 (2012): 234–47. Short (2014), 161. Hjardar and Vike (2016), 61–63. *Ólafs saga Tryggvasonar*, ch. 85 (juggle, oars).

60 **Play weapons:** Ben Raffield, "Playing Vikings," *Cultural Anthropology* 60 (December 2019). *Hervarar saga*, ch. 3 (Hervor). *Eyrbyggja saga*, ch. 40 (Kjartan). *Russian Primary Chronicle*, trans. Olgerd P. Sherbowitz-Wetzor (Medieval Academy of America, 1953), 80 (Sviatoslav). *Landnámabók*, ch. 80 (Herjolf). *Örvar-Odds saga*, ch. 2 (Arrow-Odd).

60 **miniature farms:** *Óláfs saga helga*, ch. 76.

60 **"make-believe":** *Njáls saga*, ch. 8, loosely translated. In the saga, the girl is not directly quoted, though she is "chattering" with the boys.

61 **fight at Tunsberg:** *Haralds saga hárfagra*, ch. 35.

61 **"king-slayer":** *Hákonar saga góða*, ch. 31.

5: QUEEN ASA'S REVENGE

65–66 **Queen Asa:** *Ynglinga saga*, ch. 48. *Hálfdana saga svarta*, ch. 1. Lee Hollander, trans., *Heimskringla* (University of Texas Press, 1964; rpt., 2009), 48 ("deep-wrought wiles").

67 **buried in the Oseberg ship:** Holck (2006). Nina Nordstrom, "The Immortals," in H. Williams and M. Giles, eds., *Archaeologists and the Dead* (Oxford University Press, 2016), 204–32. Niels Bonde and Arne Emil Christensen dated the burial chamber to 834; see "Dendrochronological Dating of the Viking Age Ship Burials at Oseberg, Gokstad, and Tune, Norway," *Antiquity* 67 (1993): 575–83. To deduce the date of Queen Asa's death, we must assess Snorri Sturluson's claims that Harald Fairhair became king at age ten and ruled for more than seventy years. We must also guess Asa's age when she gave birth to Halfdan and how long she ruled in Agdir. I find she could have died in about 839 at age thirty-five to forty. Gwyn Jones in *A History of the Vikings* (Oxford University Press, 1968), 8, believes Asa died after 858. On the DNA tests, see Price (2020), 199.

67–68 **Oseberg grave mound:** Thorleif Sjøvold, *The Oseberg Find* (Oslo Universitetets Oldsaksamling, 1969), 10. Anne Stine Ingstad, "The Interpretation of the Oseberg Find," in O. Crumlin-Pedersen and B. M. Thyre, eds., *The Ship as a Symbol in Prehistoric and Medieval Scandinavia* (Copenhagen Nationalmuseet, 1995), 146–47. Frands Herschend, "Ship Grave Hall Passage," in G. Barnes and M. Clunies Ross, eds., *Old Norse Myths, Literature and Society* (University of Sydney Centre for Medieval Studies, 2000), 142–51. Robert Ferguson, *The Vikings* (Viking Penguin, 2009), 15–16. Kirsten Ruffoni, *Viking Age Queens* (master's thesis, University of Oslo, 2011), 20, 28. Niels Bonde and

Frans-Arne Stylegar, "Between Sutton Hoo and Oseberg," *Danish Journal of Archaeology* 5 (2016): 19–33. Eva Andersson Strand, "Northerners," in M.-L. Nosch et al., eds., *Global Textile Encounters* (Oxbow Books, 2014), 77. Heide Eldar, "The Early Viking Ship Types," in *Særtrykk fra Sjøfartshistorisk Árbok 2012* (Bergen, 2014), 81–83. Lisbeth Weichel, "The Viking Ship That Couldn't Sail Is Headed for Roskilde," Viking Ship Museum press release, July 6, 2015. The retrieved contents of the Oseberg mound are curated at the Viking Ship Museum, Bygdøy, Norway, and listed online by the University of Oslo's Museum of Cultural History at www.khm.uio.no.

68 **"wave runes"**: *Völsunga saga*, ch. 21.

69–71 **burial ceremony**: Neil Price, "Passing into Poetry," *Medieval Archaeology* 54 (2010): 123–56. *Haralds saga hárfagra*, ch. 8 (three summers). *Ibn Fadlan and the Land of Darkness*, trans. P. Lunde and C. Stone (Penguin, 2012), 49, 51. *Ynglinga saga*, ch. 8 (burned). *Sigurðarkviða in skamma* ("Build me a pyre") and *Helreið Brynhildar* ("two pyres"). *Heimskringla Prologus* ("Uppsala").

71 **"women are silenced"**: Robert MacFarlane, *Underland* (W. W. Norton, 2019), 191.

72 **grave robbers'**: A. W. Brøgger and H. Shetelig, *Viking Ships* (Twayne, 1951; rpt., 1971), 67. Herschend, "Ship Grave Hall Passage," 144–45. Holck (2006), 190. Moen (2010 [2011]), 37. Ruffoni, *Viking Age Queens*, 23, 34. Gardeła (2013), 291. Terje Gansum, "Role the Bones—from Iron to Steel," *Norwegian Archaeological Review* 37 (2004): 41–57. Back Danielsson (2007), 247–48 ("bone coal").

72 **"rode on the wind"**: *Helgakviða Hjörvarðssonar*, prose after st. 9.

73 **Gokstad mound**: Marianne Moen, interviewed August 20, 2018, compares it to Oseberg; Moen (2010 [2011]), 39–43, 73, 96, 245.The retrieved contents are curated at the Viking Ship Museum, Bygdøy, Norway, and listed online by the University of Oslo's Museum of Cultural History at www.khm.uio.no. On the date of the burial, see Bonde and Christensen, "Dendrochronological Dating." On the skeleton, see Holck (2009).

6: THE WINTER NIGHTS FEAST

76–79 **Winter Nights:** I based my reconstruction of the ritual on Terry Gunnell, "The Season of the *Dísir*," *Cosmos* 16 (2000): 117–49. Eldar Heide, "Spinning *Seiðr*," in A. Andrén, K. Jennbert, and C. Raudvere, eds., *Old Norse Religion in Long-Term Perspectives* (Nordic Academic Press, 2006), 164–70. Price (2019), 35, 129, 168. Gavin Lucas and Thomas McGovern, "Bloody Slaughter," *European Journal of Archaeology* 10 (2007): 7–30. Lectures by Einar Selvik at the Midgardsblot in Borre, Norway, August 17–18, 2019 ("power of poetry"). *Ynglinga saga*, ch. 15 ("kings' blood," Domaldi), 29 (Adils). *Örvar-Odds saga*, ch. 3 ("wrestle"). *Eiríks saga rauða*, ch. 4 ("worthy family").

79 **staff of power:** Leszek Gardeła, "A Biography of the Seiðr-staffs," in L. Slupecki and J. Morawiec, eds., *Between Paganism and Christianity in the North* (Wydawnictwo Uniwersytetu Rzeszowskiego, 2009), 121–64 and 190–219. Price (2019), 84, 132–47. Eldar Heide ("mind-threads"), quoted in Leszek Gardeła, "Into Viking Minds," *Viking and Medieval Scandinavia* 4 (2008): 49. Ingrid Gustin, "Of Rods and Roles," in C. Theune et al., eds., *Zwischen Fjorden und Steppe* (Leidorf, 2010), 343–54.

80 **men are named witches:** Astrid Ogilvie and Gísli Pálsson, "Weather and Witchcraft in the Sagas of Icelanders," presented at the Thirteenth International Saga Conference, Durham and York (August 2006). Miriam Mayburd, "Helzt þóttumk nú heima í milli," *Arkiv för Nordisk Filologi* 129 (2014): 135.

80 **dísablót:** *Egils saga*, ch. 44 (led by Gunnhild). *Hákonar saga góða*, ch. 14 ("sprinklers"), 17, 18. *Eyrbyggja saga*, ch. 37. *Gísla saga Súrssonar*, ch. 20. Gunnell, "Season of the Dísir." Jane-Anne Denison, *Rituals in the Viking World* (master's thesis, University of the Highlands and Islands, 2016), 24.

81 *dísir*: Maria Kvilhaug, *The Maiden with the Mead* (master's thesis, University of Oslo, 2004), 38. Judith Quinn, "Mythological Motivation in Eddic Heroic Poetry," in P. Acker and C. Larrington, eds., *Revisiting the Poetic Edda* (Routledge, 2013), 173. Anne Irene Riisøy, "Eddic Poetry," *Journal of the North Atlantic* Special Volume 8 (2016): 157–71. Terry Gunnell, "*Blótgyðjur, Goðar, Mimi,* Incest, and Wagons," in P. Hermann et al., eds., *Old Norse Mythology: Comparative Perspectives* (Harvard University Press, 2017), 113–38.

83–84 **goddesses:** Gro Steinsland (creation myth), cited by Back Danielsson (2007), 57. Gardeła, "Into Viking Minds," 64 (chairs). *Edda,* 1:13, 21 (Frigg), 21 ("no less holy"), 23–24 (Skadi), 24 (Freyja), 29–30 (Eir, Vor, Syn, Hlin, and Gna); 2:61 (Skadi). John Lindow, *Norse Mythology* (Oxford University Press, 2001), 126 ("lust").

84 **Odin:** *Ynglinga saga,* ch. 6 (berserks). Terry Gunnell, "From One High-One to Another," in L. Slupecki and R. Simek, eds., *Conversions* (Fassbaender, 2013), 153–78. Price (2019), 59–62.

85 **Gullveig:** Kvilhaug, *Maiden with the Mead,* 135–40.

86 **Freyja:** *Ynglinga saga,* ch. 6 (magic), ch. 10 ("lady"). Kvilhaug, *Maiden with the Mead,* 37 (Great Goddess). Anne Irene Riisøy, "Performing Oaths in Eddic Poetry," *Journal of the North Atlantic* Special Volume 8 (2016): 146 (sun).

86 **"god house":** Søren Diinhoff of the University Museum of Bergen, quoted by Tom Metcalfe, "1,200-Year-Old Pagan Temple to Thor and Odin Unearthed in Norway," *Live Science* (October 8, 2020). Katherine Morris, *Sorceress or Witch?* (University Press of America, 1991), 2, 5–6, 129–30. Neil Price and Bo Gräslund, "Excavating the Fimbulwinter?" in F. Riede, ed., *Past Vulnerability* (Aarhus University Press, 2015).

7: THE VALKYRIES' TASK

90 **"trolls' foe":** *Egils saga,* ch. 44.

91–93 **cup bearer:** Michael J. Enright, *Lady with a Mead Cup* (Four Courts Press, 1996; rpt., 2013), 7 ("ritual of lordship"), 2 ("cohesion"). Christopher Abram, *Myths of the Pagan North* (Continuum, 2011), 68, 105. Price (2019), 279. *Edda,* 1:30–31 ("serve in Valhalla"). *Hákonarmál* in *Hákonar saga góða,* ch. 32 ("ale from the Aesir"). *Eiríksmál,* st. 1 ("What did I dream?"). Sandra Ballif Straubhaar, *Old Norse Women's Poetry* (D. S. Brewer, 2011), 16 (Gunnhild as poet). John Lindow, *Norse Mythology* (Oxford University Press, 2001), 104 ("Lone-Fighters"). Luke John Murphy, *Herjans Dísir* (master's thesis, University of Iceland, 2013), 118 ("recalcitrant teenagers").

93–94 **"women drinking":** Back Danielsson (2007), 81 ("How close"). *Ynglinga saga,* ch. 36 (King Ingjald), 37 (pairs, Hildigunn). *Ólafs saga Tryggvasonar,* ch. 43 (Sigrid). *Egils saga,* ch. 48 ("lots"); Sandra Ballif Straubhaar translated the poem "Who said" in *Old Norse Women's Poetry,* 24.

94–95 **kitchen:** Moen (2019), 261 (graves). Daniel Serra and Hanna Tunberg, *An Early Meal* (ChronoCopia Publishing, 2013), 139 ("time and effort"), 179 (joints). *Helgakviða Hundingsbana II. Grottasöngr,* st. 15 ("As heroes").

96–97 **beer and ale:** Merryn Dineley and Graham Dineley, in Serra and Tunberg, *An Early Meal* (2013), 134–36; "Where Were the Viking Brew Houses?" presented at the Seventh Experimental Archaeology Conference, Cardiff University and St. Fagans Museum (January 11–12, 2013). Geir Grønnesby, "Hot Rocks! Beer Brewing on Viking and Medieval Age Farms in Trøndelag," in F. Iversen and H. Petersson, eds., *The Agrarian Life of the North 2000 BC–AD 1000* (Portal, 2016) 133–50. Jenny Jochens, *Women in Old Norse Society* (Cornell University Press, 1995), 121. Stephen Law, "Berserkir Beer," presented at the 46th International Congress on Medieval Studies, Western Michigan University, Kalamazoo (May 12, 2011) ("stupefying," "whopping"). *Hymiskviða,* st. 2–3 (Aegir). *Sigurdrífumál,* st. 7, 29, 30. *Hávamál,* st. 12–13.

8: THE FEUD

101 **The feud:** *Egils saga*, ch. 44–45, 48–49, 56–57.

101-2 **women and wisdom:** Judith Jesch, *Women in the Viking Age* (Boydell Press, 1991), 156. Friðriksdóttir (2013), 115; Jóhanna Katrín Friðriksdóttir, "Hyggin ok Forsjál," in M. Arnold and A. Finlay, eds., *Making History* (VSNR, 2010), 73.

102 *Saga of Hrolf:* *Hrólfssaga Gautrekssonar*. Hermann Pálsson and Paul Edwards, *Hrolf Gautreksson: A Viking Romance* (University of Toronto Press, 1972), 7 ("unacceptable"), 20 ("realistic"). Michael Chesnutt ("late," "frivolous"), quoted in Friðriksdóttir, "Hyggin ok Forsjál," 69, 70. Marianne Kalinke, *Bridal-Quest Romance in Medieval Iceland* (Cornell University Press, 1990), 6. Emily Lethbridge, "Some Observations on Íslendingasögur Manuscripts and the Case of Njáls Saga," *Arkiv for Nordisk Filologi* (January 2014): 84–88.

102 *"skrifaði í tabula":* *Hrólfssaga Gautrekssonar*, ch. 37. Pálsson and Edwards, *Hrolf Gautreksson*, 148 ("committed to vellum"; I've substituted the more common term "parchment"). Normann (2008), 1–3, 31 ("to weave").

106 **"submission":** Pálsson and Edwards, *Hrolf Gautreksson*, 9. *Hrólfssaga Gautrekssonar*, ch. 11.

109 **"Grim Gunnhild":** *Egils saga*, ch. 57.

109 **Hakon the Good:** *Hákonar saga góða*, ch. 1–3.

110 **"absolute chronology":** H. Pálsson and P. Edwards, trans., *Egil's Saga* (Penguin, 1976), 248.

110 **possibly not Bloodaxe:** Clare Downham, "Eric Bloodaxe—Axed?" *Medieval Scandinavia* 14 (2004): 51–77.

9: THE QUEEN OF ORKNEY

114 **Horse Island:** Now Mainland, Orkney. That Gunnhild and Eirik lived at Stone Ness (Stenness) is my guess. James H. Barrett et al., "Diet and Ethnicity During the Viking Colonization of Northern Scotland," *Antiquity* 75 (2001): 145–54. Jane Harrison, "Settlement Landscapes in the North Atlantic," *Journal of the North Atlantic* Special Volume 4 (2013): 129–47. Raymond C. Lamb, "Carolingian Orkney and Its Transformation," in C. E. Batey et al., eds., *The Viking Age in Caithness, Orkney and the North Atlantic* (Edinburgh University Press, 1993), 260–71. Olwyn Owen, "The Scar Boat Burial," in J. Adams and K. Holman, eds., *Scandinavia and Europe 800–1350* (Brepols, 2004), 3–34. *Orkneyinga saga*, ch. 4–10.

116 **Aud the Deep-Minded:** *Landnámabók*, ch. 95–110, 170.

116 **marriages:** *Njáls saga*, ch. 97 ("find you a good wife"). Jenny Jochens, *Women in Old Norse Society* (Cornell University Press, 1995), 21, 29, 37. Thomas Bredsdorff, *Chaos and Love: The Philosophy of the Icelandic Family Saga* (Copenhagen: Museum Tusculanum Press, 2001), 22. Else Mundal, "The Double Impact of Christianization for Women in Old Norse Culture," in K. E. Børresen et al., eds., *Gender and Religion* (Carocci, 2001), 237. Birgit Sawyer, "Marriage, Inheritance, and Property in Early Medieval Scandinavia," n.d., posted on her Academia.edu page. *Orkneyinga saga*, ch. 8–9.

117-23 **textile arts:** The costumes described are my speculation, based on many sources, chiefly: Moen (2019), 33–34. Elizabeth Wayland Barber, *Women's Work* (W. W. Norton, 1995), 35, 87, 191, 194, 202, 234, 282. Thor Ewing, *Viking Clothing* (History Press, 2012), 24–58, 65–69, 79, 90–99, 123, 131, 144, 154–57, 164, 167. Jenny Jochens, "Before the Male Gaze," in L. Lönnroth, ed., *The Audience of the Sagas* (Gothenburg University, 1991), 1:250–51. Colleen Batey et al., eds., *Cultural Atlas of the Viking World* (Facts-on-File, 1994), 67. Michèle Hayeur-Smith, *Draupnir's Sweat and Mardöll's Tears* (Hadrian Books, 2004), 71, 92; "Weaving Wealth," in A. L. Huang and C. Jahnke, eds., *Textiles and the Medieval Economy* (Oxbow Books, 2015), 27–28. Marta Hoffman, *The Warp-Weighted Loom* (Oslo Universitetsforlaget, 1974), 247, 269. Agnes Geijer, "Textile Finds from Birka," in N. B. Harte and K. G. Ponting, eds., *Cloth and Clothing in Medieval Europe* (Heinemann Educational Books, 1982), 81, 86. Penelope Walton Rogers, *Textile Production at 16–22 Coppergate* (Council for British Archaeology, 1997), 1735, 1744–49, 1769. Bertil Almgren, *The Viking* (Tre Tryckare, Cagner, 1966), 200. Nobuko Kajitani, "A Man's Caftan and Leggings from the North Caucasus of the Eighth to Tenth Century," *Metropolitan Museum Journal* 36 (2001): 106. Eva Andersson Strand, "Northerners," in M.-L. Nosch et al., eds., *Global Textile Encounters* (Oxbow Books, 2014), 77. Price (2020), 392 (slave labor); he warns that the discovery of the Hårby "valkyrie" in 2012 and another figurine at Revninge, Denmark, in 2014 "have shifted, indeed undermined, scholars' presumed understanding of Viking-Age clothing," 129. *Örvar-Odds saga*, ch. 19 (magic shirt).

123–24 **tapestry:** Barber, *Women's Work*, 227–29. Normann (2008), 1–2, 3 ("*bók*"), 31 ("wrote on it"), 80, 174 ("memory peg"). *Orkneyinga saga*, quoted by Normann (2008), 100 ("make a verse").

10: THE TRAGEDY OF BRYNHILD

125–30 **Brynhild:** In Old Norse, the tragedy is told in prose in *Völsunga saga* and referred to in seventeen poems in *The Poetic Edda* (*Eddukvæði*), as well as in Snorri Sturluson's *Edda*. Brynhild also appears in *Þiðreks saga af Bern* (a Norse translation of German tales), the German *Nibelungenlied* and *Das Lied vom Hürnen Seyfrid*, and several Faroese ballads. Theodore M. Andersson reconstructs the oldest version of the story in *The Legend of Brynhild* (Cornell University Press, 1980), 72, 239–49. My retelling relies on *Völsunga saga*, ch. 21–31 ("I am a shield-maid," "The fire flared," "How dare you," "stitching," "skillful"), *Fáfnismál*, st. 42–43 ("High on Hindarfell"), and *Sigurdrífumál*, st. 23 ("Swear no oaths"). Brynhild gives advice in both *Völsunga saga* and *Sigurdrífumál*. I have added details about oaths from *Völundarkviða*, st. 32, and *Helgakviða Hundingsbana II*, st. 33. See also Jóhanna Katrín Friðriksdóttir, "Women and Subversion in Eddic Heroic Poetry," in P. Acker and C. Larrington, eds., *Revisiting the Poetic Edda* (Routledge, 2013), 117–25. Anne Irene Riisøy, "Performing Oaths in Eddic Poetry," *Journal of the North Atlantic* Special Volume 8 (2016): 141, 147–48.

130 **dyeing:** Penelope Walton Rogers, *Textile Production at 16–22 Coppergate* (Council for British Archaeology, 1997), 1766, 1768–70. Thor Ewing, *Viking Clothing* (History Press, 2012), 154–57. Ester S. B. Ferreira et al., "The Natural Constituents of Historical Textile Dyes," *Chemical Society Reviews* 33 (2004): 329–36.

131 **loom:** Marta Hoffman, *The Warp-Weighted Loom* (Oslo Universitetsforlaget, 1974), 5–6, 39. Ewing, *Viking Clothing*, 137–39. I discuss the making of wool cloth in *The Far Traveler* (Harcourt, 2007), ch. 9.

132 ***Valkyries' Song:*** *Darraðarljóð*, in *Njáls saga*, ch. 157. Most translators apply "naked" to the horses, not to the swords. Stirrups, as found in Bj581, were invented to improve the force of a sword or spear thrust from horseback. Having these valkyries ride bareback is another instance of the tendency to read Viking warrior women as myths. Nora Kershaw dates the poem to 919; see Russell Poole, *Viking Poems on War and Peace* (University of Toronto Press, 1991), 120–22. Chihiro Tsukamoto, "What Did They Sound Like? Reconstructing the Music of the Viking Age" (master's thesis, University of Iceland, 2017), 36 (working songs).

133–34 **tapestries:** Rogers, *Textile Production*, 1757–60. David J. Bernstein, *The Mystery of the Bayeux Tapestry* (University of Chicago Press, 1987), 14, 78–79. The Overhogdal tapestries are described on the website of the Nationalmuseum Jamtli, Östersund,

Sweden ("learned the trick"). Normann (2008), 124–26, 130–75 (Brynhild). Eva-Marie Göransson, "Människor i rum av tid," *Fornvännen* 90.3 (1995): 129–38 ("androgyny"). Gardeła (2013), 301–4 ("gender boundaries"); (2018), 402–8.

134–36 **settling down:** *Hervarar saga*, ch. 3–4 (Hervor). *Grettis saga*, ch. 3 and 8 (Onund). *Egils saga*, ch. 1 (Ulf).

136 **York's throne:** Clare Downham, "The Chronology of the Last Scandinavian Kings of York, AD 937–954," *Northern History* 40 (2003): 25–51.

11: SHIELD-MAIDS

137–39 **Jorvik:** Richard Hall, *The Viking Dig* (Bodley Head, 1984), 49–52, 78, 94–97. Anthony Burton, *The Yorkshire Dales and York: Landranger Guidebook* (UK Ordnance Survey, 1989), 8–26. Jelmer Dijkstra, *Rulers of Jorvik* (master's thesis, University of Utrecht, 2013), 1, 101, 125. *Egils saga*, ch. 59–61 ("taut bowstrings," "King Eirik that way"), ch. 78 ("king reigned"). *Njáls saga*, ch. 152, and *Grettis saga*, ch. 82 ("bare is back"). *Fáfnismál*, st. 30 ("courage bests").

139–43 **shield:** Hedenstierna-Jonson (2006), 28, 32; interviewed March 12, 2019. Short (2014), 34, 38–41, 133, 139; interviewed March 12, 2019. Williams (2019), 29, 35, 42, 47, 53. S. Sinnett et al., "Grunting's Competitive Advantage," *PLoS One* 13.2 (2018): e0192939. Roger of Howden ("tenaciously"), quoted by Hedenstierna-Jonson (2006), 61. Libby Liburd ("accepting the pain"), quoted by Lyndsey Winship, "Female Boxers' Battle Stories," *The Guardian* (April 23, 2019). Ariel Levy ("open, inquisitive"), describing boxer Claressa Shields in "A Ring of One's Own," *New Yorker* (May 7, 2012).

144 **family affair:** Megan McLaughlin, "The Woman Warrior," *Women's Studies* 17 (1990): 201–2. Hedenstierna-Jonson (2015), 77. Price (2020), 352–58.

144–45 **Aethelflaed:** Tom Shippey, *Laughing Shall I Die* (Reaktion Books, 2018), 170. Pauline Stafford, "The Annals of Aethelflaed," in J. Barrow and A. Wareham, eds., *Myth, Rulership, Church, and Charters* (Ashgate, 2008), 101–16. The *Fragmentary Annals* ("large army," "slaughtered"), quoted by Kim Klimek, "Aethelflaed: History and Legend," n.d., posted on her Academia.edu page. *Anglo-Saxon Chronicle*, quoted by Betty Bandel, "The English Chroniclers' Attitude Toward Women," *Journal of the History of Ideas* 16 (1955): 115 ("got into her power").

145–46 **Church's new focus:** Else Mundal, "The Double Impact of Christianization for Women in Old Norse Culture," in K. E. Børresen et al., eds., *Gender and Religion* (Carocci, 2001), 249 ("unclean," "against nature"). R. I. Moore, *Formation of a Persecuting Society* (Blackwell, 2007), 4, 8–9, 12, 86, 95 ("transformation").

146–49 **warrior women:** McLaughlin, "The Woman Warrior," 199 (Richilde). Saxo Grammaticus, trans. P. Fisher, *The History of the Danes, Books I–IX* (D. S. Brewer, 1970–80; rpt., 2008), 212 ("women in Denmark"); 238–44 (Battle of Bravellir); 280–84 (Lathgertha). Pamela D. Toler, *Women Warriors* (Beacon, 2019), 20–21 ("counterhistorical"); see also 7–9, 61, 81n, 208–9. Adrienne Mayor, *The Amazons* (Princeton University Press, 2014), 11, 29, 64, 82, 196. Birgit Strand, "Women in *Gesta Danorum*," in K. Friis-Jensen, ed., *Saxo Grammaticus: A Medieval Author Between Norse and Latin Culture* (Museum Tusculanum Press, 1981), 149 ("mirror").

149 **"later history of England":** Shippey, *Laughing Shall I Die*, 95, 106.

12: THE RED GIRL

151–52 **Eirik's defeat:** *Hákonar saga góða*, ch. 5. *Orkneyinga saga*, ch. 8. The Headland of Cats is modern Caithness, the Southlands is Sutherland, the Turning Point is Cape Wrath (from *hvarf*, "to disappear"), Big Bay is Stornoway on Lewis, and the Southern Isles are the Hebrides.

152 **coastal sailing:** Barbara Crawford, *Scandinavian Scotland* (Leicester University Press, 1987) 16, 20–26, 135. Benjamin Hudson, *Viking Pirates and Christian Princes* (Oxford University Press, 2005), 15–17. Griffiths (2012), 16–18, 39.

152–53 **Dublin:** Griffiths (2012), 64, 120–27. Clarke et al. (2018), 80, 88. Ben Raffield, "The Slave Markets of the Viking World," *Slavery & Abolition* 40 (2019): 682–704.

154 **Saxo Grammaticus:** P. Fisher, trans., *The History of the Danes, Books I–IX* (D. S. Brewer, 1970–80; rpt., 2008), 5 ("copying"), 211 (Alvild), 246 (Rusila); on Rusila's connection to the Inghen Ruaidh, see Hilda Ellis Davidson, "Introduction to Book Eight," 236–37 ("misty world"). I explore Saxo's connection to Bishop Pall and Pall's attitude toward women in *Ivory Vikings* (St. Martin's Press, 2015), ch. 2–3. Saxo considered the Sagas of Ancient Times to be "historical"; see Annette Lassen, "*Origines Gentium* and the Learned Origin of *Fornaldarsögur Nordrlanda*," in A. Lassen, A. Ney, and Á. Jakobsson, eds., *The Legendary Sagas* (University of Iceland Press, 2012), 46.

156 *War of the Irish*: J. H. Todd, trans., *Cogadh Gaedhel re Gallaibh* (Longmans, Green, Reader, and Dyer, 1867), 39–43.

157 **"lock held":** *Poem About Haraldr harðráði* by Valgarðr á Velli, st. 9.

157–59 **enslaving:** John Gillingham, "Women, Children, and the Profits of War," in J. L. Nelson, S. Reynolds, and S. M. Johns, eds., *Gender and Historiography* (Institute of Historical Research, 2012), 61. Neil Price, "The Vikings in Spain, North Africa, and the Mediterranean," in Brink and Price (2008), 466 ("blue men"). Price (2020), 141–54. Griffiths (2012), 100–101. Clarke et al. (2018), 55. Raffield, "Slave Markets." I use Raffield's estimate of a *cumal*. Bronagh Ni Chonaill estimates it as six heifers or three milk cows; see "Child-Centred Law in Medieval Ireland," in R. Davis and T. Dunne, eds., *The Empty Throne* (Cambridge University Press, 2008), 7n. Poul Holm, "The Slave Trade of Dublin," *Peritia* 5 (1986): 329. Hudson, *Viking Pirates*, 92. Clare Downham, "The Viking Slave Trade," *History Ireland* (May–June 2009): 15–17. Charlene M. Eska, "Women and Slavery in the Early Irish Laws," *Studia Celtica Fennica* 8 (2011): 29–39. Janel M. Fontaine, "The Scale of Slave Raiding and the Slave Trade in Britain and Ireland, 7th–11th Centuries," presented at the International Medieval Congress, Leeds, UK (July 9, 2014). *Annals of Ulster*, quoted by Griffiths (2012), 41 ("half dead").

159 **Cuerdale Hoard:** Griffiths (2012), 41, 44, 107. Angus A. Somerville and R. Andrew McDonald, *The Vikings and Their Age* (University of Toronto Press, 2013), 27. Clarke et al. (2018), 97.

159 **silver coin:** Christoph Kilger in Skre (2008), 264, 283, 286, 291. Gene W. Heck, "Gold Mining in Arabia and the Rise of the Islamic State," *Journal of the Economic and Social History of the Orient* 42 (1999): 371. Marek Jankowiak, "Dirhams for Slaves," presented at the Medieval Seminar, All Souls College (February 27, 2012). Maya Shatzmiller, "The Role of Money in the Economic Growth of the Early Islamic Period (650–1000)," in V. Klemm and N. al-Sha'ar, eds., *Sources and Approaches Across Disciplines in Near Eastern Studies* (Uitgeverig Peeters, 2013), 290.

160–61 **"slave hunts":** Gillingham, "Women, Children, and the Profits of War," 67. Hjardar and Vike (2016), 67–69, 230. *Cogadh Gaedhel re Gallaibh*, trans. Todd (1867), 159 ("shouting"), 163 ("swimming"), 79–81 ("soft," "fit for a slave," sack of Limerick), 83 ("line of the women"). Saxo Grammaticus, trans. Fisher, *History of the Danes*, 280 ("abuse").

162 **"everyone's going":** *Egils saga*, ch. 32.

13: SLAVE GIRLS

163–64 **traces her left foot:** In 2009, Hanne Lovise Aannestad of the University of Oslo's Viking Ship Museum discovered footprints carved into the deckboards of the Gokstad ship. See also Ole Crumlin-Pedersen, "The Sporting Element in Viking Ships," in G.

Sjøgaard, ed., *Sailing and Science* (University of Copenhagen, 1999), 29. Sven Kalm-ring, "Of Thieves, Counterfeiters, and Homicides," *Fornvännen* 105.4 (2010): 282 (sea chests). Clarke et al. (2018), 31.

165 **Findan:** R. T. Christiansen and K. O'Nolan, "The Life of Saint Findan," *Lochlann: A Review of Celtic Studies* 2 (1962): 155–64.

166–67 **eunuchs:** Ibn Hawqal, trans. P. Lunde and C. Stone, *Ibn Fadlan and the Land of Darkness* (Penguin, 2012), 173 ("*Saqaliba*"). F. A. Wright, trans., *The Works of Liudprand of Cremona* (Routledge & Sons, 1930), 208 ("*carzimasia*"). Al-Jahiz, quoted by Marek Jankowiak, "Dirhams for Slaves," presented at the Medieval Seminar, All Souls College (February 27, 2012).

167–68 **women captured:** *Ynglinga saga*, ch. 28 (Yrsa). *Ólafs saga Tryggvasonar*, ch. 1–6, 52. *Laxdæla saga*, ch. 9, 12–13, 16, 20–22 (Melkorka); "headstrong," trans. Keneva Kunz, *The Saga of the People of Laxardal*, in Ö. Thorsson, ed., *Sagas of Icelanders* (Viking, 2000), 284.

170–71 **Arab travelers:** Ibn Rustah, trans. Lunde and Stone, *Ibn Fadlan and the Land of Darkness*, 126 ("treat their slaves well"). Ibn Fadlan, quoted by Hraundal (2013), 100–106 ("sex," "washes," "girl kills herself").

171 **sacrifices:** Clare Downham, "The Viking Slave Trade," *History Ireland* (May–June 2009): 15–17. Leszek Gardeła, "The Dangerous Dead?" in L. Slupecki and R. Simek, eds., *Conversions* (Fassbaender, 2013), 117. Price (2019), 19. Hedenstierna-Jonson et al. (2017), 6 ("not questioned").

172 **graffiti:** Hanne Jakobsen, "Dealing with the Doldrums on a Viking Voyage," *Science Nordic* (April 23, 2013). Images of the graffiti on the Oseberg ship were posted by the University of Oslo on the Vikingskipshuset Facebook page (February 26, 2020).

172–73 **fetters:** Emperor Constantine VII, *De administrando imperio*, quoted by Robert Ferguson, *The Vikings* (Viking Penguin, 2009), 124–26 ("slaves in chains"). Ben Raffield, "The Slave Markets of the Viking World," *Slavery & Abolition* 40 (2019): 682–704. Jankowiak, "Dirhams for Slaves," 9. *Harðar saga ok Hólmverja*, ch. 17. *Njáls saga*, ch. 89. *Edda*, 1:28 ("cat"). First Merseburg charm, quoted by John Jeep, *Medieval Germany: An Encyclopedia* (Routledge, 2001), 112–13. *Hávamál*, st. 149 (runes).

174 **"two buckets":** *Grettis saga*, ch. 17.

174 **sleep ashore:** Anton Englert, "Ohthere's Voyages Seen from a Nautical Angle," in J. Bately and A. Englert, eds., *Ohthere's Voyages* (Roskilde Viking Ship Museum, 2007), 117–29. *Örvar-Odds saga*, ch. 32 (tents). *Eyrbyggja saga*, ch. 39 ("cooking").

14: THE SLAVE ROUTE TO BIRKA

177 **stranger shows up:** This scene is loosely based on *Egils saga*, ch. 49, *Hrólfssaga Gautrekssonar*, ch. 15, and *Njáls saga*, ch. 5. The Red Girl and her brother Trond are found in Saxo Grammaticus, *Gesta Danorum*, Book 8. There is no proof Hervor and the Red Girl sailed to Burnt Island.

179 **Viking slave route:** *Laxdæla saga*, ch. 9 ("Burnt Island"). Anders Winroth, *The Age of the Vikings* (Princeton University Press, 2014), 109, 116 (Hedeby). *Njáls saga*, ch. 5 (Oresund). Ben Raffield, "The Slave Markets of the Viking World," *Slavery & Abolition* 40 (2019): 682–704 (Gotland).

179 **reclaimed Viken:** *Hákonar saga góða*, ch. 7–8. Dagfinn Skre, "Towns and Markets," in Skre (2007), 468; "Kaupang: Between East and West," in Skre (2011), 446. Tenaya Jorgensen, *The Scandinavian Trade Network in the Early Viking Age* (master's thesis, University of Oslo, 2017), 21.

181–82 **Gunnhild led:** *Hákonar saga góða*, ch. 7–8, 10, 19, 22–26, 29–32. *Haralds saga gráfeldar*, ch. 1, 3. *Nóregs konunga tal* ("Age of Gunnhild"), 202.

182 **barricades:** Bengt Wigh, *Animal Husbandry in the Viking Age Town of Birka and Its Hinterland* (Kulturhistoriska Forskningsinstitute Stockholm, 2001), 135. Charlotte Hedenstierna-Jonson, Lena Holmquist, and Michael Olausson, "The Viking Age Paradox," in J. Baker, S. Brookes, and A. Reynolds, eds., *Landscapes of Defence in Early Medieval Europe* (Brepols, 2013), 291.

182–84 **Birka:** Helen Clarke and Björn Ambrosiani, *Towns in the Viking Age* (Leicester University Press, 1991), 68, 73–75. Björn Ambrosiani, "Birka," in Brink and Price (2008), 98. Hedenstierna-Jonsson (2006), 48–51, 92; (2015), 85. Elin Ahlin Sundman and Anna Kjellström, "Signs of Sinusitis in Times of Urbanization in Viking Age–Early Medieval Sweden," *Journal of Archaeological Science* 40 (2013): 4460. Holmquist (2016). T. Douglas Price et al., "Isotopes and Human Burials at Viking Age Birka and the Malaren Region," *Journal of Anthropological Archaeology* 49 (2018): 19. *Hrólfssaga Gautrekssonar*, ch. 10, 13.

185 **Adam of Bremen:** *History of the Archbishops of Hamburg-Bremen*, trans. F. J. Tschan (1893; rpt., Columbia University Press, 2002), 51–52, 199, 207–8. While archaeologists have not found the temple at Uppsala, one excavated at Uppåkra in Skåne, Sweden, was indeed "decked out in gold" and flanked by sacrificial deposits; see Price (2020), 210–13.

185 **"singing":** At-Tartushi, quoted by Chihiro Tsukamoto, *What Did They Sound Like? Reconstructing the Music of the Viking Age* (master's thesis, University of Iceland, 2017), 19–20.

185–86 **Anskar:** Rimbert, *Vita Anskarii*, ch. 10, 11, 17, 26, 28, trans. C. H. Robinson, *Anskar, the Apostle of the North* (Society for the Propagation of the Gospel in Foreign Parts, 1921). Sven Kalmring, Johan Runer, and Andreas Viberg, "At Home with Herigar," *Archäologisches Korrespondenzblatt* 47 (2017): 1–27. Hedenstierna-Jonson (2016), 190. T. D. Price et al., "Isotopes and Human Burials," 29 (Thor's hammer). Price (2020), 461 (crucifix).

187 **Warriors' Hall:** Hedenstierna-Jonson (2006), 51, 63–64 ("defiance"); (2015), 75; (2016), 190–91 ("identity," "external threat"). Hedenstierna-Jonson, Holmquist, and Olausson, "Viking Age Paradox," 296, 298–99. Holmquist (2016), 41–42.

15: RED EARTH

188–90 **all the women:** The people Hervor meets are based on Birka graves Bj943 (amber carver), Bj463 (little girl), and Bj644 (couple). Hedenstierna-Jonson and Kjellström (2015). Hedenstierna-Jonson, "She Came from Another Place," in M. H. Eriksen et al., eds., *Viking Worlds* (Oxbow Books, 2015), 90–101. Elin Ahlin Sundman and Anna Kjellström, "Signs of Sinusitis in Times of Urbanization in Viking Age–Early Medieval Sweden," *Journal of Archaeological Science* 40 (2013): 4463. Anne Stalsberg, "Women as Actors in North European Viking Age Trade," in R. Samson, ed., *Social Approaches to Viking Studies* (Cruithne Press, 1991), 78–79. Eva Andersson Strand and Ulla Mannering, "An Exceptional Woman from Birka," in S. Bergerbrant and S. H. Fossøy, eds., *A Stitch in Time* (Gothenburg University, 2017), 301–16.

190 **Bj644:** The contents of the grave are curated by the Swedish History Museum in Stockholm; see https://historiska.se/upptack-historien/context/845-grav-kammargrav-bj-644/. Eva Hjärthner-Holdar, "Iron: The Metal of Weapons and Wealth," in Olausson and Olausson (2009), 142. Karyn Bellamy-Dagneau, *A Falconer's Ritual* (master's thesis, University of Iceland, 2015), 28.

191 **Saaremaa:** Price (2020), 275–79. T. Douglas Price et al., "Isotopes and Human Burials at Viking Age Birka and the Malaren Region," *Journal of Anthropological Archaeology* 49 (2018): 19–20.

191-92 **iron:** Website of the Stiftelsen Ekomuseum Bergslagen, Sweden, https://ekomuseum .se/en/ ("red earth"). Hjardar and Vike (2016), 20 ("durable"). Eva Hjärthner-Holdar, Lena Grandin, Katrina Sköld, and Andreas Svensson, "By Who, for Whom? Landscape, Process, and Economy in the Bloomery Iron Production AD 400–1000," *Journal of Archaeology and Ancient History* 21 (2018): 2–51. Hjärthner-Holdar, "Iron," in Olausson and Olausson (2009), 133–42. Terje Gansum, "Role the Bones—from Iron to Steel," *Norwegian Archaeological Review* 37 (2004): 41–57. Back Danielsson (2007), 247–48.

193 **smith's art:** Hjardar and Vike (2016) cite *Svarfdæla saga* and *Ásmundar saga kappabana* for superior swords, *Eyrbyggja saga* and *Laxdæla saga* for useless swords, 159, 171. Short (2014), 113–16. Anne Stalsberg, "Swords from the Carolingian Empire to the Baltic Sea and Beyond," in Callmer, Gustin, and Roslund (2017), 262–64. Eleanor Susan Blakelock, *The Early Medieval Cutting Edge of Technology* (doctoral thesis, University of Bradford, UK, 2012), 62, 245. The PBS *Nova* TV special "Secrets of the Viking Sword" (first aired October 10, 2012) re-creates the "flaming sword" quench.

194 **Sword fighting:** Anne Pedersen, "Viking Weaponry," in Brink and Price (2008), 204. Short (2014), 105, 161. Sixt Wetzler, *Combat in Saga Literature* (doctoral thesis, Eberhard Karls Universität Tübingen, 2017), 115. Williams (2019), 43, 51–52. *Atlamál in grænlensku*, st. 47–49 (Gudrun).

194-96 **Swords were special:** Susan Elaine Brunning, *The "Living" Sword in Early Medieval Northern Europe* (doctoral thesis, University College London, 2013), 143 (faces), 185, 190, 195. *Laxdæla saga*, ch. 29 (Leg-Biter). A. Faulkes, trans., *Snorri Sturluson: Edda* (Everyman, 1987; rpt., 1995), 158, 168 ("spear clash"). *Gísla saga Súrssonar*, ch. 1 (broke). *Hervarar saga*, ch. 1 (Tyrfing). *Kormáks saga*, ch. 9 (dragon). Hedenstierna-Jonson (2015), 81, 84–85 (sword-chapes).

196 **Type E:** Fedir Androshchuk, "Vikings and Farmers," in Olausson and Olausson (2009), 93–95. In the Swedish History Museum's online catalogue of Birka grave Bj581, the sword is listed as Petersen Type V; Price et al. (2019) identify it as Type E. Both types are more commonly found in Russia and Ukraine than in Sweden, although Type V is common in Denmark.

16: A BIRKA WARRIOR

197-98 **horse archer:** Based on grave Bj1126b, described by Fredrik Lundström, Charlotte Hedenstierna-Jonson, and Lena Holmquist Olausson, "Eastern Archery in Birka's Garrison," in Olausson and Olausson (2009), 106–12. The goose-shooting episode comes from P. Lunde and C. Stone, trans., *Ibn Fadlan and the Land of Darkness* (Penguin, 2012), 20.

199-200 **Warriors' Hall:** Hedenstierna-Jonson (2006), 51; (2015), 73–75, 78–81. Holmquist (2016), 38–42. *Hervarar saga*, ch. 4 ("any warrior").

200-202 **Viking chess:** Helena M. Gamer, "The Earliest Evidence of Chess in Western Literature," *Speculum* 29 (October 1954): 734–50. Sten Helmfrid, "Hnefatafl, the Strategic Board Game of the Vikings," April 23, 2005, http://hem.bredband.net/b512479/. *Hervarar saga*, ch. 9 (riddle). *Grettis saga*, ch. 70 ("difficult"). *Þorgils saga skarða* ("swept the pieces"), quoted by Willard Fiske, *Chess in Iceland* (Florentine Typographical Society, 1905), 12–13 (slightly revised). *Droplaugarsona saga*, quoted by Ármann Jakobsson, "Troublesome Children in the Sagas of Icelanders," *Saga Book* 27 (2003): 9 (fart). *Morkinskinna*, quoted by Marilyn Yalom, *Birth of the Chess Queen* (HarperCollins, 2004), 156–57 ("sore foot"). Oskar Spjuth, *In Quest for the Lost Gamers* (master's thesis, Lund University, 2012), 13. Mads Ravn, "The Use of Symbols in Burials in Migration Age Europe," in D. S. Olausson and H. Vandkilde, eds., *Form, Function & Context* (Almqvist & Wiksell International, 2000), 275–96. Helene Whittaker, "Game Boards and Gaming

Pieces in Funerary Contexts in the Northern European Iron Age," *Nordlit Tidskrift for Kultur og Litteratur* 20 (2006): 103–12. Gavin K. E. Davies, *From Rules to Experience* (doctoral thesis, Swansea University, 2015), 26, 33–40, 43–61 (luck).

202–3 **tested:** *Bósa saga ok Herrauðs*, ch. 3 (ball game). *Ævidrápa* in *Örvar-Odds saga*, st. 66 ("I never shot"). *Egils saga einhenda og Ásmundar saga berserkjabana*, ch. 4 (sword fight).

203 **Jomsvikings:** *Jómsvíkinga saga*, ch. 16. Tom Shippey, *Laughing Shall I Die* (Reaktion Books, 2018), 215 ("have a woman"), 230 ("lads"). N. F. Blake, trans., *The Saga of the Jomsvikings* (Thomas Nelson and Sons, 1962), vii ("monastic-type").

204 **falcon symbol:** Hedenstierna-Jonson (2015), 81, 84; "Rus', Varangians, and Birka Warriors," in Olausson and Olausson (2009), 161, 167, 169–73. Björn Ambrosiani, "Birka," in Brink and Price (2008), 21.

205–7 **weapons:** Hedenstierna-Jonson (2006), 38–39 ("plain"), 55 ("rare"), 56, 58, 61, 68. Lundström, Hedenstierna-Jonson, and Holmquist Olausson, "Eastern Archery," 106–12. K. A. Mikhailov and S. Y. Kainov, "Finds of Structural Details of Composite Bows from Ancient Rus," *Acta Archaeologica Academiae Scientiarum Hungaricae* 62 (2011): 229, 236. Charlotte Hedenstierna-Jonson, "Traces of Contacts," in B. Tobias, ed., *Die Archäologie der Frühen Ungarn* (Verlag des Römisch-Germanischen Zentralmuseums, 2012), 31–32, 37, 40–41; "Close Encounters with the Byzantine Border Zones," in O. Minaeva and L. Holmquist, eds., *Scandinavia and the Balkans* (Cambridge Scholars Publishing, 2015), 140–45. O'Brien Browne, "Medieval Weapons: The Composite Bow," *Warfare History Network* (October 11, 2018) ("most effective"). Adam Clarke, "Psalm 78:57," in *Commentary on the Bible* (Emory and Waugh, 1831), 3: 244 ("string one"). John Man, *Empire of Horses* (Pegasus, 2020), 13–14, 84 ("arms and shoulders").

17: THE KAFTAN

209 **kaftan:** Nobuko Kajitani, "A Man's Caftan and Leggings from the North Caucasus of the Eighth to Tenth Century: A Conservator's Report," *Metropolitan Museum Journal* 36 (2001): 85–124. Elfriede R. Knauer, "A Man's Caftan and Leggings from the North Caucasus of the Eighth to Tenth Century: A Genealogical Study," *Metropolitan Museum Journal* 36 (2001): 125–54. Charlotte Hedenstierna-Jonsson, "Borre Style Metalwork in the Material Culture of the Birka Warriors," *Fornvännen* 101 (2006): 315–16. Fredrik Lundström, Charlotte Hedenstierna-Jonson, and Lena Holmquist Olausson, "Eastern Archery in Birka's Garrison," in Olausson and Olausson (2009), 111. Charlotte Hedenstierna-Jonsson, "Traces of Contacts," in B. Tobias, ed., *Die Archäologie der Frühen Ungarn* (Verlag des Römisch-Germanischen Zentralmuseums, 2012), 31–34.

210–12 **silk:** Larsson (2011), 125. Vedeler (2014), 7–8, 27 ("queen"), 35, 38, 68, 77–80, 85, 90, 116. Elena S. Zubkova, Olga V. Orfinskaya, and Kirill A. Mikhailov, "Studies of the Textiles from the 2006 Excavation in Pskov," in E. Andersson Strand et al., eds., *North European Symposium for Archaeological Textiles X* (Oxbow Books, 2010), 291–98. N. M. Brown, *The Far Traveler* (Harcourt, 2007), 93. Larsson (2007), 194. *Egils saga*, ch. 67, 79. *Njáls saga*, ch. 123.

212 **East Way:** Mägi (2018), 165, 190. Larsson (2007), 194; (2011). Ingrid Gustin, "Trade and Trust in the Baltic Sea Area During the Viking Age," in J. H. Barrett and S. J. Gibbon, eds., *Maritime Societies of the Viking and Medieval World* (Maney Publishing, 2015), 25–40.

213–14 **urban style:** Charlotte Hedenstierna-Jonson, interviewed June 14, 2018. Hedenstierna-Jonson (2006), 79, 82; "Borre Style," 312–22; "Rus', Varangians, and Birka Warriors," in Olausson and Olausson (2009), 159–61, 168; "Traces of Contacts," 31; (2016), 189–90; "Creating a Cultural Expression," in Callmer, Gustin, and Roslund (2017), 94–96.

214–16 **Rus:** *Homilies of Photius Patriarch of Constantinople*, trans. Cyril Mango (Harvard University Press, 1958), 82, 84, 88, 96–99 ("obscure"), 101 ("swords raised"). Photius, encyclical of 867, quoted by Wladyslaw Duczko, *Viking Rus* (Brill, 2004), 83 ("Rhos"; I added "the"). Ibn Rustah, trans. P. Lunde and C. Stone, *Ibn Fadlan and the Land of Darkness* (Penguin, 2012), 126 ("fight best," "slaves"). Mägi (2018), 192 ("Ruotsi"). Liudprand, quoted in Androshchuk (2013), 46. F. A. Wright, in *The Works of Liudprand of Cremona* (Routledge & Sons, 1930), considers their skin to be red, not their hair, 185. Ibn Khurradadhbih, trans. Lunde and Stone, *Ibn Fadlan and the Land of Darkness*, 111 ("farthest reaches," "camel"); I amended "Slav" to Saqaliba, per Mägi (2018), 199–201. Ibn Hawqal, trans. Lunde and Stone, *Ibn Fadlan*, 173 ("eunuchs").

216 **Buddha:** Helen Clarke and Björn Ambrosiani, *Towns in the Viking Age* (Leicester University Press, 1991), 70–71. Eleanor Rosamund Barraclough, *Beyond the Northlands* (Oxford University Press, 2016), 173–77. Knauer, "A Man's Caftan," 144.

216 **Islamic world:** Duczko (2004), 62–63. Gene W. Heck, *Charlemagne, Muhammad, and the Arab Roots of Capitalism* (De Gruyter, 2006), 285. Sebastian Wärmländer et al., "Analysis and Interpretation of a Unique Arabic Finger Ring from the Viking Age Town of Birka, Sweden," *Scanning* 37 (March/April 2015): 131–37.

217 *Annals of St-Bertin:* trans. Janet L. Nelson (Manchester University Press, 1991), 44. See also Mägi (2018), 195–99.

218–19 *Russian Primary Chronicle:* trans. Olgerd P. Sherbowitz-Wetzor (Medieval Academy of America, 1953), 64–69, 71–73 ("innumerable ships"), 236.

219 **Viking silk:** Vedeler (2014), 57, 75, 77, 85, 90 (Jurjan), 98–104 (*Book of the Eparch*).

220 **bezant:** The dinar-to-dirham rate in Baghdad in 970 was 1:15, according to the project "Measuring the Medieval Islamic Economy," directed by Maya Shatzmiller at Western University, Ontario, Canada.

220 **"fire-throwers":** Wright, *Liudprand of Cremona*, 184–86.

18: THE EAST WAY

221 **little boats:** I based Hervor's boat on the Viks Boat, as reconstructed by Larsson (2007) and by Lennart Widerberg, "Med Fornkåre til Novgorod 2012," *Situne Dei: Årsskrift för Sigtunaforskning och historisk arkeologi* (2013): 4–10, and "Med Fornkåre genom Ryssland 2013," *Situne Dei* (2014): 82–87. Larsson (2007), 65 (coin). Christian Keller, "Furs, Fish, and Ivory," *Journal of the North Atlantic* 3 (2010): 1–23. Larsson (2011).

223 **Bengtsson:** Lars Lönnroth, "Det våras för Bengtsson och hans vikingar," *Svenska Dagbladet* (February 9, 2012): 63 ("enjoy"). Joan Klein, "A Distant Mirror," in George Whitley-Smythe, ed., *A Round-up of Recent Essays in Twentieth Century Cultural Issues* ("Viking heritage"). Both cited from "The Long Ships" Wikipedia page.

223 **mighty vessel:** Larsson (2007), 24 ("fantasy"), 25 ("dragging beer," "not possible"); she translates the conclusions of experimental archaeologist Rune Edberg, 223 ("unproven," "improbable"). John R. Hale, "The Viking Longship," *Scientific American* (February 1998): 57 ("ideal form"). Magnus Magnusson, *Vikings!* (Elsevier-Dutton, 1980), 40 ("poem").

225–26 **Viks Boat:** Larsson (2007), 34–39, 85, 93–95, 115, 169, 223–33. Widerberg, "Med Fornkåre genom Ryssland 2013," 87 ("proved"). Ernst Manker in Larsson (2007), 225 ("whistled").

226–29 **women:** Frans G. Bengtsson, *The Long Ships* (1955; rpt., New York Review Books, 2010), 382, 431, 503. Larsson (2007), 231 ("set a *drag*"), 367 (quoting Arne Emil Christiansen, "male field"), 368 ("myth"), 369 (Tacitus, *Germania*, ch. 45–46), 370–73 ("different picture").

229 **ice roads:** Larsson (2007) 60 (seal products), 115, 142 (salt). Price (2020), 103 (tar).
230 **Birka to Russia:** Adam of Bremen, *History of the Archbishops of Hamburg-Bremen*, trans. F. J. Tschan (1893; rpt., Columbia University Press, 2002), 201n. Widerberg, "Med Fornkåre til Novgorod 2012."
230–31 **first stage:** Larsson (2007), 57–59, 93, 99, 151–60. Helen Clarke and Björn Ambrosiani, *Towns in the Viking Age* (Leicester University Press, 1991), 68. Elin Ahlin Sundman and Anna Kjellström, "Signs of Sinusitis in Times of Urbanization in Viking Age–Early Medieval Sweden," *Journal of Archaeological Science* 40 (2013): 4460. *Ólafs saga helga*, ch. 7 ("Logrinn").

19: AT LINDA'S STONE

233 **Saaremaa:** Mägi (2018), 101, 173, 181 (*kura*), 428. *Njáls saga*, ch. 119. *Ólafs saga Tryggvasonar*, ch. 6 (Astrid). T. Douglas Price et al., "Isotopic Provenancing of the Salme Ship Burials in Pre-Viking Age Estonia," *Antiquity* 90 (2016): 1022–37. Ashot Margaryan et al., "Population Genomics of the Viking World," *Nature* 585 (September 17, 2020): 390–96. Price (2020), 275–79.
235–36 **Aland:** Yiyun Li, "A Mother Journeys Through Grief Across Finland's Many Islands," *T: The New York Times Style Magazine* (November 12, 2019). Ingmar Ögren, "Pilgrim Sail 'Following the Franciscans' from Norrtelje/Arholma to Kökar the 26th June to the 5th July 2009," posted on his personal website, http://fridhem.etanet.se/pilgrim_english.html ("substantial stillness"). Larsson (2007), 170–80 ("high sea"). Max Vinner, "Unnasigling—The Seaworthiness of the Merchant Vessel," in B. Clausen, ed., *Viking Voyages to North America* (Roskilde Viking Ship Museum, 1993), 104 ("worst").
236–37 **Finland:** David Kirby, "Skerries, Haffs, and Icefloes," in P. Miller, ed., *The Sea: Thalassography and Historiography* (University of Michigan Press, 2013), 235–36. Sami Raninen and Anna Wessman, "Finland as a Part of the 'Viking World,'" in J. Ahola et al., eds., *Fibula, Fabula, Fact: The Viking Age in Finland* (Finnish Literature Society, 2014), 329–36. Ingrid Gustin, "Contacts, Identity, and Hybridity," in Callmer, Gustin, and Roslund (2017), 216–24. Mägi (2018), 98, 112, 272–73, 330, 335, 410. Torsten Edgren, "A Viking Age Resting Place and Trading Post on the Sailing Route to the East," http://vikingislands.com/historik.htm (Hitis). *Ólafs saga helga*, ch. 9 ("watchfire coast").
237–39 **Kalevipoeg:** *The Hero of Esthonia*, trans. W. G. Kirby (Nimmo, 1895), 7–31. On the brooch bound with thread, see Edgren, "Viking Age Resting Place."
239–40 **Rafala:** Heiki Valk, "The Vikings and the Eastern Baltic," in Brink and Price (2008), 492. Mägi (2018), 99–100, 112, 122–26, 174, 258–60, 273–79, 282, 331. *Ynglinga saga*, ch. 12 (Sveigdir), 32 (Yngvar). Price (2020), 278–79 ("one wonders").
241 **Estonian society:** Joonas Ahola, "Kalevalaic Heroic Epic and the Viking Age in Finland," in Ahola et al., *Fibula, Fabula, Fact*, 381. Mägi (2018), 41–45, 80–88, 83n ("sounds irrelevant"), 86–87 ("his goods follow"), 134, 154–55, 423–24.

20: "GERZKR" CAPS

242–47 **Ladoga:** The people Hervor sees in the fictional scene are based on burials excavated near Staraja Ladoga and Gnezdovo. Duczko (2004), 65–70, 76, 86–89. Androshchuk (2013), 18 ("prince's palace"). Mägi (2018), 162, 261. Tatjana N. Jackson, "*Aldeigjuborg* of the Sagas in the Light of Archaeological Data," in A. Ney, H. Williams, and F. C. Ljungqvist, eds., *Á Austrvega: Saga and East Scandinavia* (Gävle University Press, 2009), 438–42. Søren Sindbaek, "A Site of Intersection," and Johann Callmer, "The Rise of the Dominion of the ar-Rus," in Callmer, Gustin, and Roslund (2017), 76–90 and 136–67. T. Douglas Price, Vyacheslav Moiseyev, and Natalia Grigoreva, "Vikings in Russia," *Archaeological Anthropological Sciences* 11 (2019): 6093–109. Anatoliy N. Kirpichnikov,

"A Viking Period Workshop in Staraya Ladoga," *Fornvännen* 2004 (99): 183–96. Helen Clarke and Björn Ambrosiani, *Towns in the Viking Age* (Leicester University Press, 1991), 120. Dan Carlsson and Adrian Selin, *In the Footsteps of Rurik* (Northern Dimension Partnership on Culture, 2012), 39. D. A. Avdusin and Tamara A. Pushkina, "Three Chamber Graves at Gniozdovo," *Fornvännen* 83 (1988): 24–28. *Hervarar saga*, ch. 1–3. *Óláfs saga helga*, ch. 66 ("fine cloth," "furs"). *Laxdæla saga*, ch. 9 (Gilli Gerzkr). In the *Jomsvikinga saga*, an earl not otherwise linked to Russia is called Strut-Harald for the elaborate *strútr*, or "cone," on the top of his hat.

248 *chëln*: Anne Stalsberg, "Scandinavian Viking-Age Boat Graves in Old Rus," *Russian History* 28 (2001): 368–76.

249 **Rurik**: *Russian Primary Chronicle*, trans. Olgerd P. Sherbowitz-Wetzor (Medieval Academy of America, 1953), 58. Zena Harris and Nonna Ryan, "The Inconsistencies of History: Vikings and Rurik," *New Zealand Slavonic Journal* 38 (2004): 105–30; they quote August-Ludwig Schlötzer (1735–1809), 115 ("boorish").

250–51 **Novgorod**: Duczko (2004), 66. Mägi (2018), 108, 117, 202 (Ibn Rustah, "waterlogged").Clarke and Ambrosiani, *Towns*, 121, 124. Robert Wernick, *The Vikings* (Time-Life Books, 1979), 104. Carlsson and Selin, *In the Footsteps*, 46–51. *Ólafs saga Tryggvasonar*, ch. 8, 21.

251–52 **Gnezdovo**: Alexander M. Schenker, "The Gnezdovo Inscription in Its Historical and Linguistic Setting," *Russian Linguistics* 13 (1989): 210. Carlsson and Selin, *In the Footsteps*, 74–75, 79–81. Tamara Pushkina, "Viking-Period Pre-Urban Settlements in Russia and Finds of Artefacts of Scandinavian Character," in J. Hines, A. Lane, and M. Redknap, eds., *Land, Sea, and Home* (Maney, 2004), 49–51. Charlotte Hedenstierna-Jonson, "Rus', Varangians, and Birka Warriors," in Olausson and Olausson (2009), 164. Avdusin and Pushkina, "Three Chamber Graves," 20–33. Olga Orfinskaya and Tamara Pushkina, "10th Century AD Textiles from Female Burial II-301 at Gnezdovo, Russia," *Archaeological Textiles Newsletter* 53 (Fall 2011): 35–51.

252 **silver cone**: Charlotte Hedenstierna-Jonson, interviewed June 14, 2018; "Women at War?" *SAA Archaeological Record* 18 (May 2018): 29, 31. Wladyslaw Duczko, *The Filigree and Granulation Work of the Viking Period: Birka Untersuchungen und Studien 5* (Almqvist & Wiksell International, 1985), 66, 98–100. For the example found near Kyiv, see Fedir Androshchuk, "Female Viking Revised," n.d., posted on his Academia .edu page.

21: QUEEN OLGA'S REVENGE

253–56 **Kyiv**: Androshchuk (2013), 31, 52. Olgerd P. Sherbowitz-Wetzor, "Introduction," in *Russian Primary Chronicle*, trans. Olgerd P. Sherbowitz-Wetzor (Medieval Academy of America, 1953), 43 (Könugarðr, or "King's Fort"). Kevin Alan Brook, *The Jews of Khazaria* (Rowman & Littlefield, 2018), 25–27 ("settlement on the river bank"). Anabella Morina, "Pochaina River: Legendary Place of Baptism of Kyivan Rus-Ukraine," *Public Movement Pochaina* (April 20, 2018), www.ukinform.net. I. I. Movtjan, "Royal Guard Grave in Kiev," in K. Berg and O. Olsson, eds., *Olga & Ingegerd* (Statens Historiska Museum Stockholm, 2004–5), 54–57. The fictional archery demonstration comes from Al-Masudi's 934 account of Magyars in battle, quoted by Hedenstierna-Jonsson (2006), 56. I base some details on the description of the Saqaliba by Ibn Rustah, trans. P. Lunde and C. Stone, *Ibn Fadlan and the Land of Darkness* (Penguin, 2012), 124–25.

256–57 **Khazars**: Duczko (2004), 2. Brook, *Jews of Khazaria*, 2–4, 12, 61, 73–75, 135 (King Joseph). Miskawayh, trans. Lunde and Stone, *Ibn Fadlan and the Land of Darkness*, 151 ("swords").

257 **Pechenegs**: Androshchuk (2013), 216–17.

260–61 **Queen Olga:** Androshchuk (2013), 5 ("fabulous"), 65–68, 73, 84. I base Olga's description in the fictional scene on the eleventh-century fresco in Sofia Cathedral, Kyiv, assumed to depict her meeting with the emperor in Constantinople. Some details of her dress are from G. J. Ivakin, "Scandinavian Grave Finds in Kiev," in Berg and Olsson, *Olga & Ingegerd,* 53. *Russian Primary Chronicle,* trans. Sherbowitz-Wetzor, 78–81 ("hunting-grounds"); "Introduction," 31 ("picturesque," "largely legendary," "empty years," "scanty data," "tradition"). Elisabeth Löfstrand, "Olga: Avenger and Saint," in Berg and Olsson, *Olga & Ingegerd,* 15.

261 **Dniepr:** Androshchuk (2013), 119, 122. Constantine VII, *De administrando imperio,* quoted by Robert Wernick, *The Vikings* (Time-Life Books, 1979), 106 ("high rocks," "lay their boats"); quoted by Robert Ferguson, *The Vikings* (Viking Penguin, 2009), 124–26 ("Ashore they go"). Hraundal (2013), 27 (rapids).

262–63 **Constantinople:** While there is no consensus on the date of Olga's visit or her baptism, neither is in doubt. Androshchuk (2013), 176–79, 218 ("handmaidens"). Constantine VII, *De ceremoniis,* quoted by Jonathan Shepard, "The Viking Rus and Byzantium," in Brink and Price (2008), 502 ("nodded"). *The Works of Liudprand of Cremona,* trans. F. A. Wright (Routledge & Sons, 1930), 209 ("golden bowls"). *Russian Primary Chronicle,* trans. Sherbowitz-Wetzor, 82 ("her intellect").

263 **world was shifting:** Mägi (2018), 336.

264–65 **Sviatoslav:** *Russian Primary Chronicle,* trans. Sherbowitz-Wetzor, 83–84 ("laugh," "light as a leopard," "kettles"), 87–88 ("head falls," "carnage"), 90. Alice-Mary Talbot and Denis F. Sullivan, trans., *The History of Leo the Deacon* (Dumbarton Oaks Research Library and Collection, 2005), 126 ("hot-headed"), 194–99 ("die gloriously," "white horse," "intelligent general").

22: DEATH OF A VALKYRIE

267 **Blue Men:** Neil Price, "The Vikings in Spain, North Africa, and the Mediterranean," in Brink and Price (2008), 466. Caitlin R. Green, "A Man of Possible African Ancestry Buried in Anglo-Scandinavian York," posted at CaitlinGreen.org (December 28, 2019).

268 **"women who had fought":** John Skylitzes, *A Synopsis of Byzantine History, 811–1057,* trans. John Wortley (Cambridge University Press, 2010), 290.

269 **language of bones:** Anna Kjellström, "Type Specific Features and Identification of War Graves," in Olausson and Olausson (2009), 184–86. Kjellström, "Tracing Pain," in F. Fahlander and A. Kjellström, eds., *Making Sense of Things* (Stockholm University, 2010), 60. Fiona Shapland, Mary Lewis, and Rebecca Watts, "The Lives and Deaths of Young Medieval Women," *Medieval Archaeology* 59 (2015): 279–80. Guðný Zoëga and K. A. Murphy, "Life on the Edge of the Arctic," *International Journal of Osteoarchaeology* 26 (July–August 2016): 574–84.

269–70 **trauma:** Charlotte Hedenstierna-Jonson, "Grave Bj581: The Viking Warrior That Was a Woman," Forsyth Lecture, Assumption College, Worcester, MA (March 12, 2019). Holck (2009), 45 ("two persons"). Martin Biddle and Birthe Kjølbye-Biddle, "Repton and the Vikings," *Antiquity* 66 (1992): 36–51 ("a massive cut"). Hjardar and Vike (2016), 106 (amputations). *Hávamál,* 34 ("the lame").

270 **"crushed leeks":** *Óláfs saga helga,* ch. 234.

270 **dysentery:** *The Annals of St-Bertin,* trans. Janet Nelson (Manchester University Press, 1991), 129 ("discharged"). Elizabeth Ashman Rowe, *Vikings in the West,* Studia Medievalia Septentrionalia 18 (Fassbaender, 2012), ch. 3, unpaged electronic copy provided by the author (French account, "Garments").

271 **Egil:** *Egils saga,* ch. 85. Jesse Byock, "Egil's Bones," *Scientific American* (January 1995): 82–87.

271 **Gunnhild:** *Ágrip af Nóregskonungasögum,* trans. M. J. Driscoll (VSNR, 1995), 21. The bog body is now known as the Haraldskaer Woman.

272 **how she was buried:** See the online Supporting Information for Hedenstierna-Jonson et al. (2017) and the online Supplementary Material for Price et al. (2019); the exact dimensions of the Bj581 chamber are 3.45 meters long by 1.75 meters wide by 1.8 meters deep. No signs of a bonfire were recorded by Stolpe when he excavated grave Bj581. Holger Arbman, *Birka I: Die Graber* (K. Vitterhets Historie och Antikvitets Akademien, 1943), 188–90. Anne-Sofie Gräslund, *The Burial Customs: A Study of the Graves on Björkö* (Almqvist & Wiksell International, 1980), 7, 27–34, 37, 41. Helena Victor, "The Archaeological Material Culture Behind the Sagas," in A. Ney, H. Williams, and F. C. Ljungqvist, eds., *Á Austrvega: Saga and East Scandinavia* (Gävle University Press, 2009), 992–95. D. A. Avdusin and Tamara A. Pushkina, "Three Chamber Graves at Gniozdovo," *Fornvännen* 83 (1988): 20–33. Olga Orfinskaya and Tamara A. Pushkina, "10th Century AD Textiles from Female Burial II-301 at Gnezdovo, Russia," *Archaeological Textiles Newsletter* 53 (Fall 2011): 35–51. Neil Price, "Mythic Acts," in C. Raudvere and J. P. Schjødt, eds., *More Than Mythology* (Nordic Academic Press, 2012), 19–20 ("Note the detail").

272 **Christian burial:** *Sigurdrifumál,* st. 33–34 ("Care"). *Eyrbyggja saga,* ch. 51. Guðný Zoëga and Douglas Bolender, *Keflavík on Hegranes: Cemetery Excavation Interim Report* (Byggðasafn Skagfirðinga/UMass Boston, 2017), 8–22.

272–73 **pagan burial:** Alison Klevnäs, "Robbing the Dead at Gamla Uppsala," *Archaeological Review from Cambridge* 22.1 (2007): 27–29 ("poor condition"). Ibn Fadlan, quoted by Neil Price, "Passing into Poetry," *Medieval Archaeology* 54 (2010): 131–37 (Malak al-Maut as "Valkyrie"). Ibn Rustah, trans. P. Lunde and C. Stone, *Ibn Fadlan and the Land of Darkness* (Penguin, 2012), 127. *Helgakviða Hundingsbana II,* st. 43–44 ("Helgi's burial mound"). *Egils saga einhenda ok Ásmundar berserkjabana,* ch. 6 ("whichever lived longer").

275 **cremations:** Ingrid Gustin, "Contacts, Identity, and Hybridity," in Callmer, Gustin, and Roslund (2017), 230–31. Back Danielsson (2007), 66.

276 *She was a valkyrie:* *Helgakviða Hjörvarðssonar,* prose after st. 9. *Hervarar saga,* ch. 3. Saxo Grammaticus, trans. P. Fisher, *The History of the Danes, Books I–IX* (D. S. Brewer, 1970–80; rpt., 2008), 238, 280. *Völsunga saga,* ch. 29. *Grottasöngr,* st. 15. *Darraðarljóð,* in *Brennu-Njáls saga,* ch. 157.

276–77 **unknown conquerors:** Hedenstierna-Jonson (2006), 69. Olausson and Olausson (2009), 8. Price et al. (2019). The latest coin found in the garrison area dates to 965.

277 **Sigtuna:** Charlotte Hedenstierna-Jonson, "'Rus', Varangians, and Birka Warriors," in Olausson and Olausson (2009), 169. Mägi (2018), 273. Elin Ahlin Sundman and Anna Kjellström, "Signs of Sinusitis in Times of Urbanization in Viking Age–Early Medieval Sweden," *Journal of Archaeological Science* 40 (2013): 4460.

277–78 **Stolpe:** Stewart Culin, "Hjalmar Stolpe," *American Anthropologist* 8 (1906): 150–56. Gräslund, *Burial Customs,* 63 ("duller sound"). Charlotte Hedenstierna-Jonson, "Women at War? The Birka Female Warrior and Her Implications," *SAA Archaeological Record* 18 (May 2018): 28–31. Hedenstierna-Jonson (2006), 16–18 ("meticulous," "exceptional"). Price et al. (2019), online Supplementary Material.

INDEX

Note: Page numbers in *italics* refer to maps and illustrations.

68, 218–219, 222, 225; myth of the mighty ship, 223; portaging, 221–226, 261–262; Russian *chëln*, 248; sailing, 173–174, 179–182, 231, 235–238; Sami-style boats, 228; to "set a drag," 229; women and, 154–155, 227–229, 245. *See also* Viks boat

Sigurd the Dragon-Slayer, 93, 124, 129. *See also* Brynhild

silk, 164, 166, 180, 184, 188–190; from Baghdad, 219; Byzantine, 13, 210–220; caps, 14, 15, 153, 188, 190, 196, 243, 245, 253, 256, 274; from China, 219, 252; gowns, 91, 212; kaftans, 210, 213, 216, 243; *kropin'nyya* (light silk fabric), 218–219; lining, 118, 255; *pavolochity* (heavy silk fabric), 218; Prince Bahram Gur design, 211; riding coat, 197, 210–211; sails, 218–219; scarves and shawls, 153, 252; shirts, 120, 122; "slider" (silk gown), 212; Sogdian, 219

Silk Roads, 204, 212, 213, 216, 218, 244, 256

Skylitzes, John, 268

slavery: chains and fetters, 95, 153, 172–173; children in, 54, 250; clothing and, 120; in Dublin, 157–162; eunuchs and, 121; human sacrifice and, 71, 171–172; in Ireland before arrival of Vikings, 159; in Kaupang, 48–49, 174, 179; in Ladoga, 243; in Rafala, 240; Rus and, 170–172, 216; sex slavery, 169–171; slave labor, 95, 121; slave markets, 153, 158, 168–169, 179, 182, 245; slave routes 48–49, 162, 170, 174 179–180, 182; status of enslaved, 48–49, 100, 120, 156, 246; women and, 95, 159–160, 161, 164, 168–171, 179, 223, 240. *See also* Melkorka, Red Girl

Snorri Sturluson: biographical details, 4, 22, 33; Christianity and, 33, 241; chronological uncertainty in, 110–111; foster brother (Pall Jonsson), 155–156; on goddesses, 82–83; misogyny and biases of, 33, 82–83, 92, 93, 101, 241; re-created dialogue in works of, 53–54; on truth in poetry, 22; on valkyries, 4, 92. *See also* Edda; *Egil's Saga*; *Heimskringla*

Song of the Seer, 29

Stoksund (Stockholm), 230–231

Stolpe, Hjalmar, 277–278

Sviatoslav, Prince, 15, 60, 259, 260, 268; described, 255, 264–265; death of, 266

sword-chapes, 187; bearing falcon symbol, 196, 204–205, 243, 248, 251, 254, 258

swords, 2–3, *4*, 5, 48, 59, 60, *66*, 86–87, 129, 139, *143*, 166, 172, 194–196, *195*, *215*, 234, 237, 240, 252, 258, 261; in Bj581, 1, 3–4, 10, 26, 196, *272*, 275; faces of, 196; fighting with, 38, 54, 73, 104, 106, 140, 180, 193–194, 203, 269; as gifts, 27–28; grave robbing for, 26–27, 257; Jokul's Gift, 27; Leg-Biter, 56; making of, 72, 79, 191–193, 245; names of, 195; passed down through generations, 27; personalities of, 195–196; in poetry, 28, 76, 94, 126, 132, 134, 138, 142, 276; Slicer, 27; types of, 10, 196; women and, 2–8, 20, 23, 25, 26, 29, 60, 67, 104, 106, 134, 143, 194–195, 200. *See also* Tyrfing

Synopsis of Byzantine History (John Skylitzes), 268

Tacitus, 228

tapestries: Bayeux Tapestry, 102, 132–133; color and, 130; gender and, 58, 133–134; legend of Brynhild and, 128, 134; looms for, 131, 132; as memory pegs, 123–124; Oseberg tapestries, 69, 70, 71, 75, 80, *81*, 133; Overhogdal tapestries, 133–134, *135*; snare weaving (soumak), 133; storytelling through, 102, 121, 123–124, 129–130, 143

textile arts: dyeing, 113, 119, 121, 130–131, 219; embroidery, 18, 22, 54, 105, 106, 107, 130, 132–133, 134, 143, 151, 189, 246, 255, 274, 276; flax and nettle fibers, 122, 123, 189, 225; gender and, 43, 58, 59, 102, 105, 117–118, 121, 134, 136; geography and, 119; looms, 40, 69, 118, 121, 125, 131–133, 138; hemp fiber, 225; as magical, 121–122, 132; as mothers' work, 117, 134; Oseberg ship burial and, 69; ring-woven cloth, 119, 123; *skemma* and, 105, 107, 151; slave labor and, 121; spinning, 58, 119, 122–123; textile workshops, 42, 121–124, 130, 144, 189, 210; weaving sword, 131, 132; wool fabrics, 48, 68, 69, 118, 120, 122, 130, 188; working song, 131–132. *See also* linen; silk; tapestries

Thjodolf of Hvin, 65

Thor the Thunderer (god), 5, 29, 85, 96, 187, 189–190, 247; hammer of, 187, 189, 247

Thorbjorn Horn-Cleaver, 35, 37–38

Thorfinn Skull-Splitter, 116, 117, 162